THE UNIVERSITY OF
WINCHESTER

Martial Rose Library
Tel: 01962 827306

To be returned on or before the day marked above, subject to recall.

DELUXE

How Luxury Lost Its Lustre

DANA THOMAS

PENGUIN BOOKS

PENGUIN BOOKS

Published by the Penguin Group
Penguin Books Ltd, 80 Strand, London WC2R ORL, England
Penguin Group (USA) Inc., 375 Hudson Street, New York, New York 10014, USA
Penguin Group (Canada), 90 Eglinton Avenue East, Suite 700, Toronto, Ontario, Canada M4P 2Y3
(a division of Pearson Penguin Canada Inc.)
Penguin Ireland, 25 St Stephen's Green, Dublin 2, Ireland (a division of Penguin Books Ltd)
Penguin Group (Australia), 250 Camberwell Road, Camberwell, Victoria 3124, Australia
(a division of Pearson Australia Group Pty Ltd)
Penguin Books India Pvt Ltd, 11 Community Centre, Panchsheel Park, New Delhi – 110 017, India
Penguin Group (NZ), 67 Apollo Drive, Rosedale, North Shore 0632, New Zealand
(a division of Pearson New Zealand Ltd)
Penguin Books (South Africa) (Pty) Ltd, 24 Sturdee Avenue, Rosebank, Johannesburg 2196, South Africa

Penguin Books Ltd, Registered Offices: 80 Strand, London WC2R ORL, England

www.penguin.com

First published in the United States of America by The Penguin Press,
a member of Penguin Group (USA) Inc. 2007
First published in Great Britain by Allen Lane 2007
Published in Penguin Books 2008
008

Printed in England by Clays Ltd, St Ives plc

978-0-141-01967-3

www.greenpenguin.co.uk

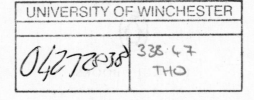

For my grandparents,
O.R. and Anne Strackbein

CONTENTS

INTRODUCTION

*D*OWN THE DUSTY ROADS of Xi'an the motor scooters zoom, weaving around potholes and rickety bicycles, bip-bip-bipping their horns as they circle the city's sixteenth-century bell tower. Xi'an, pronounced *Shee-ahn,* is one of China's oldest cities, settled by humans since prehistoric times. From 221 BC to AD 907, Xi'an served on and off as the capital of the vast Chinese empire. The famed Silk Road, the trade route that linked the Far East to Europe, started there in the second century BC and turned the city, then known as Chang'an, into a throbbing metropolis of nearly two million and an epicenter for culture and politics. Painting, poetry, dance, and music thrived in Xi'an, and *l'art de vivre*—the refined art of living—was an essential component of everyday existence. Xi'an was so beautiful—with its elaborate Buddhist temples, mosques, bustling souks, and eighth-century walled imperial city—that Japan's emperors used it as a model for their imperial capitals of Kyoto and Nara. It was said that Xi'an was as cosmopolitan and influential as Baghdad, Constantinople, and Rome. Many considered it the greatest city in the world.

It is hard to imagine today. With a population of 8 million, Xi'an is a small city by Chinese standards, compared to Shanghai (17.8 million), Beijing (15 million), and Chongqing (12 million). Unlike Beijing and Shanghai, which, thanks to China's market reforms, have become vibrant international capitals, Xi'an suffers from the blight of communism. The people, many dressed in faded Mao suits, seem downtrodden. Nothing has been painted in decades; scooters are held together with string, tape, and hope; and everything is covered in dust and soot. The new wealth of China has not trickled down to Xi'an—at least not yet. It has some local industry—cotton textiles, chemicals, and high tech—but its most important business is tourism. Half an hour away by car is the site of the Terracotta Warriors, the eight thousand life-size soldiers and horses that were buried in the tomb of Shi Huang Ti (259–210 BC), the first emperor of Qin (or China), for more than two thousand years and discovered in 1974 by a farmer digging a well. Each year, more than twenty million tourists—primarily Chinese—travel to Xi'an to see the warriors, making the site one of the country's most popular tourist destinations.

In April 2004, my husband and I traveled to China for the first time. I was there to cover the opening of Giorgio Armani's new retail complex on the Bund, the waterfront promenade in Shanghai. Afterward, we went to Xi'an to see the Terracotta Warriors. We arrived in the spanking-new airport on the outskirts of the city and took a beat-up cab down the factory-lined highway and tenement-lined streets to the historic center. We checked in to the Hyatt Regency, one of the two "Western" business hotels at the time, and as we stood there in the polished marble lobby and plant-filled atrium, I remembered that the word *Xi'an* means "western peace": the Hyatt seemed transplanted directly from any American urban center.

On the way to breakfast the first morning, we came across a couple of Chinese vendors selling clothes in a small conference room on the mezzanine. Not just any clothes: spread out across a half dozen folding tables were Gucci and Versace men's loafers, Givenchy men's shirts and socks, Versace sweaters, Calvin Klein underwear, Gucci sweaters with tags in them that read "Designed in Italy," and hanging on a garment rack in the corner, a couple of Burberry men's trench coats. Some of the items were obviously fake—several of the Versace shirts were labeled "Verla" in the same font—and I knew that Chinese factories turned out counterfeit goods of every sort. But some looked suspiciously authentic. I picked up the Gucci loafers. They were made of good-quality leather, well stitched, with a slight mod design to them, just like the shoes you find in Gucci stores on Rodeo Drive or Madison Avenue. My husband tried on one of the alleged Burberry trenches. It, too, was well made and with all the Burberry details just right. We asked the price. No one in the room spoke English, but a thin twentysomething Chinese girl pulled out a calculator and tapped out the price: $120. The regular retail price for a Burberry men's classic trench is $850. My husband said he'd think about it. We stopped by the concierge desk to ask about the provenance of the goods. Most were legitimate, the concierge told us, and had slight defects, were from an overrun, or simply didn't fit into the shipping container.

The next morning we went by the room to buy the trench. The entire operation had disappeared.

What, I wondered, was this all about?

THE LUXURY GOODS INDUSTRY, as it is known today, is a $157 billion business that produces and sells clothes, leather goods, shoes, silk scarves and neckties, watches, jewelry, perfume, and cosmetics that convey status and a pampered life—a luxurious life. Thirty-five major brands control 60 percent of the business, and dozens of smaller companies account for the rest. Several, including Louis Vuitton, Gucci, Prada, Giorgio Armani, Hermès, and Chanel, have annual revenues in excess of $1 billion. Most luxury goods companies that we know today were started a century or more ago as simple one-man or one-woman shops that sold beautiful handcrafted pieces. Today those companies still carry the founders' names but are, for the most part, owned and run by tycoons who in the last two decades have turned them into multibillion-dollar corporations and omnipresent global brands. They cluster their stores on main city avenues, in airports, in outlet malls. Their advertisements fill magazines and blanket billboards. Their primary customers are upper-income women between thirty and fifty years old. In Asia, the customer base veers younger, starting at twenty-five.

Walk up to a luxury brand store and a dark-suited man with a listening device tucked in his ear will silently pull open the heavy glass door. Inside there is a hush as slim, demurely dressed sales assistants await you in a posh minimalist space in neutral tones with chrome accents. The first thing you'll encounter are shelves full of the brand's latest fashion handbags as well as its classic designs, displayed like sculptures, each lighted with its own tiny spotlight. Glass cases are filled with monogram-covered wallets, billfolds, and business card holders: the lower-priced, entry-level items aimed at aspirational middle-market customers. Chances are, the slim assistants will make the sale right there in the very first room. Through calculated marketing strategies and with the support of fashion magazines, luxury companies in the last ten years have created the phenomenon of the handbag of the season—the must-have around the world that will catapult sales and stock prices. Louis Vuitton's sales of Japanese artist Takashi Murakami–designed smiling cherry purses were almost single-handedly responsible for double-digit growth for Louis Vuitton in the first quarter of 2005. The average markup on a handbag is ten to twelve times production cost. And Vuitton prices are never marked down.

Many luxury stores end right there: handbags and accessories. If it is a "flagship"—the industry word for a store that carries the complete range of products—then there will be a gleaming counter offering perfume and cosmetics. Perfume has, for more than seventy years, served as an introduction to a luxury brand. It has allowed folks who couldn't afford the more expensive things in the shop to own a small piece of the brand's dream. It also provides luxury brands with substantial profits. Cosmetics serve the same purpose but, like handbags, are more showy: pulling a Chanel lipstick from a handbag gives the instant impression of wealth and savoir faire.

In the next room—often upstairs or down in a converted basement—you'll find a small selection of ready-to-wear clothes and shoes. Back in the old days, when luxury was still an intimate, elegant business for an elite clientele, shopping for clothes, be it couture or ready-to-wear, was a pleasurable affair. You chose what you liked, often during a fashion show or a personal viewing, retired to a spacious, comfortable dressing room, tried on the garments leisurely, and had the seamstress on hand to do whatever retouching was necessary. Couture and high-end department-store saleswomen were counselors and confidantes. They knew who was wearing what to which event, they knew what suited you, and they advised you accordingly. Today, by contrast, shopping for luxury brand clothing is an exercise in patience. Usually there are only a few pieces of clothing and only in the smallest sizes. This is where the slim sales assistants come in: they scurry into the back storeroom for ten, fifteen, twenty minutes to find your size, or perhaps another style that isn't on the floor, or even a dress that no one else has seen. If it doesn't please you, they scurry off again for another ten or twenty minutes. And so on. This, in the minds of luxury executives, is attentive, specialized service.

Whatever the purchase, you'll walk out with a rope-handled paper bag in the brand's signature color and with the brand's logo emblazoned on the side. The product will be wrapped in tissue paper and, if it's a handbag, wallet, or other leather item, stuffed into a soft felt pouch, also in the brand's signature color.

And what will you have gotten?

THE WAY WE DRESS reflects not only our personality but also our economic, political, and social standing and our self-worth. Luxury adornment has always been at the top of the pyramid, setting apart the haves from the have-nots. Its defining elements—silk, gold and silver, precious and semiprecious stones, fur—have been culturally recognized and sought after for millennia. In prehistory, humans set themselves apart by decorating their furs with bits of bone and feathers. The Chinese enriched their appearance with silk embroidery as long as twelve thousand years ago, as did the Persians and the Egyptians in the second century BC.

The display of luxury signified one's power and achievements and brought on both scorn and envy. " 'Is it a waste or not?' was argued as far back as 700 BC," Kenneth Lapatin, an antiquities curator at the J. Paul Getty Museum in Los Angeles, California, told me. The Etruscans wore gold and imported amber from the Baltics and had beautiful engraved gemstones like jasper and carnelian. But it was this love of luxury that led to their downfall, according to social conservatives of the era.

The Greek aristocrats, Lapatin explained, "were flashy. They'd wear their gold and their fancy clothing out and would be aped by the masses." This drove the rich to live more opulently, simply "to stand out" from the ordinary folk. Rulers passed sumptuary laws—social restrictions that dictated what you could display in terms of wealth, usually clothing, jewelry, and other luxury items—thus preventing commoners from imitating nobles and reining in conspicuous consumption. "In some places, if you brought gold and jewelry to a sanctuary, you had to leave it as an offering," Lapatin said. "You dedicated your luxury to the gods and often indicated your name through an inscription or label. And when people would go into the temple and see it, they would say, 'What good taste and generosity he has.'" Faking luxury was considered the ultimate disgrace. According to one ancient tradition, the sculptor Phidias offered to build the statue of Athena in the Parthenon in Athens out of cheap materials—gold-gilded marble—but the proposal was vetoed by the Athenian assembly. "Shame! Shame!" its members cried, and insisted on gold and ivory. "They didn't want to save their money," Lapatin said. "They wanted to show it off."

It was during the reign of the Bourbons and the Bonapartes in France that luxury as we know it today was born. Many of the luxury brands we patronize, such as Louis Vuitton, Hermès, and Cartier, were founded in the eighteenth or nineteenth century by humble artisans who created the most beautiful wares imaginable for the royal court. With the fall of monarchy and the rise of industrial fortunes in the late nineteenth century, luxury became the domain of old-moneyed European aristocrats and elite American families—such as the Vanderbilts, the Astors, and the Whitneys—who moved in closed social circles. Luxury wasn't simply a product. It denoted a history of tradition, superior quality, and often a pampered buying experience. Luxury was a natural and expected element of upper-class life, like belonging to the right clubs or having the right surname. And it was produced in small quantities—often made to order—for an extremely limited and truly elite clientele. As Diana Vreeland noted in her memoir, *D.V.*, "Very few people had ever breathed the pantry air of a house of a woman who wore the kind of dress *Vogue* used to show when I was young."

When Christian Dior, considered by many to be the father of modern fashion, was interviewed by *Time* magazine in 1957, he pondered the importance of luxury in contemporary society. "I'm no philosopher," he said, "but it seems to me that women—and men too—instinctively yearn to exhibit themselves. In this machine age, which esteems convention and uniformity, fashion is the ultimate refuge of the human, the personal and the inimitable. Even the most outrageous innovations should be welcomed, if only because they shield us against the shabby and the humdrum. Of course fashion is a transient, egotistical indulgence, yet in an era as somber as ours, luxury must be defended centimeter by centimeter."

Dior believed that Europe was still the epicenter of luxury creation and production because of its steady stream of megalomaniacal kings and popes who, over the centuries, commissioned the construction of sumptuous palaces and cathedrals. "[We] inherited a tradition of craftsmanship rooted in the anonymous artisans who . . . expressed their genius in chiseled stone gargoyles and cherubs," he said. "Their descendents—skilled automobile mechanics, cabinet makers, masons, plumbers, handymen—are proud of their métiers. They feel humiliated if they've done a shoddy job. Similarly, my tailors [and] seamstresses constantly strive for perfection."

And there luxury stayed, a domain of the wealthy and the famous that the hoi polloi dared not enter, until the Youthquake of the 1960s. The political revolutions throughout the Western world at that time pulled down social barriers, including those that separated the rich from the rest. Luxury went out of fashion, and it stayed out of fashion until a new and financially powerful demographic—the unmarried female executive—emerged in the 1980s. The American meritocracy came into full bloom. Anyone and everyone could move up the economic and social ladder and indulge in the trappings of luxury that came with this newfound success. Disposable income has risen significantly in industrialized nations in the last thirty years. Both men and women have put off getting married until later in life, freeing them to spend more on themselves. The average consumer is also far more educated and well traveled than a generation ago and has developed a taste for the finer things in life.

Corporate tycoons and financiers saw the potential. They bought—or took over—luxury companies from elderly founders or incompetent heirs, turned the houses into brands, and homogenized everything: the stores, the uniforms, the products, even the coffee cups in the meetings. Then they turned their sights on a new target audience: the middle market, that broad socioeconomic demographic that includes everyone from teachers and sales executives to high-tech entrepreneurs, McMansion suburbanites, the ghetto fabulous, even the criminally wealthy. The idea, luxury executives explained, was to "democratize" luxury, to make luxury "accessible." It all sounded so noble. Heck, it sounded almost communist. But it wasn't. It was as capitalist as could be: the goal, plain and simple, was to make as much money as heavenly possible.

To realize this "democratization," the tycoons launched a two-pronged attack. First they hyped their brands mercilessly. They trumpeted the brand's historical legacy and the tradition of hand-craftsmanship to give the products an air of luxury legitimacy. They encouraged their designers to stage extravagant or provocative fashion shows—at a million dollars a pop—to drum up controversy and make headlines. They spent billions of dollars on deliberately shocking advertising campaigns—Dior's grease-smudged lesbian ads to sell purses, Yves Saint Laurent's full-frontal male nudity shot to sell perfume—that made their brands as recognizable and common as Nike and Ford. They dressed celebrities, who in return told every reporter lining the red carpet which company had provided their gown, jewels, handbag, tuxedo, or shoes. They began to sponsor high-profile sporting and entertainment events such as Louis Vuitton at the America's Cup and Chopard at the Cannes Film Festival. The message was clear: buy our brand and you, too, will live a luxury life.

Then the tycoons made their products more available, economically and physically. They introduced fashionable lower-priced accessories that most anyone could afford. They expanded their retail reach from the original polished-oak-paneled family shop and a few overseas franchises to a vast global network, rolling out thousands of stores that are as ubiquitous and approachable as Benetton or Gap. They opened outlets to sell leftovers at bargain prices, launched e-commerce sites on the Internet, and ramped up their share of duty-free retailing. In 2005, travelers purchased $9.7 billion worth of luxury goods, accounting for one-third of all global travel retail sales. And travel experts say it's only going to increase: according to the International Civil Aviation Organization, annual global air traffic is expected to reach 2.8 billion passengers by 2015, up from 2.1 billion today.

Luxury companies funded the expansion of their reach by listing themselves on the world's stock exchanges. Going public brings many advantages to a luxury company: it raises capital, elevates the brand's status, creates management incentives such as stock options, and makes the company more transparent, thus attracting a higher caliber of executive management. But it also makes the company beholden to stockholders who demand increases in profits *every three months*. "Going public does force you to change the way you do business," former Gucci designer Tom Ford told me. "It forces you to be aware of how you are spending and where it's going, to make some short-term decisions because that's what shareholders respond to, and to juggle the long-term benefits with the short-term." To meet those profit forecasts, the luxury companies have cut corners. Some use inferior materials, and many have quietly outsourced production to developing nations. Most have replaced individual handcraftsmanship with assembly-line production, much of it done on machines. Simultaneously, most luxury companies have raised their brands' prices exponentially, and many justify the move by falsely claiming that their goods are made in Western Europe, where labor is expensive. To further pump up their numbers, luxury companies have introduced cheaply made, lower-priced accessories—such as logo-covered T-shirts, nylon toiletry cases, and denim handbags—and expanded their range of perfume and cosmetics, all of which bring in substantial profits when sold in great volume. The average consumer certainly can't afford a $200,000 made-to-order couture gown, but she can drop $25 on a tube of lipstick or $65 on a bottle of eau de parfum spray to have a piece of the luxury dream.

All this hyped-up marketing of dreams has made luxury companies wildly successful and their shareholders extremely happy. In their best year—1999—luxury indexes rose a remarkable 144 percent, according to the investment banking firm Bear Stearns. And analysts predict that luxury sales will soon surpass those record pre–September 11, 2001, levels. There have never been so many wealthy in the world. In 2005, there were 8.3 million millionaires—an increase of 7.3 percent over 2004—who possessed $30.8 trillion in assets, according to the 2006 "World Wealth Report" (published annually by Merrill Lynch and Capgemini). The Swiss bank UBS's wealth-management division had an influx of $76 billion in new money in 2005, an increase of 57 percent in one year. NetJets, the private jet-share company, saw a business increase of 1,000 percent from 2001 to 2006. The private security firm Kroll reported that its business from clients with at least $500 million in assets increased by 67 percent in just two years. And the "World Wealth Report" added that there has been a rise in "middle market millionaires" with assets of $5 million to $30 million.

But for some on the wrong side of this growth, those dreams are nightmares. Luxury brands are among the most counterfeited products today—the World Customs Organization states that the fashion industry loses up to $9.7 billion (€7.5 billion) per year to counterfeiting—and most of the counterfeiters' profits fund illicit activities such as drug trafficking, human trafficking, and terrorism. Luxury incites other illegal activities, too. Japanese girls work as prostitutes in order to buy luxury brand handbags. Chinese "hostesses" accept shopping visits with their clients at luxury brand stores, which stay open until midnight, as payment for services rendered. The next morning, the hostess returns the purchase for cash, less a 10 percent "transaction fee," thus inflating luxury brands' sales figures in China and washing away any illegal cash transactions between the woman and her client. A true story, told to me over a summer lunch on the French Riviera in 2004: A rich, hip New York banker met a pretty Russian girl in the bar of the Hôtel Byblos in Saint-Tropez late one night and took her home with him. The next morning, she told him pointedly: "I could really use a new pair of Gucci shoes." He understood immediately that she was a working girl and took out his wallet. "No," she said, "Gucci shoes." And to the store they went.

The tycoons' marketing scheme has worked. Today, luxury is indeed democratic: it's available to anyone, anywhere, at any price point. In 2004, Japanese consumers accounted for 41 percent of luxury sales, Americans 17 percent, and Europeans 16 percent. Expansion continues in India, Russia, Dubai, and of course China, luxury's new El Dorado. While parts of China, like Xi'an, are still dusty and blighted, a new big-spending class is emerging at warp speed. When I visited the country in the spring of 2004, luxury companies considered China to be an immature market and an investment for the future. Eighteen months later, China accounted for 12 percent of all luxury sales—and this figure was expected to grow exponentially. Luxury companies are opening stores not only in Beijing and Shanghai but also in rapidly growing second- and third-tier cities such as Hangzhou, Chongqing, and even Xi'an. By 2011, China is expected to be the world's most important luxury market.

And luxury's barons have reaped the wealth. Bernard Arnault, chairman and CEO of the Paris-based luxury-brand group LVMH Moët Hennessy Louis Vuitton, is the most successful of them all. In 2006, *Forbes* named him the seventh richest man in the world, with a net worth of more than $21 billion. His fellow LVMH shareholders aren't doing badly either. When Arnault took control of LVMH in 1990, it had sales of about $3.65 billion (about €2.8 billion) with net profit of

$621 million (about €480 million). In 2005, it recorded $17.32 billion (€13.91 billion) in sales and net profit of $1.79 billion, or €1.44 billion. "What I like is the idea of transforming creativity into profitability," Arnault once said. "It's what I like the most."

The luxury industry has changed the way people dress. It has realigned our economic class system. It has changed the way we interact. It has become part of our social fabric. To achieve this, it has sacrificed its integrity, undermined its products, tarnished its history, and hoodwinked its consumers. In order to make luxury "accessible," tycoons have stripped away all that has made it special.

Luxury has lost its luster.

PART ONE

CHAPTER ONE

AN INDUSTRY IS BORN

"Luxury is a necessity that begins where necessity ends."

—COCO CHANEL

ARC JACOBS is the most influential creative voice in luxury fashion today. As creative director of Louis Vuitton, the world's largest luxury goods company, Jacobs oversees the studio that in the last decade has produced sumptuous and witty versions of the classic Vuitton monogram handbag—like the denim jacquard one trimmed in chinchilla—that have sold by the millions. Yet Jacobs sees what he does at Vuitton as the antithesis of luxury today. "The way I define luxury isn't by fabric or fiber or the amount of gold bits hanging from it," Jacobs says, sitting in his Paris office, sucking on his umpteenth cigarette of the day as his bull terrier Alfred gnaws on a soup bone. "That's an old definition. For me, luxury is about pleasing yourself, not dressing for other people."

The contradiction between personal indulgence and conspicuous consumption is the crux of the luxury business today: the convergence of its history with its current reality. For most people, Louis Vuitton represents true luxury. The suitcase or handbag covered with its intertwining LV logo implies that its carrier appreciates the fine-quality craftsmanship, has the money to afford it, and travels in the same circles as other Louis Vuitton customers—in first class. Long ago, that assumption was true. Louis Vuitton supplied kings and queens, high-society matrons, and business titans. It was the luggage of the rich and famous. Today, however, millions of people from a wide range of economic backgrounds own Louis Vuitton products, ranging from a $120 money clip to a trunklike humidor that holds a thousand cigars. Louis Vuitton is the greatest example of what executives in the fashion business call democratic luxury: it's big, it's broad-reaching, and it sells wildly expensive stuff that nobody really needs. "When you look at [Louis Vuitton], you see it is mass-produced luxury," Jacobs tells me. "Vuitton is a status symbol. It's not about hiding the logo. It's about being a bit of a show-off."

Louis Vuitton is the cornerstone of a publicly traded luxury conglomerate called LVMH Moët Hennessy Louis Vuitton—or LVMH for short—run by French tycoon Bernard Arnault. In 2005, it had more than fifty brands—including Moët & Chandon champagne, Givenchy couture, and Tag Heuer watches—fifty-nine thousand employees and seventeen hundred stores, and did $18.1 billion (€14 billion) in sales and made $3.5 billion (€2.7 billion) in profits. Its flagship is Louis Vuitton, which does an estimated $3.72 billion in sales annually, accounting for approximately one-quarter of the group's total business. Vuitton is the McDonald's of the luxury industry: it's far and away the leader, brags of millions sold, has stores at all the top tourist sites— usually steps away from a McD's—and has a logo as recognizable as the Golden Arches. "Luxury is crossing all age, racial, geographic and economic brackets," Daniel Piette, an LVMH executive, told *Forbes* in 1997. "We've broadened the scope far beyond the wealthy segments."

The heart of Louis Vuitton is the trunk. Back in the mid-nineteenth century, when Louis Vuitton started his business, trunks were an integral part of travel, like suitcases on wheels are today. A traveler left for months at a time, with as many as fifty trunks in tow filled with everything from petticoats to porcelain. Today Louis Vuitton makes about five hundred trunks annually. Rarely are trunks used for travel anymore. If so—and it's usually for nostalgic reasons—they're often sent ahead by mail or boat, or loaded on private jets. More often Louis Vuitton trunks, old or new, are displayed in homes like art or used as shelves, coffee tables, or bars.

Louis Vuitton trunks are still made more or less the same way they were 150 years ago, mostly at the Louis Vuitton compound in the working-class Paris suburb of Asnières-sur-Seine. Entering the Vuitton compound is like stepping from drab, monochromatic Kansas into the rich Technicolor world of Oz. Across a thick green lawn framed by strong old trees and well-tended rose beds sits a simple two-story white stucco country house with gingerbread trim and a silvery zinc roof. Louis Vuitton, a hardworking artisan of humble roots, built the place in 1859 to move his family out of filthy, crowded Paris. Out back is a century-old, two-story, L-shaped workshop where 220 artisans build hundreds of trunks and sew thousands of handbags every year. It is one of fourteen official sites—eleven in France, two in Spain, and one in San Dimas, California—where Vuitton leather goods are produced.

The trunk's structure is built out of okoumé, a hard, lightweight wood from Africa, by craftsmen in the big lumber shop on the ground floor. For the hinge, Vuitton craftsmen glue a piece of sturdy canvas to the inside, and another on the outside. Louis Vuitton invented this method in 1854 to replace the bulky metal brackets of the period. The canvas hinge doesn't break, opens and closes easily, and creates a flat surface on the back of the trunk. The trunk's exterior material—usually Vuitton's waterproofed monogram or Damier check canvas—is glued onto the wood box and hinge. The corner covers are made of brass or of leather shaped by hot and cold pressure in a mold. The edge trim, known as *lozine*, is made of many layers of paper and cloth pressed together and dipped in a zinc solution. Upstairs, workers nail on the poplar belts around the middle, the *lozine* trim on the edges, the corner covers, and the hardware. The banging is so loud that most of the eight workers in the "hammering department" wear earplugs. The lining, made of a pearl gray cotton canvas called Vuittonitte, or a synthetic suede called Alcantara, is glued inside; khaki woven cotton straps that read "Louis Vuitton" are attached to hold items in place. The trunk is then cleaned up, inspected, and sent off to be packaged and shipped.

Thousands of handbags are made at the Asnières compound each year as well. The steamer bag—originally designed in 1901 as a laundry sack for steamship travel and today one of the Vuitton's most popular items—is made by hand. Steamer bags, handbags made of exotic leathers such as crocodile and ostrich, and special-order items are all made by one artisan rather than on the assembly line. Vuitton gets about 450 to 500 special orders each year. Some are simply new editions of an existing model, like the trunk bed first designed for French explorer Pierre Savorgnan de Brazza in 1868 for his African travels through the Congo; others are a reworking of something that already exists, like a jewelry box covered in an exotic skin instead of the monogram toile, or something designed to the customer's specs. When I was in Asnières, one artisan was finishing up a tennis bag in Damier canvas that holds two rackets; it took two weeks to produce and would be the only one in the world.

The rest of Vuitton's production is assembly-line work, most of it done on machines. In a big sunlit room on the second floor, a dozen seamstresses were running up hundreds of LV monogram denim Pleaty handbags on their machines. These bags would sell for $1,150 apiece and be so popular they'd be back-ordered within weeks. "High profitability comes . . . in the atelier—the factory," Bernard Arnault once explained. "Production is organized in such a way that we have unbelievably high productivity. The atelier is a place of amazing discipline and rigor. Every single motion, every step of every process, is carefully planned with the most modern and complete engineering technology. It's not unlike how cars are made in the most modern factories. We analyze how to make each part of the product, where to buy each component, where to find the best leather at the best price, what treatment it should receive. A single purse can have up to 1,000 manufacturing tasks, and we plan each and every one."

Today, there are three Vuitton family members employed by the Louis Vuitton company: Patrick-Louis, a fifth-generation descendent of the founder, who oversees special orders and serves as a house ambassador; his youngest son, Benoit-Louis, born in 1977, who is watch special orders manager at the headquarters in Paris; and Pierre-Louis, his oldest son, who works as a craftsman in Asnières. I ran into Pierre-Louis as I visited the workshop in the spring of 2006. Pierre's a kind-looking fellow, rather pale, with hazel eyes, closely clipped dark hair, and protruding ears. He was dressed in a white lab coat over a checked shirt and jeans. On the pocket of his coat was an LV logo embroidered in brown thread. He was walking some bits of canvas for jewelry boxes from one station to another. Pierre had joined the company about a year and a half earlier, after a short stint in computers. He had visited the Vuitton factories in the provinces and was so moved by the craftsmanship that he asked Vuitton owner Bernard Arnault for a job. Arnault said, "Of course."

"I love this company," Pierre told me. "It's in my veins."

And then he got back to work.

LUXURY AS WE KNOW IT today is rooted in old Europe's royal courts—primarily those of France, which set the standards for lavish living. In the seventeenth century, French king Henri IV's second wife, Marie de Medicis, wore for the baptism of one of her children a gown embroidered with thirty-two thousand pearls and three thousand diamonds. Louis XIV dressed in satin suits with velvet sashes and frilly blouses, high-heeled shoes or boots, and wigs of flowing curls topped with ostrich-plumed chapeaux. To maintain control over his courtiers, he dictated to them what they could wear, when to wear it, and how to wear it. He declared what height necklines should be, and the length of gown trains. To please the king, the ladies of the court wore wigs so tall that their servants stood on ladders to assemble them.

Madame de Pompadour, the mistress of Louis XV, personally encouraged and supported the luxury artisans and helped found the Sèvres porcelain factory to provide the Château de Versailles with its royal services. Louis XVI's wife, Marie-Antoinette, overran her annual clothing budget of $3.6 million by buying gowns encrusted with sapphires, diamonds, silver, and gold—but according to observers, it was money well spent. She was "an object too sublime and beautiful for my dull pen to describe," wrote John Adams, a U.S. diplomatic envoy to France in the late 1770s and later the second American president. "Her dress was everything that art and wealth could make it." Napoleon's wife, the empress Josephine, spent half of the $15 million France earned selling the five-hundred-million-acre Louisiana territory to the United States in 1803 on clothes in ten years. "French fashions must be France's answers to Spain's gold mines in Peru," declared Louis XIV's finance minister Jean-Baptiste Colbert, for whom today the Committee Colbert, the French luxury brand trade association, is named.

It was in the world of nineteenth-century French aristocracy that Louis Vuitton was able to rise from nothing to the world's most famous luxury travel brand. Louis Vuitton himself was born in 1821 to a family of farmers and millers in the Jura, a mountainous region at the foot of the Alps in eastern France. At the age of thirteen, Vuitton set out by foot for Paris, then the city of opportunity. The 292-mile trek took two years; along the way, Louis earned his keep by working as a stable boy or kitchen hand. When he finally arrived, Paris was a booming town of one million, a city of opulent palaces and horrific slums. "Here you find at the same time the greatest luxury and the greatest filth, the greatest virtue and the greatest vice," the pianist Frédéric Chopin wrote to a friend, according to Paul-Gérard Pasols in his book *Louis Vuitton: The Birth of Modern Luxury.*

Vuitton became an apprentice to a master trunk maker named Monsieur Maréchal on the corner of the rue Saint-Honoré and the rue du 29 Juillet—the site today of the trendy fashion boutique Colette. In 1854, Vuitton quit, opened his own business on the rue Neuves-des-Capucines (now known simply as the rue des Capucines), and set about reworking the basic design of the trunk. He changed the traditional domed lid to a flat top (to allow for easy stacking on the backs of coaches) and replaced the leather, which turned moldy and cracked, with lightweight poplar covered with a waterproof dove gray cotton canvas he developed called Trianon gray, after the Grand Trianon Palace at Versailles.

Trunk makers back then not only built trunks but also packed and unpacked them. Throughout the mid-1800s, women wore voluminous gowns with layers of petticoats known as crinolines, made of wool and horsehair, under their skirts or, later, with bustles. The master of such creations was a young Englishman named Charles Frederick Worth, an acquaintance of Louis Vuitton's who had a dress shop in Paris on the rue de la Paix. Today Worth is known as the father of haute couture. Rather than producing dresses to order like his confreres, Worth designed seasonal collections from which his clients could choose. He was one of the first to stage fashion shows to present his collections, and the first to put a signature label on his clothes. He became luxury fashion's first true arbiter of style: he dictated what the fashion would be, and the public followed. "Women will stoop to any depths to be dressed by him," wrote historian Hippolyte Taine at the time. "This arid, nervous, dwarfish creature receives them nonchalantly, stretched out on a couch, a cigar between his lips. He growls, 'Walk! Turn! Good! Come back in a week and I will have an appropriate toilette for you!' It is he, not they, who chooses. They are only too content to be dominated by him—and even so they need references." Worth's dresses required some fifteen yards of fabric—such as floss silk, painted chiffon, or lamé gauze—and could take three to four hundred hours to embroider. Buttons were embroidered, too, each one requiring three to ten hours of work. His dresses were so popular that he could have a team of thirty seamstresses working full-time for one client all year long. His prices were stratospheric, his vanity legendary: he considered himself a "great artist," on par with Delacroix. He snidely dismissed clients who questioned his skills, and shamelessly catered to aristocrats above all others. Vuitton so excelled at packing these delicate frocks and baubles that he became the official packer and trunk maker for the empress Eugénie, the extravagant Spanish-born wife of Napoleon III. Having her royal warrant was the ultimate seal of approval.

Louis Vuitton's business was doing well enough that by 1859 he needed to expand. He bought an acre of land in Asnières, a northeastern suburb situated on both the rail line to Paris and the river Seine, which allowed for easy receipt of raw materials as well as easy shipping to the store, and constructed a workshop of brick and glass with iron frames and trusses, like those used by French architect Victor Baltard at Les Halles. On the ground floor, Louis had about twenty artisans making trunks. Upstairs, he had a small apartment where he would stay when visiting the site.

Today, that two-room space serves as the Louis Vuitton Museum of Travel, which can be viewed only by appointment. The windowless gallery is clean and modern, with high-gloss blond wood floors; it traces the evolution not only of Vuitton but also of modern luxury goods. The tour begins with a stack of four old beat-up trunks. The first is the revolutionary Trianon Gray. Shortly after it was introduced, it was copied by the competition. So Louis Vuitton came up with a new canvas design—the second trunk—of red and beige stripes. He later changed the stripes to brown and beige, which have been the house's signature colors ever since. The third trunk on display is a chocolate brown and beige checkerboard print known today as Damier, designed by Louis's thirty-one-year-old son, Georges, in 1888. The words "Marque Louis Vuitton Deposée"—or "registered trademark"—were written in white inside a few of the checks, thus launching luxury branding. And the fourth trunk is the monogram pattern of interlocking LVs interspersed with naïf-style diamonds, stars, and flowers, which Georges designed in 1896 also in response to counterfeiting and registered it as a trademark in 1905. No one knows for sure where Georges found his inspiration, though it is believed that the blossoms came from the Japonisme movement of the late nineteenth century. What is certain today is that the Japanese adore the Vuitton monogram. By 2006, 40 percent of all Japanese owned a Vuitton product, primarily from the monogram line.

At the end of the nineteenth century, monarchy around the world was giving way, through social or bloody revolution, to more equitable—or democratic—societies, and the Industrial Revolution made inventors and entrepreneurs as rich as kings. This allowed the increasingly wealthy bourgeoisie to share the lifestyle and tastes of the aristocracy—and they did, wholeheartedly. As American economist Thorstein Veblen argued in his famous treatise *The Theory of the Leisure Class* in 1899, spending became the way people established their social position in an affluent society. American Industrial Revolution families such as the Carnegies, Fords, Vanderbilts, Rockefellers, Guggenheims, Pierpont Morgans, and Hearsts showed their social might by building gargantuan homes filled with uniformed staff and European antiques, underwriting public institutions such as libraries and universities, and buying gobs of luxury goods. In Europe, most reigning monarchy had been abolished, but not the aspiration to emulate it. Aristocrats continued to live grandly, as before, and a new bourgeoisie spent liberally to acquire all the same trappings, from fully staffed manor houses to complete sets of Vuitton luggage.

To keep up with the demand at Vuitton, Georges added another two rows of workshops in Asnières. He opened a shop in Nice—a favorite winter destination on the French Riviera for wealthy English, Russians, and Americans—moved the Paris store from the Opéra district to the far-wealthier Champs-Élysées, and negotiated distribution deals in the United States. Soon Vuitton became the luggage of choice for such Hollywood stars as Mary Pickford, Marlene Dietrich, Lillian Gish, Ginger Rogers, and Cary Grant. Among the star pieces in the Vuitton museum collection is actor Douglas Fairbanks's smart Roma suitcase from 1925, covered with natural cowhide and lined with pigskin.

It was a glamorous time, perhaps the last true golden period for luxury, and you can feel the gaiety and refinement in the Vuitton collection in such items as singer Marthe Chenal's crocodile toiletry case with tortoiseshell-handled grooming utensils; crystal flasks with gold stoppers; and the ever-popular drawstring Noé bag, designed in 1932 to hold five bottles of champagne—four upright and a fifth upside-down in the center. "In those days, fully furnished houses meant fully stocked households," wrote Maria Riva in *Marlene Dietrich: By Her Daughter,* of a home Dietrich rented in Los Angeles in 1930. "Our inventory lists never had fewer than eight complete dinner services for fifty, six separate lunch and tea services, all of bone china, dozens and dozens of crystal goblets, and linen enough to stock Buckingham palace. This house also boasted fourteen-karat gold cutlery; the sterling silver was for lunch."

In the 1920s, France's luxury fashion business was composed of an astounding three hundred thousand workers, including cutters, fitters, seamstresses, embroiderers, furriers, shoemakers, weavers, spinners, and milliners. In five years in the 1920s, the esteemed embroiderer Albert Lesage turned out fifteen hundred elaborate pieces for the Paris couture house Vionnet. In the 1930s, Lesage used hand-blown Murano glass to make flowers to decorate dresses, and couturier Elsa Schiaparelli flecked her gowns with semiprecious jewels set in gold. At Chanel, the atelier turned out hundreds of glittering gowns for the smart set. Diana Vreeland remembered ordering one: "The huge skirt was of silver lamé, quilted in pearls, which gave it a marvelous weight; then the bolero was lace entirely encrusted with pearls and *diamanté*; then underneath the bolero was the most beautiful shirt of linen lace. I think it was the most beautiful dress I've ever owned."

THAT ALL CHANGED with World War II. When the Germans arrived in Paris in 1940, many luxury businesses and couture houses—including Chanel—closed shop. But couturier Lucien Lelong, head of the French couture association at the time, persuaded several to remain open to save jobs and preserve pride. During the Occupation, the Germans ransacked the association's headquarters and confiscated its archives. They closed some houses—Madame Grès and Balenciaga among them—and tried to shut down the industry fourteen times. Their plan was to move couture houses to Berlin and Vienna, which were to be Europe's new cultural capitals. Lelong and his confreres would have nothing of it. "You can force us to do anything you like," Lelong declared, "but Paris haute couture will never move, neither as a whole nor bit by bit. Either it stays in Paris or it ceases to exist." To keep going, some luxury companies and couture houses sold their products to the wives of German officers and collaborators. Vuitton was among them. It is a part of the family history that the company does not mention anywhere. In fact, it was effectively buried until

Vuitton biographer Stéphanie Bonvicini exposed it in her book *Louis Vuitton: une saga française,* in 2004.

The Vuittons were as divided as France. Georges's grandson Claude-Louis joined the Second Armored Division in 1944 and fought against the Germans. Granddaughter Denyse Vuitton's husband, Jean Ogliastro, was sent to a concentration camp, and survived; a cousin named René Gimpel, a respected art dealer, died while being deported in January 1945. Their father, Gaston-Louis, however, sided with French general Philippe Pétain's German-backed government in Vichy for both political as well as business reasons, and instructed his oldest son, Henry-Louis, to work with Pétain's regime to keep Vuitton going. The company had a store on the ground floor of Vichy's elegant Hôtel du Parc next to other luxury goods shops, including the jeweler Van Cleef & Arpels. All were shut down by the Germans except Vuitton. Furthermore, Vuitton opened a factory to produce propaganda items, including more than twenty-five hundred busts of General Pétain, and Henry-Louis was decorated by Pétain's regime for his loyalty.

When the war concluded, it took some time for the luxury business to get going again. Materials were scarce, and some workers never came home. Most shuttered houses started up again and a few new ones opened, including Pierre Balmain, Givenchy, and Christian Dior; the latter kicked off the revival of couture with his New Look in 1947. "The styles [during the Occupation] were incredibly hideous and I couldn't wait to do something better," Dior said. "I revived the ripe bosom, the wasp waist and the soft shoulders, and molded them to the natural curves of the feminine body. It was a nostalgic voyage back to elegance."

French actress Leslie Caron remembers the period well. In 1953, fresh from her success in *An American in Paris,* the twenty-one-year-old Caron was escorted to Dior by her former ballet master Roland Petit because, he told her, "you need to be dressed properly." As Caron told me one summer evening in the salon of her Left Bank apartment in Paris, "It was as important to be well dressed as it was to be educated, have good manners, eat well."

Caron and Petit met with Christian Dior and his head vendeuse at the avenue Montaigne headquarters salon. "Roland knew very well the première vendeuse, who was a *grande dame de la societé*—the vendeuses moved in those circles," Caron said. "They knew what to wear to which event and wouldn't let any dress be worn by two clients for the same event. Never. And they had great authority. When they said, 'No, darling, that simply does not suit you!' you listened." After picking out a white satin duchesse gown with a knot in the front and a little black velvet dress trimmed in grosgrain, Caron, like so many others, became a devoted couture client.

More than two hundred thousand women worldwide wore couture in the 1950s. It was an expected part of a bourgeois woman's everyday life. Today, in comparison, a mere two hundred women worldwide buy haute couture. Suits start at $25,000, gowns $100,000, and are worn sparingly. I remember Ivana Trump telling me in 1988 that she wore her couture gowns a couple of times in New York and Palm Beach and then, rather than be accused of the social faux pas of being seen too many times in the same outfit, sent them to her mother in Czechoslovakia. And this was before the fall of the Berlin wall.

Buying couture in the postwar years was an exercise in high protocol. Twice a year, Dior sent out three hundred gold-embossed invitations to good clients, magazine editors, reporters, retailers, and celebrities to attend the showing of Monsieur Dior's latest creations, which were presented each January and July in the couture salons of the early-nineteenth-century gray granite headquarters—or "house"— at 30, avenue Montaigne. Guests were seated in rows of delicate chairs; behind them in alcoves sat giant urns of roses, gardenias, and carnations whose scent perfumed the air. The shows started precisely on time, and no special accommodations were made for latecomers. Once the duchess of Windsor arrived after the show began and was relegated to the staircase.

The swanlike models glided regally through the gold and olive rooms as an announcer called the name and number of the dress or suit, paused under the enormous crystal chandeliers, posed arms akimbo, twirled with great purpose, effortlessly slid off the jacket or wrap, twirled again, and continued. The American and European department store and boutique retailers seated in the front row scribbled potential orders in their notepads, and the chic Parisian and celebrity clients—many dressed in last season's Diors with pearl chokers, hats, and gloves—occasionally nodded approvingly. Shows lasted three hours; today they're twenty minutes—half an hour is considered long. The show concluded with a elaborate bridal gown, and the models would receive a thunderous applause punctuated with *"Bravo!"* and *"Magnifique!"* Dior himself was rarely there. "After all the horrors of preparing a collection," he explained, "I wouldn't think of attending a show."

After the show, Caron remembers, "if you decided to buy, you stayed. The ladies would be strewn out in the big salon, and there were several salons. The vendeuse called and asked the mannequin to put on the dress you liked. You looked at it, at all its sides, and you'd say, 'I like it, but I'd like it longer, shorter, whatever.' Then you had a rendezvous and you went into the *cabines"*—or dressing rooms—"and there were three fittings for each dress."

The Parisian clients were, as Dior himself put it, "singularly difficult." "At a fitting she behaves like a contortionist," he told *Time* magazine in 1957. "She stands up, sits down, bends and wriggles around; actually she is testing a dress because, she knows, an unhinged strap or a clasp could mean disaster at a fancy soirée. Often she brings along her husband or her lover, and they fidget as well over stitches, seams and buttonholes. They exasperate us, but we cannot afford to ignore their fussing, however petty it may seem. Unless they leave *chez* Dior in complete self-confidence, we have blundered and our image will be tarnished as a consequence."

The couturiers were often personally involved in fittings, and the clothes were constructed solidly so that they could be worn often and for years. "A dress or a suit was built on you, taking into consideration your own shape and above all, made to make you feel comfortable and at your best. You could relax and think of something else," Caron said. "The dress behaved well, served you well, whether you stood or sat for long hours. Dior, Marc Bohan, Givenchy, Yves Saint Laurent would ask you, 'What are you going to be doing in this outfit? Do you need to run or dance? Don't choose velvet if you're going to sit long hours at a gala, it makes a mark on the seat. Let's not make it tight at the seat, it wrinkles when you stand. This length is good for you, that one is not.'

"Sometimes you see women today wearing suits where the arms are tight," she told me. "I think, 'Oh my God. Nobody knows that you have to take into consideration the upper arm!'" She picked up the catalog from the sale of some of her vintage couture at Sotheby's in June 2006 and flipped it open to a photo of a Saint Laurent red and pink wool tweed suit that she wore in the 1965 film *A Very Special Favor* to show me what she meant. "Look how beautifully molded it is," she said. "It fits just exactly to your measurements." Then she pointed to a picture of her in a Saint Laurent tangerine silk and sequin gown presenting Mike Nichols with the Best Director Oscar in 1968. "This was a difficult dress to make because there was no bra," she explained. "It was silk jersey and it was worked in a way so there were no seams. That takes a lot of imagination. Couturiers had their tricks." She turned a few more pages to a photo of Saint Laurent's famous pop art minidress from 1966: simple shifts made of geometric and flowing shapes in Crayola-like colors. The form, she said, "was all in the wave, which was all different pieces. The advantage is, the bust is worked in the seam and there's a lining, in Jap silk. Everything was lined in Jap silk. This had a complete underdress in Jap silk."

Couture houses sold their patterns to American department stores such as Saks Fifth Avenue in New York or I. Magnin in San Francisco for one-year reproduction rights. That way, American society ladies who couldn't make the trip to Paris could order up a new couture creation in their hometown. It wouldn't be a Paris creation per se, but pretty close. And the American department stores did their best to re-create the ambiance of the Paris couture salons, with private fittings in spacious dressing rooms. Middle-market garment manufacturers would pay a fee—in 1957, it was $2,000—plus royalties to Dior to incorporate elements of Dior's design into dresses and suits that retailed for $50 to $60 in the United States. "If you don't come to Paris, you're missing the boat," one New York ready-to-wear manufacturer said at a Dior show in 1957. "There are more ideas in a thimble here than in all of America."

Dior understood that the middle market was the future of luxury fashion, and sold not only his ideas but also his name to companies that could spread the Dior gospel to those who could not afford a made-to-measure frock. He started with American-made stockings, since the French industry still hadn't quite recovered from the war. "I have the girls wear American stockings," Dior told his backer Jacques Rouët in 1948. "Why not use our own name?" Dior hosiery was born, as was the notion of licensing of fashion as a viable business option.

The Walt Disney Company turned licensing into a megabusiness in the 1930s and 1940s by having outside companies produce Mickey Mouse books, toys, and other kitsch. Dior saw licensing as a way to extend a luxury brand business to a wider audience without taking on the cost or management responsibilities. Dior contacted leading manufacturers in particular domains and negotiated deals for them to produce items with Dior's name. In return, Dior was paid a royalty on the sales. By 1951, Dior had licenses for handbags, men's shirts, gloves, scarves, hats, knitwear, sportswear, lingerie, and even eyeglasses.

Soon licensing was the hottest business move in the luxury fashion business. Couturiers licensed their names for perfumes. In 1959, Pierre Cardin, a former Dior assistant who started his own business, revolutionized fashion by licensing the mass production of women's designer ready-to-wear. Instead of going to a department store to have a Cardin dress made for you with the store's label inside, you could buy it off the rack and it would bear the label "Pierre Cardin—Paris." Cardin's name was stamped on everything from umbrellas to cigarettes, making his signature a coveted logo.

Another former Dior assistant—and later Dior's heir—Yves Saint Laurent, took licensing one step further in 1966 by introducing a lower-priced ready-to-wear line called Rive Gauche that targeted young people. Rive Gauche changed the fashion paradigm. Before it was simple: couturiers made exquisite clothes and sold a bit of perfume and some accessories. Now there was a new pyramid model: made-to-order couture on the top for the truly rich, ready-to-wear by the same designers for the middle class, and a broad array of fragrances and accessories for those at the bottom. With the advent of licensing names, the fragrance business began to grow, and couture diminished rapidly.

"I stopped buying couture because, frankly, it was considered really old-fashioned," Leslie Caron told me. "I remember one of the fashion magazines asked me to do a layout in about 1968, and they came up with people I had never heard of like Biba. You were supposed to look like a flower child. You couldn't wear hats anymore, you couldn't wear gloves or a bra, and you looked really old-fashioned if you wore couture dresses."

Master couturier Cristobal Balenciaga was so disillusioned by the dressing down of society that he abruptly announced the closure of his house. "I was staying with Mona Bismarck in Capri when the news came," Diana Vreeland recalled in her book. "Mona didn't come out of her room for three days. I mean . . . it was the end of a certain part of her *life*!"

It was also an end to a certain part of the luxury business. From then on, luxury was no longer simply about creating the finest things money could buy. It was about making money, a lot of money. Couturiers licensed their names liberally, and not just on perfume and eyewear. Givenchy and Pucci both did special designer editions of Lincoln Continentals. Quality dropped. "I bought ready-to-wear made of really bad quality material for a while," Caron remembered. "I have pictures of me going to the Oscars or premieres in really horrible rags that were considered fashionable." Service evaporated. "Bloomingdale's is the end of shopping because there isn't anyone to wait on you," Diana Vreeland wrote in 1984. "Then you see a man; you think he's a floor-walker: 'I'm sorry, lady, I can't help you. I'm like you, I'm just looking for somebody to help *me*.' So you go out into the street with tears in your eyes: you've accomplished nothing and you've lost your health! . . . Or I go into, say, Saks Fifth Avenue, and there on a rack on wheels are two dozen $5,000 dresses. On a rack! It shocks me . . . $5,000 dresses, dangling there . . . Of course a lot of people enjoy the variety. They go home empty-handed. But they've shopped. It's a sport."

VUITTON WAS OUT of step with the times, and this is evident when visiting the museum. From the postwar era to the early 1980s, there is little on display. Henry-Louis, who was in charge of sales, and Claude-Louis, who oversaw production, were gatekeepers, not innovators. Vuitton made old-fashioned luggage the old-fashioned way for a limited—and aging—clientele. The business foundered, the workshop in Asnières could barely meet the meager demands. By 1977, the company had two shops—one on the avenue Marceau and the other in

Nice—a piddly 70 million FF (approximately $12 million) in sales and 7 million FF (approximately $1.2 million) in profit.

Finally, in 1977, Renée Vuitton, the eighty-year-old family matriarch, asked her sixty-five-year-old son-in-law Henry Racamier to take over. Racamier was quite a presence: he stood six feet two and was regally handsome, with a manner both polite and genial. Like Louis Vuitton, Racamier was from the mountainous Jura region in the east of France. In 1943, he married Gaston-Louis and Renée's third daughter, Odile. He then started his own sheet steel company, called Stinox, and ran it so efficiently that it became the leader in its market sector. In 1976, just as the steel business was taking a downturn, Racamier sold his company to the German firm Thyssen and retired. He was too dynamic to be content doing nothing, so when his in-laws asked for help, he agreed.

Racamier looked at the books and discovered that retailers— mostly franchisees—were making the biggest profits. At the time, most luxury companies were still small, run by the original founders, and their expertise was in creation and production, not merchandising. It made more sense, particularly overseas, to let someone else risk putting up the money for the store and its stock. The local merchants knew their clientele far better than any Paris-based designer ever would. The merchants bought the product wholesale from the brand, sold it for twice as much—or more—at retail, and made a killing.

Racamier wasn't a fashion person; he was a businessman. He decided to implement a strategy called vertical integration at Vuitton: he cut out the middleman and opened Vuitton–owned-and-operated stores. It was revolutionary in luxury fashion and a roaring success financially. Within a few years, Vuitton was enjoying a whopping profit margin of 40 percent when most of its competitors were still earning 15 to 25 percent. Today most luxury companies follow Racamier's model and are now vertically integrated.

Racamier expanded production at the Asnières compound and built new workshops in the provinces. He introduced a new, popular line called Epi, whose products were made of leather with fine, uneven horizontal stripes; arranged for Louis Vuitton to sponsor the qualifying races for the America's Cup regatta to raise the brand's profile; and opened stores throughout Asia and on Fifty-seventh Street in New York. In 1984—only seven years after Racamier took over—sales at Vuitton had increased fifteen times, to about $143 million, and profits by almost thirty times, to about $22 million. That same year, Racamier listed Vuitton on the Paris Bourse and the New York Stock Exchange. Going public forced the company's executives to work more professionally, but it also made the company vulnerable for takeover.

In 1986, Louis Vuitton acquired Veuve Clicquot, a champagne and perfume group that included Parfums Givenchy, the perfume and cosmetic company that was aligned with but independent of the Givenchy fashion house. The following summer Racamier orchestrated a merger between Louis Vuitton and Moët-Hennessy, creating the group LVMH, then the sixth largest company listed on the French stock market. In 1988, he added the Givenchy fashion company to the portfolio—at the then-astronomical price of $45 million—and promised its founder, Hubert de Givenchy, that he could remain as designer until he wanted to retire.

In less than a decade, Racamier had turned Louis Vuitton from a small family business that sold to an elite clientele to a powerful, publicly traded brand with substantial sales and even more potential. By merging it into an existing and stable corporate group, and then by adding Givenchy to create a luxury fashion division, Racamier gave Vuitton the heft and the organization it needed to conquer the world. Racamier saw globalization as luxury's future, and used the synergy among brands in the group to map out and launch their expansion; he turned luxury fashion from a one-man or family-run affair to a corporate industry focused on the bottom line, and he managed to do so while maintaining the brands' integrity. Racamier made one wrong move: he turned to someone outside the family for help, someone who had no emotional attachment to Vuitton or the other brands in the group, someone who had a fearless ambition and absolutely nothing to lose. It was a move that would change the course of luxury forever.

CHAPTER TWO

GROUP MENTALITY

"War destroys man, but luxury destroys mankind; at once corrupts the body and the mind."

—JOHN CROWNE, SEVENTEENTH-CENTURY
ENGLISH PLAYWRIGHT

*E*ARLY ON A COLD February morning in 1999, I met with Bernard Arnault, chairman of LVMH, at the group's headquarters in Paris to interview him for an article I was writing for *Newsweek* magazine. In ten years, Arnault had turned LVMH into a luxury monolith with dozens of brands earning millions of dollars. Arnault was in the midst of an attempted hostile takeover of Gucci, the publicly traded Florentine leather goods house that had, under the guidance of CEO Domenico De Sole and designer Tom Ford, in five years rebounded from near bankruptcy to become one of the most successful luxury brands ever. Arnault wanted Gucci in the LVMH group, and he invited me to his office that morning to explain why.

He walked in quietly. Though tall, he stoops slightly, as if embarrassed by his stature. He was nattily attired in a tailored gray suit, which set off his ice blue eyes, and his long, thin hands moved with grace, conveying his love of piano. Since his English is halting, we spoke in French, he in a hushed tone. His voice was surprisingly nasal and solidly tenor, with an appealing lilt that makes it dangerously reassuring. His manner reminded me of the old Teddy Roosevelt adage: speak softy and carry a big stick. Except Bernard Arnault carries a club, and during the last decade he had used it to beat luxury's players into submission. Luxury was his game now, and he had written a new set of rules.

With Arnault's guiding hand, luxury had gone corporate. Most of its major brands were now part of groups run primarily by executives who had little or no background in luxury but knew plenty about business. These executives included Johann Rupert, chairman of Richemont, which owned Cartier, Chloé, and Dunhill; Patrizio Bertelli, husband of Miuccia Prada and chairman of Prada, who had purchased a sizable chunk of Gucci stock; Jean-Louis Dumas, the chairman of Hermès, which controlled John Lobb shoes and Puiforcat silversmiths, and, as a descendent of the founder, one of the few luxury heads who had been raised, as the French say, with the culture of luxury; and Domenico De Sole, the Harvard-educated lawyer who had guided Gucci to its success and was positioning it for a much bigger future.

Arnault and I sat down at his conference table and got down to business. Why, I asked, was he trying to take over Gucci?

"Because, first of all, the company is doing well, and the shares were undervalued," he told me. "Gucci is a brand with a lot of potential, in development and in amelioration of its business activities, and it has a good team. For us, it is evidently complementary: it's an Italian brand in a portfolio that is primarily French, and it's one of the best businesses in the world."

And what, I continued, was his plan for Gucci if he succeeded?

"We want to bring ideas to improve profitability," Arnault explained frankly. "The profitability of Gucci is half that of Vuitton. So there is still room for improvement."

If there is one thing that has changed in luxury in the last thirty years, it is the single-minded focus on profitability. In the old days, when luxury brands were privately held companies, owners cared about making a profit but the primary objective in-house was to produce the finest products possible. Since the tycoons have taken over, however, that objective has been replaced by a phenomenon I call the cult of luxury. Today, luxury brand items are collected like baseball cards, displayed like artwork, brandished like iconography. Arnault and his fellow luxury tycoons have shifted the focus from what the product *is* to what it *represents*. To achieve this, they "enhance [the] timelessness" as Arnault likes to say, by trumpeting a company's heritage; hire a hip, young designer to give it a sexy, modern edge; strengthen the branding by streamlining the name (Christian Dior has become simply Dior, Burberry lost its 's) and splashing the logo on everything from handbags to bikinis; and advertise the entire package relentlessly to spread the new gospel to the masses.

Arnault plays up the cachet of his brands that much more by attending their fashion shows with his striking blond second wife, a Canadian-born pianist named Hélène Mercier. The pair arrives in a chauffeured sedan, and bodyguards usher them through the crowd to their front-row seats. There they hold court, greeting high-profile guests such as France's former first lady Bernadette Chirac or actress Sharon Stone, who are seated immediately to their right and left. They pose for pictures and chat with magazine editors and newspaper reporters until the show begins. Most other luxury-group chairmen do not attend their brands' shows, and if they do, they sit in back rows and are unrecognizable. Few bring their spouses.

The result of all this hype is a product line that, Arnault says, "fulfills a fantasy. It is so new and unique you want to buy it. You feel as if you must buy it, in fact, or else you won't be in the moment. You will be left behind."

BERNARD JEAN ETIENNE ARNAULT was born on March 5, 1949, in Roubaix, an industrial town in the north of France not far from the Belgian border. The France of big families and industrial fortunes, it is perhaps the most conservative region of the country. Arnault's father, Jean, ran a family-owned construction business; his mother, Marie-Jo Savinel, was a pianist. As a boy, Arnault took up piano and showed great promise, though not enough to make it a career. "You have to be super-gifted," he said, "and I wasn't." Instead, Arnault enrolled in the École Polytechnique, one of France's prestigious *grandes écoles* that produce the country's business and political elite, and took a degree in engineering. Upon graduating, he joined the family business, called Ferret-Savinel, and in 1973 married Anne Dewavrin, a pretty blond from a prominent textile manufacturing family in Roubaix. According to Nadège Forestier and Nazanine Ravaï in their book *The Taste of Luxury: Bernard Arnault and the Moët-Hennessy Louis Vuitton Story*, Arnault kept the marriage a secret from the employees at Ferret-Savinel. (Full disclosure: while researching this book, I discovered that I was related to Dewavrin through marriage; this has had no impact on my coverage of Arnault.) He didn't wear a wedding band, and when his daughter was born, his secretary didn't even know.

Arnault was just as secretive about business. At twenty-seven, he negotiated to sell Ferret-Savinel's construction division to the Rothschilds' Societé Nationale de Construction for the impressive sum of 40 million French francs; he sought approval from his father only after the deal was agreed in principle. Jean Arnault stepped down, and Bernard Arnault took over Ferret-Savinel. Within five years, the company's development arm, Férinel, had become one of the top private home developers in France, specializing in vacation homes.

In 1981, François Mitterrand, the first popularly elected socialist president of France, swiftly nationalized banks and major industrial businesses. The new socialist economic policies made business conservatives like Arnault nervous. Arnault fled France with his wife and two small children, Delphine and Antoine, to the United States, where he bought a splendid Mediterranean-style home facing New York's Long Island Sound, enrolled his children in good schools, and began building vacation homes in Florida with moderate success. "It's tough in the United States if you haven't moved in the right circles from the start," he later said. After a few years, the socialists loosened their economic policies and Arnault decided it was time to return. But he didn't want to return as a property developer. He called his counsel Pierre Godé in France and instructed him to find a company to buy.

Like Arnault, Pierre Godé comes from the north, the city of Lille, where he worked as a lawyer for Arnault's father at Ferret-Savinel. Like Arnault, Godé is tall—he stands six feet four—and dashing. And like Arnault, Godé is wily, determined, and unafraid of confrontation. The pair circled each other at first, but once they bonded, it was for good. Godé served as Arnault's hatchet man: he would deliver the bad news and handle the difficult situations swiftly, if not painlessly.

I experienced this personally during my rendezvous with Arnault back in 1999. When I arrived for my appointment, I was informed by an assistant that I would get the bonus of talking to Maitre Godé about the Gucci takeover situation and was ushered into a conference room. Godé swaggered in like a French John Wayne, bore into me with his piercing eyes, and calmly proceeded to spin me dizzy with a well-versed tale about how awful Gucci was behaving and how LVMH was the victim. Never mind that LVMH had launched the takeover bid. I left the conference room worked over, worn out, and without a shred of useful information: mission accomplished. "I can be very un-pleasant," Godé once admitted.

In July 1984, Godé called Arnault in New York with a proposal: Boussac.

The Boussac textile empire had been acquired by a holding company called Société Foncière et Financière Agache-Willot and was in the midst of the second largest industrial bankruptcy in France. Most of its holdings were worthless. But there was one gem waiting to be dusted off: Christian Dior, the stalwart French couture house long known as the General Motors of fashion. Textile manufacturer Marcel Boussac was Christian Dior's original backer back when the house opened in 1946 and was an integral part of the Boussac Group. (Marcel Boussac died in 1980.) By the early 1980s, Dior was a fiscal mess: the main boutique was losing money, and 90 percent of Dior's sales were licenses. In 1983, Dior's own sales plus license royalties were 437 million FF ($85 million), and its net profits were a paltry 38 million FF ($7.5 million).

Its only hope was to be bought out. Cartier made overtures in the late 1970s, offering approximately $300,000. Moët-Hennessy was interested, too, as it already owned Parfums Christian Dior. But Christian Dior as a lone entity wasn't for sale. The French government insisted that Agache-Willot be sold as a whole. Godé convinced Arnault to return to France and put in a bid. Though Arnault was un-known in the luxury business community, he had a leg up on the other suitors. His wife was a distant cousin of the Willots, who were also from the north of France, and Arnault knew them socially: they all collected art and saw each other regularly at auctions. Arnault decided to deal with the Willots directly rather than through bankruptcy courts.

He had the social connections, but he needed financial might, too. He convinced Lazard Frères, the investment bank referred to then as the "second industry minister" for its close ties to the French government, to work with him and help raise the majority of the reported $80 million purchase price. It was perhaps the wisest move Arnault could have made: the link with Lazard gave the thirty-five-year-old Arnault the heft and legitimacy he needed to convince the French government he was a capable buyer. It worked: by the end of 1984, Arnault controlled Agache-Willot and, with it, Christian Dior.

Arnault immediately began to ruffle feathers both in French business circles and at Dior. Until the 1980s, business in France was a gentleman's game, governed by scruples and politesse. He was a new breed of French executive, the sort who would exhibit the kind of ruthlessness commonplace in America, where profit was the main if not only goal, but which to date had not been seen in France. He shocked the French business establishment—and the French government—by divesting the Agache-Willot conglomerate of many of its holdings. Within five years, Arnault had sacked some eight thousand workers and sold most of the company's manufacturing assets for nearly $500 million—making Arnault one of the richest men in France.

At Dior, Arnault's behavior was taken more personally. He had a very different way of working compared with Dior's gregarious former chairman, Jacques Rouët. Arnault did not feel it necessary to mix with workers and aspects of his reported behavior added to the distance between them: for example, shortly after taking over Dior, Arnault, because of his sensitivity to noise, reportedly claimed that the sewing machines in the ateliers above his office disturbed him and ordered the room to be soundproofed. He reportedly also insisted that the staff could no longer use the corridor in front of his office and that an elevator from the boutique to the executive offices upstairs was now reserved for only his use. His weak handshake and his habit of looking away when he spoke were seen by some as insulting, and his attire to others an embarrassment. The latter he eventually corrected when he turned himself over to the fashion department to be restyled.

Like Racamier, Arnault was a businessman, not a fashion person. When he took over Dior, there were 260 licenses worldwide for Dior products made by other companies, many below luxury standards. Dior handbags sold in the United States, for example, were made of cheap leather in Asia. Arnault reined all this in and began to apply Racamier's method of vertical integration—the business strategy of controlling production, distribution, and marketing in-house. Sales increased, and so did profits.

Most important, Arnault's devotion to the brand was unquestionable.

A colleague asked him one day what he would do if he were offered $500 million for Dior.

"I don't want to sell," Arnault responded. "The company's priceless."

FROM THE MOMENT Arnault got hold of Dior, he dreamed of building a luxury group, with the couture house as the cornerstone. His model was the Moët-Hennessy group, which included Moët & Chandon champagne, Hennessy cognac, and Parfums Christian Dior. Arnault's first move came in late 1986: he secretly met with Christian Lacroix, the critically acclaimed designer of the classic couture house Patou, and convinced Lacroix to leave with no advance notice, take several of his assistants, and open a new house called Christian Lacroix. In 2002, Procter & Gamble completed the purchase of Patou from the founding family. Today Patou continues to sell perfume, including its 1931 classic, Joy, but it never produced another couture or ready-to-wear collection after Lacroix's departure.

The way Arnault created the house of Lacroix stunned the luxury fashion community. It would soon prove to be Arnault's modus operandi: move in stealthily and conquer quickly, the luxury equivalent to the American military's "shock and awe" approach to war. Arnault and Lacroix's deal had comebacks for both of them. In 1988, French courts ordered Lacroix to pay $2 million in damages to Patou. And despite Lacroix's critical acclaim, by the time Arnault sold the company to the Miami-based Falic Group in 2005, it had never turned a profit.

In 1987, Arnault moved to acquire Céline, a forty-year-old luxury women's wear and leather goods company from its founders. Céline was a small family business: Madame Céline Vipiana designed, and her husband, Richard, handled the books. The company did a meager $20 million (1.2 billion FF) in sales and $5 million (26 million FF) in profits annually. Like Dior and other luxury companies back then, Céline's shops were often franchises, owned and managed by local merchants who paid Céline a percentage of the sales. It was the franchises that made the money. It was an easy way for brands to expand their presence, particularly in foreign markets like Japan, and earn a lot of money without much effort.

The Vipianas, well into their sixties, were thinking about retirement, and their son had no interest of taking over. In 1987, Arnault proposed to buy Céline but, according to the Vipianas, allow them stay on and help run it. They agreed and sold him two-thirds of their shares. However, within months of signing the deal, the Vipianas say, they were unexpectedly ousted by Arnault. "You can stay at home, Grandpa and Granny," Pierre Godé reportedly said, according to the Vipianas. "We'll call you if we need you."

Feeling beaten, they sold Arnault the remainder of their shares. A few months later, the Vipianas ran into Arnault and Nan Legeai, Céline's new beautiful blond CEO, at a restaurant in Monte Carlo. "If you'd told me that you would put us out into the street after three months, I'd not have sold you the company for twice what you paid us," Richard Vipiana hissed at Arnault. "You treated us very badly."

Maybe so, but Arnault had not broken any laws and in a matter of three years he had achieved his goal: he owned a luxury goods group.

In the spring of 1988, LVMH's vice chairman Henry Racamier—in a move he would later regret—rang Arnault and proposed that they meet to discuss Arnault's possible involvement in LVMH. Racamier was in a power struggle with LVMH chairman Alain Chevalier and thought that aligning himself with Arnault would tip the balance in his favor. Arnault had other ideas. Once Racamier believed that he had Arnault as an ally, Arnault met with Chevalier and negotiated another deal that allowed Arnault to acquire a major stake in the group. After several months of battles with Racamier, Chevalier was worn out and stepped down as chairman of LVMH. Arnault, by then the main shareholder of LVMH, became chairman of the group, and Racamier served its as vice chairman and managing director as well as chairman of the Louis Vuitton brand. For the next fifteen months, Racamier and Arnault fought for control of the group—in the boardroom, the courtroom, and the press—in what became known as the LVMH Affair. A top private investigator was hired to look into Racamier's and the Vuittons' lives, and French daily newspapers published stories that alleged—falsely—that Racamier supported radical right-wing politician Jean-Marie Le Pen and that his grandchildren goose-stepped like Nazis in the backyard. At one point criminal charges were filed against Racamier for allegedly committing fraud with a Vuitton distribution partner, prompting police to raid Racamier's Sixteenth Arrondissement home the morning of a Givenchy couture show; the charges were later dismissed. The French daily *Libération* called Arnault "the Machiavelli of finance."

Finally, in April 1990, following a judicial ruling in favor of Arnault, seventy-seven-year-old Racamier resigned from Vuitton and LVMH. At forty years old, Arnault had it all, closing one of the most venomous business takeovers in France; it later contributed to French takeover regulation reforms. The Vuittons packed up their belongings and left the avenue Montaigne headquarters, with Racamier's wife, Odile Vuitton, in tears. "One always recognized that one day the business might pass out of the family's hands," Denyse Vuitton's husband, Jean Ogliastro, told reporters. "It's just hard that it happened in this manner . . . One couldn't say that Bernard Arnault behaved to us in a gentlemanly way."

Three months later, Arnault and his wife were divorced.

RACAMIER HAD JUMP-STARTED Louis Vuitton. By the time he resigned, in 1990, the company had expanded to 125 stores and $4.167 billion FF (about $765 million at exchange rates then) in sales. But Bernard Arnault took Vuitton, and all of LVMH, to another level altogether. His motivation was simple: the luxury goods industry, he said, "is the only area in which it is possible to make luxury margins." He expanded his group, focusing on what he calls "star brands"—brands such as Vuitton, Givenchy, and Dior, which he described as "timeless, modern, fast-growing, and highly profitable [companies built] for eternity."

Some brands he bought easily, others through bold, acrimonious takeovers. With each new brand, Arnault saw opportunity for exploitation. The younger brands like Bliss, Michael Kors, and Marc Jacobs were easy: he streamlined them and folded them into the LVMH production, distribution, and retail network. The older brands were another story. They needed to be renovated top to bottom. To do it, Arnault implemented the new luxury model he helped develop: enhance timelessness, jazz up the design, and advertise like crazy.

At Vuitton, he began in 1990 by hiring an ebullient forty-two-year-old French businessman named Yves Carcelle as his new head of strategy and development; after a few months, Carcelle was promoted to CEO and chairman of Louis Vuitton. Carcelle was the only son of a civil servant and, like Arnault, had studied at the elite École Polytechnique. Rather than pursue mathematics, Carcelle went into marketing. He worked briefly as a traveling salesman hawking sponges and spent nine years with a German consumer products group. In 1985, he was hired by a big French textiles group to turn around its failing luxury linens brand, Descamps. In eighteen months, through staff layoffs and production reorganization, Carcelle brought Descamps back into the black.

Even so, Arnault and Carcelle had their work cut out for them. "You think of Vuitton and you think of airports," *Vogue*'s editor in chief, Anna Wintour, told the *New Yorker*. "Until now, it has had no fashion cachet, no status. Vuitton's image has been—it has been Palm Beach."

To refurbish the company's heritage, Carcelle and his number two, Jean-Marc Loubier, launched Vuitton ad campaigns that romanticized luxury travel; organized and sponsored antique car rallies, such as the Vintage Equator Run in 1993 across Southeast Asia; and invited journalists on tours of the Asnières workshop to write stories about how a Vuitton trunk was made. They reintroduced the century-old Damier checkerboard canvas and launched a retro handbag design called the Alma that was inspired by a luggage line from the 1930s.

Once they had manufactured the dream, they livened up the design side. For the centennial of the monogram canvas in 1996, they hired seven cutting-edge designers to reinterpret the canvas and ran the creations as an ad campaign. Spanish designer Sybilla came up with a backpack with an umbrella sprouting from it. Azzedine Alaia wrapped a monogram handbag in leopard skin. Vivienne Westwood came up with a bustle-like fanny pack. But Arnault wanted more. One of the best ways to garner attention is the women's ready-to-wear shows held twice a year in New York, Milan, and Paris. Covered by more than a thousand journalists and photographed by dozens of newspapers, wire services, and photo agencies, these shows get immediate headlines—and pictures of the outfits appear in magazines and newspapers all year long. "What counts with critiques is not whether they're good or bad," Arnault told me, quoting Christian Dior. "It's whether they're on the front page."

Arnault wanted a women's ready-to-wear line at Vuitton and told his staff to find a hip, hot designer to do it. After reviewing various suggestions, Arnault hired Marc Jacobs. It was a curious choice. In his midthirties, Jacobs was scruffy and bohemian, a New Yorker deep in his bones. A few years earlier, as the designer for New York–based Perry Ellis sportswear line, Jacobs shook up the fashion world with a ragtag collection of clothes inspired by rock star Kurt Cobain and dubbed grunge. The collection won Jacobs the Council of Fashion Designers of America women's wear designer-of-the-year award—and got him sacked from Ellis. For the eponymous company he started with his Ellis settlement, Jacobs made pretty, modern, and dizzyingly expensive clothes for cool rich girls like his pals Sofia Coppola and Kim Gordon, guitarist and singer for the rock band Sonic Youth. What could he bring to the staid, bourgeois house of Vuitton?

Attention, that's what. Jacobs's Vuitton ready-to-wear collections immediately became the most popular and critically lauded during Paris's fashion week and are now seen as a style bellwether for the industry. But the clothes are produced in small quantities, sell for extremely high prices, and are available only in Vuitton boutiques. The ready-to-wear line's main function, it seems, is to garner headlines and dress up ads to sell leather goods: while it gets a great deal of attention, according to analysts it constitutes a meager 5 percent of Vuitton sales.

While revitalizing the image of Vuitton, Arnault and Carcelle simultaneously strengthened its business side. During Racamier's reign, Vuitton outsourced 70 percent of its production. Carcelle pulled it all back in-house and increased the number of factories from five to fourteen in ten years. Carcelle also continued Racamier's effort to take control of distribution by buying out the brand's U.S. franchisees. "If you control your factories, you control your quality," Arnault explained. "If you control your distribution, you control your image." By 2004, analysts believed that, with its fully owned distribution network of three hundred stores, Vuitton earned gross margins of 80 percent.

Arnault was to come in for more criticism over the way he went about the renovation of Dior. Dior's sixty-three-year-old couturier, Marc Bohan, allegedly learned of his dismissal from his job of twenty-nine years in May 1989 when a reporter from *Women's Wear Daily* called for comment. "I was thrown out as abruptly and brutally as if I had been an incompetent valet," Bohan told the press. Arnault replaced Bohan with Italian ready-to-wear designer Gianfranco Ferré, a move that offended the French as well as those in the couture business, many of whom believed that a ready-to-wear designer knew nothing of the art of made-to-measure clothes.

At Givenchy, Arnault also made radical changes. After a series of tenuous negotiations that played out in the press, Arnault and Hubert de Givenchy reached an impasse, causing the distinguished couturier to retire from the house he had founded forty-three years earlier. Arnault ignored Givenchy's handpicked choice as successor and hired British designer John Galliano, the thirty-five-year-old plumber's son and darling of the fashion press who was known as much for his wild partying as for his bias-cut flamenco dresses and 1950s-inspired tulle confections. Givenchy learned of the appointment at the same time as journalists, through a release from his own press office. When I asked Galliano about the longtime, primarily American Givenchy clientele, he snapped in his working-class-accented English, "I don't *intend* to please them. I'm not going there to please them, and probably a lot of them will move away."

In 1996, Arnault didn't renew Ferré's contract at Dior, and moved Galliano from Givenchy to Dior. Arnault interviewed Jean-Paul

Gaultier, the bad boy of French fashion best known for designing Madonna's cone-breast corsets, for the Givenchy job. Gaultier turned it down; he wanted Dior. Arnault then took a look at Alexander Mc-Queen, the twenty-seven-year-old son of a London cabbie. McQueen was an anathema in luxury fashion, with his soft pudgy body, hard East End accent, and enough rage to make Johnny Rotten seem sweet. He made his name in fashion with shows like Highland Rape, in which models in kilts and shredded lace dresses were splattered with blood. But as he proved during his studies at Central Saint Martins in London and his apprenticeship on Savile Row, McQueen had great talent and, if he could direct his rage, even greater potential. That's what Arnault was banking on. More than once during negotiations, McQueen stood up and told Arnault off.

"Look," McQueen's lawyer said, trying to calm his client down, "they're the cart, and you're the only horse who can pull it."

"I'm not their *horse!*" McQueen exploded. He turned to Arnault.

"I don't need you!" he blasted.

Then he stormed out of the room.

McQueen later changed his mind and took the job.

I met McQueen a few weeks before his Givenchy ready-to-wear debut in Paris for a cover-story profile for *Newsweek International*. He sat at Hubert de Givenchy's desk, which overlooked the avenue George V. He had just shaved his hair into a Mohawk for the cover picture, and the trimmings were scattered across the white Formica desktop. During our talk, McQueen told me, "My clothes are out there on a limb, and I get slagged for it. It's like Hitler and the Holocaust. He destroyed millions of people because he didn't understand. That's what a lot of people have done to me because they can't understand what I do." He quickly sought to shift away from the house's longtime muse: "[Audrey] Hepburn is dead," he told another reporter.

Arnault was just as cold-blooded when reorganizing the executive offices. In 1996, he replaced Parfums Givenchy's longtime head Jean Courtière with former Procter & Gamble executive Alain Lorenzo, and Parfums Christian Dior head Maurice Roger, known as the "Philosopher-King" for his disavowal of marketing studies, with Patrick Choel, a no-nonsense executive who had worked for Unilever for thirty years, most recently as CEO of Chesebrough-Pond's in the United States. Not surprisingly, the press dubbed Arnault the "Terminator." "For a European, I have a U.S. approach," Arnault explained. "That is, I face reality as it is and not as I would like it to be. I build for the long term." A longtime colleague put it more succinctly: "[Arnault] is 100 percent capitalist in a country that has never accepted capitalism. And he has rubbed everybody the wrong way."

The new designers fulfilled their mandate—they grabbed headlines with crazy stunts like the Dior collection of newsprint dresses inspired by the homeless—and the new marketing executives made the most of the hoopla. Not surprisingly, many longtime old couture clients fled to more traditional houses such as Yves Saint Laurent and Chanel.

"There I was sitting in a row of the Dior show with French first lady Bernadette Chirac and former first lady Claude Pompidou, and they looked like they had been hit in the face with a cold dead fish," New York socialite and lifelong Dior client Nan Kempner told me after a Dior couture presentation of Edwardian-style getups in 1997. "They couldn't believe what they were looking at: this conservative house where they've all bought their clothes for years. How much was there that Madame Chirac or Madame Pompidou could wear?"

Arnault didn't care; couture lost money, heaps of it. A new generation of Dior customers flooded the LVMH brand stores to buy something linked to the newly hip brands. Perfume and handbag sales doubled, tripled, and that's where the big profits were. "Selling to the right clients isn't an issue anymore," couture client and American socialite Susan Gutfreund conceded. "When it's all filtered down, it sells to the masses. You walk through the airport and buy a pair of

Dior sunglasses that you can afford and you feel like you have a bit of the magic."

FOR MUCH OF THE 1990S, Arnault's only real competitor on the group level was a conglomerate now known as Richemont, the Swiss-based firm that owns Cartier, Van Cleef & Arpels, Dunhill, Montblanc, and Chloé, and is controlled by Johann Rupert, an Afrikaner businessman from Johannesburg, South Africa.

Richemont began modestly: during World War II, Rupert's father, Anton, took over a small tobacco factory in Johannesburg with two friends. But after the war, Anton's entrepreneurial skills took over: he licensed cigarette brands from Rothmans, a well-known London tobacconist and, in the 1950s, went global. In the 1970s, Anton bought stakes in Cartier and Alfred Dunhill, which owned Montblanc writing instruments. Like Vuitton at LVMH, Cartier became the cornerstone and cash cow for what would become a luxury group. Cartier added a moderately priced contemporary line called Les Must de Cartier, which fueled growth and expansion.

In 1985, Johann Rupert, a banker who had worked for Chase Manhattan and Lazard Frères in New York and had run his own merchant bank in South Africa, joined the family-run firm. At the time the group was growing rapidly: it acquired Chloé, a fashion house known for its hippie-chic clothes, and Piaget and Baume & Mercier watches. In 1988, partly in response to trade sanctions against South Africa's apartheid rule, Rupert reorganized the business. He separated the luxury brands from the family's tobacco and mining assets, moved them to Luxembourg and Switzerland, and became CEO of the new group. He became chairman of Richemont in 2002.

Johann Rupert is as elusive as Bernard Arnault is known. He rarely appears in public and grants few interviews. The one time he made headlines in the British papers was for telling Margaret Thatcher to "stop interrupting me while I'm interrupting you." He travels incessantly, logging seven hundred hours a year on his two company jets. "In order to judge the mood and judge the future, you've got to go to the East," he once said. "You've got to go to South America. You've got to walk the streets of New York." He never attends fashion shows. "You are the star," he explained to Chloé's chairman Ralph Toledano, "not I."

When Rupert visits his brands' stores, it's informally: he drops in, unannounced and often unrecognized. He gives his CEOs complete autonomy but knows what's going on. Though his background is in finance, when he meets with his executives, he talks marketing and strategy, not figures. He looks long-term and rarely sells off his brands or trades them like Monopoly properties when they don't perform. He invests in them, sometimes quite heavily, and waits however long it takes for the return. Most of Richemont's sales are in jewelry and watches. "We concentrate on style rather than fashion," he explained. "We do not want to sell things that we have to discount two times a year."

While Arnault and other luxury tycoons were busy snapping up brands in the late 1990s, Rupert played the game conservatively. He made two major deals: he bought 60 percent of the legendary Paris jeweler Van Cleef & Arpels in 1999 for $265 million from the Van Cleef family, and he paid $1.86 billion in 2002 for three luxury watch brands—Jaeger-LeCoultre, International Watch Co., and A. Lange & Söhne—from Vodaphone. And he acquired controlling stakes in two smaller companies: Old England haberdashery and Lancel luggage. Rupert received—and turned down—offers by Tag Heuer, Ebel, Chaumet, and Zenith; each in turn was quickly picked up by LVMH. "It's not just about what you buy," he explained. "It's also a question of whether you can support the brands you have when times are bad . . . In my view, you ultimately create shareholder value better by building goodwill, rather than buying goodwill."

Unlike LVMH, Gucci Group, the Prada group, and other luxury conglomerates that clump their brands together to get better prices for retail leasing and advertising and produce their different brands at the same factories with the same workers, Rupert keeps his companies independent of one another. "Product integrity has to be more important than synergies," he said. "David Ogilvy [the advertising executive] used to say, 'The consumer's not a bloody fool; she's your wife.' The consumer wants to know that Piaget watches are made in the Piaget factory. [That's] what makes it special. Otherwise it's just another brand."

The Ruperts own 9.1 percent of Richemont—the rest is traded on the Swiss exchange—and control the company with 50 percent of the voting rights. As a result, Rupert says he does not feel pressure to deliver substantial profit increases each quarter. "We are not in a hurry," he has said. Indeed, when analysts said he paid too much for Van Cleef, he shrugged. "In five to ten years' time, it will turn out to be a good acquisition," he said shortly after the purchase. He is so cautious that banking analysts have nicknamed him "Rupert the Bear."

The strategy has worked well. In 2005, Richemont did $5.25 billion (€4.31 billion) in sales. Cartier accounts for about half of Richemont's revenues, and a staggering 85 percent of its operating profits, according to analysts. About 60 percent of Cartier's earnings reportedly are from sales of watches.

WITH ITS BRANDS growing exponentially, and the money rolling in from the sales of perfume and accessories, LVMH was flush and Arnault was feeling omnipotent. In 1998, he quietly began to buy up large chunks of stock of Gucci, one of the hottest brands at that moment.

Gucci has had a roller-coaster ride of a history. The company started in 1923 as a small shop in Florence selling imported luggage. As the business grew, owner Guccio Gucci added a workshop to produce his own designs. During supply shortages in the 1930s, caused by economic sanctions imposed by the League of Nations on Mussolini's Italy, Gucci started experimenting with new materials like canvas and bamboo, and making smaller items such as belts and wallets. In the 1950s and 60s, under the guidance of Guccio's sons Rodolfo and Aldo, the company flourished; its floral scarves, bamboo-handled handbags, and horse-bit loafers were favored by such icons as Jacqueline Kennedy and Grace Kelly.

The 1970s brought family infighting and overlicensing of the brand. By the late 1980s, more than twenty-two thousand products, from cigarette holders to scotch, carried the Gucci name. "It was pretty much trading on its past reputation," said Brian Blake, who joined the company in 1987 and a decade later became its president. "A very large proportion of business at that time was driven by the 'interlocking G' canvas material, which was very inexpensive to produce and had very low price points. No truly discerning luxury goods client would shop at Gucci." Famed marketing strategist Faith Popcorn put it more bluntly: "When you see [Gucci's signature red and green] stripe, you want to throw up."

In the 1980s, Rodolfo's son Maurizio took over the company, and brought in Domenico De Sole, an Italian-born, Harvard-educated lawyer at a top Washington law firm, as president and managing director of Gucci America to right its course. Over the next few years, De Sole fired 150 of Gucci's 900 employees, hired managers with serious retail experience, brought distribution in-house, reined in licensing, and bought back franchises—in effect, applying Henry Racamier's model of vertical integration. In 1989, Maurizio convinced legendary retailer Dawn Mello to quit her job as president of Bergdorf Goodman in New York and become Gucci's creative director in Milan. Mello discarded most of the existing products and hired a new design team, including Tom Ford, a twenty-nine-year-old former model/actor who studied interior architecture and had a few years experience in the Seventh Avenue rag trade, to revive and update great old classics as well as create a sleeker image for the house. "The bamboo-handled knapsack was the first thing I did when I came to Gucci," Ford told me. "The first *day*."

Gucci had a new staff, a new look, and a new business plan. But it wasn't enough. Maurizio's astronomical spending combined with an economic downturn caused by a war in the Middle East and a recession in the United States—both big Gucci markets—nearly did the company in. Losses were reportedly $102 million between 1991 and 1993, and the company was on the verge of bankruptcy. Investcorp, a Bahrain-based investment group that had bought out a number of family members in the late 1980s, paid $170 million for Maurizio's remaining 50 percent share in 1993. A year and a half later Maurizio was shot dead in Milan by a hitman hired by his ex-wife. Mello left, Tom Ford became creative director, and De Sole was named chief operating officer of the company.

One of De Sole's first moves was to drop the price on all Gucci products by 30 percent, putting them lower than Chanel and Hermès and on par with Louis Vuitton and Prada. Then Ford worked his creative magic to draw the public to Gucci. When he presented the first Gucci collection under his complete control in March 1995, he shattered Gucci's staid aristocratic image and established a more modern and blatantly sexy voice. "Before I sent that first women's show down the runway with the hip-hugger pants and the metallic shirt, I remember being so terrified because it was a dramatic change," Ford told me in 1996. "I really had to rethink Gucci, and what Gucci should be. And a lot of [editors and retailers] said, 'Oh, it's great, but it's not Gucci.' " It didn't matter. The public loved it. Gucci sales shot up from $264 million in 1994 to $880 million in 1996. Smaller houses and mass-retail chains like Gap and Zara followed Ford's design lead. Investcorp floated Gucci on the stock market, making it one of the most successful initial public offerings in fashion ever.

Back in 1991, Arnault had taken a good long look at Gucci with the idea of buying it. But after reportedly doing a great deal of due diligence, he backed off, telling associates that the brand wouldn't go anywhere. Instead Arnault watched it blossom into a star brand, and now he wanted it, badly. In early 1999, after quietly spending $1.4 billion to buy 34.4 percent of Gucci stock—10 percent of which he purchased from Prada—Arnault launched a takeover bid. Tom & Dom, as Ford and De Sole were known in the fashion press, fought back. Arnault was called "the wolf in cashmere" and "a snake." *Women's Wear Daily* dubbed the confrontation "The War of the Handbags." Ford threatened to quit if Arnault succeeded in his takeover; the clause in his contract that allowed this quick exit was called the Tom Bomb. De Sole declared, "Arnault is trying to steal this company."

On Friday, March 19, 1999, it all came to a head. At 8:30 a.m., Arnault held a meeting of his top executives at the Disneyland outside of Paris. After that, he was to meet with De Sole again. But De Sole had other ideas. He and Ford called a press conference in Paris to announce the formation of Gucci Group with the help of their white knight—and Arnault rival—François Pinault, a French financier who controlled a group called Pinault-Printemps-Redoute (PPR), which included the auction house Christie's, the Printemps department store chain, and La Redoute catalog. Pinault bought 40 percent of Gucci, for $2.9 billion—or $75 a share, $10 less than Arnault was willing to pay. Pinault also bought the Yves Saint Laurent Rive Gauche ready-to-wear and cosmetics companies for $1 billion. Arnault said he found the move "stupefying." "[Pinault] came to my home with his wife, and my wife was seated next to him at the wedding of his son," Arnault whined to *Women's Wear Daily*. He was particularly bent out of shape that Pinault didn't have the good grace to consult him first on the deal.

Pinault laughed. "What, do you think I was going to ring him up and say, '*Cher ami,* I'm stealing Gucci away from you?'"

Ford was soon designing both Saint Laurent and Gucci, and he and De Sole applied the vertical integration model to Saint Laurent to turn it into a global luxury brand. It took a lot of work. Saint Laurent's former business head Pierre Bergé was of the old licensing school. When PPR took over Saint Laurent, it had 167 contracts with licensees for everything from clothing to cigarette lighters. It only had thirteen directly owned stores worldwide. PPR acquired a few more classic houses—including Balenciaga, Bottega Veneta, and the jeweler Boucheron—which were renovated (with a new designer at the helm) and streamlined. It also financed the launch of two new labels: Stella McCartney, who left her design post at Chloé, and Alexander McQueen, who quit Givenchy. In April 2004, Ford and De Sole left Gucci Group because PPR wanted to take away their autonomy and have them report to senior group executives—in other words, more corporatization.

Gucci's victory against Arnault was significant: it was the first time Arnault was beaten at his own game. The loss was stinging: "Bernard Arnault hates to lose," a close Arnault associate told me. Before the creation of Gucci Group, there were a handful of groups, but they didn't really compete; LVMH was far and away the leader. Now with the formation of Gucci Group, Arnault had a direct competition for brands, for designers, and for customers. It was a new game, and Bernard Arnault no longer dictated the rules.

THE BIGGEST WINNER of the LVMH–Gucci battle was Prada: with the $140 million profit its chairman Patrizio Bertelli made from selling his 10 percent share of Gucci to LVMH, he went shopping for luxury brands. In 1999, Bertelli bought 51 percent of the trendy New York–based ready-to-wear company of Austrian designer Helmut Lang, a stake in the British shoemaker Church & Co., and (after years of wooing) controlling interest in German designer Jil Sander's highly successful ready-to-wear company. In a mere six months, Bertelli had put together a substantial privately held luxury goods group; combined, the brands did more than $1 billion in sales turnover annually.

It's hard to tell from the outside of the Milan-based headquarters that Prada is one of the world's most successful luxury brands and the cornerstone for an important luxury group. When you arrive at the company compound at Via Bergamo, 21, you think the cab driver has made a mistake. The street is gray and dreary, a deeply industrial section of a deeply industrial town. (LVMH's corporate headquarters, by contrast, are now in a sleek new building on the avenue Montaigne, across the street from the posh Hôtel Plaza Athénée.) You enter Prada through an anonymous portal-like oak door—there is no name, no plaque, nothing—and are greeted by a security guard dressed in gray. Everything is gray: the security office, the cobblestone courtyard, the various factory-like buildings surrounding it, and many of the cars parked in it. The only thing that gives the place away is the guard's uniform: it is not the typical formless security garb but tailored Prada with its stark—some would say neofascist—lines. That, and the clocks behind him showing the time in Milan, New York, Los Angeles, Tokyo, Sydney, and Hong Kong. When I was there in the spring of 2006, several of them were off by more than a few minutes.

I was taken to a room I had read about often. It is officially Miuccia Prada's office, and it is as stark and contrived as her designs: poured concrete; a slew of orange and yellow molded plastic Eames chairs; and, sticking up in the center of the floor, a metal tube slide— by artist Carsten Höller—that runs three floors down to the parking lot and is titled The Slide No. 5. Prada has whizzed down it when asked to by reporters.

Prada entered the room as if it were her salon and she had been ushered in by her trusted butler rather than her communications director. This was a woman who had been raised in haute bourgeois society, with servants and grandeur and politesse. Unlike her competitor Donatella Versace, who came from nothing, Prada's airs are not airs at all: her snobbery is in her bones. She was wearing a tightly belted full-skirted dress like 1950s matrons used to wear—think of Lucille Ball in *I Love Lucy*—but made of navy blue silk faille that rustled when she walked, with a light blue Oxford-like shirt underneath. On her feet was a pair of bamboo platform shoes that squeaked as she crossed the painted cement floor and made her teeter like a Chinese woman with bound feet. In her graying chestnut hair, cut sensibly at the shoulder, she had the requisite bourgeois headband, in dark green knit. She didn't have a stitch of makeup on, not even lipstick, but her brows were well brushed. Her aristocratic profile is the sort that has been rendered in marble by masters, and her sharp nose is well freckled. On her ears were big dangling antique diamond earrings—somebody's heirloom, if not her own—and just above her left breast a big, gaudy 1950s-like brooch.

She told one of her attentive assistants to bring her a pot of fennel tea, which she poured delicately like a proper English lady, and reluctantly told me a bit about the roots of her family and her company. Her grandfather Mario Prada came from a family of civil servants. "They must have had money, because they traveled," she said, and Mario soaked in the luxury lifestyles of Europe's upper classes. In 1913, he opened a shop called Fratelli Prada with his brother Martino in the Galleria Vittorio Emanuele II, a late-nineteenth-century shopping concourse next to the Duomo with mosaic tile floors and a domed glass roof. With the help of La Scala's set designer Nicola Benois, Mario decorated the shop like an English aristocrat's library, with rich woods, brass railings, and leather-bound books. Miuccia Prada told me that, contrary to the oft-recounted tale, Fratelli Prada was not a luggage shop or "travel company," like Louis Vuitton, but a boutique that specialized in "luxury objects." Indeed, the door of the Galleria shop still has the original sign, which reads *Oggetti di Lusso* (Objects of Luxury).

"He went to Vienna to find the best leather for cases, Poland for crystal for bottles," she said. "He sold watches and evening bags. He worked with artists as well as artisans." She showed me images of some of his products: a small lizard handbag with a marcasite-and-lapis-lazuli buckle from 1918, a black silk handbag with a hand-carved ivory monkey clasp from 1925, a toadskin wallet with a silver flower from 1927, a tortoise and enamel watch from 1938. "He had very grand ideas," she said.

Miuccia said she doesn't know how the shop weathered World War I, but it did, and sometime afterward Martino got out of the business. Mario opened a second shop on the nearby Via Manzoni, not far from La Scala. The company survived World War II, too, though Mario did close the Via Manzoni store then for good. After that, Miuccia became vague about family details. She claimed it was because she's not interested in the past, which may be somewhat true: the only thing historically referential in her designs is the little enamel triangle label, which is based on her grandfather's trunk labels. Her reticence could stem in part from her traditional upbringing. But I felt there was also a bit of mystery, something the family—or at least Miuccia—was hiding. When I pressed her on it, she bristled and answered hesitantly, if at all. What she wouldn't tell me, I discovered from sources close to Prada.

Mario married a woman named Fernanda—Miuccia wouldn't tell me her name—and they had two daughters, one being Luisa, Miuccia's mother. (Miuccia wouldn't tell me her aunt's name either.) Sometime in the 1940s, Luisa married a man named Bianchi, "from a wealthy, eccentric family," Miuccia said. She wouldn't tell me anything further about him—if he worked, if he supported the family, if he underwrote the company—except to repeat that he was "eccentric." She wouldn't even tell me his first name. "My mother would be very upset. She would think I've already said too much," Miuccia explained. His name, I later learned, was Luigi, and everyone called him Gino.

The Bianchis had three children, Alberto, Marina, and Maria—
who later became known as Miuccia—and they lived in a four-story,
late-nineteenth-century palazzo on the Corso Porta Romana where
Miuccia, as well as other family members, still resides today. When I
asked then why she was Miuccia Prada, and not Miuccia Bianchi, she
said, "My name is Miuccia Bianchi Prada. Some women keep their
name. It's done in Italy." In fact, according to sources at Prada, Miuccia Prada was officially named Maria Bianchi until the late 1980s,
when she had her elderly unwed maternal aunt adopt her, thereby
officially changing her name to Miuccia Prada.

After World War II, Mario Prada lost interest in his business, and
it continued on unremarkably until 1958, when he died and Luisa took
it over. The notion of a married, haute bourgeois mother of three working in a shop was unthinkable in Italy at the time. Miuccia explained
it this way: two businessmen actually ran the shop and "my mother
worked there. It was her little thing on the side." When I asked Miuccia if she ever helped out—ringing up sales, sending out orders—she
looked at me incredulously. "I was a student," she said in a tone that
made it clear that students of her rank did not work, even part-time in
the family shop. Miuccia remembers going to the Galleria boutique
once or twice in her youth. "It was not a woman's place," she said
firmly, though it was—at least in theory—her mother's shop. Her
father, Gino, had little if any involvement with the company or the
shop. At one point he produced lawn mowers for golf courses.

Her mother's "little thing" limped along for another twenty years,
draining the family's finances. "We passed from being rich to being
just well-off," Miuccia told an Italian paper. Finally in 1978, the
twenty-eight-year-old Miuccia took over, and she was about as unpre-
pared as one can be. She had a doctorate in political science from the
University of Milan and had studied five years with the Piccolo Teatro
to be a mime. Her only luxury experience was living it: she was a fashion addict, wearing Yves Saint Laurent, Biba, and André Courrèges.

She had moral objections to taking over the business: she was a feminist and a communist, albeit an Yves Saint Laurent–wearing, haute bourgeois feminist communist who had never worked a day in her life. "I loved fashion like mad, but I didn't like it as an idea," she told me. But then, she reasoned, the company "wasn't clothes, so it wasn't frivolous." When I asked her why she thought she could run a company without so much as one class in business management or one day of on-the-job experience, she waved off the question like an annoying gnat.

A year into it, she nearly threw in the towel. Then she met Patrizio Bertelli, a leather goods manufacturer from Arezzo, in Tuscany. Fashion legend has it that she caught him at a trade show in Milan in 1978 selling cheap knockoffs of her bags, legally pursued him to stop, then decided to bring him on board to handle her manufacturing instead. I asked her to recount the tale, and she came up with another one altogether. Bertelli—she always calls him Bertelli, never Patrizio—came into the Galleria shop and told her, "Why don't we work together?" She was taken by his "acute eyes" and said she'd think about it. "Probably had I not met him," she continued, "I would not have gone on. I couldn't have bought a factory then. Now I could do it, but then? A woman opening a factory? I didn't see it as very possible. He had a factory. He was already doing it. He had everything. So I could do the creative side. It took the company immediately to another level." When I asked about the trade show story, she said tersely, "I knew his company. I met other people, then him. I don't know if I noticed him there or met him in the store." The couple's relationship evolved rapidly from businesslike to romantic. They lived together for eight years, then married in 1987 and had two sons.

What is clear is that Bertelli pushed Miuccia to do things she would have never done otherwise. Within a decade, Miuccia Prada was overseeing the design of shoes and women's wear, which was often inspired by her bourgeois upbringing and tastes. In the mid-1990s,

Prada launched Miu Miu, which was a secondary, more youthful line, as well as men's wear and Prada Sport—all, Miuccia insists, against her will. "Shoes, I didn't want to do them," she told me. "Clothes either. I never wanted to do more." When Miuccia balked, Bertelli responded, "Fine, then we'll do them without you." And that, Miuccia says, was "impossible" for her to allow. In retrospect, she is pleased he pushed her. "If I had only done bags I would have been bored," she says now. "You enlarge your mind, you learn more."

As Miuccia tells it, she has always struggled to accept what she does for a living. "It's a very big conflict," she explained. "I am tempted to say what is luxury: servants and sixteenth-century service. If you want to talk about rare beauty, I know what that is. To fake luxury today is easy. You put some details from the brand's past, you put a little bit of gold, and that's it. I can't bear that . . . Real luxurious people hate status. You don't look rich because you have a rich dress. When you look at a person, do you see the spirit or the sexiness or the creativity? Just to see a big diamond, what does it mean? It's all about satisfaction. I think it's horrible, this judgment based on money. It's all an illusion that you look better because you have a symbol of luxury. Really, it doesn't bring you anything. It's so banal."

At one point, Miuccia was nearly saved from her daily torment: she was asked to run for the Italian parliament, though of course she wouldn't tell me when or by which party. She chickened out. "I'd have to stop doing my work," she explained. "Can you imagine a famous designer doing politics?" I was about to mention that the porn star Ilona Staller, known as Cicciolina, served in the Italian parliament in the late 1980s, but I bit my tongue.

As MIUCCIA PRADA reluctantly designed clothes, shoes, and handbags, Patrizio Bertelli focused on the business side of Prada. His method was absolute control through fear. He is a short, stout man with a bulldog face and well-trimmed wavy white hair. He wears mod retro glasses—like Peter Sellers but more narrow—which make him look like a hip intellectual. He is not known to have a sense of humor, and his temper is legendary. He explodes at the slightest mistake, "and not for one minute but for half an hour," remembers one former staff member. No one ever speaks back. Except Miuccia. They can fight like cats and dogs all day at the office, then go home together for dinner.

Bertelli is involved in every company detail: he has chosen the company's stationery, dictated the menu in the employee cafeteria, and personally hired much of the staff. When he opened the American subsidiary in New York, he had the office furniture sent over from Milan as well as a huge supply of pasta and his favorite olive oil for the employee kitchen. The porcelain and the cutlery in the New York office were the same as in Milan and Tokyo, and the receptionists all wore the same uniforms. At midday, cleaning people would come through the office to empty ashtrays and trash cans. Everything was always shipshape, one employee told me.

Bertelli's business methods are at times unconventional. In the early 1990s, for example, he killed the company's best-selling handbag line because he didn't want Prada to be associated with just one product. "He'll cut off business even if it's profitable at the time when he knows it's holding back growth," Leslie Johnsen, Prada's former director of public relations in New York, said. He can become so involved in design that he has been known to redo an entire handbag collection himself. Publicly, Miuccia welcomes his meddling. "It can be annoying," she once said, "but when he puts his hands on a product, I have to admit, it becomes better."

Once Bertelli had steered Prada into a thriving business—from $25 million in 1991 to $750 million in 1997—he started spending money like those nouveau riche clients whom Miuccia so loathes. In the late 1990s, he sank more than $50 million into the construction of *Luna Rossa*, a sleek gray and red yacht, for the America's Cup. Bertelli, an avid sailor, reasoned that the high-profile competition would bring a new sort of customer to Prada, as well as promote Prada Sport—now known as Linea Rossa—a line of overdesigned, overpriced athletic clothing launched in 1997. In the late 1990s, the Prada store architect Roberto Baciocchi was hired to turn the Via Bergamo building, which was a former gramophone factory, into the company's new headquarters and the Fondazione Prada, the couple's contemporary art foundation. The hall, with its exposed steel beams and bare cement walls, is the setting for Prada's women's and men's ready-to-wear wear shows as well as two art exhibits each year. Artists have included Mariko Mori, Barry McGee, and Carsten Höller. When I was there, New York artist Tom Sachs was setting up a show.

Then, in 2000, things began to go bad for Bertelli. *Luna Rossa* made the America's Cup finals only to be soundly beaten by New Zealand. Jil Sander up and quit as CEO and designer of the company she had founded thirty years earlier. "Quite simply, Bertelli and I had different visions about how to run the company," Sander told me later. Without Sander at the design helm, the company foundered and the brand quickly became worthless. And Prada's nonstop expansion—including the construction of a $40 million Rem Koolhaas–designed epicenter store in downtown Manhattan due to open in late 2001—was sinking the company further into debt. To raise capital, Bertelli decided to take the company public in late September 2001. When the September 11 terrorist attacks on New York and Washington happened, the Prada initial public offering was called off, and the luxury market deflated, literally overnight. By the end of 2001, Prada Group reportedly had debts of about $1.9 billion, approximately what it did in sales.

It was discussing the IPO that Miuccia Prada took me truly by surprise. I told her I had read in the morning papers that, now that the company had shed the Jil Sander and Helmut Lang brands, it was rumored in the business world that Prada might attempt an IPO again. No, she said, it wasn't true. I asked, "How many times have you attempted it? Three, right?" No, she said, once. On September 18, 2001. The other times, she continued, were invented by the press.

I stopped writing in my notebook and looked straight at her. I had heard that the accounting firm PricewaterhouseCoopers had prepared dossiers for two separate attempts since the first one in 2001 and, in 2002, Bertelli had held a press conference to announce one of them.

In her reluctance to be forthcoming, Prada had unwittingly exposed the Achilles heel of luxury today: in becoming leaders of global corporations, luxury executives must now conceal from the public not only how their products are made but how the individual brands are doing. The truth, if widely known, could shatter consumer confidence in the brands: they'd stop buying, profits would plummet, and the companies—and their parent groups—could face bankruptcy. Publicly traded companies are required to be transparent—that is, they must publish their financial data in their annual reports. But when luxury brands are consolidated into groups, they can lump all their figures together to disguise what's really happening. Overall, LVMH is raking in profits and its brands, thanks to the hype, seem highly successful. What you don't know is that, as Vuitton is doing record sales each year, the Givenchy and Kenzo fashion houses are muddling along.

In the last decade, more groups have formed, including the Bulgari Group, the Ferragamo Group, and the Valentino Fashion Group, and those that existed previously have added substantially to their portfolios. Today, there are very few European luxury brands that remain independent and privately held. Among them are Sonia Rykiel in France and Giorgio Armani, Versace, and Dolce & Gabbana in Italy, though Versace has talked about going public since before its founder, Gianni Versace, was murdered in 1997. Giorgio Armani, now in his seventies and with no apparent heirs, has over the years contemplated various options, including selling to LVMH and going public. Yet he resists.

I once asked him why. "I can allow myself to go back to the office at night, to change whatever I want without having to justify it to anyone, and without any anxiety about achieving certain financial results because investors—who understand nothing—decide that today its ten of something, then twenty then thirty. That's the problem," he said. "Sometimes results take a while, and most of the time, the market requires that the results be felt immediately. Psychologically, this isn't good for our work, because it puts a damper on our enthusiasm."

CHAPTER THREE

GOING GLOBAL

"He is poor who does not feel content."

— JAPANESE PROVERB

KYOICHI TSUZUKI, a Japanese photojournalist and publisher, has spent nearly a decade taking pictures of luxury-brand-obsessed Japanese in their tiny apartments surrounded by their collections of clothes, ties, scarves, jewelry, handbags, and shoes for the *Fashion News,* one of Japan's oldest fashion magazines. Tsuzuki calls his subjects "happy victims" because, while they are victims of brand marketing, the items seem to bring them a sort of happiness. On a cool November morning in 2005, I visited Tsuzuki in his apartment in Tokyo and, over cups of jasmine tea, he told me about these happy victims. There is the Hermès collector, a patent executive who lives in a tiny fourth-floor walk-up flat. He keeps all of his Hermès shirts, ties, and leather goods in their original boxes and bags, which are stacked up on his tatami floor. He spent half a million yen (about $4,000) on an Hermès briefcase that he carries with an Hermès towel wrapped around the handle to avoid damaging the leather with his hand perspiration.

There is a Buddhist monk who collects Comme des Garçons religiously. Once a month, Tsuzuki told me, the monk sheds his robes, dons Comme des Garçons' avant-garde constructionist clothes, and heads from his temple to Tokyo to pick up a few more pieces. He is so convinced of their miraculous powers that he says his delinquent sister cleaned up her act when she started wearing Comme des Garçons. There's an English teacher at a prep school who started wearing Gianni Versace's flamboyant designs to keep the attention of his students. After ten years, he had one hundred pieces of Versace as well as an impressive Bulgari jewelry collection. He lives in a shoebox apartment with his unemployed girlfriend, who spends her days organizing the collection. There's a Tom Ford collector (she has both Gucci and Yves Saint Laurent), an Armani man, a McQueen girl, and a Martin Margiela manic who is so fastidious about his collection that he never cooks at home because he doesn't want the clothes to retain the odors. The only thing in his refrigerator is eyedrops. "When he gets thirsty," Tsuzuki said, "he goes to a convenience shop and drinks there then goes back home. He does not want to put any kind of trash in the room."

Tsuzuki's subjects seem extreme. But in fact they are representative of the Japanese preoccupation with luxury goods. Analysts estimate that 20 percent of all luxury goods are sold in Japan and another 30 percent to Japanese traveling abroad—meaning Japanese buy half of all luxury goods. Today, approximately 40 percent of all Japanese own a Vuitton product. They claim in market studies that they buy luxury goods for a logical reason: durability. Experts believe, however, there is a far deeper sociological meaning. According to polls, the Japanese consider themselves to be a classless society—in one study, 85 percent stated they were middle class. At the same time, in Japan, conformity is prized. By wearing and carrying luxury goods covered with logos, the Japanese are able to identify themselves in socioeconomic terms as well as conform to social mores. It's as if they are branding themselves.

Their impact on the business is immeasurable. Their tastes influence product and store design. Their travel habits dictate where brands expand, and their exigencies affect how stores are run. "We never make any decision on our worldwide strategy without asking our Japanese colleagues what Japan would think of it," said Louis Vuitton CEO Yves Carcelle. The Japanese, in other words, homogenized luxury. And by doing so, they prepared it for globalization, which effectively is the homogenization of the world.

THE JAPANESE LOVE of Western luxury goods is a relatively recent phenomenon. In the 1960s and 70s, the Japanese economy flourished, giving birth to a newly flush middle class that wanted to live a more ostentatious life. Grand homes or vast real estate holdings—generally the most blatant way to enjoy as well as exhibit one's riches—was a near impossibility in the densely populated island-nation of Japan. Instead, the Japanese chose to show their wealth by dressing richly, and for the postwar generation, Western luxury items such as leather goods, silk scarves, furs, and jewels were the ultimate status symbols.

Unfortunately, there was little to be had in Japan; distribution was extremely limited. To satisfy the surge in demand, entrepreneurial Japanese merchants traveled to Europe, bought items at full retail price, shipped them back to Japan, and sold them for three to four times more in shops around Tokyo, creating what is known as a parallel market. The parallel market confounded luxury executives back in Europe: their flagship stores were getting cleaned out of stock, and they had no control over how the product was being sold overseas.

In February 1976, Louis Vuitton's great-grandson Henry-Louis invited Kyojiro Hata, consultant for the international accounting and consulting firm Peat Marwick, to his office at the avenue Marceau store to discuss the problem. Hata, in Paris on unrelated business, knew nothing of the luxury industry and had never heard of Louis Vuitton. But he was impressed by Henry-Louis Vuitton's manner—"He was a very shy, sincere person and extremely discreet," Hata told me—and by the genuine refinement of the store and its products. "The serenity and the high ceilings of Henry Vuitton's office were worlds away from my experience," Hata later wrote in his memoir, *Louis Vuitton Japan: The Building of Luxury.* "The long room had a small window from which to view the sales floor, and the walls were embedded with antique trunks. I felt the long history of Louis Vuitton and the depth of French tradition through my body for the first time. It was an awakening for me."

Vuitton explained to Hata his exasperation: the Japanese were buying so much that Vuitton had placed a limit on the number of products that could be sold to Japanese customers. Through the small window in Vuitton's office, Hata watched the frenzied Japanese customers in the avenue Marceau store, buying like they were at a fire sale. Intrigued by the phenomenon, Hata turned to Vuitton and proposed to do a research project assessing the Japanese luxury goods market. Vuitton agreed.

When Hata returned to Tokyo, he found Vuitton monogram bags in shop windows all over town for sale at astounding prices. At the time, there was only one Vuitton wholesale importer in Japan, and one official retailer: the Ann International store in the Akasaka Tokyu Hotel shopping arcade. When Hata visited the store, he recalled, "there was no stock at all and nobody knew when the next shipment would arrive." Hata wrote up his report for Henry-Louis Vuitton, concluding it was time for the company to embrace the Japanese market and expand properly there. Vuitton concurred and hired Hata to oversee it. Until then, luxury companies had opened stores in a few international capitals, often as franchises, and sold a limited amount of product in department stores; it was a niche retail business. Hata had much bigger ambitions: to conquer a foreign territory by selling not only to Japan's upper crust but also—and primarily—to its large and increasingly wealthy middle class. Vuitton's expansion in Japan was luxury's first bold step toward globalization, and it took an outsider—a businessman—to make it happen.

Hata came up with and implemented a two-pronged business model. First, Louis Vuitton Paris would distribute directly to Japanese retailers rather than through wholesalers—a business move unheard of in the luxury industry at the time. Second, Louis Vuitton would establish a management service contract stipulating that its Japan office would conduct all operations to maintain the brand's image, protect the trademark, and handle quality control, advertising, and publicity. In return, Vuitton would charge franchise and management service fees to the department stores. Louis Vuitton headquarters in France would dictate everything to the Japan operation, from uniforms to wrapping paper, to create a synergy with the home base. Vuitton's products would be excluded from department store members-only discounts and gift catalogs, all in an effort to buff up the company's brand image. "We wanted to accurately communicate not only the name of Louis Vuitton," Hata explained, "but the brand's values, which are its history and tradition."

In March 1978, Vuitton made its official Tokyo debut in five different department stores, followed in September by one in Osaka. Each shop was only seven hundred to one thousand square feet but stocked every size of steamer trunks—"the symbol of Louis Vuitton's craftsmanship," Hata told me.

Next, Hata tackled the pricing problem. When Vuitton opened its first Japanese store in 1978, prices were about two and a half times higher than in Paris, due to a difference in currency rates and to government restrictions. To even the playing field a bit and stop parallel trade, Hata implemented a floating-rate system so that prices in Japan would be no more than 1.4 times those in Paris, and would fluctuate with the exchange rate. Prices in Japan immediately dropped by half or more, and Japanese shoppers suddenly saw Louis Vuitton as a good value, especially compared to its competitors. That first year, the six stores sold $5.8 million worth of Vuitton products. "This surprised the whole industry," Hata remembered. Within two years, sales had doubled to $11 million. Vuitton appointed Hata the Japanese branch manager, and converted the branch into a corporation, called Louis Vuitton Japan. In 1981, Hata opened Vuitton's first freestanding store, in the posh Ginza district.

Furthermore, the Japanese demonstrated an unparalleled predilection for quality. "Their attention to detail and demand for quality is unmatched and unyielding," says Chanel Japan's president Richard Collasse. "The Japanese have zero tolerance for flaws."

He tells a story to illustrate point. Back in the 1980s, when Collasse worked for another luxury brand, a Japanese woman brought a dress in and said it had a defect. Collasse looked and looked and finally saw a two-inch thread dangling from the hem. It was absolutely unacceptable to her. Collasse exchanged the dress, bowed repeatedly, and sent her a big bouquet of flowers. Then he decided to do a test. He took the dress to a French woman. She tried it on, liked it, saw the thread, and said, "I can cut it." He took the dress to an American woman. She tried it on, liked it, and never saw the thread.

Vuitton's Hata ran into the same thing. "During the first ten years, we have often found ourselves having to return products to Paris saying, 'This level of quality is unacceptable in Japan,'" he recalls. "At first we had a very hard time being understood. If we returned a product because the fastener was attached the wrong way, they argued that we should sell it to a left-handed customer. If we complained that the stitches were not straight, they said it was because of the nature of hand stitching and that they could sell the products in Paris without a problem. On one occasion we returned all the products, saying, 'Please sell these in Paris.' " Finally, in 1991, Hata opened a Vuitton repair center in Japan; today, there are two.

LOUIS VUITTON'S expansion in Japan led the way; soon its competitors began to expand their presence there, too, selling in major department stores and opening boutiques in Tokyo's Ginza shopping district and in Osaka. The timing couldn't have been better. In the early and mid-1980s, the Japanese economy was soaring: it grew by 3.7 percent annually, and Japan's postwar generation experienced a dramatic increase of disposable income. Some of the investments were dizzying: Mitsubishi forked out $1.4 billion for 80 percent of Rockefeller Center in New York in 1989 and 1990; Sony bought Columbia Pictures in 1989 for $3.4 billion; Matsushita electronics took over MCA, which included Universal Studios, in 1990 for $6.1 billion; Japanese businessman Ryoei Saito spent $82.5 million for Van Gogh's *Portrait of Dr. Gachet* in 1990.

But the economic boom also created a new sociological phenomenon in Japan known in banking circles as Parasite Singles: unmarried university-educated women, ages twenty-five to thirty-four, who worked in good-paying jobs—as secretaries, teachers, executives— and lived with their parents. Their economic power was and still is impressive: analysts estimate that Parasite Singles account for nearly one-tenth of Japan's population of 130 million. With few living expenses, Parasite Singles use their ample disposable income to shop. Their favorite items: luxury brand leather goods, preferably covered with logos. Indeed, 23 percent of all luxury brand sales in Japan today are leather goods such as wallets and handbags.

When they first emerged, Parasite Singles shopped like mad in Japan, driving luxury brands to expand their presence and stock there.

Even after the bubble burst in the early 1990s, and the Japanese economy plunged into a decade-long recession, Parasite Singles' appetite for luxury brands did not wane. They were the only demographic group to increase spending during the 1990s, and they became responsible for up to 80 percent of Japan's consumer spending.

When they found they could buy more overseas with their strong yen, Parasite Singles embarked on international shopping trips, usually organized by charter companies, inciting brands to open stores in new markets and to add Japanese-speaking sales staff. One of Parasite Singles' favorite destinations was Hawaii: it was close, it was beautiful, and the yen went far.

In the early 1980s, Rolf Vogel, then president of Chanel in Japan, went to Hawaii on vacation and was stupefied to see the number of Japanese there, shopping. "Let's stop playing golf and look for a location," he told his colleagues.

Vogel rang Chanel executives in New York to inform them of his idea.

"Hawaii?" they responded incredulously. "Are you crazy?"

He wasn't. In 1984, Vogel opened Chanel's first freestanding store in the United States—before New York, before Beverly Hills—in the Royal Hawaiian Shopping Center, a mall at the entrance of the famed hotel's drive. The store carried accessories as well as a small selection of ready-to-wear by Chanel's new designer Karl Lagerfeld. The Japanese flocked to it, snatching up quilted leather purses, gold chain belts, and two-toned shoes like crazy. Throughout the 1990s, the Waikiki boutique was the number one Chanel store in the world, with $60 million a year in sales.

The success of Chanel drew other brands to open on Kalakaua Avenue. All the usual suspects arrived, each building a large, lush boutique with Japanese-speaking staff. It was a wise business move: within five years of its 1992 opening, the Louis Vuitton store on Kalakaua Avenue was doing nearly $100 million in sales annually.

Several brands reported that their Waikiki stores were among the most successful in the world, enticing more brands to open there and those who were there to upgrade their locations. In 2002, Chanel moved out of its Royal Hawaiian digs down Kalakaua Avenue into a twelve-thousand-square-foot flagship; Cartier moved into the old space.

The new Chanel store is a luxury shopping palace with expansive salons, high ceilings, plush carpeting, and gobs of handbags, sunglasses, shoes, suits—and security video cameras that are viewed at headquarters in New York. Of the seven hundred to eight hundred customers who enter the Chanel boutique on Kalakaua every day, most are Japanese and most buy accessories. Sometimes a Japanese customer will take a picture of an item in the store with her cell phone and zap the image to a friend in Japan with a note asking, "What do you think?" If the friend says yes, then the customer will make the purchase. If the desired luxury brand product is not available in the Waikiki store, the brand's salesclerk can find it in one of the mainland U.S. boutiques and have it overnighted to Hawaii before the customer heads back to Japan. Joyce Okano, regional vice president for Chanel in Hawaii, tells me that "more than half the sales of Chanel in Hawaii are to Japanese."

THERE WAS ANOTHER great attraction that drew the Japanese to Hawaii: buying luxury goods duty-free. Duty-free shopping allows shoppers holding boarding passes to buy tax-free goods that have never entered the local stream of commerce, thus providing a discount of 10 to 30 percent off full retail price. Hermès products in Japan, for example, cost 30 percent more than in France and 15 to 20 percent more than in duty-free stores. In 2005, about 10 percent of all Hermès sales were duty-free.

Today, according to the Tax Free World Association, annual duty-free sales are about $25 billion—$9.1 billion of which are luxury goods.

There are several duty-free companies in the world today, but the largest by far is Duty Free Shoppers (DFS), which operates primarily in Asia and the Pacific, and is majority-owned by LVMH. In 2006, DFS did about $2.2 billion (€1.7 billion) in sales—30 percent more than its nearest competitor.

The notion of selling items duty-free dates back as far as commerce itself. In Britain during the 1500s, seamen were offered liquor duty-free—or tax-free—for consumption on board ships in international waters. In the nineteenth century, liquor, cigarettes, and perfume were supplied duty-free to crew members and travelers on ships for voyages that took weeks or months. The modern version of duty-free retailing began with the International Civil Aviation Organization at the Chicago Convention of 1944, which allowed the selling of articles duty-free on ships in international waters and on aircraft on international flights, and created "customs-free" zones in airports. Soon after, Brendan O'Regan, the head of the Shannon Airport Catering Service in Ireland, opened a kiosk at the airport to sell gifts and souvenirs tax-free to departing passengers on transatlantic flights that stopped to refuel. Business started slowly—on a good day, it would do £5 in sales. But as international travel grew in the 1950s, so did O'Regan's business: in 1953, it did £120,000 in sales.

In 1960, two Americans college buddies named Robert Miller and Chuck Feeney, both graduates of Cornell University's hotel management school, were drinking in a bar in Barcelona and dreamed up a business to sell liquor tax-free to GIs ending their tours in Europe. They called their business Duty Free Shoppers and opened shops in Hong Kong and at the Honolulu airport in Hawaii to target Asian tourists. Business went so well that they eventually hired a British accountant named Alan M. Parker and an American tax lawyer named Anthony Pilaro to help optimize the profitability of the company and gave them each a small stake. Between 1977 and 1995, DFS generated some $3 billion in dividends, 90 percent of which the four partners

received in cash or funneled into their tax-driven trusts or foundations; both DFS and Feeney's foundations were then based in
Bermuda, an offshore tax haven. "This was not just a nice cash cow
they milked," said lawyer who knew the company. "The size is more on
the magnitude of Godzilla and King Kong."

Feeney, the more conservative of the pair, set up a foundation
called the Atlantic Philanthropies and donated generously to Cornell,
underprivileged youth programs, and Sinn Féin, the political wing of
the Irish Republican Army. He gave anonymously, and most recipients
never knew who their benefactor was. "I simply decided I had enough
money," he explained. "It doesn't drive my life. I'm a what-you-see-is-
what-you-get kind of guy." Miller, by contrast, lived large, with stately
homes reportedly in New York, Gstaad, Paris, Hong Kong, and York-
shire, England, and a taste for the extravagant: he once threw a three-
day party for which his Ecuadorian wife, Chantal, dressed as a South
American princess, arrived in a hot air balloon. For his daughter
Marie-Chantel's marriage to Crown Prince Pavlos of Greece, Miller
hosted a wedding for fourteen hundred guests that reportedly cost
$1.5 million and included a reception at the posh Claridge's Hotel in
London officially hosted by Queen Elizabeth II.

In 1994, Feeney decided to sell his stake to LVMH, DFS's largest
supplier. Miller was dead-set against it. "Despite his promises,
Bernard Arnault has a pattern of exploiting the assets of partially acquired companies for the benefit of LVMH with no concern for the
best interests of the minority shareholders," Miller charged in court.
Feeney and Parker sold their majority stake of the company to Arnault
for $2.47 billion. Eventually Pilaro sold his 2.5 percent to Arnault, too.
Arnault abruptly stopped negotiations for Miller's 38.75 percent—said
to be worth $1.6 billion at the time—and Miller remained a minority
shareholder of the company. Arnault told financial analysts it was "not
necessary at this stage to invest an additional 9 billion francs [$1.58 bil-
lion] to take advantage of the synergies that already exist between

[LVMH and DFS]." In other words, the world's leading producer of luxury goods controlled the world's leading purveyor of luxury goods.

AS WITH LUXURY, Bernard Arnault changed the way duty-free business was done. Traditionally, duty-free stores had been in airports or at ports, on airborne planes, or on ships at sea—places where it was guaranteed that the goods would not be entering the local stream of commerce. Arnault had another idea: targeting tourists in town. You still need a boarding pass, and your purchases will be delivered to you as you board the plane. But you are shopping in town, just across the street from your hotel.

In Waikiki in 2001, Arnault opened on the site of the old Woolworth's a $65 million, three-floor, gleaming white shopping-mall-like store on Kalakaua Avenue called the DFS Galleria to sell luxury goods at both duty-pay and duty-free prices. Compared to the usual stark, stock-laden duty-free stores in airports, the DFS Galleria was a veritable palace. To enter, you can either walk through a sixty-five-thousand-gallon aquarium filled with black tip reef sharks, spotted eagle rays, parrot fish, and other colorful Hawaiian reef fish or drift in through the sidewalk openings into an atrium loaded with Hawaiian floral perfumes, macadamia nut candies, and other Polynesian kitsch. The second floor is a regular duty-pay section that features hip fashion; logo-covered accessories from a few luxury brands, as well as more reasonably priced labels like Le Sport Sac; and the largest cosmetics section in the state. DFS doesn't charge the state's 4 percent sales tax in the duty-pay sections of the Galleria—the company pays it—to make their prices more competitive than those of the other retailers on Kalakaua Avenue. The third floor is exclusively duty-free—there you'll find luxury brands as well as perfume, liquor, and cigarettes. Since you must possess a boarding pass to a foreign destination to shop in the duty-free section, there are very few Americans. And a great many Japanese.

DFS has always used crafty tactics to get the Japanese into its stores—way back when, Chuck Feeney learned Japanese to negotiate deals with Japanese tour operators so that they would steer their customers into the stores. But DFS under Bernard Arnault's guidance has taken Feeney's stratagems to another level altogether. Flights arrive from Japan early in the morning, long before the hotels are ready for check-in. If the Japanese come on a package tour—and 85 percent do—they already have their return boarding pass and a DFS shopping card, which allows them to enter the duty-free zone of the store. If they are traveling with a tour company that receives commissions from DFS, they are bused straight from the airport to the Galleria, where they are ushered into a conference room for a briefing on Hawaii and DFS. Following the discussion, they are guided to the duty-free floor, which is set up like Ikea: there is only one way out and you have to pass through every section of the store—luxury goods, jewelry, perfume, liquor, and tobacco—to get there.

Most of the top luxury brands are represented: Prada, Hermès, Dior, Céline, Fendi, Ferragamo, Bulgari, Burberry, Cartier, and Van Cleef & Arpels. On the duty-free floor, all the major luxury brands have miniature versions of their regular boutiques and primarily sell accessories such as handbags, wallets, jewelry, watches, and shoes or small fashion items like T-shirts and bathing suits—things that can be carried on an airplane. Many of the shops, as well as the tobacco and liquor sections, have signs announcing reduced prices written only in Japanese. Some brands have boutiques on both the duty-pay and duty-free floors but are careful not to carry identical items. The boutiques on the duty-free floor rarely carry shoes larger than size 7½ for women, or clothes larger than size 8, because Japanese women are small. What they primarily sell, though, is leather goods. In 2003, 42 percent of

Japanese travelers around the world purchased a high-end or branded handbag or leather good.

Generally, the Japanese only look during their maiden visit to the Galleria. They prefer to return in the evening, after dinner, to do their serious shopping. Because of this, the Galleria—and most luxury stores on Kalakaua Avenue—stay open until 11:00 p.m. DFS provides a free Trolley Express that cruises up and down Kalakaua Avenue, making stops at Louis Vuitton, Gucci, Cartier, Chanel, and the DFS Galleria. DFS will reimburse taxi fare for those who buy in the duty-free section. And the charter bus depot is directly behind the Galleria, giving Japanese tourists yet another chance to pass by the store. The goal of DFS is to get the Japanese into the store as much as possible.

Though the secret to duty-free sales success is moving product in volume, there are some exclusive items. In 2000, for example, Céline—an LVMH brand—created a line of handbags just for DFS, which is also an LVMH company. And on occasion Hermès gets one of its coveted Kelly or Birkin bags to sell—normally they are made to order and there's a several-months-long waiting list. Not surprisingly, they sell almost immediately. In February 2005, Hermès received a small black crocodile Birkin with a diamond clasp and a price tag of $82,100. A Japanese customer bought it within a matter of days. Galleria Hawaii is DFS's biggest retail outlet, and the Japanese are by far its—and DFS's—biggest-spending clientele.

Today, of Hawaii's 7 million visitors each year, 1.5 million are Japanese. They stay for four or five days or long weekends, and most come to shop; tourism is secondary. "The Japanese know what they are going to do from the time they land until they leave," says Okano of Chanel. "They come with an agenda and know what they are going to buy in each store."

The Japanese obsession with luxury goods—and the luxury companies' obsession to satisfy it—has dramatically changed Waikiki's landscape. When I went there in the mid-1980s—not long after Chanel

arrived—Kalakaua Avenue was a party scene, with teenagers cruising
in shiny low-riding Japanese pickups, a few working girls available for
lonely conventioneers, five-and-dimes like Woolworth's, local bars
with cover bands playing Hawaiian-twanged pop, and a couple of old
movie theaters. I went to catch Clint Eastwood's *Heartbreak Ridge*
at one.

When I returned in 2004, it was a different ambience altogether:
there are no more local bars, no movie theaters at all; the one I went
to in the mid-1980s was bricked up, ready for demolition. In their
place were glistening luxury brand temples, Japanese travel agencies,
and sushi bars. The only thing slightly Waikiki-ish left on the strip
were ABC Stores—a chain of convenience shops that sell sunscreen,
film, flip-flops, and Hawaiian souvenirs made in China. When I mentioned this to Kellyn Kubo, the director of Cartier's Royal Hawaiian
and Ala Moana boutiques, she sighed. "It's true," she admitted.
"Waikiki doesn't have much to offer locals anymore."

THE SUCCESS with the Japanese emboldened and enriched luxury
brands; they had the courage as well as the cash to expand globally.
The plan was to roll out to the world's cosmopolitan capitals—places
such as Paris, London, New York, Rome, Milan, Beverly Hills, and
Hong Kong, where there were both a rich local clientele and a steady
flow of Japanese tourists. The stores would be flagships: big, flashy
showcases that would sell the brand's lines as well as its image. Put
simply, brands had to "build a fantasy world for those clothes and accessories—create the life that your customers aspire to," Tom Ford explained to me. Wildly extravagant displays of wealth and creativity that
have nothing to do with everyday life, flagships not only evoke the
dream of old cultured luxury but also embody the new opulent luxury
of today. In essence, they feel unreal.

To achieve this, luxury companies called in architects to create their new stores. Gucci hired respected American interior designer Bill Sofield. Prada brought on Milan-based architect Roberto Baciocchi. And in 1996, Bernard Arnault placed a call to a New York–based architect named Peter Marino, best known for his work for Barneys.

Marino is quite a character. He stands about five feet nine, speaks with a "Noo Yawk" accent, dresses like a biker in black leather, has a nutty sense of humor, and is as chatty as your inconvenient neighbor. He studied at Cornell's architecture school and began his career working for such traditional firms as Skidmore, Owings & Merrill and George Nelson & Associates. In the early 1970s, he hung out with Andy Warhol, and later redecorated Warhol's uptown townhouse and his infamous Factory studio on Union Square—assignments that established Marino's reputation among the fashionable set. "Andy was quite a good calling card," Marino later admitted.

In 1978, Marino opened his own firm, now known as Peter Marino & Associates Architects, and started doing the homes of wealthy jet-set clients such as couturier Yves Saint Laurent, Chanel owner Alain Wertheimer, and Fiat chairman Gianni Agnelli. Marino's style is deeply French, and he travels the world with his big-bucks clients to buy the finest antiques and art. For those who hire Marino, price is no object: the cost of redoing one client's living room and library was $57 million. "Mine is very much a couture house," he has said.

When Arnault called, Marino told me, "I wasn't quite sure who he was at first."

But when Arnault started talking about his companies, Louis Vuitton and Christian Dior, Marino clicked in.

"This is the beginning of something big," Marino thought to himself.

"Well, can you come to Paris tomorrow?" Arnault asked.

"I don't think so," Marino said.

But he did go the day after that.

Marino's first assignment was the renovation of Dior's original avenue Montaigne store. I remember visiting the old boutique back in 1982, before Bernard Arnault had contemplated buying Dior. Still a teenager, I walked in to buy perfume for my mother and grandmother for Christmas. The place reminded me of the drawing room of an old-moneyed mansion. The walls were painted dove gray with snow white moldings. The carpeting was dark gray and cushy. Crystal chandeliers hung from the ceilings, and mannequins dressed in elegant gowns, dresses, and chapeaux dotted the salons. There was no music, no chatter. Customers talked in hushed tones. The salesclerks were middle-aged women in prim suits and heels, their hair pulled up in neat chignons: the epitome of chic Parisiennes, serving you while setting an example. The perfume room was off to the right and bathed in natural light, the classics displayed on an old-fashioned wood-and-glass sales counter. I chose Diorissimo and Miss Dior, which the salesclerk silently wrapped in sheets of matte gray paper without tape or glue and tied up with white ribbon. They were the most beautiful gifts I had ever purchased, and it was the most refined shopping experience I have ever experienced.

When Marino got done with the store, I barely recognized it. What was once a foyer had become a vast, two-story-high round emporium-like space for handbags and scarves—the items that tourists and middle-market customers buy en masse. To the right, where the demure perfume counter once was, Marino put the shoe department with tiger-stripe carpeting, mirrors draped in gray and cherry red taffeta and a zebra-legged console. That led to the women's wear department: a mishmash of neo–Louis XVI and rococo Louis XV styles, tea rose satin chairs with silver raffia pompoms, ivory leopard damask poufs on grooved gold-leafed legs, fluted silver velvet armchairs, and two tea tables sheathed in snakeskin. There were sales tables in bronze with mica inlay, gray silk fitting rooms with black Chantilly lace trim, stone flooring with silver molten glass insets in Dior's signature caning design, and Marino's favorite item, a stool with bronze goat legs. The perfume and cosmetics room had been moved to the back left section of the store, and one passed through it, like a hallway. It was entirely fitted in silver-gray mirrors with black and gold arabesques and floral motifs painted on the silver foil lining. Marino said he wanted to evoke a jewelry box. To me, it was plain gaudy and light-years away from the refinement and quiet elegance of Dior pre-Arnault.

Dior executives were thrilled with Marino's transformation of the space. Its nouveau riche extravagance lured tourists as well as shoppers from all economic classes, and Marino became luxury fashion's favorite boutique designer. Along with Dior, he has produced opulent, highly designed stores for Chanel, Donna Karan, Calvin Klein, Fendi, and Louis Vuitton, as well as Valentino's New York home and his 152-foot yacht, *TM Blue One*. While most businesses would shy away from having the same designer as nearly all their competitors, luxury fashion industry executives sees it as a validation of their impeccable taste. Luxury fashion is a clubby world—designers all know each other, many intimately so, support staff such as press attachés and assistant designers move freely from one company to another, everyone dines in the same restaurants and vacations in the same locales. They refer to themselves as "the fashion tribe."

Back in the old days, when luxury companies were run by their owners or heirs, each house had its own distinctive style that reflected the founder's creative vision, right down to the boutique, normally just below the designer's studio. Now individualism has given way to homogenization, not only among stores within a brand but also among brands themselves. Like Hollywood studios hiring the same handful of bankable stars to lure middle-market audiences to see their blockbuster movies, luxury brands tend to hire the same architects and use the same design tricks to get crowds into the stores. Luxury brands used to be innovative: they were revolutionary in design, they'd come up with something *new*. Now, they try to avoid leading the way for fear of alienating customers.

Marino was the perfect compromise: he was crazy creative, but since they all hired him, the Marino look has become the standard. Though Marino claims that each brand's team of designers never knows what the others are up to—"I'm the only link," Marino told me—Marino-designed boutiques most definitely have a common look about them: shiny and clean, with lots of gold, silver, sparkle, and gloss. The year-long remodeling of Chanel's original rue Cambon flagship, for example, included oxblood-hued epoxy-resin panels flecked in gold, mirrors wrapped in a mile's worth of antique silver and gold ribbon, and faux-ivory marquetry that evokes piano keys. And Marino's decors make handbags radiate like movie stars on the red carpet. "Rule No. 1 is: don't ever let the merchandise be subservient to the architecture," he says.

Though Marino-designed luxury brand boutiques cost a substantial fortune—$20 million to create or renovate a flagship is not unusual—the investment seems to be worth it. Sales at the Osaka and Hong Kong boutiques that Marino did for Fendi increased by 300 percent within months of their openings. After Marino renovated Vuitton's store on the Champs-Élysées for a second time in 2005—for an estimated $20 million—it was expected to generate $90 million to $115 million (€75 to 95 million) a year in sales. "We saw a phenomenal difference in sales before and after Marino—a 20 to 40 percent increase," Françoise Montenay, former president of Chanel in Europe, told me. "And it takes us two years to recoup our investment." By 2006, Marino had done all of Chanel's European and most of its Asian stores.

Luxury continued its global march, expanding in secondary cities such as Monte Carlo, Venice, Chicago, Miami, São Paolo, and Osaka, and the store decors echoed the opulent flagships. The idea—a central tenet of globalization—was to market a cohesive image throughout the world. Back in Japan, where luxury's globalization began, its founding father, Louis Vuitton's Kyojiro Hata, grew frustrated with this marketing policy. "All the stores were 'consistent' wherever you went in the world, which meant they looked the same, and it was getting boring," he told me. He wanted to do something to shake luxury up and make it a voice in creativity again.

Hata has long been interested in architecture—his brother-in-law Masayoshi Yendo is former president of the Japan Institute of Architects—so Hata decided to host a competition to select an unknown architect to build something fantastic. "We wanted it to be a Vuitton store, not an architect's monument," he explained, and "if you commission a star you cannot argue." Vuitton selected Jun Aoki's proposal of a building with "fuzzy external walls, like air, mist, or mirage." When completed in 1999, the store was "an oblong cube, resembling a transparent jewelry case placed in the middle of the city," as Aoki described it, with a glass facade re-creating Vuitton's Damier check pattern. In 2002, Aoki produced another architectural masterpiece for Vuitton in the pretty, tree-lined shopping district of Omotesando: a store of "randomly stacked Louis Vuitton trunks," Aoki said, each "trunk" creating an airy, modern rectangular space to display and sell Louis Vuitton products.

The Omotesando store set out to be the most glamorous shopping address in Japan. It offered a concierge who would help with store orientation as well as book restaurants or taxis and provide information about Tokyo. On the top floor, there is a VIP salon, which you access via private lift, for special customers to try on clothes or place custom orders for luggage and accessories out of view of the masses. To celebrate the opening, Vuitton threw a splashy party attended by movie stars, local celebrities, and important clients who sipped Veuve Clicquot—an LVMH brand—as they mingled among the glass display cases and posed for the paparazzi.

The strategy worked. For two days leading up to the Omotesando store's opening, fourteen hundred Japanese Vuitton groupies camped out front, waiting to shop. On the first day of business, the store's clerks rang up a staggering $1.04 million in sales. When I visited it in November 2005, a middle-aged Japanese woman was trying on a pair of LV monogram–covered blue jeans and a matching monogram denim shoulder bag with chinchilla trim as her husband sat in an armchair talking on his cell phone. His shirt cuffs were held together with Vuitton cufflinks. In a stroller next to them sat their dog, watching contentedly. On the fourth floor, a group of large, loud Russians checked out Vuitton suitcases as a posse of Japanese fashion guys with blond-streaked hair, tight shiny suits, wide-open shirts, and cowboy boots chatted up a pair of local girls in little jackets, microskirts, and stiletto boots. I got the feeling that trendy Japanese cruise the Vuitton store in Omotesando like young Americans hit happy hour.

The truly fashionable set, however, bypass all of that and go to Celux—pronounced "say luxe" like the French phrase "It's luxury"—a private club tucked in the back upper corner of the building where trendy Japanese pay one-time membership of about $1,850 and annual dues of $215 for the privilege to buy modern art, vintage jewelry, luxury fashion, and leather goods not found anywhere else in Tokyo. Members enter through a discreet side door and take a private lift that they access with their Celux swipe card to the eighth-floor lounge with blood-red carpeting, exotic wood paneling, and hip jazz. LVMH brands are all around you: mod pink Pucci-print sofas by Cappellini, Kenzo aromatherapy products on the coffee table, a wet bar on top of an upright Vuitton trunk. There is an impressive collection of fashion books and modern art. Down a dramatic curving staircase, the double-height suite is done up with red velvet armchairs, colored crystal fruit chandeliers, and baroque gold-framed mirrors, displaying everything from vintage-inspired sunglasses by Oliver Goldsmith of the United Kingdom to filmy Lanvin blouses.

Some young designers create items for Celux, like the British brand Filth, which came up with a vintage-style green army jacket with the word "Celux" painted down the sleeve. Naturally, everything from the artwork to the armchairs is for sale. Members are "people with taste and fashion sense, like artists, entrepreneurs, deejays, and musicians," says Chiaki Tanabe, Celux's public relations rep. "Trendsetters." To become one, you must be recommended by an existing member. By the fall of 2005, Celux had met about half of its membership goal of two thousand.

The Vuitton stores kicked off a luxury architecture war in Japan. In 2001, Hermès inaugurated a stunning $137 million twelve-story glass-brick tower designed by Renzo Piano in Ginza with fourteen hundred square feet of rich retail space, a workshop, executive offices, an art gallery, and a forty-seat film screening room. The first dramatic architectural luxury tower in Tokyo, it replaced a small café. In 2003, Prada built an $80 million six-story temple to postmodernism on Omotesando designed by the Swiss architecture firm of Herzog & de Meuron—the folks who did the Tate Modern in London. With its striking five-sided facade of clear bubble-like glass in a twisted harlequin pattern, the Prada store seems to draw more tourists snapping pictures than shoppers laying out the plastic. And in December 2004, Chanel christened its Ginza building. The property, previously a Warner Bros. store with a giant TV screen playing Bugs Bunny shorts, cost Chanel a staggering $117 million at auction. It took three months to knock down the existing building and another fourteen and a half for Peter Marino to construct a new one.

It's quite a building. There are ten floors, including about fourteen thousand square feet of shopping space done up in absurdly expensive materials. There is glittering silver dust on the pillars, woven gold-ribbon panels on the walls, and an underground customer parking lot (a rarity in Tokyo) with Andy Warhol's *Chanel No. 5* image to greet you when you pull in. Above the store there are plush executive office suites with expansive windows; a vast multipurpose cultural space called Nexus Hall that hosts classical music concerts and photography exhibits in conjunction with the Bibliotèque Nationale de France; a rooftop terrace with Japanese bamboo and water gardens; and on the top floor, with a commanding view of the city, the Alain Ducasse restaurant Beige Tokyo. "I wanted the best chef in the world," Richard Collasse, Chanel Japan's president, says quite simply.

Marino's pièce de résistance is the facade, which took up half of the building's construction budget: a gigantic curtain wall of Privalite glass with seven hundred thousand embedded light-emitting diodes (LEDs) that at night project swirling black-and-white images of Chanel symbols such as the interlocking Cs, the tweed pattern and camellias, making it effectively the largest television screen in the world. The total cost of the building was reportedly $240 million. Collasse will only say that it cost twice as much as "good-quality building" in Tokyo. A year and a half after it opened, there were still lines out front. Former Chanel president Françoise Montenay told me that she expected the store to recoup its investment in three years.

PART TWO

CHAPTER FOUR

STARS GET IN YOUR EYES

"Luxury lies not in richness and ornateness but in the absence of vulgarity."

— COCO CHANEL

ACHEL ZOE blew into the Jimmy Choo Oscar Suite on the fifth floor of the Peninsula Beverly Hills hotel on a rainy February morning in 2005 like she owned the joint. Dressed in a black fitted Roberto Cavalli jacket with fur cuffs, tight skinny jeans, a Chloé belt, and five-inch-high stiletto boots with buckles, she air-kissed Sandra Choi, niece of the London-based luxury shoe company's namesake, and clocked the crowd in a swift 360-degree glance. Choi, the company's creative director, and Tamara Mellon, its glam jet-set founder and president, booked the suite to receive socialites, starlets, and A-list stylists looking for shoes to borrow for the myriad dinners and parties later in the week, culminating with the seventy-seventh Academy Awards on Sunday night. Swishing her long Botticelli ringlets out of the way, and with notebook-wielding Choi by her side, Zoe cut through the sea of tea- and champagne-sipping faux blondes and headed straight into the bedroom of the buttercup yellow suite. The bed, dresser, desk, and armoire had been replaced with long banquet tables, each covered with white linen tablecloths, huge bouquets of white roses and tulips, and scores of dangerously tall and wildly expensive women's shoes.

"For Salma"—as in Hayek—"I need size-wise 6," Zoe instructed Choi in her acute northern New Jersey accent. "She called me this morning. 'Rachel, I need *five* inches!'" Choi nodded and jotted it down. Zoe picked up a strappy gold leather stiletto, handed it to Choi to note, and pointed out others in silver and bronze. They were for Julie Delpy, who was nominated for best original screenplay for *Before Sunset*. "I'm not sure what her jewelry is going to be," Zoe explained, "so I'd like to keep it open."

She scanned the table again. "These are fabulous," she declared of a bronze pair that tied around the ankle. She picked out a pair of black platforms, too. "Can we do a jewel on the platform?" she asked pointedly. Choi nodded and scribbled. "Great," Zoe concluded. She turned to leave but spied another table in the back corner. "Holy crap! Holy crap!" she wailed as she cradled a pair of purple satin pumps with big jeweled buckles. "This is incredible! And look at this," pawing a pair of five-inch silver-strap stilettos. "I could *cry!*"

Zoe—pronounced *Zo*, like *snow*—is one of Hollywood's top celebrity stylists, the fashionistas who are paid thousands of dollars a day to dress film, TV, and music stars. A decade ago, the job of celebrity stylist didn't even exist. But with the onslaught of premieres, charity galas, and awards programs, all of which require stars to look as if they have stepped out of the pages of *Vogue,* stylists have become as essential in Hollywood as publicists, personal assistants, trainers, and chefs. Stylists attend fashion shows and visit showrooms in Paris, Milan, New York, and Los Angeles, scan fashion Web sites like Style.com, and shop incessantly to pull together the hippest, sexiest, most glamorous wardrobes possible for their clients. For big events, like the Oscars or Golden Globes, stylists are on hand to dress the celebrity, add jewels, and tie sashes just right. Whenever a top celebrity does a "public appearance"—from a chat on *David Letterman* to a stroll before cameras on a red carpet—you can be sure a stylist has helped create the look. The result for the luxury brands, Zoe explains, is "a million dollars of free advertising."

For most of their existence, luxury brands had not advertised. Leather goods houses such as Louis Vuitton and Gucci ran some ads in magazines, and couture houses such as Chanel and Yves Saint Laurent hawked their perfumes and cosmetics. But, as Arie Kopelman, former president of Chanel Inc., explained to me, luxury executives and designers "thought it an anathema to advertise fashion, that it would cheapen the business." The generation of designers that hit big in the 1970s, including Giorgio Armani and Gianni Versace in Milan, and Ralph Lauren and Calvin Klein in New York, changed that perspective. They hired fashion's top photographers such as Richard Avedon and Bruce Weber and supermodels such as Janice Dickinson, Jerry Hall, and Brooke Shields to star in their campaigns, which ran in fashion and art magazines. In 1987, Chanel couturier Karl Lagerfeld, an accomplished amateur photographer, started shooting the house's fashion ads himself. Other brands followed. "The industry became more competitive, and you had to be more aggressive," Kopelman explained. "Advertising played a role in that marketing."

As the industry grew in the 1990s, so did advertising. Gucci nearly doubled its ad expenditure from $5.9 million, or 2.9 percent of revenues, in 1993 to $11.6 million, or 4.6 percent, in 1994. By 1999, Gucci's advertising and communication budget had grown to 7 percent, or about $86 million, of its $1.2 billion sales turnover. In 2000, advertising for the entire group reached approximately $250 million, or 13 percent of sales. LVMH spent more than $1 billion in advertising— or 11 percent of sales—in 2002, making it the largest advertising buyer in fashion magazines. "We are the largest luxury goods advertiser in the world," Arnault once boasted. "I cannot tell you the exact savings—I cannot give away my secrets—but it is obvious that the more you buy, the better [deal] you get."

Designers, or creative directors as they rechristened themselves in the 1990s, became an integral part of the process. They dreamed up ad concepts, chose the models and photographers—Lagerfeld continued to shoot Chanel fashion campaigns himself—and became the spokesmen for their brands. At Gucci, for example, "Domenico [De Sole] and Tom [Ford] sat down and said, 'How are we going to turn Gucci around?' " recalled Gucci's then–chief financial officer Robert Singer in 2001. "And they said, 'We'll make Tom a star.' " Ford sat for magazine profiles and TV interviews—often at one of his spectacular homes—held news-making press conferences, and swirled with the jet set, his goings-on tracked by gossip columns. Soon Ford and Gucci became synonymous for a hedonistic lifestyle that, Singer said, "became the platform for selling incredible quantities of handbags."

It worked for a while. But soon, as Claus Lindorff of the BETC Luxe advertising agency in Paris explained, luxury brands realized they needed more than "a pretty girl in a pretty picture." They needed real people who had an air of glamour about them.

They needed Hollywood.

HOLLYWOOD HAS A LONG and deep relationship with luxury. During the Golden Age, from the 1920s to the early 1960s, when powerful moguls such as Jack Warner and Louis B. Mayer were in charge of the studios and ran them like kingdoms, movies were rich. Characters had posh accents, lived in grand homes, employed staff, dressed extravagantly, and made audiences dream. The primary creators of these dreams were the costumers—the studios' in-house designers who came up with and produced the outfits for everyone in a film from the leading lady to the extras. Back in the 1930s, the bias-cut gowns that MGM's costumer Adrian designed for Greta Garbo were so sublime that fans wrote to her begging to buy them. Paramount costumer Travis Banton's glittering gowns and slim tuxedos "made Dietrich," Diana Vreeland declared, and Edith Head's structured, voluminous couture turned several of Alfred Hitchcock's blond heroines into style role models. Columbia Studios' French-born costume designer Jean Louis designed with such flair that he became known as Hollywood's Prince of Glamour. Among his masterpieces were Rita Hayworth's black satin hourglass gown in *Gilda* and the sheer beaded chiffon second skin that Marilyn Monroe wore to sing "Happy Birthday" to President John F. Kennedy. When Kim Novak went to the Cannes Film Festival in 1956 for *Picnic,* she told me, "I had two trunks of incredible wardrobe, these fabulous gowns that Jean Louis at the studio designed and they were absolutely magnificent. I swept Prince Aly Khan off his feet."

Stars relished this *richesse.* Silent-screen siren Gloria Swanson swathed herself in liquid satin gowns, sparkling diamonds, mink, and ermine, both on and off screen; Pinkerton security guards would arrive at her studio dressing room with chests of gems to dress up her costumes. "The public wanted us to live like kings and queens," Swanson explained, "and we did." Joan Crawford was known to change her clothes up to ten times a day. "She had a special outfit for answering the fan mail," cracked director Joseph Mankiewicz. She'd travel with more than three dozen suitcases and had her hip flasks made to match her ensembles. She had her favorite hats copied a dozen times in different colors and at one point she owned sixteen fur coats. "I look at them and I know that I'm a star," she pronounced. Crawford once claimed that more money was spent on her wardrobe, per movie, than on the script.

"Actresses had a lot of taste themselves—and if they didn't have it initially, they developed it," actress Olivia de Havilland, best known for her role as Melanie in the 1939 epic *Gone with the Wind,* told me over tea in her Paris townhouse one winter afternoon. "You absorbed a lot. You knew it was an essential part of being in that profession because there was the public expectation. I remember I went to a film and during the intermission, the actress Frances Farmer—long before her breakdown—wasn't carelessly dressed but underdressed and under-made-up and I heard someone say, 'That's Frances Farmer—oh, my.' I myself was much more careful after that. It was such a responsibility to be impeccable."

Movie stars' marketing power was formidable. When Crawford wore a white Adrian-designed gown with organdy ruffled shoulders in *Letty Lynton* in 1932, Macy's sold half a million copies. Grace Kelly's wedding dress, designed by MGM's Helen Rose for Kelly's 1956 marriage to Prince Rainier III of Monaco, was one of the most copied ever. Hollywood stars endorsed clothes for the Sears Roebuck catalog and sold their signatures for labels. To have a dress with Shirley Temple's or Joan Crawford's embroidered autograph on the label was the bee's knees.

When it came time to choose the wardrobe for a film, French actress Leslie Caron, who arrived in Hollywood in 1950 to star in *An American in Paris,* remembers, "You went to the salons, which was like a couture salon with two dressing rooms, and everything was brought to you. Helen [Rose] was capable of gently persuading you if this or that was fitting, but you certainly had a say. Every star had her own style. I was forever trying to do French fashions and get away from the Hollywood look, which had a lack of simplicity and too much froufrou. The studio made my premiere dresses, too, and if you had to go to the Oscars, they would do a dress for you, especially if your film was nominated."

The best shoemaker in town was Salvatore Ferragamo, an ambitious cobbler from a remote village east of Naples, Italy. He originally settled in Santa Barbara, California, in 1914, where he and his brothers opened a shop and made cowboy boots and shoes for the American Film Company's movies. The studio's actresses—Mary Pickford and her sister Lottie, Pola Negri, and Dolores del Rio—so loved Ferragamo's shoes for their film roles that they went by the shop and ordered pumps for their personal wardrobes. In the early 1920s, Ferragamo moved to Los Angeles and opened the Hollywood Boot Shop on the corner of Las Palmas and Hollywood boulevards. He created "Roman" sandals for Cecil B. DeMille's epics, including *The Ten Commandments* and *The King of Kings,* and shod the floor-show dancers at Grauman's Egyptian and Chinese Theaters. He made shoes to order for Rudolph Valentino, Lillian Gish, Clara Bow, and John Barrymore, and he created a pair of one-of-a-kind pumps covered in hummingbird feathers for a princess visiting from India, for which he was paid a staggering $500, the highest price he ever received for a pair of shoes.

Ferragamo got caught up in Hollywood's social swirl. "Valentino would drop into my house on Beachwood Drive to eat a bowl of spaghetti cooked as he had liked it in Italy. He was a beautiful boy, always impeccably debonair," Ferragamo wrote in his memoir, *Shoemaker of Dreams.* "John Barrymore, that perfect actor, used to drop into my shop for a drink as well as to buy shoes. It being the time of Prohibition, drink was difficult to obtain, and anyone who was lucky enough to come across a spare bottle promptly drank it." At parties "attended by virtually every star in Hollywood—those who could tolerate one another—from Mary Pickford and Douglas Fairbanks downward," Ferragamo recalled, he played barman, whipping up his own concoctions like "Green," made of mint and rum, and "Roscata," which was gin, bitters, a dash of brandy, and a lot of ice. Though he was friendly with his clientele, Ferragamo understood that "the world's stars do not come to my salon to buy my reputation; they come to buy shoes that fit and flatter them."

Paris couture's relationship to Hollywood back then was limited and at times downright tenuous. Coco Chanel traveled there in the early 1930s to costume a handful of pictures but quickly grew frustrated and returned to Paris. Dior made clothes for a few of his favorite clients, including Marlene Dietrich for Alfred Hitchcock's *Stage Fright* and Olivia de Havilland and her co-star, Myrna Loy, for Norman Krasna's *The Ambassador's Daughter.* But in 1955, Dior refused to provide a wedding dress for Brigitte Bardot to wear in the French film *La Mariée est trop belle.* "There was no way Dior would risk incurring the displeasure of some of his most elegant clients by allowing his dresses to be put on vulgar display on the screen," wrote biographer Marie-France Pochna in *Christian Dior: The Man Who Made the World Look New.* "Dior was a snob. He ranked living, breathing aristocrats far higher aesthetically than their pale imitations on stage and screen."

Only French couturier Hubert de Givenchy saw how Hollywood stars could serve as ambassadors for luxury brands—and even then it took him some time to figure it out. In 1953, Paramount telephoned Givenchy in Paris to make an appointment for "Miss Hepburn" to pick out a few clothes for her new movie, *Sabrina.* When the waif in a bob, T-shirt, gingham trousers, and no makeup came by for her fitting, Givenchy was aghast. He thought he would be receiving *Katharine* Hepburn, who was not only a huge Hollywood star but a Bryn Mawr girl, the American equivalent to Givenchy's aristocratic background and clientele. Givenchy politely told the gamine Audrey to paw through the racks of the previous season's clothes and pick out what she wanted. "I had no time to meet with her," he said. "I was in the middle of making my second collection, and I didn't have too many workers then." It was only over dinner that evening, when Audrey Hepburn flaunted her social charm—she, too, had come from a good European family—did Givenchy see the possibilities of an alliance. He dressed her for several of her movies, including *Breakfast at Tiffany's* and *Charade,* and convinced her to pose for the advertising campaign for his perfume L'Interdit. It was the first time a movie star allowed her face to be used to promote a scent. Thanks to Hepburn's unparalleled endorsement on and off screen, Givenchy was able to turn his small couture house into one of luxury's first globally recognized and genuinely successful brands. Yet it took decades for his confreres in the luxury business to understand and exploit the force of celebrity.

IN THE 1950S, following the advent of television and a U.S. Supreme Court ruling known as the Hollywood Anti-Trust Case that forced studios to sell off their theater chains, the industry suffered a financial slump and changed the way business was done. Actors and technical staff—including costumers—were gradually released from their studio contracts; many costume departments were shut down. To make matters worse, films began to take on a more realistic tone, with actors in more everyday, normal clothes—no ermine-trimmed peignoirs or sequined siren gowns required. By the mid-1960s, movie costumer designers were nearly an extinct breed. "They closed their workrooms down, they got rid of their designers," the designer Bob Mackie, who started as an assistant in the early 1960s for Jean Louis and Edith Head, told me. "Paramount got rid of Edith Head; it was all changing at that point. I had always wanted to be the designer at a studio but when I got into the business I realized it was over."

With no more Edith Head or Helen Rose or Jean Louis to provide glamorous wardrobes gratis, stars were forced to shop themselves for premieres and awards shows, including the Oscars. They'd frequent local designers such as Don Loper or James Galanos, department stores such as Bullock's and I. Magnin, and a trendy European-style fashion boutique called Giorgio Beverly Hills on Rodeo Drive. For most of the twentieth century, Rodeo Drive was an unpretentious street, with pharmacies, bookstores, and a few good restaurants, including the Brown Derby and Romanoff's. In the 1950s, there were handful of haberdasheries where actors such as Tyrone Power and Cary Grant shopped, and a divine lingerie boutique called Juel Park, where Beverly Hills' most soigné ladies, including Joan Crawford and Gene Tierney, would have their silk and lace negligees made to measure. But in general, "Rodeo Drive wasn't a fashion street," Fred Hayman told me—at least until he arrived.

The only way to understand Hollywood dressing, or in fact luxury retail in the United States today, is to talk to Fred Hayman, the man who introduced modern luxury shopping to Americans with his fashion boutique Giorgio Beverly Hills. In October 2004, I rang Hayman's office in a five-story building with his signature yellow and white striped awnings on Canon Drive, two blocks east of Rodeo. In his early eighties, Hayman is retired now but still goes to the office a couple of days a week to manage his store's legacy. He immediately proposed we lunch at Spago next door a few days later. When I arrived at the famous Beverly Hills eatery at the appointed time, I was ushered to what was obviously Hayman's regular table. He had arrived early and was busy receiving good wishes from other patrons. Dressed nattily in a perfectly pressed shirt, trousers, and a jacket—a rarity in Los Angeles, especially at lunch—Hayman stood to greet me. He is a small, elegant man with silver hair parted neatly on the side, a crisp continental accent, and gracious manners, all of which indicate not only his upbringing but also the secret to his success.

Born in 1925 and raised in Saint Gall, a small textile town in Switzerland, Hayman immigrated as a boy to New York with his mother and stepfather. At seventeen, he went to work as an apprentice in the kitchen at Conrad Hilton's famed Waldorf-Astoria Hotel, and over the years rose through the ranks to become banquet manager. In 1955, Hilton asked Hayman to move to Los Angeles to oversee the dining rooms of the new Beverly Hilton. Hayman brought with him a staff of fifty, primarily from the Waldorf, and demanded of them what would become his signature managerial style: personalized service, impeccable manners, quiet perfection. Soon the Beverly Hilton became the place to be, with stars such as Clark Gable, Norma Shearer, and Irene Dunne dropping in regularly for drinks or dinner.

In the late 1950s, Hayman invested in a building on Dayton Way just off Rodeo Drive that housed a women's clothing boutique called Giorgio. Surprised to find out how much he enjoyed retailing, Hayman quit the hotel, bought out his partners, and took over the store. He acquired the shop next door, number 273 Rodeo Drive, connected the two, dressed them up with cheerful yellow and white striped awnings, and put in a pool table and an oak bar "with a few bottles of booze," he told me. Uniformed barmen served complimentary tea, cappuccino, wine, and cocktails to customers as they shopped. There was a denlike corner with a fireplace, comfortable chairs, and a newspaper rack. Hayman's third wife, Gale, was the store's buyer. Hayman chatted up customers such as Elizabeth Taylor, Barbra Streisand, and Natalie Wood, while Gale and her pretty salesgirls modeled the latest creations by Halston, Diane von Furstenberg, Oscar de la Renta, and Christian Dior. The modus operandi at Giorgio, as at the Beverly Hilton, was personalized service. "We wrote thank-you letters when customers shopped at our store," Hayman told me. "We had files on all the customers, thick files, and if they hadn't bought anything in a while, we followed up," usually with a handwritten note that would be delivered by a Silver Wraith Rolls-Royce with the license plate number 273. Giorgio "wasn't a ladies' store," Hayman explained. "It was like a home."

The Haymans' only true competition was Gucci, the first European luxury brand to open its own boutique on Rodeo Drive, in 1968. Aldo Gucci, son of the founder and head of the company at the time, sensed that Rodeo Drive was going to evolve into an important luxury shopping street. The Gucci store was impressive: an imposing glass-and-bronze door gave way to a spacious main salon with Gucci green carpeting and eight Renaissance-style Murano glass and Florentine bronze chandeliers. Upstairs there was a couture salon called the Galleria that VIP shoppers accessed via a glass elevator. Gucci had a good celebrity following: Grace Kelly, Sophia Loren, and John Wayne were regular customers. Frank Sinatra so loved Gucci loafers that he sent his secretary over to the new Rodeo Drive store to buy a pair even before it had opened to the public. By the late 1970s, celebrities, locals, and tourists were snapping up Gucci handbags—ranging in price from $100 for basic leather to $11,000 for eighteen-karat-gold-trimmed lizard—so fast that the store manager complained, "Our biggest problem is shortages." "Gucci was as hot as could be," remembers Hayman. "There were lines around the block." Beverly Hills became so "Guccied out" that students at nearby Beverly Hills High School raised a faux Gucci flag on campus.

Within a few years, Giorgio and Gucci had turned Rodeo Drive into a destination address for luxury shopping, attracting not only wealthy customers but also other brands. Ralph Lauren opened his first Polo store there in 1971. Yves Saint Laurent, Céline, Courrèges, and Fred Joaillier soon followed, replacing local merchants and even a gas station with their expensive, exclusive boutiques. The superrich flocked to the street, and spent voraciously. Hayman was once forced to close Giorgio after an Arab client arrived with his harem and bought every evening gown in the store. In 1977, Giorgio Beverly Hills grossed $5 million, which meant that it sold four times more merchandise per square foot than Bloomingdale's flagship in Manhattan, then the country's most successful department store, according to Anthony Cook, who charted the rise of Rodeo Drive in *New West* magazine. "The times were good and we were right for the times," Hayman said with a laugh. In 1985, Chanel opened its first store on the American mainland on Rodeo Drive. Its decor lived up to the street's growing reputation of ostentatious luxury: crystal shelves, suede walls, and a skylight inspired by the crystal stopper of the Chanel No. 5 perfume bottle. Writer Judith Krantz, who set her best-selling 1978 novel

Scruples on Rodeo Drive, called the street "the most staggering display of luxury in the Western world."

It only could have happened in Los Angeles. L.A. was a young, liberal city, settled by people who fled their conservative roots to start anew. Its primary business—cinema—was new. Its money was new. There was no pretension, no snobbism, no traditional class rules—yet. To shop in luxury boutiques, you didn't have to come from a good family or dress well, as was the case in America's old, traditional cities. If you had the dough, you could go.

Oscar time was the busiest, with stars crisscrossing Rodeo Drive from boutique to jeweler to beauty salon. "Stars would spend months deciding what they were going to wear to the Oscars," remembers Gale Hayman. "Nobody sent them clothes." The problem was, most stars didn't have cultivated taste and they didn't have the studio costumers to guide them anymore. L.A.'s reputation as a laid-back city accentuated the problem. Folks knew how to dress down, but no one knew how to dress up anymore. The society ladies such as Betsey Bloomingdale and Nancy Reagan still had James Galanos to dress them in southern California couture, and Bob Mackie designed spangly getups for Cher and comedian Carol Burnett. But most other celebrities were on their own, sometimes with disastrous results. Who could forget when Demi Moore walked the Oscars' red carpet in 1989 in a black cape and spandex bicycle pants?

They needed guidance, someone with good taste to dress them as elegantly as their predecessors. And Giorgio Armani was happy to oblige.

BACK IN THE MID-1970S, a new generation of Italian ready-to-wear designers emerged, turning the industrial city of Milan into an important fashion capital almost overnight. Among them were Gianni

Versace, who came from the southern town of Reggio di Calabria, and made his name with sexy sequin and leather clothes that were inspired by hookers; Gianfranco Ferré, an architect by training who made highly structured clothes; and Giorgio Armani, a handsome, quiet man who invented what has become known as the soft suit.

To understand Giorgio Armani, and the austerity of his clothes, you have to go back to his childhood. He was born in 1934, the middle child of three, in Piacenza, an industrial town forty miles outside of Milan that was bombed relentlessly by the Allies. "Sometimes I would find myself with my little sister, who was three years old, hiding in a hole while a plane tried to gun us down," he remembers. Often, when he was out playing with his friends, the bomb alerts would sound and they'd scurry into shelters. But one day, he wasn't with them—he had something else to do, he doesn't remember what—and "they died and I lived," he told me during an interview in his office in Milan. "It was just good luck." Another day, he wasn't so lucky. The neighborhood boys were playing with gunpowder from an Allied cartridge they had found, and it exploded as Giorgio bent over to look. He was covered in flames. He spent forty days in the hospital, where he was submerged in vats of pure alcohol. He still carries a scar on his foot where the buckle of his sandal burned into his skin. "Those were disagreeable times," he says in his understated way, "and their memory remains."

But even as a child, with the world coming down on his head, Armani's talent for visual aesthetics emerged. One Christmas shortly after the war ended, his mother set the table for the holiday feast of roast chicken. Little Giorgio looked on with displeasure—he did not approve of her arrangement. "There were too many things—the centerpiece, with flowers, and then small flowers everywhere. I remember telling my mother, 'Do one of these things, not both.'" His mother reeled at first, but after her son left the room, she removed the centerpiece. "She understood that there was something different about me, that I had a sensitivity for certain things, for aesthetics, for exteriors," he says. "She realized that I could tell if something was beautiful or ugly." From then on, she asked his opinion on decor. Looking back, Armani says that she was the only woman "who really influenced the direction of my work and my life . . . with her way of being, so simple but rigorous and severe at the same time. She spoke very little but with words that counted."

In 1955, Armani enrolled in medical school in Milan, but he soon realized he was not suited to be a doctor and got a job at a local department store called La Rinascente. During his eight years there, Armani worked as a photographer, a window dresser, an assistant men's wear buyer, and the fashion coordinator. It was a good job, but a lousy fashion job. Men with money and taste had their own tailors in Italy back then. Those who didn't had to buy off the rack from the sorry selection of baggy, saggy suits churned out by manufacturers in few sizes. Armani was appalled by this and decided to do something about it. He went to work for Cerruti as an assistant men's wear designer for a collection drolly named Hitman, and learned the essentials of suit construction and manufacturing. He came up with several new approaches to men's suits, including dabbling in deconstruction. After a few years, Armani left Cerruti to launch a freelance career. "I was ready to pursue my own path," he told me. "I wanted to discover my own aesthetic."

In 1975, Armani and his boyfriend, Sergio Galeotti, scraped together $10,000 in start-up capital, rented a two-room office on Corso Venezia, and launched the Giorgio Armani fashion company. Galeotti handled the business; Armani designed. For his first men's wear collection, which he presented to buyers in a first-floor apartment in the building where he and Galeotti lived, Armani introduced his new silhouette: the unstructured suit. Armani abandoned the traditional stiff English wools and flannels in navy, black, and charcoal in favor of lighter, pliable fabrics such as linen, wool jersey, and woven textiles in muted tones such as olive, mauve, slate blue, and a gray-beige dubbed "greige" that later became his signature. Three months later, he did the same for women in traditional men's fabric. "This was the time of feminism," Armani told me. "Women needed clothing that went much further than the little dress or a tight little suit—clothing that provided strength and power. Yves Saint Laurent did it, and it worked well, but I thought it should be translated into things that were easier to understand, more adaptable to a greater number of people. So I tried to alter this spirit a bit, with the help of women in my office who saw men's clothing and said, 'Why can't we have this, too?' "

Fred Pressman, the visionary owner of the New York men's wear store Barneys, thought Armani's suits were genius and, according to Joshua Levine in *The Rise and Fall of the House of Barneys,* Pressman flew to Milan in June 1976 and offered $10,000 to sell Armani's clothes—an enormous amount for a fledging company. In return, Armani gave Barneys exclusivity to sell the brand in the New York market. "That meant Saks won't get it, Bloomingdale's won't get it, Bergdorf couldn't get it, the specialty stores couldn't get it," Barneys executive Ed Glantz told Levine. "It was a real coup." Armani's early American customers were the in-the-know sorts, like director Martin Scorsese, Columbia Pictures president Dawn Steele, *Top Gun* producer Don Simpson (who, since Armani had limited L.A. distribution, would order twenty black suits at a clip from Barneys in New York), and Bob Le Mond, a talent manager who represented John Travolta, star of the recent hits *Saturday Night Fever* and *Grease.*

In 1979, when Travolta was hired to play a high-end Hollywood hustler in director Paul Schrader's film *American Gigolo,* Le Mond told to Schrader that Giorgio Armani's suits would be the perfect look for Travolta's character: a suave, vain male prostitute in Los Angeles. Schrader and Travolta met with Armani in his studio in Milan and put together a wardrobe for the role. Days before shooting was scheduled to begin, Travolta pulled out to do *Urban Cowboy* and was replaced by the little-known Richard Gere. It was a perfect fit. Armani's soft suits swayed with Gere's swagger, his tight shirts sculpted Gere's buff torso. Gere was casually formal and heart-stoppingly sexy. The movie lifted Armani's fashion reputation, but his distribution was still limited to Barneys and a few other department and specialty stores. When *Time* put Armani on its cover in 1982, only the second designer after Yves Saint Laurent to receive such an honor, his U.S. sales were close to $14 million, a mere 10 percent of his worldwide total. Armani wanted to dress more than Hollywood and Wall Street hotshots. What about the rest of America? They needed great suits, too.

In 1985, Sergio Galeotti died of AIDS. Armani was bereft and poured himself into his work. Not only was he now in charge of design, but he had to come up with and implement the company's business strategy as well. Looking back at the impact that *American Gigolo* had publicity-wise, Armani realized that the best way to reach that middle-American audience was to dress its stars. In 1987, he designed the retro-1930s costumes for Brian De Palma's gangster flick *The Untouchables,* and suddenly crowds of Americans poured into Armani's Madison Avenue store, his first in the United States. The following year, Armani opened a thirteen-thousand-square-foot, glass-front luxury emporium on Rodeo Drive and inaugurated it with a splashy, exclusive benefit at L.A.'s Museum of Contemporary Art for three hundred of Hollywood's most powerful and famous, with Spago catering and Peter Duchin's orchestra playing. The tone was set. There was just one thing missing: "I needed to have the right people wearing my clothes the right way," he said.

For New York, Armani hired Lee Radziwill, sister of Jacqueline Kennedy Onassis, as his "special events coordinator." Radziwill wore Armani everywhere she went—the ballet, the opera, charity galas—and soon enough, her much-photographed socialite friends were wearing Armani, too. But what about the West Coast, what about Hollywood? Radziwill told her sister's niece, Maria Shriver, who lived in Los Angeles, about the job, and Shriver told her friend, the *Los Angeles Herald-Examiner* society editor Wanda McDaniel, who had served as a bridesmaid in Shriver's 1986 marriage to Arnold Schwarzenegger. McDaniel, it seemed, had just the right mix of conservative smarts and Hollywood savvy for Armani. She was born and raised in Macon, Missouri, attended the University of Missouri's famed journalism school, and had worked as society editor first for the *Dallas Times-Herald* and, since 1977, for the *Los Angeles Herald-Examiner*. "I remember my first week here I went to an event at the Beverly Wilshire and there was Jimmy Stewart, Cary Grant, and Gene Kelly," McDaniel told me over lunch at the Beverly Hills Hotel's Polo Lounge. "And I thought, 'Oh my God, I'm so out of my league here.' I mean, in Dallas it was the Cowboys' football coach Tom Landry and quarterback Roger Staubach. Those were the big stars. So I walk up to Cary Grant and said, 'I just want to say hello because I don't think I'm going to last past the first week of this job.' "

Instead, Cary Grant took her out and introduced her to all of his friends, and within a matter of months she had the town wired. Her scooplike approach to society reporting triggered an old-fashioned newspaper war with her competitor, *Los Angeles Times* society columnist Jody Jacobs, and she rattled the entire state of California with a frank and not terribly flattering five-part series about its former first lady Nancy Reagan that came out during the presidential campaign and included a rare interview with her father, Loyal Davis. "I tell you I thought [Nancy Reagan] was going to have my head chopped off," McDaniel remembered, "and there were several people who opened up to me a lot and were axed from the friends' list." The following year, McDaniel married Albert Ruddy, the producer of such 1970s box-office hits as *The Godfather* and *The Longest Yard* (and most recently Clint Eastwood's *Million Dollar Baby*), with a swank star-studded reception at the Beverly Hills Hotel. They became a Hollywood power couple, and she became a far-better-dressed reporter.

In May 1988, Armani hired McDaniel to be the director of entertainment industry communications. Her job: to get Hollywood players to wear Armani. McDaniel lunched with celebrity publicists, managers, and agents, and wore and preached Armani at dinner parties. Armani swiftly became the uniform for producers, executives, agents, and powerbrokers in town. But Giorgio Armani wanted more: he wanted movie stars to wear his clothes in public and cause a stir that would be captured by the paparazzi and run in papers around the world. McDaniel snagged the first one: Jodie Foster.

In 1989, Foster accepted her Best Actress Academy Award for her role as a rape victim in *The Accused* in a baby blue taffeta ball gown with a giant bow on the derriere that she bought while window-shopping in Milan. "Everyone blasted her for it," remembered McDaniel. "I knew Jodie would go back to the Oscars the following year to be a presenter, so I thought, why not call her right now and say, 'You want to commit for next year? Why don't we get you going and know that decision is done.' And Jodie said, 'You know what? You can do this for the rest of my life.'"

Armani found the second one while watching a video of Brian De Palma's 1983 epic *Scarface:* the willowy blond moll, Michelle Pfeiffer. McDaniel contacted Pfeiffer and offered to dress her for the Oscars, too. Together they picked out a perfect navy blue sheath. "Before I went over to her house to get her organized the afternoon of the Oscars," McDaniel remembers, "I called and said, 'What else are you going to be wearing?'"

"I don't know," Pfeiffer responded. "You'll figure it out."

McDaniel threw some of her own handbags and jewelry in the car, and when she arrived at Pfeiffer's old Spanish home in Santa Monica, Pfeiffer came downstairs dressed in her Armani gown and a tiny sea pearl necklace that her boyfriend, Fisher Stevens, had given her.

"Michelle," McDaniel said almost disapprovingly, "this is the Oscars."

McDaniel pulled out of her sack a string of large baroque pearls and a black alligator clutch evening bag.

"But I don't *sparkle,*" Pfeiffer wailed.

McDaniel slid her big diamond wedding ring off and handed it to Pfeiffer.

"Is that weird?" Pfeiffer asked.

"No one is going to know," McDaniel responded.

The next morning, *Women's Wear Daily* ran the headline "The Agony and the Ecstasy." Under it there were two pictures: Kim Basinger in a freakish self-designed one-sleeve white number, and luminous Pfeiffer in her understated, utterly tasteful Armani.

She wasn't the only one. Armani also dressed Best Actress winner Jessica Tandy, Best Supporting Actress nominee Lena Olin, Best Actor nominees Dan Aykroyd and Tom Cruise, Best Supporting Actor winner Denzel Washington, Steve Martin, Jeff Goldblum, Dennis Hopper, and the ceremony's host Billy Crystal. "We were the only people calling," McDaniel remembers. "We were the only game in town."

Women's Wear Daily dubbed the event the "Armani Awards." *Vogue*'s Anna Wintour declared it "a revolution . . . the end of that glitzy, over-the-top, rather vulgar way of dressing. Armani gave movie stars a modern way to look." More important, it gave Americans a glamour they could actually imagine wearing. Sales for Armani soared: between 1990 and 1993, worldwide turnover doubled to $442 million, much of the surge coming from the United States. Jennifer Meyer, Ralph Lauren's West Coast liaison at the time, said, "[McDaniel] single-handedly changed the paradigm."

THE MESSAGE WAS CLEAR: dressing celebrities for the red carpet was the best, and cheapest, advertising a luxury business could do. The following year "everybody tried to hire me," McDaniel says with a laugh. "Valentino tried to get me. I met Gianni Versace in a cabana here at the Beverly Hills Hotel, hiding out. He said, 'You are working for Armani, come work for me!' " She turned them all down and kept wrangling celebrities for Armani. Calvin Klein began staging an exclusive West Coast salon at the Beverly Wilshire Hotel twice a year where a select group of celebrities—including Meg Ryan, Anjelica Huston, and Goldie Hawn—could pick up his frocks at discount prices. Houses started luring stars to sit in the front row of their fashion shows in Paris and Milan by offering them and their loved ones free trips, hotel accommodations, and clothes. All the stars had to do was smile for the paparazzi for a couple of minutes and attend a champagne-infused postshow dinner or party. This way, the houses had a good relationship with the stars when it came time to dress them for the Oscars or the Golden Globes or some other big red-carpet event.

The sales impact was enormous. When Madonna wore a sapphire satin shirt and black velvet hipsters from Gucci to the MTV awards in 1995, sales exploded: within days there were waiting lists for the pants in Gucci stores worldwide. After the world's top celebrity, Princess Diana, was photographed in 1995 carrying a Dior handbag—dubbed the Lady Dior in her honor—the company sold a hundred thousand at $1,000 apiece, single-handedly raising Dior's 1996 annual revenues by 20 percent. Magazines devoted to celebrity style sprouted, beginning with *In Style* in August 1993. The goal of *In Style,* founding editor Martha Nelson told me, was to show that "style was accessible. Readers feel that they 'know' the celebrities in a way that they'll never know models. There's glamour there but not a distant glamour. Celebrities are in TV, movies, and pop music. They are in people's lives and in people's living rooms. They are not that mysterious." Fashion magazines such as *Vogue* and *Harper's Bazaar* began to put celebrities instead of models on their covers. "The bottom line is celebrities sell much better," *Vogue*'s editor in chief, Anna Wintour, explained to me.

The Academy Awards ceremony is by far the biggest celebrity event and the most important for luxury brands. "Hundreds of millions of people watch the Oscars, all over the world," Lisa Schiek, former director of communications for Gucci Group, told me. "If you've got the right actress or actor walking up the red carpet, saying that designer's name over and over, you get the heat, it's validation and you've got the world. The magnitude is awesome." Indeed, Dana Telsey, former luxury goods analyst of Bear Stearns in New York, declared: "The highly anticipated red-carpet arrivals [are] arguably the most important moment for fashion and jewelry designers." Carol Brodie, who was working for jeweler Harry Winston when I met with her during Oscar week 2005, told me that if a celebrity is photographed on the red carpet of the Academy Awards wearing your product, "You'll get a hit once a month" for years. "Harry Winston's advertising budget in the U.S. is slightly over a million a year," she said. "But if you ask nine out of ten people in this country about Harry Winston, they'll say, 'Oh yeah, they are the jeweler who dresses the stars.' Dressing celebrities is an overwhelming way to gain awareness. Uma Thurman put Prada on the map. Charlize Theron put Vera Wang on the map. Halle Berry made Elie Saab. Americans spend billions of dollars on luxury brands because celebrities wear them."

Though it was quickly becoming "a crowded field," as McDaniel recalls, dressing stars still remained an intimate affair, like it was back in those studio wardrobe-department days. "The celebrities would come in directly to see us," McDaniel said. They'd have tea and chat in the third-floor VIP lounge as they tried on the latest evening wear, then afterward maybe go down to the store and do a little shopping. It was a friendly business arrangement, a personal service.

"Then suddenly," McDaniel remembers, "somebody else came in for them."

STYLISTS ARE A RELATIVELY new phenomenon in fashion. Originally, stylists worked as fashion editors, dressing—or "styling"—models for fashion shoots for magazines and catalogs. But as the number of formal affairs exploded in the 1990s, from the Oscars and a few premieres to an avalanche of paparazzi-lined red-carpet events, stylists saw the birth of a new niche: dressing celebrities. Stylists went freelance and started signing up movie, television, and music stars. A stylist's job, as Rachel Zoe explains, is to do "everything": shopping, putting outfits together, dressing the star, creating a coherent look that reflects what the star's image is, or what he or she wants their image to be, in the public mind. When a star embarks on a media tour, the stylist will put together a notebook filled with Polaroids of outfits—"from bra to shoes," Zoe says—with notes indicating which one to wear to which event as well as which to wear if it rains or if it is nice out. "No matter how beautiful actresses are, they don't know how to dress," says Kelly Cutrone, founder of the fashion public relations firm People's Revolution. "They need to be told how to say the designer's name—it's *Jeee-van-shee,* not *Ga-vin-chee*—and how to put a dress on—what's the front and the back—and how to walk in that shoe. They are in way over their heads. And that's where the stylist steps in: they are replacing what studios used to do."

Soon the stylists began to take credit for their work and became fashion stars themselves. Jessica Paster made her name at the Oscars in 1998 when she dressed two Best Supporting Actress nominees: Kim Basinger in an Escada pistachio silk taffeta ball gown and Minnie Driver in a Halston blood-red jersey column with a matching fur stole. When Basinger won for her role in *L.A. Confidential*, Escada's— and Paster's—profile soared. Since then, Paster has dressed Cate Blanchett, Uma Thurman, Naomi Watts, Joan Allen, and Kate Beckinsale. L'Wren Scott, the six-feet-four raven-haired girlfriend of Mick Jagger, is a former model who started her styling career doing photo shoots for Helmut Newton and Herb Ritts. Scott's signature style is sophisticated and very haute couture—more aspiration than accessible. Her premier client is Nicole Kidman, but she has also dressed Marisa

Tomei and Sarah Jessica Parker. Phillip Bloch, a former model turned fashion stylist, famously dressed Halle Berry for the 2002 Oscars in a sheer burgundy gown with sarong-like skirt by the then–relatively unknown Lebanese designer Elie Saab. The move simultaneously catapulted Berry, who won the Best Actress award, to best-dressed lists and Saab to the level of Paris couturier. Bloch wrote a book called *Elements of Style: From the Portfolio of Hollywood's Premier Stylist,* became a spokesman for Lycra and Visa, and in 2007 was launching a luxury shoe and a middle-market lifestyle collection that he described as "Hollywood glamour for the masses."

Rachel Zoe was perhaps the hottest stylist in the business when I met her at the Jimmy Choo Oscar salon in 2005. Her client list read like Page Six of the *New York Post:* along with Salma Hayek and Julie Delpy, she handled Lindsay Lohan, Nicole Richie, Mischa Barton, and Jessica Simpson. Some have great style and simply needed help putting everything together. Others need a complete workup: a total, seamless new look. For a reported $6,000 a day, Zoe provides it, turning T-shirt-and-jeans devotees into luxury brand fashion plates.

"Those girls get photographed going to dinner," Zoe explained. "They get photographed going to lunch. They get photographed from the minute they leave their houses in the morning till the minute they go to sleep." As New York designer Michael Kors noted, "We've never lived in such a paparazzi moment. So many women get their fashion information by looking at a tabloid, and [Rachel] has found a way of making those girls look intriguing and fabulous when they're running out for a Starbucks." By the summer of 2006, Zoe had become so influential that you could see references to her trademark look on luxury brand runways. And her fans are legion. At the Armani couture show in Paris, one girl standing behind me gasped, "There's Rachel Zoe!" when Zoe dashed in at the last minute. "She's the best stylist in Hollywood today!" At some shows, Zoe has been asked for an autograph.

Rachel Zoe Rosenzweig—her agent convinced her to lose the complicated last name in 1997—was born in New York in 1971 to an engineer and his Berkeley-grad wife and raised in Short Hills, New Jersey, the younger of two daughters. Early on, Zoe realized she had champagne tastes. "I was reading *Vogue* at thirteen and was always attracted to luxury," she says. "My father always said he could drop me in a five-and-dime and I could find the one thing that was a dollar." During a family vacation to Paris when she was thirteen, Zoe took her savings and bought a messenger-style monogram satchel at Louis Vuitton. She still has it, and keeps it in a closet with her several hundred other Vuitton bags. She studied sociology and psychology at George Washington University in Washington, D.C., and worked as a hostess at the Mona Lisa restaurant in Georgetown, where she met a dashing waiter named Rodger Berman and fell in love. They married in 1998. He worked for a few years as an investment banker. Now he is president of Recognition Media, a company that owns awards shows, such as the Webby Awards for excellence on the Internet. After Zoe finished her undergraduate studies, she thought about pursuing postgraduate work to become a psychiatrist but opted instead to look for a job. A friend of a friend told her about an opening as a fashion assistant at *YM* magazine. She thought, "Why not?" and got it: three days a week at $75 a day. Within three years, she was *YM*'s senior fashion editor. "I loved it so much, I decided to do it the rest of my life," she says. In 1997, she went freelance, styling for fashion magazines. Often her subjects were celebrities and on occasion they asked if she could help them dress for red-carpet appearances. Soon Zoe had a host of private clients, including the Backstreet Boys, Britney Spears, and Enrique Iglesias.

Zoe's trademark style—for herself as well as her clients—is *Saturday Night Fever* meets early Cher: for day, skinny cropped jeans, little fitted jackets, reptile-skin stilettos, and gobs of chains; for night, clingy goddess gowns. Her favorite designers are Karl Lagerfeld at Chanel, Christian Lacroix, John Galliano, Marc Jacobs, and Tom

Ford. "If I ever got a tattoo it would be 'Tom Ford Lives Forever,'" she gushed to *Harper's Bazaar* in 2005. She also collects and uses a lot of vintage clothing, particularly from Halston, Pucci, and Yves Saint Laurent. Zoe has even reached into her personal wardrobe of free clothes to dress her "girls" Lindsay Lohan, Nicole Richie, and Jessica Simpson, prompting the fashion press to dub them "Zoe Clones."

She's parlayed her styling into other gigs, including contributing regularly to *Cosmopolitan,* appearing on *Oprah,* and designing a capsule collection of handbags for Judith Leiber. She is so famous for her taste that now she gets requests from the rich and unfamous to help them, too. "People come in to L.A. for three days and want to pay me $20,000 a day to take them shopping," she says incredulously. "I have someone who wants to fly me to Paris to take their daughter shopping." She also consults for various luxury designers for red-carpet appearances, giving them design suggestions. "The designers don't have time to know their clients—they're too busy with their collections," Zoe explains. "And the media pressure is immense. That's why I have my job, because the media feels there is a sense of power and influence of style. Clients come to me now—or their agents and publicists—and say, 'Help! Help! Help!'" In March 2007, she joined the advisory board and signed on as the creative consultant for Halston, the legendary 1970s American fashion brand that movie mogul Harvey Weinstein had just purchased.

While Zoe is constantly busy dressing her clients, Oscar season is "colossal mayhem," she says with a laugh. "You can forget sleeping between January and March. A million fittings, gathering accessories. Me and my two assistants drinking coffee at midnight. I get three hundred phone calls and two hundred e-mails a day." She has one primary rule: "There should never be more than two dresses from the same house on the red carpet." To avoid this, Zoe normally asks for exclusivity from a brand. "It protects the brand from overexposure," she said, "and most importantly, it protects my client." In 2006, Zoe had Jennifer

Garner, who was presenting; Keira Knightley, who was nominated for Best Actress; and six clients attending the *Vanity Fair* party who needed to be as glamorous as the movie stars. On Oscar day, Zoe personally helped dress her highest-profile client, Knightley, in a Vera Wang one-shouldered burgundy taffeta gown, while her assistants were dispatched to attend to her other clients. "You need to have someone on hand in case of a fashion emergency, like a broken zipper or a popped button," Zoe explained.

Luxury brands go to extraordinary lengths to get their products on those red-carpet arrivals. They send unsolicited packages of goodies—known as "swag" in the biz—to celebrities year-round, usually via their publicists. "That's what I'm here for—to handle the avalanche," Troy Nankin—publicist for such stars as Hilary Swank, Angie Harmon, and Selma Blair—told me. "I send it to the mom or to a charity. Escada sent these purses around before Christmas, and then *US Weekly* runs a photo of Selma Blair with a caption that reads 'Selma Blair loves her new Escada bag.' No, Selma Blair's *maid* loves her new bag." The Oscars traditionally have been the ultimate swagfests. Presenters received gigantic baskets of freebies—including exotic trips, luxury watches, and camcorders—that were worth hundreds of thousands of dollars from the Academy until the IRS came down on them. The Academy voted to discontinue the practice as of 2007. Luxury brands, on their own, swag nominees and presenters too. In 2005, the London-based leather goods company Anya Hindmarch, for example, gave each Best Actress and Supporting Actress nominee a Bespoke Ebury chocolate leather tote embossed with a personal message from their director or co-star and stuffed with Revlon products.

Perhaps the most visible effort luxury brands make to dress celebrities for the Oscars is to set up salons at the finest addresses around town, such as the Jimmy Choo Oscar Suite at the Peninsula. They invite A-list and B-list celebrities, publicists, agents, and stylists such as Zoe to come by for lunch, tea, or drinks to check out their latest, most fabulous wares—all available to "borrow" for the red carpet. For small companies like Jimmy Choo, an Oscar salon is a bonanza of publicity. "When you put a pair of glamorous shoes on a stunning actress about to receive an award, well, you can't beat that," says Jimmy Choo creative director Sandra Choi. "Everybody who watches the show, or reads about it, knows we took part. Everything we have here is in the store and they can come in and buy a piece of that glamour." Most of the time, as Choi points out, no one can see the Choos underneath the long gowns. But every chance an actress gets, she'll mention to a television commentator or reporter that she's wearing Choos and give a little flash of ankle to prove it. She'll also say who loaned (or gave) her the dress, jewels, and handbag. The morning after a red-carpet event, Choo, like all the other major luxury brands that dress stars, e-mails a press release to reporters around the globe that details who wore which Choo shoes, often with a red-carpet photo attached. Says Choi: "The mileage for the rest of the year is phenomenal."

The impact on the public is profound. According to a study conducted by Cotton Incorporated in 2004, 27 percent of female shoppers ages twenty to twenty-four said they got clothing ideas from watching celebrities, up from 15 percent in 1994. In the twenty-five to thirty-four bracket, it jumped from 10 percent in 1994 to 18 percent in 2004. For women ages thirty-five to forty-four, it was 14 percent, up from 8 percent in 1994.

In February 2005, I decided to see the salonfest firsthand. I checked into the Chateau Marmont, a favorite old Hollywood hotel for movie and fashion sorts, got in contact with luxury brand and product placement publicists, and the invitations rolled in. Right there at the Chateau, in one of the Craig Ellwood–designed 1950s bungalows in the garden, French designer Roland Mouret showed his recent couture collection to stylists and their celebrities. He wound up dressing Cate Blanchett and Selma Blair for events during the week, and Scarlett Johansson for the Oscars ceremony. In the 1920s clapboard

Bungalow 1 overlooking the pool, the estate jewelry company Sell Jewelry hosted a ladies' luncheon for stylists, socialites, and fashion editors to try on vintage rings and brooches. At the Kwiat diamonds cocktail party at The Four Seasons Hotel in Beverly Hills, guests sipped "diamond-tinis"—turquoise-hued martinis sprinkled with gold dust. *W* magazine hosted an invitation-only "Hollywood Retreat," in a mod Hollywood Hills home, where high- as well as low-wattage stars pawed through and borrowed Rena Lange clothes, Penny Preville jewels, and Jaeger-LeCoultre watches. In the back bedroom, celebrity hairdresser Chris McMillan tended to their tresses; when I was there, Paula Abdul was in his chair getting the works. Afterward, I was invited to join guests by the pool for a light "spa" lunch by top L.A. restaurant Patina.

Over on Rodeo Drive, Chanel offered free professional makeup sessions to regular and celebrity clients at the Frédéric Fekkai Salon and Harry Winston received customers and stylists in its jewel-box salon, with butlers serving martinis. In 2003, Harry Winston provided more than $40 million worth of diamonds for the Oscars, including a $3.5 million necklace for Queen Latifah. Up the street, Caroline Gruosi-Scheufele, co-president of the Swiss jeweler Chopard, and her staff dispatched a heart-shaped diamond-studded pendant as a gift to Elizabeth Taylor, who would be the guest of honor at the post-Oscars Elton John AIDS Foundation benefit, which Chopard co-sponsored. Sir Elton and his partner, David Furnish, had Chopard diamond watches on their wrists at the gala, which the *Los Angeles Times* duly noted in its Oscar party wrap-up.

Swarovski, the one-hundred-year-old Austrian cut-crystal company, took over garden suite number 102 at the exclusive Raffles L'Ermitage in Beverly Hills, one of a dozen luxury brand salons at the hotel. Swarovski has provided crystals for the film industry since the Golden Age, when it helped create the sparkling ruby red shoes that Dorothy wore down the Yellow Brick Road in *The Wizard of Oz*.

Today, Nadja Swarovski, the company's vice president of international communications and the great-granddaughter the founder, has unabashedly pursued the Hollywood angle. In 2000, she joined the luxury onslaught during Oscar week, booking the roomy fourteen-hundred-square-foot L'Ermitage garden suite, which goes for $2,000 a night during Oscar week. She had the company ship hundreds of handbags to L.A. and sent her top staff to get those bags in the hands of movie stars. "We have shifted from the supermodel to the celebrity," Nadja told me over tea in the suite one morning. "Celebrities make it more realistic."

The large plush beige-on-beige living room was filled with long tables cluttered with evening bags: clutches covered with shimmering silver, gold, or black crystals; little handbags made of dusty rose or bronze crystal beads; plain silk clutches that could be dressed up with 1940s crystal brooches. "Americans have special needs," François Ortarix, Swarovski's international PR head, said as he showed me the collection. "Most want clutches, small, black, silver or gold. They don't want to take any risk. At the Cannes Film Festival you see crazy things on the red carpet. Here, it's traditional and conventional. There are so many critics reviewing what you wear, you aren't allowed to make any mistakes on the Oscar red carpet. You have to be perfect, and in a way that people want you to be, not as you are."

Over in the corner on the floor sat a pile of clutches, in gold, silver and black, ordered up by Jessica Paster. Swarovski sent Rachel Zoe a selection, but she dropped by without an appointment to see what else they had to offer and left with a few more. Nothing in the salon was for sale. "We are here to create a dream," Ortarix told me. "We don't want to put a price on it."

THE POWER and the money involved in dressing celebrities in luxury brands has brought out a frightening ruthlessness among stylists.

Some have been known to hoard the best looks, or an entire collection, until the night before an event so that no one else can see them, much less use them. Some ask their celebrity clients to reimburse purchases of luxury goods that were actually gifts from the houses, or neglect to tell their clients about the gifts, then resell them and pocket the cash. One prominent stylist who dressed Pink, Mary J. Blige, and P. Diddy, was reportedly convicted of defrauding eight New York jewelers of more than $1.5 million and sentenced to eighteen months to three years in prison. He allegedly sold the jewels to maintain his flamboyant lifestyle.

Stylists have a lot of leverage. Some have asked luxury brands for cash payments, mortgage payments, exotic vacations. "Seventy percent of them make it clear: 'I think I could make it happen.' And they are waiting for you to say, 'If you make this happen I'll take care of you, and I'll hook the celebrity up,' " says Kelly Cutrone of People's Revolution. "About 25 to 30 percent say, 'Yes I can make this happen, but what's in it for us? Money, clothes, trips, first-class travel, the Ritz in Paris? What's the business of this?' " One stylist reportedly demanded that a designer pay for her liposuction. The designer did, and the stylist's client was wearing the designer's dress when she picked up her Best Actress Oscar. Harry Winston's Carol Brodie remembers another story—"which I know is true," she says—about a stylist who demanded that a designer furnish her home. The designer agreed, the actress wore the dress, and the world's fashion press declared her the best-dressed star on the red carpet. "It's their lethal poker hand: 'I need a vacation and can I use your private villa and your private jet and can you pay for my liposuction?' " Cutrone says. "And you have to ante up."

Says Zoe, "I have never taken a bribe or been paid to use a brand on the red carpet. But I've been offered trips all over the world, gifts, cash, anything and everything."

And some stylists have been known simply to be caustic. For the Golden Globes in 2000, Jessica Paster wanted to dress her big client Hilary Swank in a gown by Randolph Duke. The publicist for Randolph Duke at the time remembers, "Jessica had heard we were dressing Charlize Theron in the same dress as Hilary, which was not true. At five a.m., I got this phone call. 'I will not be fooled!' Screeching. The most insane sound I had ever heard. I held the phone from my ear, and she said, 'I will ruin you! You will never work with any of my clients again!!!' So they dropped that dress and put Hilary in Versace."

When I asked Rachel Zoe about such bad behavior, she sighed. "Stylists in general are really vindictive and greedy," she said, "and I get really frustrated with this petty high school bullshit that goes on."

Traditionally, none of that effort or graft guaranteed that the star would actually wear what the brand had sent via the stylist to the celebrity. Luxury brands' Hollywood point-people would get confirmation the afternoon of the event, then see the celebrity show up with something else on that evening. "For the Golden Globes [in 2005] I sent over a collection of watches, cufflinks, and studs chosen by an A-A-A-list star," says Harry Winston's Carol Brodie. "And I loaned to his girlfriend and his manager and his manager's wife, which I never do, but I knew he was going to be the most visible person on the carpet. And I looked at the wires the next day, and he wasn't wearing it. I called the stylist and said, 'What was that about? Why did you waste my time?' And the stylist told me, 'He was all set to wear it, but he got a tray full of watches in front of him and every single one was free for him if he wore it.'"

Eventually, flacks started getting confirmation from the celebrity's publicist in the limo on the way to the event. And sometimes even that didn't mean anything. "One year I had Chloe Sevigny sorted out with Bulgari and had her going in the car with it on," remembers Cutrone, who at the time worked for Bulgari in Beverly Hills. "And when she got out of the car, she was wearing a cross by Asprey-Girard." Finally, brands started drawing up contracts stipulating that the star would wear their wares at a particular event, on press tours, or for a year. One group did even better: a few years ago, it quietly signed a contract with a top stylist stipulating that she would dress her clients exclusively in that group's clothes. Sure enough, her A-list stars began to wear clothes from that group's brands almost exclusively to premieres and gala events—one actress even wore the group's clothes to her wedding. The stylist made out, too, getting paid on both ends.

Then, a few years ago, the power quietly shifted away from the stylists and to the celebrities. It started, says Cutrone, with the celebrities asking if they could keep the clothes, shoes, jewelry, and so on: "[Then] it was, 'What else are you going to give me?' Then, 'Give me a $10,000 gift certificate.' And then it was, 'I want bank'—$100,000, $200,000, even $250,000. And the queens of the bank game are the nominees and presenters at the Oscars."

Celebrity agents at William Morris, CAA, ICM, and others negotiate the contracts, and the luxury brands state their requirements. A brooch must be visible in an above-the-waist shot. Earrings have to be visible, so hair has to be up. The celebrity must say the brand's name two to four times on a national television channel. When asked to talk about his or her look, the celebrity must refer to the brand in an audible and clear manner. "I thought it was amazing to put their star's name on an e-mail," says Armani's Wanda McDaniel, of agents shopping their clients for luxury brand deals. "But [the agents] are clear that it is an interesting component for a star's career. It's part of the star's branding."

Without much coercing, I heard several stories of actors or actresses getting paid to wear luxury brand goods to the Oscars and Golden Globes. The most famous was when Charlize Theron and Hilary Swank reportedly decided at the last minute to replace the loaned Harry Winston jewels they were to wear to the Golden Globes in 2005 with dangling earrings and six-figure checks from Chopard, but said nothing publicly about it. Other celebrities and Hollywood insiders have revealed that Chopard regularly offered "a boatload of money," as one put it, to wear Chopard jewels. Chopard's U.S. spokeswoman Stephanie Labeille told the *Los Angeles Times* that the house did not have formal contracts with the stars but that the company had used money as an incentive in the past. However, Chopard seems to be having a hard time with its official position regarding celebrity remuneration: two days after the *Los Angeles Times* piece, Labeille said she didn't know whether the company paid stars to wear its jewelry.

"If you are a contractor, and you hire one company over another because they paid you, it's called bribery—that's illegal in the United States," says Carol Brodie. "So if you are a celebrity and somebody is paying you to wear their goods and you choose it because they are bribing you, is that illegal? It's a tough ethical question. I think it's all fine as long as you don't deceive the public and fess up that you are under contract with the company to wear their goods. I think in a few years each brand will have a face associated with it, something where some money has been exchanged to use the likeness of a celebrity, and the stars will wear the brand from shoes to hats. Celebrity dressing will purely be product placement, openly and outwardly."

CHAPTER FIVE

THE SWEET SMELL OF SUCCESS

"A woman enveloped in luxury has a special radiance."

—COCO CHANEL

ESTLED IN THE HILLS near the town of Grasse, in the south of France, is a peaceful valley divided by a single winding country road. Along one side runs a small gentle river called the Siagne. Along the other are flat fields of rose and jasmine bushes. The farm, known as Le Petit Campadieu (The Little Camp of God), is run by Joseph Mul, a fifth-generation farmer in Grasse. Mul tends to one hundred hectares of flowers, five hectares of which are Centifolia roses and another five jasmine. Mul and his family have farmed this land exclusively for Chanel since 1986. Each May, he harvests fifty tons of Centifolia roses, and each September, twenty-five tons of jasmine. In the hills surrounding the valley there are several hectares of mimosa, which he distills for other perfume companies. Le Petit Campadieu is one of the last major flower farms in Grasse.

Monsieur Mul is a jolly French *paysan*, the sort that Doisneau photographed back in the 1950s, with a round, red-cheeked face, twinkling clear gray eyes, and a broad, deep smile. He dresses usually in a polo shirt, work trousers cinched up under his belly, worn dark brown sneakers, and atop his slightly balding pate, a classic *casquette*. He shakes your hand firmly, his thick fingers as rough as old cracked leather. When he talks, it's in that distinct southern twang known as an *accent du Midi*. *Pain* (bread), normally pronounced *pahn*, comes out *payng*. Same with *vin* (wine): *vehn* is *veyng*.

The Mul family started out in the region in the nineteenth century growing hay. At the time, Grasse was a center for production of leather gloves. Leather back then had a vile smell, so tanneries treated it with animal fat infused with flowers. The demand for flowers increased in the region, and the Muls replaced their hay with roses and jasmine. From there, the Grasse perfume industry grew. The belle epoque for flowers in Grasse, Mul explained as he drove me in his navy Jeep Grand Cherokee to the rose fields on a dewy May morning, was from 1920 to 1950. "That was the generation that flourished," he says. "It was really a boom." But in the 1950s, labor prices began to rise in France, and the flower business, which relies on manual labor, first moved to southern Italy and Morocco, then later to Egypt. Now flowers are grown in such cheap labor markets as Turkey, India, China, and since the fall of the Berlin wall, the Balkans.

For the perfume Coco, Chanel uses another sweet, soft-smelling rose called Damascena, which is cultivated in Turkey and Bulgaria. Bulgaria's Damascena roses sell for $1 a kilo, six times less than Grasse's Centifolia. To comprehend what all this international sourcing has done to the French flower industry, consider this: In the 1920s, Grasse produced thirty tons of jasmine absolute, the rich oil that is extracted from the flower. Today, it produces about sixty-five pounds. Grasse has become like the haute couture ateliers in Paris: a boutique business kept alive by the generosity of those who understand, appreciate, and can afford the best that money can buy.

Chanel is Grasse's most important patron. It purchases all of Joseph Mul's jasmine and 40 percent of his roses. The remaining 60 percent is sold to laboratories that create perfumes, primarily International Flavors & Fragrances. The Centifolia annual production is small: 150 kilos of concrete, the waxy substance that contains the flower's absolute. Centifolia concrete from Grasse sells for three times more than Moroccan rose concrete. Chanel is "one of the only old perfumes that hasn't changed," Mul said. "As long as No. 5 exists, we'll be here."

We arrive at the fields at about ten in the morning, the moment when the rose blossoms open. It is warm, with a soft refreshing wind. "Sea breezes," Mul tells me as we walk down the rows of bushes. The variety of Centifolia that Mul grows is known as the *rose de mai,* or May rose, because it blooms only once a year, for about five weeks in May and early June. The aroma is overwhelming and very particular: the Centifolia is a fragrant rose, but not like the sweet pleasing ones in your garden. It is a far more voluptuous and serious scent, with an acrid edge to it. About forty workers, most dark-skinned and many speaking Arabic, move down the rows, quickly snapping the roses' heads off and slipping them gently in pouches slung over their torsos. When the pouches are full, they are emptied into big burlap sacks, which are loaded onto a flatbed trailer pulled by a tractor to the extraction factory, a one-hundred-by-fifty-foot, two-story warehouse-like building at the edge of the fields. For most of the twentieth century, the Mul family only farmed flowers and sent them elsewhere in Grasse for extraction. In 1986, when Joseph Mul secured the Chanel contract, he built an extracting plant on his farm "because," says he frankly, "Grasse was dying out."

The roses are brought into the plant, weighed into fifty-kilo—about 120-pound—batches, and dumped into one of Mul's four vats, called extractors. There are five levels of fifty kilos each in the extractor, each separated by a giant disklike grille so that the flowers aren't crushed. The vat is filled with a volatile chemical called hexane, which dissolves the molecules in the flowers and extracts their principal fragrance. When the process is complete, the five layers of brown, spent roses are pulled out—it looks like a giant hazelnut layer cake without icing—and discarded in a regulated compost receptacle. The syrupy liquid that remains is cooked in a still until the solvent evaporates and is captured for reuse, leaving approximately six hundred grams of concrete, a waxy burnt orange substance that smells like pungent rose candles. Concrete is stored in tin canisters and has a shelf life of about two years.

When perfumers are ready to make their perfume, they mix the concrete with alcohol—which, at Chanel, is made from beets—and chilled at −15 degrees Celsius (5 degrees Fahrenheit). The fat rises to the top, leaving the absolute in the alcohol. The potion is reheated at 40 degrees Celsius (104 degrees Fahrenheit), the alcohol evaporates, and what remains is the absolute. It takes four hundred kilos of roses to make one kilo of concrete, which itself is made up of four hundred grams of wax and six hundred grams of absolute.

Another method used to capture scent from flowers is hydrodistillation to extract essential oil. Flowers are heated with steam at 100 degrees Celsius (212 degrees Fahrenheit) until their sacs of scented oil burst. The steam carries the oil into a chilled condenser, where the steam turns back into water. The essential oil is then separated from the water and bottled. Sometimes, the fragrant water is bottled, too. Rosewater, for example, has long been known for its healing properties, and is used as a refreshing wash or antiseptic. As Chanel uses only Centifolia absolute for its perfume, the Muls do very little hydrodistillation— only enough to provide friends and visitors bottles of rosewater each May. Essence and absolute have different attributes and therefore different uses in perfume creation. Absolute is "more rich," Jean-Claude

Ellena, the perfume creator—or "nose"—for Hermès, explained to me. "Essence is more exciting, vibrant and alive."

THE PERFUME INDUSTRY does $15 billion a year in sales. Some perfumes are the old stalwarts we all know: Chanel No. 5, Yves Saint Laurent's Opium, Diorissimo, Nina Ricci's L'Air du Temps. But the majority are new. About two hundred new perfumes are launched each year—double the number from a decade ago. The reason is simple: perfume is luxury's most accessible and powerful product. It's easy to sell, and it crosses borders, cultures, and target audiences with ease. For example, 30 to 35 percent of all successful male-targeted perfumes are worn by women. Perfume serves as an introduction to, as well as a flag-bearer for, a brand—and it reaps great profits. "[Dior's perfume division's] relationship with Dior Couture is extremely important," Parfums Christian Dior's chief financial officer, Jacques Mantz, explained. "All the communication and what happens around the couture brand helps our [perfume] division, and the broad presence of the perfumes in selective retailers around the world supports the Dior couture brand." In other words, perfume allows you, as the tycoons like to say, to buy into the dream.

At the same time, perfume has a mystical, magical quality. It catches your attention, enchants you. It complements and enhances your personality. It stirs emotion, within you and others around you. "Perfume was a link between gods and mortals. It was a way to contact the gods," Hermès's Ellena told me. "Now it is a profane link: it's between you and me." French poet Paul Valéry said, "A woman who does not perfume herself has no future."

One day a few years ago, a woman went to the Osmothèque, a perfume conservatory in Versailles, and told its president, Jean Kerléo, that she wanted to find her mother, who had long ago died. Kerléo was taken aback. Her mother, the woman explained, always wore the same oriental floral scent, called Arlequinade, introduced by Paul Poiret's Parfums de Rosine in 1920. Her clothes smelled of it. The house reeked of it. A cloud of it lingered whenever she passed by. Arlequinade *was* her mother. Arlequinade disappeared in 1928 after Les Parfums de Rosine went bankrupt. The only place it still existed was in the Osmothèque's inventory of seventeen hundred perfumes. Kerléo took a *touche*—a strip of white absorbent paper used by perfumers to test scents—dipped it in the tiny brown vial, and handed it to the woman. She inhaled, then sighed. "Ah, mother."

Perfume, like luxury, has a history as long as civilization itself. Prehistoric man applied scent to his body, and the Mesopotamians burned incense for the gods. The Egyptians discovered *enfleurage*—the process of crushing aromatic plants such as roses, crocuses, and violets in oil, which they kept in elaborate glass bottles and used for massage and their daily toilette. For parties, they would throw flower petals across the floor that perfumed the room when guests trod on them. Cleopatra was so obsessed with scent that the sails of her cedar ship were perfumed. "From the barge / a strange invisible perfume hits the sense / of the adjacent wharfs," wrote Shakespeare in *Antony and Cleopatra*.

In Crete, athletes anointed themselves with specific aromatic oils before the games, wrote Diane Ackerman in *A Natural History of the Senses*. Greek writers suggested mint for the arms; thyme for the knees; cinnamon, rose, or palm oil for the jaw and chest; and marjoram for the hair and eyebrows. Alexander the Great liberally perfumed his body and had his tunics soaked in saffron essence. Romans bathed in perfume, saturated their clothes in it, drenched their horses and pets with it. Gladiators massaged their bodies with various scented lotions before battle.

In the thirteenth century, a Spanish alchemist named Arnaud de Villeneuve refined the process of distilling alcohol—called *aquae vitae* (waters of life)—and soon after, modern perfume as we know it was born. "Alcohol was used as a medicine, and to make it more agreeable, it was perfumed with lemon or herbs," Kerléo explained to me when I visited him at the Osmothèque in October 2006. Kerléo knows perfumes better than anyone else today: he served as Patou's chief perfumer for thirty-five years, and in 1990 founded Osmothèque, which he still runs.

He took out a *touche* and dipped it in a small flacon labeled Eau de la Reine de Hongrie (Queen of Hungary Water), which Kerléo said was the first aromatic alcohol, created in 1370 for Queen Elizabeth of Hungary to treat rheumatism and gout. It smelled of rosemary and burned my nostrils slightly when I inhaled. The queen used it liberally most of her adult life, and it is said to have preserved her great beauty.

French king Louis XIV had a team of servants on hand to perfume his rooms with rosewater and marjoram and to wash his clothes in a bath of spices and musk. He ordered his perfumer to create a new scent every day. For parties at the "Perfume Court" of Louis XV, the staff doused doves in scent and released them to fly about the guests, each flap of the wing filling the salons with a rich aroma. During the eighteenth century, women perfumed their clothes and bodies, dusted their hair with sweet-smelling powder, and scented their rooms with potpourris. Napoleon doused himself in two entire bottles of eau de cologne, from Cologne, Germany, during his morning toilet.

In the mid-nineteenth century, perfume as we know it today came about when French perfume houses such as Houbigant and Guerlain began creating scents for old-moneyed aristocrats and the new-moneyed industrialists. Like couture and leather goods, perfume was an independent business, its own domain, until 1910, when couturier Paul Poiret introduced his first scent, Coupe d'Or (Golden Cup), Kerléo said. He dipped a *touche* into a small flask of Coupe d'Or and handed it to me. I inhaled its spicy, floral musk. "It's very modern, no?" Kerléo said. "Something you could wear today." He was right. I wanted to dab some on right then and there.

Poiret produced thirty-six perfumes in fifteen years, straight through World War I. One, a rich sweet scent called Fruit Défendu

(Forbidden Fruit), was launched during the war, causing a great scandal. "How you could produce something so luxurious when our sons are dying in the trenches?" the public howled. They bought it nevertheless. Poiret's products sold, but he lost a fortune in the 1929 stock market crash. Shortly after, he went bankrupt and fifteen years later he died a pauper. His perfumes and his couture designs have mostly been forgotten. But his idea of couture brand perfumes lived on. Chanel, Lanvin, Schiaparelli, and Patou all launched perfumes before World War II. The scents were heavy, full of spice and flowers. The bottles were works of art, produced by fine crystal makers as Baccarat and Lalique, and the customer base was extremely limited. Perfume—known in the business as extract, because of its potency—became an essential part of upper-class dress, like made-to-measure clothes, good shoes, fine leather gloves, and elegant chapeaux. The masses wore eau de cologne, a cheaper version that was a small dose of extract diluted with orange blossom or lemon water. "Eau de cologne was very fashionable in the 1920s, 1930s, before the war," Chanel's nose Jacques Polge explained. "It was sold in the mass market and worn in great quantities. Now it has practically disappeared."

In the 1930s, luxury perfume brands introduced eau de toilette, which is 6 to 12 percent extract diluted with solvents such as ethanol and water, and it became commonplace in the 1950s. Unlike eau de cologne, it smelled like a weaker version of the extract and sold for a fraction of extract prices. "Eau de toilette was created to take perfume to the street," meaning to the middle market, Polge explained. "It was the beginning of the democratization of luxury perfume."

Shortly after Bernard Arnault purchased Dior in 1985, the luxury perfume business underwent a radical acceleration in creation, production, marketing, and consumption. At Dior, for example, in its first forty years, it created twelve perfumes—one every three or four years—including Miss Dior, Diorissimo, Diorella, and Eau Fraîche. In the twenty years since Arnault took over, Dior has introduced more than thirty. In 2005 alone, it launched four. Many are sequels: Dior's 1985 hit Poison, for example, gave rise to Tendre Poison in 1994, Hypnotic Poison in 1998, and Pure Poison in 2004.

In the 1980s, when luxury brands began to focus more on the middle market, they marketed eau de parfum, a more potent product—it is 8 to 20 percent concentrate, blended with alcohol—that sells for slightly more than eau de toilette. A 1.7-ounce bottle of Dior's J'adore eau de parfum, for example, retails for $62; the same size eau de toilette is $50. It was a wise marketing ploy: by incorporating the word *parfum* (perfume) into the name of the product, luxury brands offered to the middle market what appeared to be a true luxury product, a piece of the dream. Perfume is made of 15 to 30 percent concentrate blended with alcohol; it is still the most expensive scent product— J'adore perfume retails for $215 an ounce—and makes up for a small slice of sales. It has, in fact, become like couture: a modest portion of the business, targeted to the rich. To reach more of the middle market, and to earn more profits, luxury brands have extended their perfume scents into other product categories such as body lotion and bath oil.

Today perfume in all its many forms is an essential component of a luxury brand. Old-time luxury brands that have nothing to do with fashion, such as the jewelers Cartier and Van Cleef & Arpels, all have perfumes. Newcomers such as Narciso Rodriguez and Stella McCartney have launched scents as soon as their fledgling companies could support it. Only one major luxury brand does not have one: Louis Vuitton. The company has a policy of strict control of distribution—it sells its products only in its own boutiques and Louis Vuitton sections of department stores—and it believes that is not a large enough retail network for a viable perfume business. Original perfume brands such as Coty have become corporate behemoths that churn out perfume products like Kraft makes cheese. Luxury brands dominate the perfume market: their glossy, gleaming counters clutter department stores, and their high-design packages dominate the shelves of duty-free stores, and perfume chains such as Sephora (owned by LVMH), shoving smaller houses such as Patou out of the picture.

The greatest challenge to luxury brand perfumes today is the recent rise of the celebrity perfume, such as Sarah Jessica Parker's Lovely and Jennifer Lopez's Glow, both produced by Coty. Celebrity perfumes have a short, explosive life: they hit the market with a tsunami of publicity, sell vast amounts to the middle market, and then disappear. And they have pushed luxury brands such as Chanel, Dior, and Givenchy to do the same. "The industry has educated consumers to be volatile," said Michael Steib, a consumer goods analyst at Morgan Stanley in London. "The challenge for the big labels is to differentiate themselves from the other brands that are often discounted, have a very short shelf life, and are totally dependent upon the names associated with them."

THE GRANDDADDY of modern perfumes is Chanel No. 5. World War II GIs fighting in Europe brought it home for their sweethearts. Marilyn Monroe declared it was all she wore to bed. In 1959, the Museum of Modern Art added No. 5's packaging to its permanent collection, and Andy Warhol produced a silk-screened image of the No. 5 bottle in a rainbow of colors. No. 5's spicy oriental bouquet is the scent that young perfumers try to duplicate: it is the standard by which one measures a nose. It is said that a bottle of No. 5 sells every thirty seconds somewhere in the world every day.

In 2003, Chanel's beauty business reportedly did $1.6 billion in sales, thanks in large part to No. 5. According to *Women's Wear Daily,* No. 5 produces a profit margin of 40 percent—more than four times that of its competitors. This reliable and substantial profit allows Chanel's owners, the Wertheimer family, to grow the company cautiously and invest in long-term projects, such as the Muls' farm. "No.

5 is outside of fashion," Jacques Polge told me over dinner in Antibes following my visit to the flower fields. "It comes from another era, and each year that passes, the more strange and foreign it becomes."

Chanel's founder, Gabrielle "Coco" Chanel, came from even more humble beginnings than Louis Vuitton. She was born in Saumur in 1883, one of three daughters of a sickly mother and a philandering father who worked as a traveling salesman. After their mother died of tuberculosis when Gabrielle was eleven, their father deposited the girls at an orphanage in the rustic region of Auvergne and was never to be seen again. At eighteen, Gabrielle was sent to a Catholic boarding school where the nuns taught her how to sew. She worked as a shopgirl for a local lingerie company and moonlighted at a tailor's shop. She spent evenings at the town's cabaret, singing for soldiers stationed there. Her two standards were "Ko Ko Ri Ko" (Cock-a-Doodle Doo) and "Qui Qu'a Vu Coco?" (Who Has Seen Coco?), a ditty about a lost dog. The soldiers shouted "Coco!" when she sang them. The name stuck.

She made her way north toward Paris, where she became a courtesan and a milliner for the horse set. One of her beaux, the dashing polo player Arthur "Boy" Capel, set her up in a millinery business in 1910 at 21, rue Cambon, a block west of Place Vendôme and directly behind the Hôtel Ritz. In 1912, she opened a couture shop in Deauville, the Norman seaside resort and another in 1915 in the southwest Atlantic beach town of Biarritz. In 1918, Chanel moved the Paris shop to 31, rue Cambon, and it has been there ever since. She sold hats and couture, which she fashioned out of soft, pliable jersey like that used for Capel's polo shirts. It was a radical departure from the rigid taffetas and wools that were popular at the time.

In 1919, Chanel was introduced to respected perfumer Ernest Beaux by her new lover, the grand duke Dmitri Pavlovich Romanov. Beaux was born to French perfumers in Russia in 1881 and grew up in Moscow to become the czar's official perfumer. When the Romanov dynasty fell, Beaux fled Russia and moved to La Bocca, an inland town on the Côte d'Azur near Cannes. Chanel met Beaux at his laboratory there to discuss the idea of creating a perfume. Back then, perfumes primarily were monoflora—violet, rose, orange blossom—and packaged in extravagant bottles. Chanel found it boring. "I want everything in the perfume," she told Beaux, "and nothing in the bottle." Her brief was just as succinct: an abstract of flowers that would evoke the odor of women. Beaux whipped up a series of exotic *essais* (samples) that were so rich he needed something to balance them. He chose aldehydes, a group of organic compounds that have a chemical function like alcohol. "It was like putting lemon on strawberries," Polge explained to me. Beaux presented his concoctions to Mademoiselle. She chose the fifth proposition and called it No. 5.

Chanel No. 5 was, and still is, constructed of approximately eighty ingredients. The most important is jasmine, which since 1986 has been provided solely by Joseph Mul. There is ylang-ylang, an exotic flower that grows on the Comores Islands off the west coast of Africa, and patchouli, a dried leaf from Indonesia that was used as a repellent in silk shipments. There is orange blossom water and a variety of spices, particularly clove, which back in the 1920s was one of the most popular spices for perfume. And there is a healthy dose of Joseph Mul's Centifolia roses. For the flask, Chanel chose the most banal shape she could find, a chemist's laboratory bottle. "Now it's the Rolls-Royce of bottle design," Polge said with a laugh, "but then it was very simple." The rectangular cut-glass stopper was based on Paris's elegant Place Vendôme.

Chanel decided to introduce No. 5 slowly, anonymously. First she did a test in Cannes: she invited Beaux and a few friends to dinner at a top restaurant, placed a bottle on the table and when a chic woman walked by, Chanel squeezed the atomizer bulb and filled the air with an invisible cloud of No. 5. Each time the woman stopped, smelled, and appeared to be enchanted by the scent. Pleased with the results, Chanel returned to Paris and quietly launched No. 5. She didn't announce its arrival in the press or stock it in her store. She wore it herself, spritzed the shop's dressing rooms with it, and gave bottles to a few of her high-society friends. Soon the buzz began: "Have you heard Mademoiselle Chanel has a perfume?" When the buzz rose to a clamor, Chanel instructed Beaux to put No. 5 into production. "The success was beyond anything we could have imagined," recalled Chanel's friend Misia Sert. "It was like a winning lottery ticket."

Théophile Bader, the founder of the French department store Galeries Lafayette, wanted to sell No. 5, but to fill the order, Chanel needed to expand production. Bader introduced Chanel to his friend Pierre Wertheimer, co-owner of the Bourjois cosmetics company. In 1924, the trio hammered out a deal to incorporate Les Parfums Chanel: Wertheimer, who would produce No. 5 in his Bourjois factory, got 70 percent, Bader got 20 percent as a finder's fee, and Chanel received a mere 10 percent. It didn't take long for Chanel to realize she'd been crooked. She filed so many lawsuits to get more control and more profits—mostly to no avail—that by 1928, the Wertheimers had a lawyer on staff who dealt solely with, as Wertheimer called her, "that bloody woman."

Throughout the 1920s, Chanel added new scents to her fragrance line: No. 22 in 1922, Gardenia in 1925, Bois des Isles in 1926, and Cuir de Russie in 1927. They were popular, but No. 5 surpassed them all and the competition, too: in 1929, it was named the number-one-selling perfume in the world. By the 1930s, Coco Chanel was earning $4 million a year and reportedly had assets of $10 million. "Under her glossy façade," opined a French banker, "she is a shrewd, calculating peasant."

When the German army arrived in Paris in 1940, brothers Pierre and Paul Wertheimer—Alsatian Jews who feared persecution—fled to the United States. Once settled in New York, they sent an American named H. Gregory Thomas to Grasse to secure the formula and the primary ingredients to produce No. 5 in the United States during the war. While there, Thomas helped Pierre's son Jacques escape, via Morocco and Portugal, to New York. Thomas was later named president of Chanel in the United States, a post he held for thirty-two years.

Chanel closed her fashion house but continued to live across the street at the Hôtel Ritz, a German military headquarters during the war, where she took up with a young German officer named Hans Gunther von Dincklage. In an extraordinarily evil power play to maintain control of the company, Chanel wrote to the French collaborationist government in Vichy and denounced the Wertheimers. But the Wertheimers had anticipated her treachery. In 1943, the family bought 50 percent of an airplane propeller company run by Félix Amiot, a French Aryan collaborator who sold arms to the German military. When Chanel turned coat, the Wertheimers signed Les Parfums Chanel over to Amiot, and the Germans left the company alone. After the armistice, Amiot returned Les Parfums Chanel to the Wertheimers. Amiot's help in protecting the Wertheimers' company "saved his little neck" from the revenge-seeking Allies, Jacques's son Alain Wertheimer told *Forbes*.

Chanel, however, was arrested by French resistance forces. She was released three hours later with the help, it was said, of Winston Churchill, a friend of another of Chanel's former beaux, the Duke of Westminster. She immediately fled to Switzerland and continued to menace the Wertheimers. She threatened to produce her own perfume—which she would call Mademoiselle Chanel No.1.—and two other new scents, and she filed a suit in France that charged that Les Parfums Chanel made an inferior product and demanded that it cease production and sales, and return ownership and rights to her. The Wertheimers negotiated a new deal with Chanel: instead of 10 percent of all French sales of No. 5, she would have 2 percent of world sales.

When No. 5's sales began to lag in the early 1950s, Pierre Wertheimer paid a visit to then-seventy-year-old Mademoiselle Chanel at the Beau Rivage hotel in Lausanne. Within a few days, she was back on the rue Cambon in Paris, planning the relaunch of Chanel couture. Her first collection of slim 1920s gamine looks in the era of Christian Dior's ample New Look designs was roundly dismissed. "A fiasco!" wrote one British paper. Another called the show "a melancholy retrospective." The crowd snickered and grimaced. It was "one of the cruelest experiences I've ever witnessed," film director Franco Zeffirelli recalled.

Chanel was unruffled.

"I want to go on, go on and win," she told Pierre Wertheimer.

"You're right," he said. "You're right to go on."

She did, and each collection got stronger and better. Within a few seasons, the Chanel collarless tweed suit and the gamine flapper dress were the preferred silhouettes in fashion. Even Christian Dior went "back to Chanel's beloved 1920s for inspiration," *Newsweek* reported. "His mannequins had flattened busts, waistlines where hips usually are, and not a curve was to be seen." All this fashion success further boosted Chanel perfume sales and Mademoiselle's position in the company. In 1954, Wertheimer negotiated his final deal with her: the family would pay for the rue Cambon headquarters, her personal expenses, and her taxes for the rest of her life in return for control of her name for perfume and fashion. As she had no heirs, upon her death the family would receive her perfume royalty payments, too. That same year, the Wertheimers bought from the Bader family the remaining 20 percent of the house. When Chanel died at the Ritz in 1971, the Wertheimers became the sole owners of the company. They still are today.

WITH NO. 5, Coco Chanel had turned the idea of a fashion-branded perfume into a viable and quite remunerative business. Louis Amic, a respected French nose who ran the major perfume laboratory of Roure

Bertrand Dupont, decided to make it a business unto itself. In the 1930s and 40s, he went to couture houses such as Elsa Schiaparelli, Piguet, and Balenciaga and told them, "You have good taste and you should have a perfume. Let me do it for you." Back then, creating luxury brand perfumes was a relaxed, pleasurable assignment. Often the couturier and perfumer would meet for lunch and over a four-course meal and a bottle or two of good wine, they'd come up with the name, the basic recipe, the packaging, and the marketing plan. Louis Amic's son, Jean, continued the practice, doing perfumes in the 1960s for Paco Rabanne, Givenchy, and Pierre Cardin. Only a handful of couture houses, such as Chanel and Patou, created, produced, and distributed their own perfumes.

In 1969, Roure Bertrand Dupont hired a young nose from Saint-Rémy-en-Provence named Jacques Polge to work for its New York office. Polge had become a perfumer by chance—he was recruited by a local firm while studying English and French literature at a university in Aix-en-Provence—but he soon became a respected young talent. While at Roure Bertrand Dupont, Polge helped create perfumes for Saint Laurent and Givenchy. In 1974, Alain Wertheimer, the twenty-five-year-old grandson of Pierre, took over as CEO of Chanel. By then, the company had dwindled down to the perfume line and the original shop on rue Cambon. "Chanel was dead," Alain Wertheimer said a few years later. "Nothing was happening." Wertheimer had little business experience—he had interned at the Moët & Chandon champagne winery in Épernay not long before taking over Chanel—but he saw quickly what needed to be done to revive the brand. He reined in distribution, pulling Chanel No. 5 off drugstore shelves. He launched the Chanel Beauté cosmetics line, which was sold only in high-end stores. Then, in 1979, he called Polge.

Chanel had employed only two noses in sixty years: Ernest Beaux, the chemist who created No. 5 in 1921, and Henri Robert, who did No. 19, Cristalle, and Chanel pour Monsieur. Robert, well into his eighties, was retiring. The perfume arm of Chanel had been creatively dormant for some time. "There was a new perfume every twenty years," Polge remembered with a laugh. "People in the industry said, 'You're crazy to take this job. You'll have nothing to do!'" But this was the house of No. 5, Polge reasoned. "It's a mythical perfume."

His confreres were right. When Polge arrived at Chanel, there were a handful of perfumes at the time—No. 5, No. 19, and Cristalle—and No. 5 accounted for 80 percent of sales. "For a long time, [Chanel executives] didn't want to do any new perfumes because they were afraid it would cannibalize No. 5," Polge explained. But Wertheimer had different ideas. He told Polge to maintain the quality of Chanel's existing perfumes and to develop new scents that would follow the same olfactory path. For his first creation, Coco, introduced in 1984, Polge visited Coco Chanel's apartment in the rue Cambon headquarters. "She had died in 1971, and this was 1979, and no one had touched anything," he remembered. "I was taken by the mix of Venetian and baroque decor. What would this decor produce?" He came up with a mélange that recalls Chanel perfumes Bois des Isles, Cuir de Russie, and Sycomore—a profoundly oriental fragrance. For Coco Mademoiselle, launched in 2001, Polge revisited Coco "to see what the same ideas would produce ten years later." The scent had evolved, like fashion. For Allure, which came out in 1996, Polge created a perfume that would be the equivalent of Chanel sportswear—something comfortable, easy to wear.

Among Polge's chief responsibilities is to protect and nurture No. 5. "We care for No. 5 every day of the year," he told me one winter afternoon in his office in the Paris suburb of Neuilly-sur-Seine. "Look, there are two flacons of it here on my desk." Indeed, among the little bottles of absolute and essence clustered on his otherwise empty desktop were two marked "No. 5." He constantly tests it to make sure, as he puts it, "that it is always the same and always the best."

Polge took me into the lab next to his office. It was all white, bathed in sunlight. On metal shelves above the worktables sat old-fashioned indigo blue flacons of absolutes, essences, and synthetics. Others are kept in refrigerator-like coolers originally built to store wine. He took a *touche*, dipped it into a flacon, and held it up to my nose. "This is the jasmine of No. 5," he said as I inhaled. It was absolute made from Joseph Mul's flowers. Jasmine from anywhere else, Polge explained, would change the scent of No. 5. The liquid was thick and syrupy and the color of amber. The aroma was pungent.

"What do you smell?"

"Flowers," I said. "Rich earth, like the dirt in a kitchen garden."

"And tea," he added. "Do you smell the tea?"

Yes, he was right. A good strong Ceylon tea.

BACK IN THE EARLY twentieth century, "every luxury brand hired a nose like a restaurant hired a chef," Jacques Polge said. "Poiret had a nose who later worked for Patou. Coty had a nose. Lanvin had one, who created Arpège." Today, only a handful of perfume companies have a nose on staff. Chanel has Jacques Polge. Hermès hired Jean-Claude Ellena in 2004. Patou, which is owned by Procter & Gamble, has Jean-Michel Duriez, who took over when Kerléo retired in 1999. At Guerlain, which LVMH acquired from the family in 1994, the founder's great-grandson Jean-Paul Guerlain retired in 2002 but still consults.

Most luxury brands today do not own, create, manufacture, or distribute their perfumes. Luxury brands such as Giorgio Armani, Calvin Klein, Jil Sander, and Marc Jacobs license their names to conglomerates such as Procter & Gamble—"soap companies," sniffed Polge—or big cosmetic firms such as Coty, Estée Lauder, and L'Oréal. (In 2005, Coty bought Unilever's fragrance division, which included Calvin Klein, Vera Wang, and Chloé, for $800 million.) In return, the conglomerates produce, package, distribute, and market the perfume.

Some designers are implicated in the perfume's creation from the start; some arrive at the end of the creative process and simply choose the juice.

Most perfumes are created by a handful of big laboratories: Givaudan Roure in Switzerland; International Flavors & Fragrances in New York; Symrise in Holzminden, Germany; Firmenich in Switzerland; Quest International in Kent, England; Haarmann & Reimer in Germany; and Takasago in Japan. Together, they do about $20 billion a year in business, creating smells and tastes for everything from luxury brand perfumes to French fries. Givaudan Roure is the largest: in 2005, it did a staggering $2.1 billion in sales and possessed 13.2 percent of the business. Among its creations are Giorgio Beverly Hills, Calvin Klein's Obsession, Cindy Crawford's signature scent, and Guerlain's new women's fragrance Insolence. In late 2006, Givaudan stunned the fragrance industry when it acquired Quest for $2.3 billion (£1.2 billion), making it far and away the largest fragrance and flavor firm in the world, with expected combined annual revenues of approximately $3.26 billion. About 44 percent of the business—or $1.43 billion—would be in fragrance.

Givaundan's biggest rival is International Flavors & Fragrances, a 170-year-old global conglomerate that began as a small family business producing pure drugs and essential oils and by 2005 had grown into a $2 billion business with ninety-six perfumers and sixty-seven flavorists on staff. Among its "Hall of Fame Fragrances" are Givenchy's Organza, Lancôme's Trésor (owned by Estée Lauder), Calvin Klein's Eternity (owned by Unilever), Ralph Lauren's Polo (owned by Cosmair), and Estée Lauder's White Linen. The fragrance division of these conglomerates—which includes not only luxury perfumes but also scents for detergents, soaps, and lotions—is the most remunerative part of their business.

If a luxury brand—other than Chanel, Patou, and now Hermès—wants to launch a new perfume, the company puts together a brief that explains what it wants the perfume to achieve and invites the laboratories to compete for the assignment. Unlike luxury perfume's golden years, when perfumers and designers used to dream up a new scent together over lunch, briefs today are written by marketing executives with polls, surveys, and sales figures as their guide. Briefs often have conceptual ideas or marketing pitches. Take Dior's brief for Quest International to create J'adore in the late 1990s: it declared that the scent should be "sexy like a stiletto and as comfortable as a pair of Tod's." But generally, luxury perfume briefs all follow the same script. "Basically, it's 'We want something for women,' " a perfume executive told the *New Yorker*. "Okay, which women? 'Women! All women! It should make them feel more feminine, but strong, and competent, but not too much, and it should work well in Europe and the U.S. and especially in the Asian market, and it should be new but it should be classic, and young women should love it, but older women should love it too.' If it's a French house, the brief will also say, 'And it should be a great and uncompromised work of art,' and if it's an American brief it will say, 'And it should smell like that Armani thing two years ago that did four million dollars in the first two months in Europe but also like the Givenchy that sold so well in China.' " All of this leaves Jacques Polge resigned. "I hear the briefs of brands that declare that they want to create a 'classic,' like No. 5," he says with a sigh. "This is a false notion. We should try to create a perfume of its time, and perhaps it can become a classic."

If the labs are interested, they take on the assignment and set their noses to work. Each conglomerate works on an average of ten to fifteen briefs at a time. Three weeks later, the labs present their *essais* to the luxury brand's perfume executives. If the suits choose one of the proposals, they'll initially order two or three tons of the juice. If it sells well, they'll order more. The toughest part of the business, Polge told me, "is to beat the competition and win the brief." No matter how wonderful the scent, a perfume only exists if it is chosen. Labs are known to recycle a scent they really believe in. They adapt their discourse to make it fit the brief and include marketing studies in the pitch that show it has strong approval ratings. Perfume companies will also buy juices they think are marketable and keep them in reserve until they find the right brand for them. L'Oréal sat on one such *essai* for three years until Viktor & Rolf chose it for Flowerbomb.

ON A BRIGHT MORNING in May 2006, I visited Hermès's nose Jean-Claude Ellena at his laboratory, which is in his 1960s contemporary home tucked in the fragrant parasol pines in the steep hills behind Grasse. Ellena is a dashing Frenchman in his late fifties, tan and fit with a flop of sandy blond hair combed back, a strong chin, bright eyes, and a wicked sense of humor. Dressed in pressed khakis and a crisp white shirt, he invited me to sit in his mod living room overlooking the forested valley and, over tea, explained to me how he makes perfume.

Today, a mere 10 percent of the ingredients used to create perfumes are natural. The remaining 90 percent are synthetic. Ellena told me, surprisingly, that this is not such a bad thing. When I asked him about the quality difference between synthetics and pure ingredients, he said, "I put natural and synthetics at the same level. They are constructive materials."

Ellena ushered me into his lab—a small sunny room next to the living room—to make his point. He reached over to one of the two turning stainless-steel stands that hold the clear glass flacons of the 115 odors he prefers to work with. About 40 percent are natural, the remaining 60 synthetic. He opened a flacon containing a synthetic called alcohol phenylethylique, dipped a white *touche* into it, and handed it to me to smell. The odor was chemical and bitter. He dipped another into geraniol, put it with the first one, and I took a whiff: tea rose. He took a third *touche,* dipped it into ionone beta. Alone, it smelled of coconut oil, like Hawaiian Tropic sunscreen. But when Ellena put it with the other two, the overall odor was Chinese rose. "With a hint of sake," he added. He dipped a fourth into acetate de benzyle and added it to the mix, and we had a big, full-blossomed rose like you find at the florist. "I am an illusionist," he said with a laugh. "I make you believe."

He dipped a *touche* into essence of rose Turque, and handed it to me. It was potent and dense—far more than the synthetics. I smelled honey. "And Armagnac," Ellena pointed out. "If I'm looking for the smell of aged alcohol, I'd say, 'Ah! Rose Turque!' If I want the smell of sake it's alcohol phenylethylique. Geraniol is sparkling. If I want a perfume with bubbles—tight, compact bubbles that move—I use geraniol. I don't use materials for what they smell, but for what they do."

The first synthetic, Ellena told me, was created in 1853: aldehyde benzoic, which smells of bitter almond. By the late ninetienth century, there were loads of synthetics in perfume: Guerlain's famous perfume Jicky, introduced in 1879, included synthetics. "During the Industrial Revolution, we believed in progress, that it would solve all the problems of the world," Ellena explained, "and perfumes profited." By 1920, chemists had come up with 80 percent of the synthetics used today.

Ellena has spent his whole life immersed in the perfume business. Raised in a small town near Grasse, he quit high school at the age of seventeen because he didn't like formal studies. His father, a perfumer, helped him find a job manufacturing essences such as jasmine, clove, sandalwood, and lavender. Soon he was promoted to nose. In the late 1960s, Ellena spent a year in the United States to learn about the American market, then in the early 1970s moved to Paris, where he worked for Givaudan. He created his first luxury brand perfume, called First, for Van Cleef & Arpels in 1976. He was twenty-eight. Since then, he has produced more than one hundred scents, including Declaration for Cartier, In Love Again for Yves Saint Laurent, Eau parfumée au thé for

Bulgari, Night for Her for Emporio Armani, and Bazar Femme for Christian Lacroix. "I never know if a perfume will be a success," he says, "but I know what to do to not make a bad perfume."

Today Ellena is one of eighty noses in France, and one of the most efficient. He prefers to use 10 to 20 different odors in his formula, versus 150 to 300, which is the norm in the business, and he is known to work quickly. He came up with the basic formula for Hermès's Un Jardin en Méditerranée in two weeks and spent three months finalizing it. His initial inspiration was the scent of fig leaves lining a tray that was being used to serve champagne at a cocktail party. Ellena lives some of the legends of being a nose—he doesn't eat garlic, and his house has no scents whatsoever. But he debunks other myths, like the idea of top notes and base notes. "That's bull," he said. "When you smell perfume, you smell everything at the same time." When I asked about making different perfumes for men and women, he scrunched his nose and waved his hand dismissively. "That's just marketing."

In 1998, Ellena met Véronique Gautier, then head of perfumes for Cartier; she hired him to create Declaration. Not long after, Gautier joined Hermès, and she asked Ellena to do their new scent, Un Jardin en Méditerranée (A Garden in the Mediterranean), which launched in 2003. The company was so pleased with its success that the next year Gautier brought Ellena in-house, where he created Un Jardin sur le Nil (Garden on the Nile), which would serve as the centerpiece for Hermès's theme the following year, "As a River Runs." The brief Gautier provided was extremely brief: the name Un Jardin sur le Nil. "I had an idea in my head of what the perfume should be—jasmine, orange flower, lotus flower, spice, and saffron—because these are the smells I imagined you smell in Egypt," Ellena told me. Then he traveled to Aswan, Egypt, to confirm his idea and discovered there were no jasmine blooms, no orange blossoms, and no lotus flowers. "It caused me great anxiety," he said. "I couldn't sleep that first night because I had to wipe this idea completely out of my mind."

The next morning, Ellena set about constructing a new recipe. He went to the Aswan souk, where he saw lotus root soaking in glass bowls filled with water. He took a whiff and found that the water smelled of lotus flower. He went for a hike on Elephantine Island, across the Nile from the Old Cataract Hotel, and pulled leaves off the trees and bushes and scrunched them to release their odor. He was most taken with the scent of sycamore. "I kept that smell," he said. He went down the Nile to a Nubian village where the mango trees were covered with ripe fruit. He found that odor enchanting and decided to make it the theme of the perfume. He returned to Paris, wrote down the formula that was in his head, and gave it to his assistants. It was 70 percent of what became the final perfume in the bottle. "In the beginning of the twentieth century, perfumery was more figurative. It was floral bouquets," he told me. "Now we are in narrative: the perfume tells a story." Next, he says, perfume will be olfactive: you will be able to smell a place. Like Un Jardin sur le Nil. You can smell the souk, the mango groves, the heat, and the dry desert. "You will travel with perfume," he said.

Ellena constructed Un Jardin sur le Nil with both synthetic and natural ingredients. For naturals, Ellena turns to Laboratoire Monique Rémy (LMR), a small lab in Grasse that is the leading supplier of 100 percent pure raw materials for the perfume industry. I visited LMR a few days after meeting with Ellena. When I drove up to the headquarters, tucked in the middle of a charmless industrial park on the outskirts of town, and saw the place—two big navy corrugated metal warehouses with poured cement floors—it was hard to imagine LMR as the perfume equivalent to a couture atelier. But as soon as I stepped out of the car, there was no doubt: even there in the parking lot, I was bowled over by the aroma of flowers, grasses, and spices.

I entered the administrative office's small reception room. On the wall hung a 1997 Certified Vendor Award from Estée Lauder Companies, "presented to LMR for outstanding quality and service in providing essential oils." Displayed in glass cases were some of LMR's recent hits: Prada's signature women's fragrance, Givenchy's Very Irresistible and Organza, Viktor & Rolf's Flowerbomb, Dior Homme. LMR's general manager, Bernard Toulemonde, a kind, gentle man, walked in, introduced himself, and explained to me the LMR mission. "We work with only the most noble extracts: white flowers, roses, tuber rose, daffodil, narcissus, jasmine, mimosa, and iris, which is the Rolls-Royce of perfumery," he said. "There is a parallel between what we do and haute cuisine. The best food is only achieved by using the best ingredients." Same with perfume, he explained. "There is not a great perfume today that does not have LMR products in it."

LMR was born out of frustration. From the 1960s to the early 1980s, Monique Rémy worked for the big perfume groups, including Unilever and Pfizer, as a chemical engineer specializing in natural ingredients. It was a time when tycoons had started to take over luxury brands and demand more profits in all product areas, including perfume. "As a plant manager, she delivered what the industry wanted: the same but cheaper," Toulemonde explained. "They started stretching the product with solvents to make it cheaper to the point that nobody knew what natural was anymore." Ellena remembered that period well. "Grasse had lost its soul," he told me. "Most companies there were doing scents like ready-to-wear. If Givaudan wanted a rose at this price, the lab said, 'We'll do it, and cheaper!' They would dilute their good products with less expensive ones. The quality had changed and was uneven."

By the early 1980s, Rémy had grown so disillusioned that she decided to go into business herself. Her idea, as Ellena recalls, was "stupidly simple": 100 percent pure ingredients. Her products cost far more than the diluted ones that were in use. To sell them, she bypassed the commercial and marketing departments of the big laboratories and went straight to the noses. Once the noses got a whiff of her goods, that's all they wanted. "The perfumers started telling the buyers to buy at LMR," Toulemonde said. And the business took off. "It was very courageous of her," Ellena told me. "She did the inverse of what the market was at the time."

Like the couturiers in Paris a decade earlier, Rémy sold her company in 2000 to a big group—International Flavors & Fragrances (IFF)—with the idea of soon retiring. But she wasn't pleased with how the corporate executives were running the company, and she fought with them for LMR's autonomy. She won. In 2002, she hired Toulemonde, a food engineer who had worked for Nestlé and Sanofi, as her new general manager. The following year, she retired and left Toulemonde in charge; her daughter Frédérique, who had worked as the company's commercial director, left in 2005. LMR is small: it has thirty-four employees and does about €13 million ($16.3 million) a year in business, 40 percent of which is with IFF. The remaining 60 percent of LMR's business is with the other big groups, Hermès and Chanel. "Those two houses use more naturals than anyone else," Toulemonde told me.

He handed me a pair of plastic protective eyeglasses and guided me into the plant next door. The room is the size of an airplane hangar, with towering, mad-scientist-like contraptions of aluminum tubes and big Pyrex glass balloons that percolate and steam and drip various fragrant potions and oil-drum-sized vats filled with orange, brown, or green goo. I walked over and sniffed one and nearly sneezed. I read the label: hay. On the shelves sat canisters as small as 250 grams and up to 10 kilos. In the back was a walk-in refrigerator that contained about half a year's production, from two years ago, as inventory and insurance. "We're dealing with nature," Toulemonde pointed out as we stood in the chilly walk-in, "and nature generally delivers once a year and sometimes only a fraction."

LMR's specialty is made-to-measure ingredients, a complicated and expensive process that only a few top brands, such as Hermès, can afford. "Say I buy the best quality lavender on the market," Ellena explained to me. "Lavender has three hundred molecules in it. I tell the lab to cut it in slices for me, like a sausage. This is high tech, to slice it like this. I go and smell all the slices and choose the ones I want, the best ones, and have them put those molecules back together. I have a unique quality and it becomes the beginning of a creation. I created the essence of orange in Un Jardin sur le Nil like this with Monique Rémy. Sure, it's more costly, but that's not a problem at Hermès. The industrial level can't do this."

LMR has given birth to a small renaissance in Grasse. Toulemonde tells me that a handful of young entrepreneurs have moved to the region and are reviving the flower-growing business. It's a boutique industry: they are small firms, many of which are following practices of sustainable agriculture, like LMR. "It's very trendy, like organic vegetables," Toulemonde said with a laugh. No one, though, grows Centifolia—they leave that to Joseph Mul. "It's a high-cost flower, and yield is too small," Toulemonde explained.

The perfume business has now become like luxury fashion. There's the tiny couture division, with a handful of small producers in places such as Grasse, the Comores, Turkey, and Egypt, which supply exclusive labs like LMR. And there are the ready-to-wear producers in third-world nations such as India and China that churn out synthetics for the big boys. The reasoning for the shift is the same as in fashion: cost. "You can't earn enough in raw materials," Ellena said.

IN THE MID-1990S, luxury brands began to test-market their perfumes. "[Luxury perfume] has become such a big business that brands want to make sure their investment is worth it," a perfume lab executive explained to me. Chanel didn't start testing until the creation of Allure in 1996, and it tests only for the color of the juice and the packaging, never the scent. For Allure, the color tested badly in the United

States, so it was changed. Ellena insists that Hermès does not test its perfumes in any way before a launch. "Market testing is the best way to repeat or copy perfumes consumers already know," he told me, "not to create."

Once a perfume is ready to go, the marketing department organizes a "launch" to get the press rolling. Some launches are restrained: I remember attending one for Issey Miyake's Le Feu d'Issey in 1998 that was a low-key luncheon for fifty reporters and editors at the Musée des Arts Décoratifs in Paris with speeches by executives and samples of the perfume to take back to the office to try out. Others are less restrained. When Yves Saint Laurent, then owned by the Gucci Group, launched Nu in 2001, it threw a wild late-night party at the old French stock exchange with topless dancers in flesh-colored thongs rolling around in a giant Plexiglas corral. "All I see is an orgy," cracked American fashion designer Jeremy Scott at the fete. "[This launch] is all about money. It's in the Bourse. It's a money event."

To celebrate the launch of Un Jardin sur le Nil, in February, 2005, Hermès organized a trip to Aswan for two dozen fashion writers and editors as well as Hermès public relations and communications directors from around the world. Hermès chartered a plane from Paris on Air Egypt, brought along champagne and good bordeaux (which Hermès reps served during the flight, since it was a Muslim-run carrier), and lodged everyone in Aswan's finest hotels. For three days, there were nonstop activities: boat trips down the Nile, champagne-drenched picnics, a guided tour of the Temple of Isis, a Nubian banquet under the vaulted dining room of the Old Cataract with festive music by an orchestra and choir flown in from Cairo, and of course, at midnight, belly dancing. All of this was to give the Hermès staff who attended a flurry of ideas for marketing and advertising campaigns as well as window and store displays, and to provide the attending journalists color for their Un Jardin sur le Nil stories. Everyone went home with a bottle.

A few weeks after the Aswan trip, Un Jardin sur le Nil was everywhere. I walked through department stores in Paris and was spritzed by bottle-wielding ladies. There were ads, posters, and magazine stories. "You might spend the same amount in advertising that you'd expect in first-year sales," Tom Ford told me. "If you are expecting $25 million in sales, you'll spend $25 million in advertising." And like a mortgage, you have to keep paying. "You must invest every year in fragrance advertising," Jacques Polge said. "When you stop investing in publicity, sales drop." The investment worked for Jardin sur le Nil. In its first year, it did approximately $18 million in sales, making it the number one scent in Hermès's $100 million perfume stable. Number two was Eau de Merveille, which debuted a year earlier and sold a bit less than Un Jardin sur le Nil. "Today, it's difficult to have a success," Polge told me. "When you look at the number of perfumes that are launched and how few remain . . . The difficulty is not only to succeed, but to last."

WHEN A PERFUME does succeed, the profits are formidable all around. The laboratory sells the juice to the licensee at two and a half times the cost. The licensee retails it for two to four times its cost and earns about 30 to 40 percent in profits. The licensee then pays the luxury brand royalties for use of the name. The big money is made in volume, which is why perfumes are pushed on the mass-market level, everywhere from department stores to airport duty-free shops—two thousand points of sale in the United States for major brands such as Chanel or Dior is not unusual. Hermès, by contrast, is in fewer than three hundred.

Since the late 1990s, perfume sales have dropped, despite a dramatic increase in advertising. Like many in the business, Polge blames the crisis on what he calls the "banalization of perfumery": the industrialization of creation, which kills craftsmanship, the mass distribution in perfumery chains—which, Polge says, "focus on the ephemeral side of perfume. All that we put into perfume disappears [there]"—and the "quick hits" like celebrity perfumes. They can be very lucrative—Jennifer Lopez's Glow, launched in 2002, sold $80 million worth in its first three years—but they generally have a short life and contribute greatly to the market's saturation.

In response to sluggish sales and declining profits, luxury brands have quietly been slashing the cost of production. One of the easiest places to cut back on cost—and therefore quality—is in packaging. When Alain Lorenzo took over as CEO of Parfums Givenchy in 1996, he eliminated the cellophane inside perfume boxes. Cartondruck, a leading packaging manufacturer, has been told by luxury brands "to look at how we can execute the design at the lowest price," says Bruce Betancourt, general manager for the company's American branch in Fairview, New Jersey. "We will run four-color process instead of twelve. We can print metallics instead of restamping them. Sometimes we reduce the size of the box so we can print more boxes per sheet." Most luxury brands have also eliminated what Betancourt called "flute liners": the protective corrugated paper board around the bottle inside the box. "Now that is rarely used," he says. The same goes with bottle production. Bottles for luxury perfumes cost on average 10 percent of total production cost, a figure that luxury brands constantly strive to reduce. "Everyone cuts corners, and they do it through the production," Catherine Descourtieux, marketing director for Saint-Gobain Desjonquères, a leading maker of perfume bottles in Paris. "You can alter the shape of the bottle slightly or work with colors that cost less—subtle things that the buyer won't notice." Says Betancourt: "All brands launch their perfumes with what is more design-driven and then later make value-driven decisions to maintain the same look but reduce the aesthetics to reduce costs. This is pretty consistent."

But more and more, luxury brands are also looking for ways to produce cheaper juice. For new perfumes, luxury brands submit briefs with a final production price that is half of what it was a decade ago— a price that, Polge says, "is impossible to meet at any quality. They ask to construct jasmine without any flowers. Sure, there's been a progress in chemistry: we can reconstruct jasmine better than we would thirty years ago, but it's lower in quality than the lowest of real jasmine. No odor can replace another. Replacing one with another that is less expensive is the greatest error you can make." One company looked into taking the entire production process to China. "It was going to be produced and filled at the same location," Betancourt remembered. To lower the production cost of existing perfumes, luxury brands have done something once unthinkable: they have instructed laboratories to change legendary formulas by using cheaper flowers or synthetics, or by simply diluting the perfume. "They say, 'We need to cut costs. Do what you can to lower your prices,'" Jean-Claude Ellena told me.

Of course, brands and noses deny this. Most claim on the record that the changes in old perfume recipes are due to new government regulations on ingredients. But the watering down of good perfumes for economic reasons does happen. When I asked Jean Kerléo at the Osmothèque, who is effectively the caretaker of perfumes for the industry, if brands dilute or cheapen ingredients in classic perfumes, he looked down and quietly said, "Yes." When I asked which brands, he responded, "I don't think I should answer that."

Perhaps the greatest threat to luxury perfume sales, however, isn't cuts in costs or quality. It's a shift in marketing focus by the luxury brands themselves. "Perfume today is important," Jacques Polge told me, "but couture houses live with the handbag."

LONGCHAMP

P A R I S

CHAPTER SIX

IT'S IN THE BAG

"Contentment is natural wealth. Luxury is artificial poverty."

—SOCRATES

OOK AT A WOMAN TODAY, any woman, and what do you see? Clothes that are more or less anonymous. Shoes that are more or less anonymous.

And a handbag.

It could be made of leather or canvas or nylon. It could be a tiny clutch in her hand or a backpack slung over her shoulder. Never mind what's in it. More than anything else today, the handbag tells the story of a woman: her reality, her dreams. And thanks to luxury brand marketing, that handbag changes every few months, like the seasons, like her moods.

Since the late 1990s, handbags and other small leather goods have joined perfume as "entrance products" to a luxury brand. Once costing as much as, if not more than, ready-to-wear, luxury brand handbags now come in a wide range of materials, from nylon to crocodile, and an abundant number of styles at prices as low as $200. Unlike perfume, handbags are visible on the body, and—like Air Jordans for teenagers—give the wearer the chance to brandish the logo and publicly declare her status or her aspiration. "[They] make your life more pleasant, make you dream, give you confidence, and show your neighbors you are doing well," Karl Lagerfeld told me. "Everyone can afford a luxury handbag."

Today, when you walk into a luxury brand store anywhere in the world, you will find yourself surrounded by handbags. They are the easiest luxury fashion item to sell because they don't require sizing or trying on: you look at it, and if you like it, you buy it. Done. They are easier to create and produce than perfumes, and the profit margin is astounding: for most luxury brands the profit is between ten and twelve times the cost to make the item. At Vuitton, it's as much as thirteen times. Handbags are the engine that drives luxury brands today. According to annual consumer surveys conducted by Coach each year, the average American woman purchased two new handbags a year in 2000; by 2004, that number was more than four. At Louis Vuitton's immense four-floor global store in Tokyo, 40 percent of all sales are made in the first room, which sells only monogram handbags, wallets, and other small leather goods.

"With the bag . . . there are no leftovers because there are no sizes, unlike shoes or clothes," Miuccia Prada told me. "It's easier to choose a bag than a dress because you don't have to face the age, the weight, all the problems. And there is a kind of an obsession with bags. It's so easy to make money. The bag is the miracle of the company."

In 2004, luxury brands collectively sold $11.7 billion worth of handbags and other leather accessories, and the segment is only getting stronger. While the luxury market grew by 1.2 percent each year from 2001 and 2004, leather goods sales increased by 7.5 percent each year. A large share of those sales are "It" bags: the latest hot designs that—thanks to luxury brand ad campaigns and fashion magazine articles—

become the must-have of the season. Recent "It" bags include the Louis Vuitton Murakami, with the signature monogram stamped in rainbow tones on white leather, and the Gucci Flora, a pretty floral print taken from a scarf originally designed by the house for Princess Grace back in the 1960s. Handbags have become so important in fashion today that an English journalist wrote during London Fashion Week in 2006, "Everybody—everybody—is talking about handbags with the intensity of cardinals appointing a new Pope."

The "It" bag phenomenon is young—less than twenty years old—and has been wholly created by the marketing wizards at luxury brand companies. I remember in the early 1990s reading stories in fashion magazines that declared that if you couldn't afford to change your wardrobe each season, you could update your look with a new handbag. Even my bureau chief at *Newsweek* in Paris picked up on the trend. Back in 1996, as we sat in his office and discussed a fashion story for the spring season, he said, "Look, fashion is dead. It's about accessories." How did he know that? Because luxury brands had been pushing the message, and the product, relentlessly. "It's like you've gotta have it or you'll die," Tom Ford explained.

Leather companies launched ready-to-wear lines to make the brands—and therefore their handbags—sexier. Fashion companies pushed handbags to the forefront of their offerings and made them the centerpiece of their increasingly provocative advertising. Handbags became an intoxicating lure.

And women got hooked, some disturbingly so. As I noted in the Introduction, there are Japanese girls who work as prostitutes to earn money to buy Louis Vuitton, Chanel, and Hermès bags. I read about a woman who played backgammon for Hermès bags. In September 2005, victims of Hurricane Katrina used their Red Cross cards to buy $800 bags at the Louis Vuitton boutique in Atlanta. (Once the story hit the papers, Louis Vuitton executives instructed their salespeople to stop accepting Red Cross cards for payment and reimbursed the Red Cross for the purchases already made.) Web sites such as BagBorroworSteal.com have cropped up for women to rent luxury and designer handbags for a fashionably short time instead of buying them—that way, they can change their bags more often.

Women's obsession with logo-riddled status handbags has become such a part of Western society that contemporary artists riffed on it, often to luxury brands' great displeasure. At the Venice Biennale in 1999, French performance artist Alberto Sorbelli staged a happening called L'Agressé (The Victim of Attacks) during which he had a woman in a black minidress and spike-heeled boots and a man in a blue leather suit beat him silly with Louis Vuitton handbags. New York artist Tom Sachs produced a series of works in 1999 that included McDonald's-style value meals done up in various luxury brands' logo wrap, a black guillotine with a big white Chanel logo, and a miniature concentration camp made of Prada boxes. Surprisingly, Sachs received little backlash—only Hermès complained, he said. Indeed, the opening party at the Galerie Thaddaeus Ropac in Paris was a fashion happening, and San Francisco socialite and couture client Dodie Rosekrans bought the guillotine and donated it to the Centre Pompidou in Paris.

San Francisco artist Libby Black wasn't so lucky. When she re-created a Louis Vuitton store—replete with the entire Vuitton product line, all out of paper, paint, and glue—at the Manolo Garcia Gallery in 2003, she and her gallery owner were called to Louis Vuitton's San Francisco office, where corporate lawyers told her she was violating copyright laws and had to shut down the show. Black kept it up anyway and never heard from Vuitton again.

IN THE WORLD of luxury brand handbags, as in automobiles and clothing, there is a pyramid of quality: made-to-order down to mass-manufactured. The best—the equivalent of a Rolls-Royce or Chanel couture suit—is an Hermès handbag. Made of the finest leather and fabrics, sewed by hand, and with starting prices of more than $6,000 and years-long waiting lists, Hermès handbags are considered by many to be the last true luxury goods in the luxury fashion industry. They have long been the bag of choice for those who can afford to choose. Jackie Onassis was photographed so often with her Constance bag slung over her shoulder that customers would ask Hermès salesclerks for "Jackie O's bag." Maryvonne Pinault, wife of Gucci Group owner François Pinault, raised fashion eyebrows when she attended the Paris women's wear shows in the fall of 2001 not with a Gucci or a Saint Laurent, but with a large alligator Hermès Birkin bag on her arm. Martha Stewart showed up at her insider trading trial in 2004 carrying a buttery brown Birkin and was taken to task by the press for her indiscretion. Carrying into a jury trial "a bag that is surrounded by such a thick cloud of wealth and privilege was ill-advised," Robin Givhan opined in the *Washington Post*.

Today, buying a luxury brand handbag is an exercise in banality: you walk into the well-appointed store past the chic-suited security guards, peruse what's on display, choose, pay, and walk out with your purchase. The shopping experience may have been pleasant, but in the end it was no different from going to the Gap, except for the price. There is nothing unique about the product: the brand has churned out thousands of them, absolutely identical. Unless you place a special order to have something custom made—and that is a very limited business, available at only a few companies—what you get is a ready-to-carry bag.

Buying an Hermès handbag—or saddle, or luggage—on the other hand, is still a true experience in luxury. Hermès boutiques do receive a few bags each season to sell to customers who walk in—a bit like a good restaurant always saving a table for a regular who drops in without a reservation. But generally, if you want to buy an Hermès bag, you have to order it. The bags on display in the store are just that: display models to show you the options. You choose the material: cowhide, reptile, ostrich, or even canvas. You choose the color and the kind of hardware: silver, gold, diamond-encrusted. And for the Kelly, you choose if the seams are on the outside or turned in. And then you wait several months while it is made to your specifications. When it arrives in the shop and you are invited to come pick it up, it is your bag. Another woman may have a navy blue cowhide Kelly with gold hardware and turned-in seams, but that was her idea, just as yours was yours.

Hermès handbags are the antithesis of an "It" bag: most of the designs have been around for almost a century and are coveted not because they are in fashion but because they never go out of fashion. They don't bear ostentatious logos; the bags themselves are sufficiently recognizable. Hermès handbags convey old money and refinement—even if those who carry them have neither. They are luxury's discreet symbol of wealth and success.

To see how an Hermès bag is made is to understand what luxury once was and what it is no longer. On a cool spring morning in March 2005, I visited the Hermès special orders workshop in Pantin, a seedy suburb north of Paris, to get a glimpse. Pantin is only thirty minutes by car or Metro from the rue du Faubourg Saint-Honoré store, but it's another world altogether. Here, as in many other Paris suburbs, is where the poor immigrants—mostly Muslims from Africa—have settled. Many live in public housing. Some run small businesses, like minimarkets and sandwich shops, or work in menial jobs. A lot live on the dole. The race riots of October 2005 erupted nearby and eventually spread to Pantin.

In the middle of all this is Hermès's first subsidiary, Hermès Sellier, housed in an enormous contemporary glass-and-green-metal building constructed in 1991 and decorated by Rena Dumas, a renowned interior designer and the Greek-born wife of Hermès's longtime head, Jean-Louis Dumas, who retired in 2006. The building is the exact opposite of the traditional prewar aesthetic for which Hermès is known. The atrium of pale stone floors, glass walls, and glass elevators looks like that of a Hyatt without the fountains and tropical plants. One giant wall is covered in a checkerboard of Hermès silk scarves. Next to the lift on each floor is a closed-circuit flat-screen TV that broadcasts images from the store on rue du Faubourg Saint-Honoré to keep people in Pantin "connected," a public relations woman explained.

Pantin houses Hermès's largest leather production site—three hundred workers spread among fifteen ateliers—as well as administration for, and some production of, ready-to-wear as well as a school for leatherworking. Hermès requires that all newly hired leather artisans—most of whom have graduated from one of France's renowned leather-working academies—spend two years as apprentices in its own schools either in Pantin or in the Vosges, in eastern France, to learn from Hermès's senior leather craftsmen how to cut skins and sew the house's signature saddle stitch perfectly.

On the fourth floor is the special orders workshop. It is here that Hermès makes its gleaming crocodile- and alligator-skin Kellys, Birkins, and Constances, in all sizes, some with diamond clasps. Special orders have always been an integral part of Hermès. Among the more eccentric orders: a violinist who wanted a leather violin case lined with Hermès silk foulards, a big-game hunter who ordered luggage made with the skins of his kill, and a Japanese client who requested a Pokémon character printed on her Kelly bag. In 1957, showman Sammy Davis Jr. ordered a black-crocodile suitcase bar to take on his travels and concert tours. In 2003, a young wealthy Greek man brought the torn mainsheet from his yacht and asked Hermès to use it to make three Kelly bags. Dumas liked the result so much that he included the design in the following season's collection.

The special-orders atelier has about forty workers, all young—the average age of leather artisans at Hermès is thirty-three—and, surprisingly, many are women. Hermès, in fact, is a youthful and female-driven company. Of Hermès's 5,871 employees—from store salesclerks to leather craftsmen—61 percent are forty years old or younger, and 65 percent are women. The company is growing, too. From 2000 to 2004, Hermès created 1,230 new jobs, including adding more than six hundred leather artisans to three new leather goods ateliers. By early 2006, Hermès had fifteen hundred leather artisans. "We are frightened to grow and [frightened] not to grow," Jean-Louis Dumas once said, "or to grow so much we blow a gasket."

Indeed, that's what sets Hermès apart from its competitors. Whereas Gucci Group's CEO Robert Polet declared within months of taking over the helm in 2004 that he planned to double Gucci's annual sales, then $2 billion, in seven years, and Bernard Arnault crowed in March 2005 how his group posted $1.26 billion in profits for 2004, Hermès takes it slow and easy. In 2005, it did $1.85 billion (or €1.427 billion) in sales—a reasonable turnover compared to its competitors, considering its extremely high retail prices. Of that, 40 percent was in leather goods. During Dumas's thirty-year reign, Hermès could have increased production to eliminate the waiting lists and sell the bags ready-made in the store. It could have become a multibillion-dollar company easily. But Dumas resisted. He preferred to run Hermès like a small, intimate luxury company, and that is the same business philosophy that drives the company today. There are craftsmen in Lyon weaving silk for scarves and ties, and others in Limoges making porcelain dinner services. There are goldsmiths in Mali crafting jewelry and Tuareg tribesmen in Niger making silver belt buckles. There are Indians in the Amazonian rain forests who harvest latex sap for rubberized handbags. In 1995, Dumas took ten artisans from the Hermès stable of brands to the Thar Desert near the Pakistani border for a weeklong exploration of their creative roots. The silversmiths studied the chisels and hammers of local craftsmen. The perfume man sniffed the desert air. As tribesmen beat drums, the visitors hoisted a Saint-Louis crystal chandelier over a flickering campfire. For Dumas, the message was as clear as the desert night: "The world is divided into two," he pronounced. "Those who know how to use tools and those who do not."

The artisans in the Pantin workshop dress in aprons and white coats. Some wear earphones to listen to music on their iPods while they work. The workshop is perfectly silent except for the occasional tapping of a hammer or the short burst of stitching on a sewing machine. No one speaks. They just build bags. Even with a lot of practice, making an Hermès bag goes slowly. It takes fifteen to sixteen hours to make an average-size Birkin or Kelly. The bigger bags take twenty-five to thirty hours. In 2005, Hermès's twelve leather ateliers in France produced 130,000 handbags. Thanks to the waiting lists, Hermès didn't suffer losses after the terrorist attacks of September 11, 2001, which caused one of the worst retail years in recent memory. In fact, sales went up. "After September 11, a lot of people came in to buy that one special scarf or tie or bag," Robert Chavez, CEO of Hermès's American subsidiary in New York, told me. "They'd say, 'I just want to have one special thing.'"

The first station in the atelier is the reptile skins table. Three or four men inspect the skins for defects and cut the shapes for the bags. All materials for Hermès bags are cut by press machines except for crocodile, alligator, and other reptile skins, which are extremely fragile and valuable. The artisans in the special-orders department work with three types of reptile skin: two crocodile and one alligator. The most delicate and expensive is from the *Crocodylus porosus* of Australia. It has square scales in the middle of the belly and four to five rows of small round scales down the side. There is *Crocodylus niloticus*, raised in Zimbabwe. It has bigger square scales in the middle and then two lines of big round scales down the side. The third is *Alligator mississippiensis*, which comes from a farm owned by Hermès in Florida. The alligator has small rectangular scales in the middle and smaller, oval-shaped ones down the side. It's hard for amateurs to see the difference between *mississipiensis* and *porosus*. But there is a difference: in 2006, a *porosus* crocodile thirty-two-centimeter Kelly retailed for $19,600; the same bag in alligator cost $16,700.

An average-size bag requires three skins. Like human fingers, each crocodile or alligator has its own print, so it takes time to find skins that go well together. Only the skin from the soft underside of the reptile is used, never the back, which is scarred and rough. The belly is used for the bag's sides and flap, the underside of the tail, which has bigger scales, for the bottom or the side—or gusset. The skins are not varnished; to obtain their brilliant varnish-like shine, the artisan polishes the skins quickly with agate stone. As a result, the skin—and therefore the bag—is not water resistant. Large bags like a fifty-five-centimeter Birkin, which is the size of a suitcase, are rarely made in crocodile. "Crocodiles are not very kind animals," explains one of the artisans, "so to find one so big and with no bite marks is unusual. You have to wait ten years for a skin like that."

When I visited, one of the craftsmen was working with a ruby red crocodile skin, another with pine green. The men stand on spongy rubber mats—they're on their feet all day—and lay the skin, which still retains the shape of the animal, across big white tables. Under natural light streaming through skylights, they inspect the skin and circle the defects with a white marker. All skins have defects that must be cut out. Cows have scars from wounds or mosquito bites that can't be seen until the hide is tanned. "On crocodile and on light, bright colors you see everything," one of the artisans explained. The piece he was working on had too many marks to use for the body or flap of a handbag. Perhaps, he said, they'd use it for a gusset.

The skin men cut all the forms for each bag and put the pieces into a plastic tray, along with zippers, locks, hardware, lining, leather string for piping—everything that is required to make the entire bag. The tray is handed off to a craftsperson who will build the bag from beginning to end. Each artisan works on three or four bags at a time—same model, same size, same material. One was working on a mini Kelly in black crocodile with a diamond clasp. Diamonds are always set in white gold and come with a certificate verifying the weight of the gold and the stones. In 2004, the special-orders atelier made a ruby red Birkin with diamonds on the fittings for the Hermès store in Honolulu that sold for $90,000.

Most Hermès bags are built from the inside out. The first thing the artisan uses is a *griffe,* a handmade metal tool that looks like an Afro comb with very pointy tips. The *griffe,* which comes in several sizes, is pushed lightly along the edges of the leather to mark perfectly and evenly where the artisan will sew the seam by hand. Only the zipper and the inside pocket are sewn by machine. The artisan inserts a stiff piece of cowhide between the outer skin and the lining to give the bag strength and rigidity. Everything on the bag except the zipper is made of leather (unless of course it is a raffia or canvas bag). There are no unseen plastic reinforcements, no hidden canvas or plastic linings.

The Kelly comes in two styles: *sellier,* which means the seams are on the outside, and *retourner,* which means the seams are on the inside. The Birkin is only available *retourner.* The edges of *retourner* bags have piping, usually in the same color as the rest of the bag. The piping is made by wrapping a piece of leather cord with the skin, held together with a bit of glue. When it is all sewn together, there are eight layers of leather: the outer skin, the cowhide, and the lining on each side, plus the two edges of the piping. On the Kelly, the flap is a continuation of the back of bag. On the Birkin, it is sewn on.

The artisans sew all the leather seams by hand with a classic saddle stitch. The artisan takes two needles and one very long piece of thread, long enough to sew together all the pieces so that there are no knots on the bag. The linen thread, which comes from France, is break-resistant and doesn't burn when pulled through the leather. It is waxed with beeswax to make it strong, waterproof, and smoothe. It always matches the leather, except when the skin is gold or natural, in which case white thread is used. The artisan holds the leather together with a long wooden clamp, leaving his two hands free. He pierces each *griffe* mark with an awl, making a hole through the several pieces of leather; sticks one needle through in one direction and the other through the other direction; tugs till the stitch is tight; and moves on to the next. The beginning and end of each seam has three double stitches so it doesn't come apart. Once sewing is completed, the seams are tapped flat with a plastic hammer and the edges are shaved, sanded, and polished with wax until they are smooth and appear to be one single piece of leather. The handle is comprised of six pieces of leather and is shaped on the artisan's thigh; each one takes about three and a half hours to make. "If the handle is not perfect," said one artisan, "the bag is not perfect."

When the inside and outside of the bag are complete, the artisan puts it all together and attaches the hardware. The hardware on most handbags today is attached with screws, but, as I was told by an Hermès artisan, screws come unscrewed. Hermès has a special method for attaching its hardware called pearling. The artisan puts the clasp on the front of the leather and a metal backing on the backside, sticks a nail from the back to the front through each corner hole, and clips off the length of the nail, leaving a tiny bit. He takes a special tool that looks like an awl but with a slight concave tip and taps the bit of nail gently in a circle until it is as round as a tiny pearl. Each piece of hardware has four pearls—one on each corner—and each is exactly the same shape. The pearls hold the two pieces of metal together forever. The hardware is then covered with clear plastic film to protect it from getting scratched. The artisan turns the bag right side out and irons it into shape. Ever-delicate crocodile is ironed scale by scale. The artisan runs a skinny hot iron between seams to clean as well as define and straighten the edge.

When the bag is finished, a supervisor inspects it to see if the stitching is balanced, the pearls are well done, the lock works, the shape is perfect, and the surface is unblemished. If the supervisor approves the bag, it is marked with a stamp that identifies the artisan, the year, and the workshop. On the Kelly, the stamp is on the leather buckle. The bag is placed in the house's signature orange felt bag and sent to the logistics department, about fifteen minutes away in the suburb of Bobigny, to be inspected again. If it passes, it is wrapped in tissue paper, boxed, and sent to the store. Hermès wouldn't tell me what they do with bags that don't pass inspection.

IN 2007, Hermès had 257 stores around the world, in cosmopolitan shopping districts, suburban shopping malls, five-star hotels, and international airports. But the loveliest by far is the original flagship at 24, rue du Faubourg Saint-Honoré, just steps off the Place de la Concorde in Paris. The two-floor store in the six-story company headquarters is a throwback to the late-nineteenth-century emporium: heavy black iron-and-glass doors, well-worn mosaic tile floors, highly polished oak sales counters topped with glass display cases, deco domed lighting. On the walls hang beautiful eighteenth- and nineteenth-century equestrian prints and paintings. Among them is a stunning 1727 portrait of King Louis XV astride a high-stepping steed, one of three by Jean-Baptiste van Loo and Charles Parrocel. Another hangs in the Louvre.

Walk in any time of day and the place is humming with activity. Slim chic saleswomen dramatically unfurl silk scarf after silk scarf for clusters of Japanese shoppers and elegant Parisiennes. Tailors take measurements for made-to-order suits, and millinery experts size up chapeaus to be worn at the next big wedding or horse race. On the mezzanine, jewelers fit watches or help select the perfect pair of cuff links. In the back, salesmen in the saddle department show off bridles, hacking jackets, and saddles, which, like Hermès handbags, are made to order and by hand. Hermès has made more than forty-three thousand saddles since its founding in 1837. To be measured for one, customers make their way up the back stairs to the saddle atelier, where they straddle a leather sawhorse—just as clients have for more than a century—as one of the company's eight saddlemakers, dressed in a worn cowhide apron, takes out his tape measure and gets to work. That, in a snapshot, is what sets Hermès apart from its competitors in the luxury business. As its 2004 fall ad campaign, shot by the late Richard Avedon, declared: "Nothing changes, but everything changes."

In the center of the store is another staircase that leads to what Jean-Louis Dumas describes as the "soul of Hermès": the former office of Dumas's grandfather Émile-Maurice Hermès, which today serves as the Hermès museum. Open by appointment and curated by Hermès's director of cultural heritage, Menehould de Bazelaire, the two-room museum is a veritable time machine that whisks visitors back a century to an epoch when one still traveled by horse, and life for the rich and noble was extremely refined. On the oak-paneled walls hang equestrian prints, carriage lanterns, silver spurs, leather crops, and harnesses, some decorated with royal coats of arms. Scattered about are hand-tooled saddles, trunks, toiletry cases, and a children's carriage from the reign of Napoleon I. Today the museum serves as an inspiration for the company's designers. For example, the gold-painted waves on a Japanese saddle were reproduced recently on a silk scarf.

De Bazelaire is a tall, thin, handsome woman—she reminded me a bit of Katharine Hepburn—and an educator at heart. She began her career teaching Greek and Latin at the Lycée Français in New York. In the 1980s, she returned to Paris to become an archivist and was soon hired by Hermès to replace its retiring part-time museum curator. Today, overseeing a staff of fifteen, she is in charge of the house's archives, documentation, conservation, and museum. On a freezing

January night in 2006, she welcomed me into the museum and told me all there is to know about the house of Hermès.

Thierry Hermès was born to Dietrich Hermès, an auberge owner, and his wife, Agnes, in Krefeld, a town on the left bank of the Rhine not far from Cologne. The region was French at the time, so Thierry, the youngest of six children, had French papers. The family was Protestant, a minority that had long been persecuted in Catholic Europe. This persecution, Jean-Louis Dumas has said, contributed to Hermès's success in the luxury business: by keeping to themselves, the family learned to succeed as merchants.

Krefeld was on the road to Russia, and as a child, de Bazelaire explained, Thierry watched as Napoleon's troops passed by full of pride on their way to Moscow and returned wounded and defeated. His oldest brother, Henri, a soldier in Napoleon's army, was killed during battle in Spain in 1813, and his parents and his four other siblings died of disease, leaving Thierry orphaned at fifteen. In 1821, he walked with a Dutch friend to Paris. Thierry settled in Normandy, France's horse country, to learn the harness-making trade, married, and had three children. In 1837, he opened a harness workshop near the Madeleine in Paris. Five years later he moved around the corner to the boulevard des Capucines. Today it is the site of the Olympia theater. "It was a very cosmopolitan quarter," de Bazelaire told me. "The cafés were filled with royals, courtesans, and demimondaines, like Marie Duplessis, the woman who inspired Alexandre Dumas's *Camille,* and later Verdi's *La Traviata.* She promenaded down Paris's *grands boulevards* in a cabriolet carriage with Hermès harnesses."

In 1859, Thierry retired to Normandy and turned the company over to his second son, Charles-Émile. By then, Charles-Émile had married and had four children, including Émile-Maurice. The horse transportation business was booming: in the 1860s, there were ninety thousand horses in the streets of Paris. Charles-Émile invented harnesses that protected both horses and passengers, such as one that stopped horses from bolting. In 1880, he moved the business to a pretty two-story building at 24, rue du Faubourg Saint-Honoré, near the Champs-Élysées and the Bois de Boulogne, which, de Bazelaire noted, "was the noble horse country back then." The shop was on the ground floor, the ateliers on the first floor, and the oldest son, Adolphe, lived in the converted attic, where the museum is now located. Charles-Émile expanded the business by adding ateliers to produce saddles and jockey racing silks. In 1902, a sports newspaper writer described Hermès as "the great horse bazaar in Paris."

The dawning of the twentieth century was, as for Louis Vuitton, the turning point for Hermès. In 1902, Charles-Émile's sons, Émile-Maurice and Adolphe, took over the business. Émile-Maurice spoke English very well and was a globetrotter long before it was fashionable. Following a trip to Argentina, where he saw gauchos carrying their saddles in big satchels, he came up with Hermès's *haut à courroies* saddle-bag. He traveled to Russia and secured an order to produce harnesses and saddles for Czar Nicholas II. During World War I, he went to the United States and Canada and saw a new invention called the zipper. He secured the patent for Europe from 1922 to 1924 and integrated it into Hermès designs, such as the *sac pour l'auto,* known now as the Bolide. He remodeled the building, adding four floors, converting the old attic into his office, and turning the southwest corner of the ground floor into a big display window.

With the help of friends Louis Renault (the cofounder of automaker Renault), and Ettore Bugatti (the revolutionary Italian carmaker), Émile-Maurice introduced products for the automobile such as trunks that fit on the back of a Bugatti and leather wallets for maps. He enlisted contemporary artists Jean-Michel Frank, the Giacometti brothers, and Sonia Delaunay to design products; developed new lines such as couture and belts; and expanded the retail network to such fashionable French holiday resorts as Deauville, Biarritz, and Cannes. The Cannes boutique makes an appearance in F. Scott Fitzgerald's

Tender Is the Night when Nicole Diver buys "two chamois leather jackets of kingfisher blue and burning bush from Hermès."

In the late 1930s, Émile-Maurice bought Mi Colline, a villa in the hills above Cannes, not far from the Croisette shop. During the Nazi Occupation of Paris, most of the family fled to Mi Colline. The Hermès store on the rue du Faubourg Saint-Honoré shut down for four days and then reopened to keep the employees working and receiving wages, however small. Émile-Maurice's son-in-law Jean Guerrand took over the store and distributed potato soup to the workers because, de Bazelaire said, "everyone was starving." As in many stores that remained open during the Occupation, there were often signs in the Hermès windows reading, "Nothing for Sale," due to shortages not only of materials but also the will to sell to Nazis. General Hermann Göring ordered a big picnic trunk from Hermès, but there was no leather and no motivation, and it was never produced. Paper, cardboard, and other sorts of packaging were scarce as well; the only color available was vibrant orange. Hermès used it for boxes and bags. Almost overnight, it became the house's signature color.

In 1945, Émile-Maurice adopted the company logo based on a drawing by nineteenth-century artist Alfred de Dreux of a groom standing before a horse and open carriage. The picture still hangs behind his desk in the museum. A few years later, he introduced silk neckties and the house's first scent, Eau d'Hermès, which is still a staple at the house. In 1951, the eighty-year-old Émile-Maurice died of a stroke and his son-in-law Robert Dumas took over. With the help of Guerrand, Dumas focused on the burgeoning jet set. It was Dumas who decided to rename the *haut à courroies* the Kelly after Princess Grace of Monaco—formerly Grace Kelly—was photographed carrying it to conceal her pregnancy. Half a century later, the Kelly remains one of the most popular items at Hermès.

Most important, though, Robert Dumas groomed his son Jean-Louis to lead the company into the twenty-first century. Jean-Louis

Dumas is what the French call *un grand monsieur:* well educated, distinguished, and charming. As he likes to point out, "Oscar Wilde said elegance is power." By the time he was born—in 1938, the fourth of Robert's six children—the Dumas family not only sold leather goods to the right sort, they *were* the right sort. He attended Lycée Franklin, a preppy Jesuit school in the Sixteenth Arrondissement, and went on to France's prestigious Paris Institute of Political Science in the Quartier Latin, where he took degrees in politics and economics. Like his grandfather Émile-Maurice, he traveled extensively. In the early 1960s, he and his Greek-born wife, Rena, climbed into a beat-up Citröen and drove down the Silk Road to India. Dumas has said that the trip opened his eyes to vast gulf between rich and poor and gave him a sense of spiritualism that he would use later to guide the company.

In 1963, Jean-Louis was sent by his father to work as an assistant buyer for Bloomingdale's in New York to learn the fashion retail trade. A year later, he joined the family business as a consultant, "an ideas man," de Bazelaire explained. The 1970s were a quiet, rambling time for Hermès. Luxury was next to dead. The oil crisis, the economic recession, and high unemployment dried up spending. To make matters worse, Robert Dumas didn't push the company like his father-in-law, Émile-Maurice, had. "Robert was very discreet, from a generation where you didn't hawk your wares, you didn't sell per se," de Bazelaire explained. Instead, you waited for the good, regular customers to come in and buy. And they didn't. Sales were so slow one year that the company was forced to shut down the ateliers for two weeks.

In 1976, the company received an unexpected boost from fashion photographer Helmut Newton, known as the "King of Kink" for his sexually powerful pictures. Newton adored Hermès. He found the rue du Faubourg Saint-Honoré store to be "the most expensive and luxurious sex shop in the world," he wrote in his autobiography. "In its glass cases there were displayed great collections of spurs, whips, leather ware, and saddles. The salesladies were dressed like strict teachers, in wraparound gray flannel skirts, blouses closed to the neck, and a brooch in the shape of a riding crop pinned to their bosoms." Newton paid homage to Hermès by shooting a portfolio featuring its products at the Hôtel Raphael in Paris for *Vogue*. And what pictures they were. The most famous is of a model on all fours on a bed, with a saddle on her back, while dressed in tight jodhpurs, shiny black leather riding boots with silver spurs, and a black lace scoop bra. "After seeing the *Vogue* pages, [Robert Dumas] succumbed to a malaise," Newton recalled. "Happily," Newton added, "he recovered."

When Robert Dumas died two years later from illness, the board unanimously elected Jean-Louis as chairman. With the help of his cousins Patrick Guerrand and Bertrand Puech, Dumas got the company back in shape. He reinvigorated the silk scarf business by hiring artists to make dazzling new designs and by having salesclerks show customers creative new ways to wear them: as a belt, as a halter top, or simply tied to a handbag for a splash of color. He hired an outside firm to do ad campaigns—a first for the house—and expanded the press office, which at the time had one person for the entire company. (By 2006, there were sixteen press attachés in Paris alone.) In 1980, he hired nineteen-year-old designer Eric Bergère just out of fashion school to liven up the staid women's wear line. And then he decided to revitalize the handbag division.

THROUGHOUT the centuries, men and women have carried their belongings in some sort of bag. When the five-thousand-year-old remains of a man, known as "Frozen Fritz," were found in the ice of the Tyrolean Alps in 1991, researchers discovered that sewn onto his calfskin belt was a pouch containing small tools made of stone, lime wood, bone, and horn. In Greece, schoolchildren kept their knucklebone games in bags. In Rome, women carried small net pouches called *reticula,* and they were ridiculed for carrying their pockets in their hands. In the Middle Ages, there were drawstring alms purses. In China, Buddhist monks and pilgrims carried small pouches of amulets and icons. African medicine men kept their divining ossicles in pouches, and nomads throughout the world used bags to transport their possessions on the backs of their camels and horses. During the late eighteenth century, European women wore diaphanous high-waisted dresses without pockets and carried their essentials in small sacks that are now considered the forebears to the handbag. In the late nineteenth century, when sewing and embroidery were social activities, ladies of the upper classes had ornate sewing bags to carry their needles and thread. Carrying anything more than that was seen as socially inferior: that's why one had staff.

The modern handbag was born in the early twentieth century with the emergence of suffragettes. The handbag was "the sign of a new independence, that of coming and going at will, of being able to leave home without answering to anyone," writes Farid Chenoune in *Carried Away: All About Bags.* The handbag quickly became an essential accessory for the average consumer. "It's so infuriating, this lack of pockets in skirts that are too close-fitting," wrote one observer in *Fémina* magazine back in 1908. "All the precious things you lose— purse, notebook, handkerchief—that you end up resigned to the handbag, day and night. Wealthy women are still holding out—they can put all their bits and pieces in the car; but the others have made up their minds and the current thing is the handbag." With the arrival of the slim "flapper" silhouette, handbags became an essential fashion accessory. In the 1930s, couturiers began to quietly replace their customers' initials with their own, thus launching the practice of displaying luxury brand logos.

By the time Diana Vreeland joined *Harper's Bazaar* in 1937 as a junior editor, handbags had become an integral and important part of the fashion business, as she would quickly learn. Shortly after she arrived at the august glossy, Vreeland had what she described in her memoir, *D.V.*, as a "brainwave!"

"We're going to eliminate all handbags," she told a colleague.

"You're going to *what*?" he responded.

"Eliminate all handbags," she repeated. "Now look. What have I got here? I've got cigarettes, I've got my lipstick, I've got my comb, I've got my powder, I've got my rouge, I've got my money. But what do I want with a bloody old handbag that one leaves in taxis and so on? It should all go into pockets. Real pockets, like a man has, for goodness sake."

Then Vreeland explained how she wanted to devote an entire issue of the venerable fashion magazine to "showing what you can do with pockets and how the silhouette is improved and so on."

Her colleague ran from her office—"the way you run for the police!" she recalled—straight to *Harper's Bazaar* editor Carmel Snow.

"Diana's going crazy!" he cried. "Get hold of her."

Snow went to see Vreeland.

"Listen, Diana," Snow told Vreeland, "I think you've lost your mind. Do you realize that our income from handbag advertising is God knows how many millions a year?!"

During World War II, handbags became simple and practical, like the leather backpack and the "game bag," a largish sac worn across the torso so that one could ride a bicycle easily, the preferred method of transportation during gasoline rationing. After the war, designers embraced an array of interesting new materials such as plastic, Plexiglass, raffia, and straw. In 1947, Gucci introduced a spare U-shaped handbag made of gleaming black cowhide with a handle made of bamboo, a material that was cheap and abundant. In February 1955, Chanel launched its now-iconic 2.55 (named for the launch date), the rectangle-shaped quilted leather bag with a fold-over flap and gold-chain shoulder strap. It had no monogram; the interlocking Cs were sewn inside. Not long after, the Kelly came into vogue, thanks to Princess Grace.

During the feminist movement of the late 1960s, all the accessories that for centuries had been essential items in a woman's wardrobe— the hat, the parasol, the gloves, the muff—disappeared. All that remained was the baby of the lot, the handbag, and it moved up the arm to the shoulder, freeing up a woman's hands as she liberated her mind and her soul. "We've got into the habit of using just one bag right around the clock," reported the French fashion magazine *Jardins des Modes*. "No more changing the color to go with the clothes, no more matching sets—bag, gloves, shoes, and so on. You fine-tune your bag with what you're wearing by adjusting the length of the strap."

As women joined the workforce in droves in the 1980s, they found they needed a bag that could go from day to evening and could work as a briefcase, too—and they had the disposable income to spend to get a good one. They needed something classic, something that wasn't too flashy, that wouldn't undermine their desire to be taken seriously in a man's world. And since a good leather handbag was a hefty investment, women preferred a design that wouldn't go out of fashion too quickly.

Luxury brands had the answer. At Chanel, executives decided to push the thirty-year-old quilted 2.55 bag. "I remember being in all those meetings when we said we have to get aggressive about selling handbags," Arie Kopelman, former CEO of Chanel Inc., the company's American affiliate, told me. "You can drive the business with accessories, you can advertise it easily, you can promote it in many ways, and we said, 'How can we make this happen in the greatest way possible and really go after the business?' It was a product line that really needed a tremendous push to capitalize on the opportunity."

Kopelman was among those at Chanel who wanted to do a big ad campaign promoting the 2.55 and other similar bags. It was a bold move, since back then, as Kopelman pointed out, "[Chanel] didn't really advertise except for perfume and cosmetics." To the French, advertising fashion was considered tacky: "You don't do that" was the standard response. But Kopelman, a former ad man who had worked for the advertising giant Doyle Dane Bernbach for twenty years before joining Chanel, helped to convince his colleagues otherwise. The ad campaign ran, and Chanel handbag sales took off. "It was clearly a terrific market opportunity," Kopelman told me. "We jumped on a trend and made the most of it." Each season, Chanel reissued the 2.55 in new bold colors and materials. Chanel designer Karl Lagerfeld reinterpreted the 2.55's chain strap as a belt slung around the hips and the quilting pattern was used for everything from down-filled coats to a stamped impression on eye shadow. In 1986, Lagerfeld designed a magnificent couture evening gown embroidered with a trompe l'oeil inspired by the quilted 2.55.

At Hermès, Dumas reinvigorated the eighty-year-old Kelly. He expanded the range from dark tones to a rainbow of colors and in a variety of leathers and featured it in a snappy ad campaign. "He released the Kelly from its conservative past," de Bazelaire said. "Shook it up. Put it in front of the scene." Sales exploded. Waiting lists started, and they've never abated.

One day in 1984 on an Air France flight from Paris to London, British actress Jane Birkin pulled her Hermès datebook out of her bag and—*whoosh*—all her papers fell out all over the floor. She groused as she scooped them up about how the book needed a pocket. Beside her sat Jean-Louis Dumas.

"Let me take yours and let's see what we can do," he said.

A few weeks later, Birkin received her datebook with a pocket stitched inside the cover.

"Now they all have pockets!" she told me when she recounted the story. "Isn't it marvelous?"

During that same flight, Birkin grumbled to Dumas—she had his attention after all—that there wasn't a good leather weekend bag for women, "one that isn't too big, or too heavy when it's full of stuff," she explained.

"What would you want it to look like?" he asked.

She described it to him.

Not long after, a big package arrived at her flat. It was a leather weekend bag, just as she had imagined it. Dumas had adapted the *haut à courroies* to Birkin's specs and dubbed it the Birkin.

"You and Grace Kelly are the only ones with Hermès bags named in your honor," he told her.

HERMÈS'S BIRKIN and Kelly were big hits with the rich set, and the Chanel's 2.55 with the working woman—I remember when I was writing about fashion for the *Washington Post,* seeing the power lawyers and lobbyists on K Street with their quilted bags dangling from chains on their shoulders. But what was the young or average-income woman who wanted to be fashionable to do? I was in my twenties at the time and, though I had a good job, I shared an apartment with a roommate to make rent. I wrote about Chanel, but I shopped at the Gap. My one luxury fashion item was Chanel No. 5, but the cheapest level: eau de toilette spray. Yes, I was buying into the dream. But I wondered: How could I and my friends, most also in low-paying, starting-level jobs, be a part of the world of luxury fashion that we read about in *Vogue* and *Harper's Bazaar,* beyond perfume? And how could we do it without looking like those conservative lobbyists and lawyers?

The answer sat quietly in an eighty-year-old mahogany-and-glass display case in Milan, waiting to be discovered. When Miuccia Prada took over her grandfather's company in 1978, she didn't want to reissue a design made famous by Grace Kelly or Audrey Hepburn or Jackie Kennedy. She wanted to do new designs. Nothing at Prada would be old. She began exploring the use of different fabrics and designs and came up with a backpack made of nylon parachute fabric trimmed in leather. She had it made on sewing machines that made parachutes for the Italian army and it came in two colors: black and brown.

It didn't sell for a while. "No one wanted the backpack because it didn't scream luxury," Prada told me when I met with her in 2006. It was anonymous and simple. As Holly Brubach wrote in the *New Yorker* in 1990, "These were upstart bags: by their design they demanded to be taken seriously, but they were made of a material that, according to most people's taste at the time, undermined their credibility. Real bags, the sort of bags people were proud to carry, came in leather or crocodile or silk, not nylon." Fashion editors urged Prada to put the company's initials on the sack like Chanel or Gucci did to give it more cachet, but she refused. She had always hated logos on luxury items when she was growing up. Instead, she chose to use the tiny triangle label that her grandfather affixed on trunks. It was in black enamel, with the name Fratelli Prada, a crown that signified that the company was an official supplier to the Italian royal family and "Milano." Miuccia added a line stating that the company was founded in 1913 to validate its place among luxury brands, and attached it to the flap of the backpack.

The backpack finally got its close-up in 1988. Prada showed her first collection of women's wear, and when editors and retailers stopped by the showroom to review and order the clothes, they came upon the backpack. The next season it popped up in small articles in the glossies and on department store shelves. Prada increased the buzz by sending backpacks to key editors as a Christmas present. "Then it hit," remembers fashion public relations executive Karla Otto, who worked with Prada at the time. "It was everywhere."

The Prada backpack was the ultimate "It" bag for the average consumer: it was hip, modern, lightweight, and at $450 far less expensive than finely tooled leather bags like the Kelly and the 2.55. Prada backpacks were so popular that *New York Times* street fashion photographer Bill Cunningham stood on the corner of Fifty-seventh Street and Fifth Avenue one afternoon, shooting women walking by with the sacks slung over their shoulders, the little triangle with PRADA written neatly in an exclusive serif typeface designed for the company's logo stuck on the flap for everyone to see. The Prada backpack became the handbag design of the moment: every brand had a version. The backpack sold like crazy, made the company a fortune, and turned Prada into a household name. All the while, Miuccia Prada sat in her studio and cringed. "She hated seeing certain women carrying her handbags," recalls Leslie Johnsen, who worked as Prada's director for public relations for North America in the early 1990s. Meanwhile, Prada's husband and company CEO, Patrizio Bertelli, sat in his office and plotted the company's global expansion, funded with backpack sales.

The Prada backpack, in fact, unknowingly became the emblem of the radical change that luxury was undergoing at the time: the shift from small family businesses of beautifully handcrafted goods to global corporations selling to the middle market. When Tom Ford took over the creative direction of Gucci in 1994, he saw the potential of the youth market in luxury fashion and pushed handbags into the forefront. Models would come marching down the runway of his Gucci women's wear shows in Milan to the hip-hop sounds of Lauryn Hill or Fatboy Slim, dressed in sexy black satin suits or white liquid jersey columns, clutching or wearing a fantastic new Gucci bag. Soon fashion editors were reporting not only on Ford's new clothes but also on the new bags. The phenomenal sales of Ford's bags pulled Gucci out of near bankruptcy and helped underwrite its global expansion. "Tom Ford made beautiful dresses, but he always stuck a great bag on them," said Claus Lindorff of BETC Luxe. "How many $2,000 white satin gowns are you going to sell? Luxury brands know that clothing is a loss. The bag is the introduction to a brand. Even if it's a ready-to-wear ad campaign, what you are really selling is the handbag. Thanks to Tom Ford, prêt-à-porter is the decor for the accessory."

So essential is the handbag in the success of a luxury brand today that Gucci Group attributed the disappointing figures at Yves Saint Laurent in 2005 to the fact that the brand hadn't had a hit bag in a couple of seasons. And Yves Saint Laurent was, at least until Gucci Group took it over in 1999, a fashion house, not a leather goods company. In 2006, Gucci Group was still supporting its fledgling fashion brands, Alexander McQueen and Stella McCartney. But as Lindorff said, "It's not going to be clothes that make those brands work. Those designers are being told, 'Get a bloody handbag out there that will sell well.' "

It was an "It" bag that turned Fendi from a dowdy old fur company into a top-tier luxury fashion brand. Back in 1997, Fendi's accessories designer Silvia Fendi Venturini came up with the Baguette, a little, soft oblong pouch on a short shoulder strap that nestles comfortably under the arm. It sold out in a matter of months and soon had a long waiting list, including for the $5,000 version made of silk handwoven in the Manifattura Lisio in Florence. All together, Fendi sold more than a hundred thousand Baguettes the first year. It became such an important fashion item that it was written into an episode of *Sex and the City*: when a mugger ordered Carrie Bradshaw to hand over her purse, she responded, "It's a Baguette."

Venturini kept coming up with new spins on it—in denim, or covered in sea pearls—and stuck it on the arms of models showing Fendi's women's wear, which has been designed by Karl Lagerfeld since 1965. The Baguette gave the house such a financial and fashion boost that by the fall of 1999, the luxury barons were fighting over it. Gucci, Prada, Bulgari, and LVMH all tried to buy the company, first founded by Venturini's grandmother Adele Casagrande in 1918—she married Edoardo Fendi in 1925—and run since 1954 by their five daughters. In the end LVMH teamed up with Prada and bought 51 percent of Fendi for $520 million—valuing the entire company at nearly $1 billion. Some of Fendi's suitors complained during negotiations that Bernard Arnault and Prada's Patrizio Bertelli wanted to pay too much for Fendi. "They're throwing money around like drunken sailors," one remarked at the time.

By 2001, the Baguette was over. Bertelli wisely sold Prada's 25 percent back to LVMH for $260 million, and over the years LVMH acquired more shares from the Fendi family, for a total of 94 percent in 2007. For years LVMH has poured money into Fendi—hiring über–luxury brand architect Peter Marino for a costly renovation of the Rome store, opening more than thirty new free-standing stores in less than four years, buying back dozens of licenses—but by 2005, it was still in the red. Market sources estimated that Fendi lost approximately $31.2 million in 2004. Meanwhile, Silvia Fendi Venturini and her team offer several new designs each season, hoping one will be "It."

To meet the increasing demand for handbags they had created, luxury brands had to come up with innovative solutions. Hermès stuck with its limited distribution. For Dumas, it was a question of integrity: the heart of Hermès was fine traditional craftsmanship, and to sacrifice that would undermine the brand. The other major—and minor—luxury brands looked for ways to produce more goods faster and more efficiently. Louis Vuitton expanded its production, adding workshops in France and moving some manufacturing to the Loewe factory in Spain. When I visited the special-orders atelier in Asnières, I got a glimpse of how Louis Vuitton makes its bags: seamstresses sat behind sewing machines, stitching together scores of the new denim monogram handbag. Unlike at Hermès, where bags were crafted by hand one at a time, at Vuitton, the workers were churning them out assembly-line style, in twenty-bag batches. Vuitton executives may crow about quality, but the company's focus is obviously on productivity.

Gucci, on the other hand, went high-tech. In March 2004, I visited Gucci factory headquarters near Florence a few weeks before Tom Ford and Domenico De Sole—and much of the team that worked with them—left the company, to see how Gucci handbags were made. My guide was Gucci's product development director, Alessandro Poggiolini, an affable and polite man in his sixties who had joined Gucci in 1967 as a handbag artisan. (He retired from the company in 2005.) The original Gucci factory, Poggiolini told me, was on the river Arno in Florence. Later it moved to Via della Caldaie, in the city center, and in 1971 it moved to an industrial park called Casellina di Scandicci, about half an hour outside the city.

Back in the early 1990s, when Gucci was on the verge of bankruptcy, most of its leather goods were classics that carried over from one season to the next. De Sole wanted to introduce more creativity to design and ramp up production. To achieve this, in 1994, De Sole put Gucci production online. Poggiolini took me into a vast room in the factory filled with dozens of desktop computers on long tables to show me how it worked. "In the old days the bag went straight from design to leather, which was time-consuming and expensive and might have been right or not," he told me. Now, technicians work on the three-dimensional computer image of the bag with the creative teams in London, Paris, and Milan to perfect the design. "You can turn around the bag on the screen and really study it," Poggiolini explained. Once the design is green-lighted, the technicians print the pattern on pink cardboard for the prototype. The first prototype is made in a black rubberized fabric called Peplon so that the artisans can see the shape of the bag. The leather details are glued on to give the design team an idea of what the bag will look like when completed. When Ford approved the prototype, it went into production.

Unlike at Hermès, where artisans study the skins and figure out the best way to cut them for the handbags, at Gucci the computer makes a map that shows the technicians how to lay out the pattern on the material. Fragile skins such as ostrich, lizard, and alligator are cut with a metal press. Cowhide, however, is cut by a special machine (developed and used exclusively by Gucci) with water jets that move at twice the speed of sound. When experimenting with faster and more efficient ways to cut the leather, the technicians tried lasers, but as Poggiolini explained, "it burned the leather and smoked." They finally chose the water-jet method because, as Poggiolini said, "it's fast, it's clean, and the quality of the cut is very good." The water jet is remarkable to see because, in fact, you can't see it. All you see is the leather cut, as if by magic, and a mist from the water jet dissipating to the sides. There were three of these machines at Casellina di Scandicci factory when I visited and another six at other manufacturing sites in the area.

Since 1995, all Gucci leather goods have been designed on computers. Between 1994 and 1998, leather goods production jumped from 640,000 to 2.4 million items per year, an increase of 277 percent. In 1997, classic designs made up 60 percent of Gucci's leather goods inventory. By 1999, that had dropped to 10 percent. Production time—from prototype to warehouse—was cut from 104 to 68 days. By 2004, Gucci Group, which then included Yves Saint Laurent, Sergio Rossi, Stella McCartney, Alexander McQueen, Balenciaga, and Bottega Veneta, turned out 3.5 million leather goods a year.

After our tour of the main factory, we walked across the industrial park to a small, two-story blocklike building housing one of about ten subcontractors that produced Gucci Group handbags. It was owned and run by Carlo Bacci, who had joined Gucci in 1960 as a handbag craftsman. Back then, all Gucci leather goods were produced in-house. Bacci left in 1969 to start his own company in Florence, and two years later began to manufacture for Gucci, which by then was subcontracting to outside ateliers. When I visited Bacci's workshop during my Gucci tour in 2004, he had twenty-three people on staff—including his wife and son—many of whom had worked at the Gucci factory across the street. He only worked for Gucci Group, with a partnership contract that stipulated that Gucci would guarantee a certain number of orders each year.

The workroom was simple: white, with cement floors, long tables, and overhead fluorescent lights. On each table sat piles of bags from Gucci, Yves Saint Laurent, Stella McCartney, and Sergio Rossi in various states of completion. Gold cowhide clutches with linen lining. Bronze crocodile purses with enamel snakehead clasps. Basic bags were produced in two to three hours; more complex ones took eight or more. Most were glued together and sewn on machines. The craftsmen worked on twenty bags at a time—five times as many as at Hermès—but like Hermès workers, they made each one from beginning to end. Bacci's studio only produced handbags—wallets and belts were done elsewhere—and it only turned out about 250 bags a month because it did the most complex designs with the most precious skins. Each finished bag was stamped with a code that identified Bacci's atelier. Bacci also managed subsuppliers, who did another two thousand bags a month.

THAT'S HOW IT IS DONE in Europe. In China, luxury handbag manufacturing is a completely different business. Yes, luxury handbags are made in China. Top brands. Brands that you carry. Brands that deny outright that their bags are made in China make their bags in China, not in Italy, not in France, not in the United Kingdom. I visited a factory in Guangdong Province and held the bags in my hands. To see them, I had to promise the manufacturer that I wouldn't reveal the brand names. Each brand made the manufacturer sign a confidentiality agreement stipulating that he could not reveal the fact that he produced their products in China. Furthermore, the manufacturer doesn't let the competition know who else he is producing. When the representatives come to the factory, they are led directly to the section working on their goods, and they talk only to the team in charge of their goods. It's as complicated as keeping a slew of mistresses.

There are three or four factories that specialize in manufacturing luxury brand leather goods in China, most in Dongguan, an industrial town about an hour north of Hong Kong. Often they do low- and middle-range business, for companies like JCPenney, Sears, Liz Claiborne, and Ann Taylor that run $40 to $80. But they also produce luxury handbags. The change came in the mid-1990s when Coach decided to move a small portion of its production from the United States to China.

Coach was a new player in the luxury goods category. Originally founded by an entrepreneur named Miles Cahn in midtown Manhattan in 1941, Coach had long been a conservative stalwart of the American leather goods business: the sort of brand that suburban mothers carried before luxury brands went mass. In 1985, the family sold the company to Sara Lee Corporation, a huge American conglomerate that was known for its frozen cheesecakes and owned such brands as Hanes underwear and Wonderbra. In 1996, Coach's CEO, Lew Frankfort, decided it was time to renovate the brand. He hired Reed Krakoff, a young, savvy designer at Tommy Hilfiger, as executive creative director, and together they mapped out a new future for Coach. The idea was to reposition the brand as an American alternative to Prada and Louis Vuitton, with prices ranging from $125 to $2,000. They called it "affordable luxury."

In 2000, Coach was listed on the New York Stock Exchange and was split off from Sara Lee. In 2001, its sales were a respectable $600 million, and its customers were primarily in the United States, with some in Japan and Asia. (Coach does not sell in Europe because it believes that competition from local brands would be tough. Also, two-thirds of the luxury consumers are from the United States and Japan, which allows for plenty of growth.) That year, Frankfort and Krakoff decided to change the creative direction of the brand from traditional classics to more fashion-forward. They came up with a new Signature collection of items in leather and cheerful-colored canvas printed with the company's C logo like a checkerboard, and began shipping new designs to stores monthly instead of twice a year. The Japanese particularly loved the Signature collection and bought it so fervently that, in 2003, Coach became the second most popular imported accessories brand in Japan, after Louis Vuitton.

To continue Coach's financial growth, Frankfort focused on increasing distribution and maximizing productivity. To do this, Coach rolled out new stores throughout North America and Asia, and it switched its manufacturing from company-owned U.S.-based factories to outsourcing overseas, much of it in China. Coach has never kept its manufacturing in China a secret. Today, Coach products are manufactured in eighty-four sites in fifteen countries; "a significant majority" are made in China, a Coach spokeswoman said. In 2002, Coach closed its last company-operated manufacturing facilities. The original Thirty-fourth Street factory is now home to Coach's executive offices as well as a small prototypes workshop. "By shifting our production from owned domestic facilities to independent manufacturers in lower-cost markets, we can support a broader mix of product types, materials, and a seasonal influx of new, more fashion-oriented styles," Coach said. "All product sources must achieve and maintain our high quality standards ... and we monitor compliance through on-site quality inspections at all Coach-operated or independent manufacturing facilities."

The strategy paid off. From 2001 to 2006, Coach experienced double-digit growth every quarter; by 2006, it was doing $2.1 billion in sales. At the same time, thanks in large part to lower production costs, profits soared. Coach's stock value increased a whopping 1,270 percent in the first five years after the company's initial public offering. And contrary to conventional wisdom, the perceived quality of Coach products has risen since it shifted production from the United States to China and other countries.

Emboldened by Coach's trailblazing success, other luxury brands quietly began to look into producing leather goods in China. Luxury brands have been hesitant to outsource production to developing nations in part because they feared quality would be compromised and, more important, because of the perceived image that the goods were no longer up to snuff. During the renovation and reinvention of luxury brands in the last twenty years, executives have trumpeted the fact that their products were made by artisans in Italy and France who had not only the experience but also the heritage of luxury craftsmanship, as if making fine leather goods, beautiful fabrics, and jewelry was in their genes, in their blood. According to luxury brand executives, that extraordinary gift could not be replicated anywhere else in the world. The "Made in Italy" or "Made in France"—or for cashmere, "Made in Scotland"—labels were the cachet, the reason these goods were "luxury" and cost so much. As labor costs mounted in Europe in the 1990s, businesses began to source to cheaper labor elsewhere in the world.

Not luxury brands. They couldn't publicly move production out of Europe without damaging the brand image they had so carefully crafted. Their initial response was to raise retail prices, but only slightly, so as not to chase off all those new middle-market customers. Luxury brands that were publicly traded had to answer to their shareholders, who wanted more of a return, more profits. That meant increasing volume and lowering costs. To increase volume they ramped up production and advertising, particularly for handbags.

Lowering costs was a more delicate problem. How could luxury brands slash the production cost of their goods and maintain the same high level of quality? In fact, they couldn't. There had to be concessions. In the name of profit—or, to put it more bluntly, greed—luxury brands began to compromise their integrity. Some cut corners in ready-to-wear. "I remember being in fittings in the mid-nineties where the CEO came in and said, 'Women don't really need linings,'" one former major luxury brand assistant told me. Soon that became the industry standard. "There's a raw-edge cutting, which is deemed post-Japanese avant-garde from a design standpoint, but actually is an easy way to cut production costs," another luxury brand design assistant explained to me. "You can imagine how much less time and money it takes to make a dress or jacket if you don't have to sew the outer fabric and lining together, press them, fold them back on themselves, press them again and add another seam to keep it together. If you do a raw edge, you just cut the edge and it's done." Another Italian brand trimmed costs by cutting sleeves half an inch shorter. "When you get to a thousand, you see the savings," the assistant explained.

Many luxury brands cut costs by using cheaper materials. Example: In 1992, I bought a pink sleeveless Prada cocktail dress that was made of thick iridescent cotton and silk faille, fully lined, and finished beautifully. It cost $2,000, but it is couture quality and will last forever. Ten years later, I bought a pair of thin cotton-poplin cropped trousers at Prada for $500. I put them on, and the gentle passing of my foot ripped the hem out. I put my hand in the pocket, and it tore away from its seam. I squatted down to pick up my two-year-old, and the derriere split open. I hadn't had those pants on ten minutes and they were literally falling apart at the seams. I mentioned this to a former Prada design assistant. "It's the thread," he told me. "It's cheaper and breaks easily." When I told him about my gorgeous dress from 1992 that was as solid as a Rolls, he nodded. "That was then," he said with a sigh. Of course, not all Prada goods are shoddy, but this story shows how standards in the production of luxury products has diminished in the last decade.

The most obvious place for luxury brands to trim costs was the same place that every other industry was trimming costs: in the price of labor. And the cheapest and most plentiful labor today is in China. Once Coach proved that Chinese workers could meet luxury brand quality standards, several other brands moved a small amount of production there, too. Like Coach, they started with short runs of classic and basic designs of leather goods. To get the technique right, one major Italian luxury brand executive sent a team of leather goods artisans from Italy to teach the Chinese workers. With each successful run, the brands got braver, ordering more, and other brands joined the exodus. By 2006, hundreds of thousands of luxury brand handbags, toiletry cases, and satchels were produced in China each year, unbeknownst to customers.

Few admit to it. The small Italian leather goods firm Furla said it began to produce some of its wallets and handbags in China in 2002. Despite Bernard Arnault's declaration at a luxury conference in Hong Kong in December 2004 that only European artisans truly knew how to make luxury goods, one of his LVMH brands, Céline, produced its denim and leather Macadam handbags in China the following year. A brown leather tag inside the bag stated that it was designed in Paris and "handcrafted in China with the greatest attention to quality and detail." In May 2005, the *Financial Times* reported that Prada, who claimed that all its clothing and accessories were made in Italy, was "currently evaluating a series of opportunities" to produce in cheaper labor markets elsewhere in the world, including China. In fact, Prada had already started producing leather goods in China by May 2005.

Today, the luxury brand handbag is a study in globalization: hardware, like locks, come from Italy and China (primarily Guangzhou); the zipper comes from Japan; the lining comes from Korea; the embroidery is done in Italy, India, or northern China; the leather is from Korea or Italy; and the bag is assembled partly in China and partly in Italy. The sourcing is sometimes as questionable as the true provenance of the bag: one manufacturer told me that one supplier claims his silk is British when in fact he buys it in China, stores it in the United Kingdom, and then sells it at European prices.

Most luxury brands don't produce a lot of different styles in China. Instead they reproduce the same designs in different colors or materials. The luxury brand's design team dreams up a new bag and sends a pattern to the factory in China. The manufacturer does the research to find the materials, hardware, and, if needed, a source to do the embroidery. Sometimes the manufacturer's research pays off: one replaced an Italian-made fabric that cost $21.50 (€18) a yard with one from Korea that cost $12, and, he added, "the quality is better." The Chinese manufacturer makes the prototype. Once corrected and approved, the bag is put into production.

The luxury brands are fiercely protective of the logo and only send the number of labels needed for the amount of bags in each order. "If that label turns up on other bags, the logo is worthless," the manufacturer told me. Few bags actually carry the "Made in China" label. If they do, it is well hidden. For one bag, the tag was sewn into the bottom seam of the inside pocket. For another, it was stamped on the reverse side of a postage-stamp-size leather flap that bears the brand's logo. You need a magnifying glass to read it. The majority, however, carry a "Made in Italy," "Made in France," or "Made in the U.K." label. The brands have little tricks to get around the China label. One brand's "Made in China" label is actually a sticker affixed to the outer package. The luxury brand rips it off when the goods arrive in Italy and replaces it with a "Made in Italy" label. Another has the entire bag made in China except for the handle. The bag is shipped to Italy, where the Italian-made handle is attached. Some brands have the tops of shoes—the most labor-intensive part of the process—made in China and then attach the soles in Italy. These items can carry the "Made in Italy" label.

The craftsmanship can be complicated. I watched Chinese girls make intricately braided leather handles and tassels. "We learned the technique from Italy," the manufacturer told me. The amount of glue used to construct the bag dictates the level of luxury—and the retail price. Low-end luxury brands use a lot of glue. Higher-end brands use little. One young and highly respected European brand that produces only very fine leather goods doesn't use glue at all—but it does quietly produce most of its goods in China. When you walk into its production room, you only smell leather. "I hate glue," the manufacturer told me. "But that's how the brands can afford it." And how they make their profits.

Production in China costs 30 to 40 percent less than in Italy. "So we aren't dirt cheap," the manufacturer said. "There is a preconception in the U.S. and Europe that if the brands move to China they'll get it for 10 percent. Sure, there are factories that will do that, but the quality won't be there and the brand will suffer. If we do it right and they get good products from our effort, they will make money. In the end, we are the money generator for them."

Indeed they are. The evening after I visited the factory in China, I met some friends for a drink at the bar at the new Harvey Nichols store in Hong Kong. As I entered the store from the Landmark luxury shopping mall in the heart of the Central business district, I passed through the handbag department. To my right, on the shelf, sat the exact same bag I saw the Chinese girls making in the factory. It cost the brand $120 to produce. It was for sale at Harvey Nick's for $1,200.

A CHINESE FACTORY can be a bit like a university campus. The place is populated with thousands of unmarried young people ages sixteen to about twenty-six. They often live in dorms on the property, eat off metal trays at long tables in a cafeteria, and ride bikes or take the bus to town during their time off to hit a karaoke bar. One factory I visited has a game room with pool tables, Ping-Pong, and Foosball; a basketball court; a convenience store; and a computer room. A gym was under construction. There's a doctor onsite and day care. And the place was absolutely spotless. "If it's not a healthy environment, then the workers aren't healthy and our goods reflect it," the manufacturer told me, adding, "We are one of the few exceptions." Factories that produce luxury goods have a couple of thousand workers, small by comparison to mass brands. "A Nike factory will have twenty to thirty thousand people," the manufacturer told me. "It's a town."

Most of the workers are young women, somewhere between the ages of twenty-two and twenty-six. The legal working age in China is sixteen—though, the manufacturer noted, "there are tons of kids in regular factories here who have fake papers." Only about 15 percent of the workers in Dongguan are locals. The rest come from the poor cities in the north and from the countryside and require a permit from their hometowns to go elsewhere to work. They earn about $120 a month and send it all home. "They come to work and get out," he said. "They work enough to support a family, build a house. In five to six years, they earn between fifty and sixty thousand RMB, which is about $6,000 to $7,000. The workers have no friends. No relatives nearby. They don't mind doing overtime. They don't care if they are working long hours or don't have fun. They just work. It's a big cultural difference."

At the factory I visited in October 2005, the workday is 8:00 a.m. to 12:30 p.m and 2:00 p.m. to 7:00 p.m., and if there is overtime, 9:00 p.m. to 11:00 p.m. at one and a half times the usual hourly rate. All workers have Sunday off. This is unusual: most factories in China run 24/7, and shifts can last up to ten hours. I arrived in the early evening, just as the workers were about to go on break. In the four-floor factory there is nearly twenty-seven thousand square feet of production space. The windows were open and slatted to allow for cross-breezes. Fans sat silently in the corners; summers in the Pearl River delta are stiflingly hot and humid. It takes about ten months to build a factory in China from scratch to production—one-fourth the time it does in the United States. In one large room of fifteen thousand square feet, there were fifteen rows of long worktables. At each table stood about a dozen thin young women in pale blue short-sleeve shirts and dark trousers busily gluing, hammering, and stitching seams on sewing machines. They were surrounded by bags with coveted luxury brand logos. A room this size processes fifteen to twenty thousand units a month. Unlike at Hermès in France or Gucci in Italy, it's all assembly-line work. I watched one girl as she glued handles onto the outside of a canvas tote. She placed a cardboard pattern on top of the canvas to make sure the straps were attached in the right place, hammered them, then handed the bag off to the next girl, who in turn stitched the handles to the canvas on a machine. The glue girl did about two bags a minute. When it was dinnertime, the girls put everything neatly in its place, covered the machines—in case of rain—and walked out, single file, giggling and gossiping as they crossed the common to the six-story dorm for dinner in the ground-floor canteen. Each girl had a photo ID badge on a chain around her neck.

Not surprisingly, manufacturers in China are starting to experience problems. Supplies are going up in price. There are electricity shortages because there are so many factories. And there's a shortage of what is known as "sophisticated labor": work that requires refined skills. As workers gain more education, they demand more in wages and perks. Salaries went up 30 percent from 2000 to 2005, from $90 to $120 a month, simply to retain workers. The gyms and computer rooms help, too.

The brands aren't making it any easier. "They get all the human rights complaints," explained the manufacturer. "It's killing me because they put constraints and complain that we don't pay enough. I say, 'If you want it made same way for the same wages then just produce in your country.' We never want to treat the workers badly because we want to make the product. But the brands are helping the workers, giving them more value." Nevertheless, there are still casualties. On the way to Dongguan, we read a story in the paper of a worker who, just the day before, left the factory in an industrial zone in Guangzhou after a twenty-four-hour shift, collapsed in the street, and died. "Pure fatigue," the manufacturer told me. "It's one of thousands of cases here."

CHAPTER SEVEN

THE NEEDLE AND THE DAMAGE DONE

If there were no luxury, there would be no poor.

— HENRY HOME, LORD KAMES

"CAN YOU SMELL the silk?" Laudomia Pucci asked.

We were standing in the entrance of the Antico Setificio Fiorentino, the oldest silk factory in Italy, maybe even in the world, housed in an eighteenth-century building near the Amerigo Vespucci Bridge in Florence. Before us sat a rack of big wooden spools wrapped with luminescent silk thread in hues that only nature can produce: the dark blue of the deep Mediterranean, a gold the color of wheat at harvest, a fuchsia like French tulips in springtime.

I took a deep breath and could indeed smell the silk: a damp musky smell of forests and cocoons.

Silk is known as the queen of textiles. It has been used for Chinese emperors' robes and Catherine the Great's wedding dress, for Italian noble families' banners and the Pope's Swiss Guard flags, and for the thread that stitched war wounds closed. Skiers wear socks made of silk because it naturally wicks moisture away from the body. Ben Franklin flew a silk kite during his electricity experiments. Today silk remains the fabric of choice for couture gowns, whether they are in taffeta, satin duchesse, organdy, or tulle. "Silk does for the body what diamonds do for the hand," designer Oscar de la Renta once said.

Laudomia Pucci, a slim, elegant brunette in her early forties, is the daughter of Marchese Emilio Pucci di Barsento, the founder of Pucci, the Florentine luxury fashion brand known for its psychedelic-print silk jersey clothes that has been majority-owned by LVMH since 2000. The Puccis have deep roots in Florence. In the fifteenth century, the family served as political advisers to the ruling Medicis. Their sumptuous thirteenth-century palazzo, on Via de' Pucci, is decorated with elaborate frescos, and their family chapel in Santissima Annunziata is a Renaissance gem.

Emilio Pucci was raised with his younger brother and sister by severe nannies. An accomplished athlete, Pucci excelled in swimming, tennis, fencing, and skiing. He studied agriculture at the University of Milan and the University of Georgia, and received a skiing scholarship at Reed University in Portland, Oregon, where he earned his master's degree in social sciences. While there, he designed uniforms for the ski team. He later earned a Ph.D. in political science from the University of Florence. He was a member of the 1934 Italian Olympic ski team and served as a pilot in the Italian air force in World War II, returning "covered with medals," Laudomia boasted.

After the war, he worked as a ski instructor in Switzerland and, continuing his dual passions for innovation and skiing, designed the first slim stretch ski pants with an elastic stirrup. They appeared in *Harper's Bazaar* in 1948 and soon were the preferred look on ski slopes around the world. The following summer, Pucci opened a small boutique on Capri, the jet-set haven just off the coast of Naples, and filled it with clothes for "island life," like cropped pants, dubbed Capri pants, in cheerful colors like Mediterranean blue, bougainvillea pink, and sunshine yellow. In 1954, he officially launched the House of Pucci. With the fabric mills in Como, he created print silk jersey that clung sensually to the body. Originally production was in Florence, in little ateliers around town. He signed the psychedelic patterns "Emilio," respectfully leaving the Pucci family off and out of the limelight. "He believed women had to be free to move, no corsets, or girdles," Laudomia explained.

By the mid-1950s, the Antico Setificio Fiorentino was in a state of semi-abandonment. In 1958, Emilio Pucci purchased the majority share of the factory from a consortium of fellow Florentine noble families, effectively saving it from the wrecking ball. "It was supposed to be bought by a hotel corporation and turned into a modern hotel," Laudomia said incredulously. Pucci poured some of his sizable fortune into the factory and commissioned it to reproduce the damasks and taffetas that for centuries had been used to decorate the family's palazzo. The looms have been singing ever since.

In the spring of 2004, I rang up Laudomia and asked her to show me the Antico Setificio Fiorentino. "It's really a special place," she told me as we drove across the Arno and turned the corner onto Via Bartolini. You walk down a narrow stone path draped in wisteria, cross a small courtyard garden where for centuries the children of weavers have played, and enter a simple faded yellow houselike building with thick walls, worn brick floors, and big airy rooms with high beamed ceilings. The first room is the warping room, where the silk thread is prepared for the looms. One of the warping machines is a tall wooden cylindrical contraption called Orditoio, built in the eighteenth century according to plans by Leonardo da Vinci. It is the only one known to be in existence today. "You have to kick it to move it," Laudomia explained to me. The other warping machine at the factory is a Benninger from 1879.

In the next small room sat big plastic bags stuffed with skeins of gloriously colored silk thread. Until the 1920s, the Setificio dyed silk, most of it produced in the region. Silk production in Italy disappeared after World War II. Today silk arrives from China in bulk, already dyed and ready to be spooled. You can tell that it has not been treated chemically, because you can hear it rustle. Laudomia took a bolt of emerald green taffeta, called *ermisino*—"the grandfather of taffeta," she said— and scrunched the fabric. "Look," she said, "it stands up." The fabric held the scrunched shape, like tinfoil. "That's what silk is supposed to do," she told me. "Silk is a living thing. Today, manufacturers push it so much, they kill it and destroy it. Weaving by hand respects the body of the thread."

Next comes the pattern making. Back in the Renaissance, the noble families each had looms in their palazzi to produce silks to decorate the house and dress the family members. Laudomia tells me that when the oldest son married, the family would create a new damask pattern that would bear the family's name. A silk fabric design was also created when a first son was born, and the family owned exclusively it until he died.

The largest and noisiest room of the otherwise serene Setificio is the weaving room. It is there that all the damasks and moirés and even some linens are woven by workers on manual looms. Though it is a magical room of movement, sound, and *richesse,* it is a sad shadow of what it once was. In November 1966, the Arno flooded and the Setificio, which sits on the river's banks, filled with water and mud. Most of the patterns, designs, and archives—which included the records of what each loom had produced for centuries—were destroyed, but the looms were salvaged. All are from 1780 and are pedaled with the right leg; the hand pulls a rope, and the shuttle slides through. When I visited one woman was weaving a sixteenth-century lampas called Princess Mary of England; it is made of fine gold thread and advances only sixty centimeters a day.

Workers require five years of training to be able to weave silk and linen at the Setificio. It's a trade passed down from generation to generation. Back in the 1920s, Florentine girls came after school to learn how to weave on small looms built for them. Today, there are thirteen weavers, mostly women. Each fabric is made from beginning to end by one weaver because otherwise you would be able to see the change of hand in the cloth. Most weavers at the Setificio are in their thirties or forties. Back in the factory's heyday, the weavers' talent was considered so precious that when they decided to marry, the factory would offer handsome dowries and other concessions to get them to stay on.

The Setificio is underwritten by the noble families of Italy who are still shareholders, and it receives commissions from all over the world. In 2000, the looms produced the silk for the costumes for Siena's annual Renaissance parade. The factory has also created damasks for one of the royal palaces in Copenhagen and won the commission over Lyon to redo two rooms of the Kremlin; it continues to make silk pouches for potpourri for the Farmacia di Santa Maria Novella, the famed seventeenth-century apothecary that operates in the heart of old Florence. Next door to the factory is a shop that sells the Setificio's silks and linens. While there, I admired an ivory silk and linen weave called Spinone. It cost €125 a meter. Laudomia saw my interest. "The problem is, once you do one chair with this fabric, the rest of the room looks awful," she said with a laugh.

SILK IS CREATED through the process of sericulture, or silkworm farming. Silkworms are not worms at all, but rather caterpillars, and the *Bombyx mori* is the primary variety used for commercial silk. The *Bombyx* is raised on farms in China, Thailand, and India, where it feasts on mulberry leaves and increases its bodyweight ten thousand times in its four-week life span to about the size of an adult thumb.

After four moltings, it spins a two-inch-long waterproof cocoon, eject-
ing liquid silk at about a foot a minute. Two weeks later, it emerges as
a moth and mates like crazy for a few hours. The female lays three
hundred to five hundred eggs and dies in a few days. The eggs take six
weeks to twelve months to hatch. A few moths are allowed to hatch
to continue the process. The remaining cocoons are steamed to kill
the caterpillar, washed by hand in hot water to remove the gummy
substance called sericin, and unwound on a reeling machine, which
spools the filaments on a bobbin. The work is swift, the water filthy,
smelly, and very hot. Usually five to eight filaments are spun together
to create a thread. On some farms in India, young girls make thread by
hand, unwinding the cocoons and slapping and twisting the filaments
across their thighs.

The Chinese began to produce silk in the third millennium BC for
exclusive use by the emperor and his court. The Chinese kept sericulture to themselves for centuries—anyone found guilty of disclosing its
secrets was sentenced to death by torture—but the fabric itself made
its way westward. When Alexander the Great conquered Persia in
331 BC, he discovered swaths of the luminous silk. The five-thousand-
mile Silk Road began in Xi'an, passed through the Jade Gate, and
crossed the Turkestan desert, the Iranian plateau, and Asia Minor to
Constantinople. There, silk and other exotic goods were loaded on
ships and transported to the Mediterranean's capitals. Travel on the
Silk Road peaked during China's prosperous and culturally rich Tang
Dynasty (AD 618–907), and glorious cities along the route, such as
Tashkent, Bukhara, and Samarkand, flourished. In Rome, only the
wealthiest could afford silk—it was said to be worth its weight in
gold—and they wore it so lavishly that the government passed sumptuary laws to restrain its conspicuous display. Caesar's heir, Octavian,
eventually restricted the importation of silk because the material was
too costly.

There are many legends about how the knowledge of sericulture arrived in Italy. One recounts that in the sixth century, the Roman emperor Justinian sent two monks to China to smuggle cocoons in a hollow cane back to Italy. Another tells of an Asian princess who brought the fabric to Italy as a bride. The most generally accepted, however, is that of Italian merchants in the Middle Ages who discovered the rich iridescent fabric in Hormuz, Persia, dubbed *ormesino;* learned how it was made; took it home; and reproduced it. Today it is known today as *ermisino,* the taffeta that Laudomia scrunched.

One of the early centers for silk weaving was in the Tuscan town of Lucca. In the fourteenth century, several of Lucca's weavers settled in Florence and opened the city's first silk workshops. The city's rulers granted them tax exemptions to pursue their art. The Arte della Seta, the silk weavers' guild, was formed and drew up strict guidelines for silk manufacturing. By the mid-fifteenth century, Florentine farmers were required to plant mulberry bushes on their land to feed silkworms. The noble families of Florence, including the Puccis, wholly embraced the luxurious silks for both decor and clothing, as detailed in portraits by such Renaissance masters as Leonardo da Vinci, Raphael, and Botticelli. By the fifteenth century, silk was a symbol of Florence's wealth and refinement: when Cosimo de' Medici, the Grand Duke of Tuscany, arrived in Florence, he noted that the streets were filled with "fine tapestries and hangings . . . There was not a shop to be seen that did not put on a great show of works in silk and sumptuous gold."

The Como Lake region in northern Italy was at the time a center for wool dying and weaving. The wool came from Scotland and Spain, across Flanders, down the Rhine to Zurich, and over the Alps to Como, where the lake's pure water was perfect for dyeing. When turf wars broke out across Europe, the wool route shut down. The ruler of the region, Gian Galeazzo Sforza, and his uncle Ludovico Sforza decided to bring silk production from Florence to Como to make up the loss. Como has remained a textile manufacturing center ever since. In the fifteenth century, King Louis XI of France set up silk manufacturing in Lyon to stop French aristocrats from buying the fabric from Italy, and the industry flourished there for centuries.

ON A RAINY SPRING afternoon in 2006, I drove from Milan through the congested industrial northern suburbs to Como, the Alpine lake resort, to meet Michele Canepa, owner of Taroni, the last silk factory in the city. Canepa is one of those friendly yet elegant Italians who instantly make you feel welcome and important. When I met him, he was dressed conservatively yet impeccably in a brown herringbone jacket, charcoal gray flannel trousers, a good blue-and-white-striped shirt with French cuffs, and a conservative black knit tie. His longish chestnut hair was slicked back neatly, and his eyes were smiling. The Taroni headquarters dates to the early twentieth century; Canepa's office was filled with 1970s contemporary decor, including a glass-top table for a desk and molded plastic chairs with chrome legs. Outside his small window a strong old magnolia was in bloom, many of its petals scattered about, knocked off by the pouring rain.

Canepa's family has been in the silk and textile business for two centuries in Como. Half of Como's business then was weaving—its specialty was silk twill, the fabric used for scarves—and the other half was manufacturing. In the 1950s, it all began to change. First, since Europe no longer produced silk, Como's weavers were forced to buy their thread primarily from China. Then they started to import twill and other silk fabrics from China, and changed their business from weaving to dyeing, printing, and producing finished goods. When Canepa joined the family firm in 1968, it was third or fourth largest silk manufacturer in Como.

In 1998, Canepa decided to retire and sold the business, which is now located outside the city, to his sisters. A year later he got a call from his friend Giampaolo Porlezza, owner of Taroni.

"Would you be interested in buying my company?" Porlezza asked.

Realizing that he missed working, Conepa accepted.

Taroni by then was last silk mill in town. Silk production in the Como region is one-tenth of what it was in 1950. China is now the primary producer, followed by India and Thailand. Italian and Lyonnais silk manufacturing firms are boutique businesses, and their woven silks are still considered the finest. "If a client only wants eighteen meters' worth, that's what I'll do," Canepa told me. "I take the time to do it right." In the Como region, there are only a handful of other companies, including Mantero and Ratti, that do silk production of this quality. In Florence there is the Antico Setificio, but its production is minuscule. In Lyon there are a few factories weaving high-quality silk, including Bucol, which is owned by Hermès and produces Hermès's silk scarves as well as fabrics for other couture houses. And that's about it.

We walked up the stairs to the muffled thumping sounds of the looms. As Canepa opened the door to the factory's production room, I was hit with a gust of wind created by the whirring machines. The air had the same musky odor that I had first smelled in Florence. The sound was deafening. The shuttle on the new computer-run Grob Horgen looms moves so quickly that you can hardly see it—quite a difference from the old ones in Florence pulled through by hand. The older Benninger looms from the 1960s, Canepa shouted to me, are slower and better. "On the old looms," he hollered, "you can produce a quality that is impossible to produce with modern looms." One of the Benningers was turning out a sumptuous gold taffeta with bronze and pale pink stripes. It was for a top couture house, Canepa told me. He had me touch another soft white silk with small checks. "It's waterproof," he explained. It, too, would show up on a runway in a year. Canepa is contractually not allowed to disclose who his clients are—they like to keep their sourcing a secret—but I can say that most of the major couture houses and the top New York designers use his fabrics for their finest creations.

Many of Como's manufacturers have moved over the years to the countryside just south of the city. What were once farms are now industrial parks. One of the top manufacturers in the region is ISA S.p.A. Located in a gated compound behind a big grocery store half an hour down the *superstrada* from Como, ISA produces ties and scarves for Louis Vuitton, Christian Dior, Gucci, Fendi, and Pucci. ISA was founded by Giorgio Bianchi just after World War II. As a student, Bianchi visited Paris and was so taken with Hermès's silk scarves and ties he returned to Como and opened the factory to try to produce an Italian equivalent. He focused on one product: silk twill. He designed some print patterns himself; others he bought in Paris. One of his first clients was Céline, followed by Dior back when Christian Dior himself was at the helm. The company grew quickly, from 1 weaving machine in the late 1940s to 150 in the 1960s, but it was hard to find enough labor, especially in such an agricultural region.

Since the 1960s, ISA's business has shifted, like Taroni's, from weaving to printing and production. Today, the company is run by Giorgio's son Giambattista and his wife, Gabriella, a fashionable young couple with a lot of verve. They understand the importance of China in the manufacturing business and are adapting accordingly. Weaving accounts for a mere 5 percent of ISA's business, and that work is very specific: the company is down to thirty looms and only produces complicated fabrics like jacquard or precious taffetas and chiffons—"the luxurious fabrics," Gabriella Bianchi explained to me when I visited ISA in March 2006. "We leave the less expensive fabrics to others in Italy or to China." Gabriella is a vivacious brunette with an hourglass figure and a winning smile. When we met, Gabriella was dressed in a tight white denim dress, a black leather fur-trimmed jacket cinched with a wide belt, and a saucy pair of gold 1940s-style heels. This, in Italy, is office wear.

Gabriella grabbed an umbrella and escorted me across the parking lot from the shiny white corporate offices to the old beat-up factory. The weaving was moved off-site five years ago—about five kilometers down the road—simply because it was too loud, she explained as we entered the old loom room. The space is gargantuan—as big as an airplane hangar—with worn redbrick floors. Today it is where ISA makes all the sample ties and scarves. There are bolts of fabric, worktables, sewing machines. In the next big room, a woman attaches bar-code tags to Vuitton neckties, slides them into cellophane sleeves, and places them in a carton to be shipped. At another table is a box of Gucci twill scarves. For Vuitton and some others, the product is sent to the company, where it is boxed. For Fendi, the product is shipped directly to the stores.

"We do a lot of printing just for Pucci since LVMH took it over, because we do printing and production for many LVMH brands, including Marc Jacobs, Céline, Dior, Fendi, and Louis Vuitton," Gabriella explained. We walked up to the design studio, a small room with women at worktables and computers, adjusting scarf print designs. Luxury brand design assistants visit ISA's factory regularly and consult with the studio on designs. Sometimes they bring their own, and sometimes they alter ISA's proposed sketches. Often they peruse the old leather-bound scrapbooks that contain swatches of previous prints and weaves for ideas. "This is the history of Como," Gabriella told me as she paged through a dusty volume of plaids. The tattered pages were brown and mottled, but the fabrics were glorious, the colors pure, the weave tight, the yarn smooth and rich.

The initial hand-drawn design is scanned into the computer so that it can be copied easily to create a repetitive pattern. A prototype is produced by hand on enormous silk screens in the print room, a gigantic space with a dozen fifty-meter-long tables and big plastic tubs of ink that look like huge pots of finger paint. The place smells like a Xerox machine. I watched as two large, strong women hooked a heavy, square screen on top of a long swath of twill on the table. They poured some ink on the screen, pulled a big scraper across it, unhooked it, lifted the apparatus, and moved it to the next plain section of twill. Once the prototype is approved, the design is programmed into computer-driven silk screen machines and the scarves are printed one after another on twill affixed to the long tables. The printed scarves, still stiff with ink, are washed in huge machines until soft and inspected under hot lights for faults.

Much of the twill ISA uses comes from China. "There are three or four companies there that only do plain twill, and it is cheaper because they never stop production and that's all they do," Gabriella explained. "We buy twill from China when the quality doesn't have to be perfect and the customer wants lower prices. For the first-quality level we still do all the weaving in Como. You can see when something is printed well or woven well. This is the power of Como."

Scarves with machine-sewn edges are sent to a sewing room upstairs to be finished. Scarves with hand-rolled, hand-stitched edges are sent to freelancers in the region who work at home or to a factory that specializes in hand-rolled finishing in Mauritius, an island in the Indian Ocean just off Madagascar. Hermès has some of its silk scarves finished there, too. The Mauritius factory "has good prices and good quality," Gabriella explains. ISA produces between seven and eight hundred thousand scarves and six to seven hundred thousand ties each year. They used to do more than one million ties a year, but "ties are going out of fashion," she explained. The average twill scarf costs about $40 to $50 to produce. It retails for ten times more, and prices are rarely reduced. The production cost for a scarf in China is 40 percent less, or $25 to $30 apiece. Some brands now produce their scarves in China. But several have remained at ISA—at least for the time being—because, Gabriella explained, "we do small quantities, we are flexible, we do samples in a week, and we're nearby. We now only do the highest level of the market because it's impossible for us to make it cheaper. We don't have the prices. I don't know what it will be like in ten years, but for the moment, it's still a good business. And honestly, I don't think the Chinese are interested in doing small production. At least this is what I hope."

THE MANUFACTURING of clothing—like that of perfume, accessories, and every other luxury good—now follows the pyramid model: the exquisite work is produced in a very limited quantity by a coterie of highly skilled traditional craftsmen in France, Italy, and the United Kingdom. The middle range, such as ready-to-wear, is farmed out to big factories in places like Spain, North Africa, Turkey, and the former Eastern bloc countries. Giorgio Armani said in 2005 that it produced 18 percent of its high-end ready-to-wear line, Armani Collezioni, in Eastern Europe. Gucci makes some of its sneakers in Serbia, and Prada does the upper part of some shoes in Slovenia.

In 2004, Valentino reportedly began to outsource its $1,300 men's suits to a factory in Cairo, where they were produced by veiled Muslim seamstresses who learned their craft by watching videos on televisions in the workshop. At the time, Italian textile workers' hourly wages were $18.63; the Egyptian workers earned 88 cents. When the suits, destined for the European market, arrived in Italy, Valentino representatives ripped out the "Made in Egypt" tags—in Europe, companies do not have to declare where their goods are produced. Valentino suits for the American and Japanese markets, which have stricter laws about provenance labeling, were produced in Italy. In the United States and Japan, "perceived quality is more important than real quality," explained Valentino CEO Michele Norsa. The cut in manufacturing costs had a positive impact on the bottom line: in 2005, Valentino posted its first profit in years.

The lowest end of the luxury spectrum, like logo-covered luxury T-shirts and knitwear, are produced in developing nations such as China, Mexico, Madagascar, and Mauritius. In February 2003, I traveled to Mauritius to see the process firsthand.

Mauritius is a tropical paradise so ravishing that Mark Twain once wrote, "You gather the idea that . . . heaven was copied after Mauritius." Endless acres of lush sugarcane fields surround jagged volcanic mountains that rise out of the sea mist like peaks of meringue. Wide tranquil bays of vibrant turquoise are framed by swaths of fine white sand and swaying palms. Colonized over the centuries by the Dutch, the British, and the French, the island was the home of the legendary dodo bird. Today Mauritius is a favored winter holiday destination for Europeans and an offshore financial center for India. It has also been, for the last thirty years, one of the world's key centers for textile manufacturing. Textile manufacturing in Mauritius is a purely contrived industry. Unlike other major garment manufacturing countries, which also produce much of their raw materials, Mauritius imports everything, from the yarn to the packaging. Hundreds of factories dot the inland hills, where workers—predominantly women—produce sweaters, cashmere blankets, and T-shirts for everyone from discount retailers like JC Penney to luxury brands such as Giorgio Armani and Burberry.

Mauritius was first "discovered" by the Portuguese, shortly after Vasco da Gama's expedition around the Cape of Good Hope in 1498. In 1511, the Dutch claimed the island and named it in honor of their sovereign, Maurice. During their fifty-year stay in Mauritius, the Dutch not only wiped out the dodo but also introduced and cultivated sugarcane, which they harvested with slaves they imported from Africa. In 1715, the French arrived from the neighboring island of Bourbon (now Réunion), renamed it Île de France, and declared it French. During the Napoleonic Wars of the early nineteenth century, the French lost the island to the British, who renamed it Mauritius and developed the sugarcane business with the help of indentured laborers from their nearby colony, India. Today most Mauritians speak both French and English. In 1968, Mauritius received its independence from Great Britain, but, as Mookeshwarsing Gopal, chairman of the Mauritius Export Processing Zone Association (MEPZA), the industry's trade association, explained to me, "it suffered serious economic structural problems. It was a poor country."

The one thing Mauritius did have was abundant, unemployed manpower. In a 1975 trade agreement to boost developing nations, it received the right to export textiles duty-free and quota-free to the European Economic Community (now the European Union). The government saw textile manufacturing as Mauritius's key to prosperity and dedicated all that it could to developing the industry there. This allowed companies like Shibani Knitting Company Ltd. to flourish.

Shibani is a big block building within the barbed-wire-topped chain-link fences in Phoenix, an industrial area in the hills inland from Port Louis. As I pulled into the parking lot, I noticed a Max Mara factory across the street. Upstairs, in the clean, white retail offices of Shibani stood racks of its in-house label knitwear, T-shirts, and lingerie for the spring season one year away. If it weren't for the view of the Indian Ocean out the windows, I would have thought I was in a showroom on Seventh Avenue in New York. In walked Sunil M. Hassamal, a large-set Mauritian-born man of Indian origin. He sat down, asked an assistant to bring two cups of tea, and told me about his company, one of the largest on the island.

Hassamal's family, one of the more important textile manufacturers in Mauritius, decided in 1986 to produce sweaters for Europe and opened Shibani with a South African partner. "Unlike other Mauritian companies who had cheap labor, hand machines, handlooms—that was the traditional way of doing it—we used electronic machines from day one," he explained. "And we have kept modernizing and expanding so today we at are at the forefront of technology."

That's evident from the moment you enter the factory downstairs. The knitting room is the size of a football field, the dozens of knitting machines roaring as loudly as newspaper presses; many of the workers wear protective earphones. Most of the machines are from Stoll of Frankfurt, Germany, and bear the company slogan—"The right way to knit!"—embossed on the side. There are also two three-gauge Shima Seiki machines from Japan. "Some people cut up fabric and sew it together," explain Hassamal. "Here, the whole thing is knitted on a machine."

Among the labels Shibani produces in Phoenix and at its two other sweater and one intimate apparel factories on the island are the French catalog company La Redoute, the Paris department store Le Bon Marché, the high-fashion label Zadig & Voltaire, the French couture house Carven, Armani Jeans, Nordstrom, and Ralph Lauren. "We used to do Calvin Klein Europe," Hassamal said. "And we do all the cashmere blankets for Ralph Lauren." All of Shibani's cashmere comes from Mongolia and is then dyed and spun in China, Italy, and Scotland. Chinese cashmere is the cheapest; Scottish the finest and most expensive. "The quality used in a sweater depends on what the client wants to pay," Hassamal said. Generally, clients bring their own sketches and some supply one-off samples as patterns to follow. The sweater is drawn on a computer following specs for colors, type of yarn (cashmere, lamb's wool, Merino wool, or cotton), kind of stitch, and size or gauge of the knitting. When the test swatch is approved, the whole production is run. Then the sweaters are sent to the finishing room to have trims, collars, buttons, and labels added.

It was break time when we walked into the finishing room. The Mauritian women were chatting and drinking tea, as the Chinese girls slept on folded arms on their knitting machines. In the mid-1990s, Mauritius was at full employment and needed more textile laborers to keep the factories running. The government devised a system that grants foreign—or expatriate (expat)—workers three-year contracts.

Expats—who come from China, Bangladesh, Sri Lanka, and India—are an essential part of the Mauritian textile labor force; in 2004, there were twenty thousand expats working in manufacturing on the island, most twenty to thirty years old. Up to 25 percent of a factory's workforce can be expats. The factory owners are obliged to provide housing and board as well as pay wages. Generally, expats are limited to one three-year posting. "But they take another passport and come again two or three years later," says Michel Mayer, marketing director for World Knits, a T-shirt manufacturer in Coromandel, Mauritius, that produces for JCPenney, Guess, and Armani Jeans, among others.

Shibani has eighteen hundred workers on sweaters and four hundred on intimate wear; expat workers predominantly from China and India make up about 10 percent of the workforce in the sweater factories. Shibani's four factories run twenty-four hours, seven days a week, with four shifts each day. The legal Mauritian workweek is forty-five hours. "I'd rather give preference to Mauritius workers than deal with lodging, food, passage tickets," Hassamal admitted, but "imports are better skilled as machine operators and there is less absenteeism because of family duties. Plus they don't mind working nights and Mauritians do." When the break was over, the Chinese girls snapped up and went right back to work. Their faces were blank, their eyes empty. No one spoke. All you could hear was the deafening *sidth-sidth-sidth* of the knitting machines.

By 2003, Mauritius textile and clothing manufacturing export sales amounted to roughly $1.5 billion. The sector employed about 40 percent of the country's workforce and contributed 12 percent to the gross domestic product. As a result, Mauritius had the highest per-capita gross domestic product in sub-Saharan Africa. There's evidence of the prosperity in Mauritius everywhere you turn: new European cars, restaurants, shopping centers, and housing construction. "Textile manufacturing is a main pillar of our economy," trade chairman Gopal told me.

But that may be headed the way of the dodo. On January 1, 2005, the World Trade Organization eliminated the thirty-year-old textile quotas that gave birth to thriving manufacturing centers in developing nations such as Mauritius, Bangladesh, Madagascar, and Sri Lanka. Mauritius was perhaps the worst hit, according to apparel industry consultant David Birnbaum of Third Horizon Ltd. in "Winners and Losers 2005," a study of the economic impact of the phase-out of twenty-eight key garment-producing countries. In 2003 and 2004, Mauritius lost thirty companies employing fifteen thousand apparel and textile workers. And Birnbaum reports that textile shipments from Mauritius to the United State in 2004 were down 17.5 percent from 2003. Not surprisingly, the majority of producers have moved their manufacturing to China. "The Chinese work seven days a week, twenty-four hours a day, they live in the factory and are paid pennies an hour," Michel Mayer told me. "How can we compete with that?"

IN THE NORTHERN AREA of Hong Kong called the New Territories— far from the banking towers, the grand hotels, and the luxury shopping malls—is an old industrial area of tired warehouses and rundown factories that until a decade ago was the pulsating heart of the region. For thirty years, this section of town turned out everything from plastic dolls to cashmere sweaters with the "Made in Hong Kong" label. In the fall of 2005, I walked into the parking garage of an old factory on a crummy street, stepped into a beat-up elevator, and went up to the modern, well-appointed offices of Fang Bros., a forty-year-old manufacturing company that today specializes in knitwear. Kenneth Fang, the company's chairman, is a distinguished Chinese gentleman who speaks the Queen's English and displays impeccable manners. When we met, he was in a tailored hay-colored suit and cheerful cashmere vest in a pastel argyle pattern, his silver hair neatly combed back, his hands perfectly manicured. His card boasts that he is a commander of the British Empire (CBE), an honor just below knight bestowed by the queen. Fang's main business is knitwear manufacturing. He also owns Pringle, the luxury Scottish cashmere knitwear company, which he bought in 2000 and is trying to revitalize.

In 1949, when Mao Tse-tung established the People's Republic of China, Fang's family fled Shanghai to British-ruled Hong Kong. "Hong Kong back then was a small fishing port," Fang remembers fondly. His father set up a business to continue what the family had done in China: spinning cotton yarn. In the 1960s, the company started weaving cotton fabric, which was exported to the United States and Great Britain to be made into clothes. In 1956, Kenneth was sent to North America to study. He took a bachelor of science in chemical engineering at the University of Michigan in Ann Arbor and a master's at the Massachusetts Institute of Technology, and in 1966 returned to Hong Kong to join and expand the family business. One of his first initiatives was to move the company into knitwear.

Back then, Hong Kong was a manufacturing center of lightweight goods such as toys, plastics, wigs, and inexpensive clothing. One-fourth of Hong Kong's economy was manufacturing, and 40 percent of Hong Kong residents worked in factories. From the late 1970s to the mid-1980s, Hong Kong's manufacturing quality had improved enough to lure high-end brands such as Ralph Lauren, Calvin Klein, and Max Mara. Fang Bros. became one of Ralph Lauren's biggest Polo shirt manufacturers.

In 1978, China opened its doors, "inviting investment with cheap land and cheap labor," Fang explained. Many Chinese refugees in Hong Kong, like Fang Bros., returned to the mainland to open factories, primarily in the Pearl River Delta of Guangdong, the southeastern province that abuts Hong Kong. Most were in and around Shenzhen, a border town about an hour north of the Hong Kong port by car or train. By the mid-1990s in the Shenzhen region, more than six million workers were employed in thirty thousand factories owned and run by Hong Kong manufacturers—as many as the entire population of Hong Kong. Like Hong Kong two decades earlier, the product manufactured in Guangdong was cheap in quality and price.

As China's manufacturing base grew, Hong Kong's shrank. Chinese workers' skills improved and production quality increased, yet costs remained low. Soon high-end and luxury brands began to relocate their clothing manufacturing from Europe, the United States, Hong Kong, Mauritius, and elsewhere to China. In a matter of days in the fall of 2005, I heard from manufacturing and industry sources in China that several prestigious Italian brands manufactured ready-to-wear and knitwear there in pieces and had the items assembled in Italy to carry the "Made in Italy" label, and Christian Lacroix had knitwear made there. Fang said, "We do a lot for Ralph Lauren and a small amount for Donna Karan," which, since 2001, has been an LVMH brand.

I was told by a senior Burberry executive in Hong Kong in December 2004 that the British-based company produced "a small bit of luggage in China. It's experimental, tiny, tiny." A day later, a source who worked with Burberry at the time told me, "Burberry's production in China is more than experimental. It is big quantities," and said it was primarily leather goods and accessories. Some of the lower-priced Burberry Blue Label, a licensed line that is produced by the Japanese firm Sanyo Shokai Ltd. for the Japanese market, is manufactured in China as well. I remembered the Burberry trench my husband tried on in Xi'an and thought to myself, "Maybe it *was* real." In September 2006, Burberry announced it was shuttering a factory in South Wales that had been in operation since 1939 and produced polo shirts, leaving three hundred out of work, and moving the production to China. In November, Welsh actor Ioan Gruffudd, who had modeled in a Burberry ad campaign, protested the closure, and the *Times* of London reported that Prince Charles contacted

Welsh government ministers to "ask if there was anything he could do" to stop the move. Peter Hain, Britain's secretary of state for Northern Ireland and Wales, asked Burberry CEO Angela Ahrendts to rethink the move and the Church of England, which has a $4.9 million stake in the company, requested a formal explanation. "We found the costs of producing the polo shirts offshore were substantially lower than the coasts in Wales," Michael Mahony, Burberry's director of commercial affairs, said at the time. "In fact, they were less than half."

The only luxury designer I heard openly embrace manufacturing clothing in China was Giorgio Armani. "The 'Made in Italy' label is very important for the top line because it suggests a certain specialization," he said during his visit to China in 2004. "But to manufacture some of our other lines in China . . . as long as we control the quality, then why not?"

Today, there are more than thirty thousand apparel and textile companies in Guangdong Province, employing more than five million people. China's textiles and apparel industry is worth more than $100 billion a year; meanwhile, Hong Kong's is nearly extinct. By 2002, manufacturing made up only 5 percent of Hong Kong's economy and only one in ten Hong Kong residents worked in factories. Instead, banking, trade, tourism, and real estate were the primary businesses. "Most manufacturers have their headquarters, and some design and marketing in Hong Kong," Fang said, "but assembly has moved to China." Fang Bros. continues to produce a small amount of knitwear in its Hong Kong factory, but most of its manufacturing is done in China, where the company has four knitwear factories and ten thousand employees at one-third the cost of Hong Kong. Average garment and textile factory wages in Guangdong Province are $50 to $100 a month. (Pringle's cashmere sweaters are still made in Hawick, Scotland, but some of the ready-to-wear is now produced in Fang's factories in China.) The living standard in Hong Kong has increased so much in the last forty years, making it one of the most expensive and cosmopolitan cities in the world, that "most young people do not want blue-collar jobs."

Fang sees manufacturing in China quickly evolving into a more sophisticated and costly market, like Japan and Taiwan before it. "Everybody goes through the same track," he said. At the moment, he explained, "the Chinese are brand-contracting." But soon, he believes, "manufacturers will start to promote brands. I expect more oriental brands to emerge in the next decade, especially for the Chinese market. The Chinese government has been supporting this: there are now fashion shows in Beijing, Shanghai, and Guangzhou. And manufacturers will pay more attention to quality and consistency. You have high-quality, well-built factories. China has well-skilled labor. In ten years it will be a different market." However, Fang doesn't believe that luxury brands will ever open their own factories in China. "Why should they," he asked, "if they can have someone produce for them and guarantee the quality?"

The exponential rise in manufacturing in Guangdong province has caused a host of environmental and labor problems. In late 2005, health and environmental experts stated that the factories and population in Guangdong were drawing too much fresh water out of the Pearl River, allowing seawater to flow upstream and taint the local water supply, forcing Guangdong and Macao residents to use only bottled water for drinking and cooking. In January 2006, several provinces farther up the Pearl River opened the floodgates of their dams to flush the salt water out of the delta and slow down the damage to its ecosystem. The air in Hong Kong, which is downwind from Guangdong Province, has grown increasingly smoggy to the point that most days it seems cloudy when it's not. "When they shut down manufacturing in China for one or two days for national holidays, you can see the difference," Bonnie Brooks, president of Lane Crawford department stores in Hong Kong, told me. "We get a couple of sunny days."

The constant pressure to increase productivity has triggered a rise in human-rights violations in textile manufacturing around the world, according to the 2005 "Annual Survey of Trade Union Rights Violations," published by the Belgium-based International Confederation of Free Trade Unions. In Bangladesh, workers at International Knitwear and Apparel who demanded better working conditions were fired, beaten, and told they'd be killed if they joined a union, the report stated. In Cambodia, police armed with guns and electric prods dispersed approximately four hundred protesting workers from a garment factory. In China, police detained cotton factory workers in Shaanxi province for protesting changes in their employment contracts. In China, workers are not required to wear protective gear such as earplugs or helmets when needed. "Foreign employers in the industrial zones, mainly textile groups from South Africa, Hong Kong and Taiwan, pay wages below the statutory minimum, refuse to pay sickness benefits and make unilateral deductions from their employees' pay packets," the study said. "The authorities turn a blind eye to these infringements."

Recently, China has come under fire from human-rights and labor organizations for child labor practices. Though the legal working age in China is sixteen, children as young as eleven or twelve from poor families easily find work in factories, since they are cheaper to employ than skilled workers. Often Chinese children are forced to seek out work because their families cannot afford to send them to public school. Students at public schools in China regularly pay for their books, food, boarding, and transportation, all of which can cost up to $125 a year—the equivalent of two months of factory wages and more than some farmers make in a year. But that is slated to change. The Chinese government recently instituted a reform to largely eliminate school fees.

In response to rising costs of manufacturing in China, brands are moving production to new cheap-labor markets such as Vietnam and Cambodia. "Chinese factories are coming here more and more," said

Chinese manufacturer Chen Guohui at his factory on the outskirts of Hanoi. "Labor costs are 25 to 30 percent lower than in China." His workers earn approximately $60 a month. While in Hong Kong, I heard from a highly placed source at a well-known luxury brand that the company had begun to produce some of its knitwear in Vietnam. As Mookeshwarsing Gopal in Mauritius told me, "The textile industry has a nomadic nature and requires cheap and abundant labor."

Meanwhile, the Chinese are moving into ownership. In addition to Hong Kong manufacturer Kenneth Fang buying Pringle in 2000, Tai-wanese media magnate Shaw-Lan Wang bought the century-old French couture house Lanvin in 2001, YGM Trading Limited of Hong Kong picked up French couture house Guy Laroche in 2004, and Singaporean businessman Cheng Wai Keung owns the venerable 235-year-old Savile Row tailor Gieves & Hawkes. Chinese entrepreneur Silas Chou is co-owner of both the esteemed British jeweler Asprey and the American luxury sportswear label Michael Kors.

And Chinese manufacturers are looking to acquire textile mills in Italy, many of which are in financial trouble due to cheap labor in China. The manufacturers hope to take over established brands, set up joint ventures to launch new brands, and distribute Italian labels in China. "China is no longer content with producing goods—it wants to go to the next level, to share brand vision, to be part of a distribution plan and bring added value to a project," said Alfredo Canessa, chair-man of Ballantyne, the classic Scottish cashmere knitwear company now based in Milan, which is launching a new brand called Chinese Cashmere Company in a joint venture with the Hong Kong–based company Fenix. "We want to be part of this scenario, if and when China will no longer be a low-cost manufacturing country."

PART THREE

CHAPTER EIGHT

GOING MASS

"If you would abolish avarice, you must abolish its mother, luxury."

—CICERO

OUTSIDE IT WAS 110 in the shade. But inside the Esplanade shopping mall at the Wynn Las Vegas hotel and resort on a July afternoon in 2005, it was as cool and dry as a martini, and just as satisfying. Middle-aged Americans in T-shirts and shorts flip-flopped their way down the arcade's colorful Jacques Garcia carpet, sightseeing. They nipped into Louis Vuitton and Dior to check out the bags and scarfed down free chocolates at Frederic Robert. They snapped pictures of each other in front of Cartier, ogled dresses at Oscar de la Renta, and pawed Manolo Blahnik's towering gold sandals. Some bought, primarily small items like Vuitton credit card holders and Chanel perfume. Most looked.

Like Kris Stewart, an administrator at Miami University in Oxford, Ohio, and her sister Kathy Sorenson, a human resources executive for

Sonoco Products Corporation in Long Beach, California—a couple of nice, average, forty-something white women on holiday in Vegas shopping for "something special" for friends with birthdays coming up. They hadn't found anything by the time I met them in front of Jean-Paul Gaultier's store, but they were enjoying the tour. "We don't normally have an opportunity to stroll through these stores—we don't get to go to New York all the time," Stewart told me. "We have none of these shops in Oxford. No Chanel and Dior in Cincinnati. You see ads for the brands, so it's nice to actually see the products."

Las Vegas has always been America's everyman town. Back in the 1880s, miners set out from there, hoping to strike it rich. In the 1950s, it was the epicenter of postwar decadence: the showgirls, the mob, the Rat Pack. In the early 1990s, it improbably became a family vacation destination, with the Disneyfication of the famed Strip adding pirate ship battles and roller-coaster rides. And today, it has morphed again, into a luxury vacation resort with world-class restaurants, art museums, spas, and golf courses—and the greatest shopping in the United States. In the early 1990s, "shopping wasn't even on the charts" of how tourists passed their time in Las Vegas, says Maureen Crampton, marketing director for the Forum Shops at Caesars Palace, home of 150 "specialty shops" including Louis Vuitton, Gucci, Pucci, and Dior. By 2006, shopping was the third most popular activity, after gambling and entertainment. In fact, the Forum Shops at Caesars receive more visitors each year than Disney World.

Because of its unrelenting flow of visitors—more than thirty-five million annually, most of whom, like Stewart and Sorenson, come simply to indulge—Las Vegas has become vitally important market for the luxury fashion business. Bernard Arnault visited the Louis Vuitton and Dior stores in the Esplanade four times in the first ninety days Wynn Las Vegas was open. "Las Vegas stores are always high in performance per square foot—first, second or third best [in the United States]," says Elaine Wynn, the wife of the Vegas impresario Steve Wynn, and a member of the board of directors of Wynn Resorts.

Vegas offers everything that luxury executives dream of: space, the traffic, the favorable demographics. "It's really a broad cross-section of people," Marla Sabo, former president and chief operating officer for Christian Dior Inc., North America, told me. "We see good clients from L.A. who visit for the weekend, then you have someone walk in who comes from someplace where we don't have distribution, and then you'll have someone who has won a fortune at the gaming tables and is looking for a place to spend it. And you know the Asian clientele has really taken off in the last couple of years. Now there are nonstops from Japan to Vegas. Because of this, we can see what works and what doesn't work . . . and to get your brand image across to that many people is an incredible gift. Vegas is exposure."

In the old days, when European luxury brands expanded to the United States, they primarily sold their goods in fine department stores in New York, Los Angeles, Philadelphia, and Chicago—cities with industrialist and entertainment fortunes and a vibrant social life. Back then, there was still a strict class structure in the United States. Luxury merchants, be it Bergdorf Goodman in New York or the local fine jeweler or silversmith in a smaller city, were considered the domain of the rich, a frontier that the middle class didn't dare cross. "We don't belong there," mothers would whisper to their daughters.

The barriers came crashing down with the civil rights movement and social upheaval of the 1960s. Not only did blacks have the right to enter establishments once reserved solely for whites, the middle class could emulate the wealthy, including patronizing their finest addresses, without fear of admonishment or ridicule. America's dream of a capitalist democracy was finally fully realized: nothing was off limits to anyone anymore.

Luxury executives responded to America's social and economic liberalization conservatively by opening boutiques in New York and Beverly Hills and expanding their product lines in department stores to include lower-priced items such as scarves, ties, perfumes, and handbags. Old European luxury firms were still small, family-run affairs.

Growth was not the top priority. After all, business was good, the families lived well, and no one worked too hard. What more did one need?

But in the 1980s, when growth became not merely a priority but the sole objective, and Japan had proved that luxury brand products could sell very big overseas, the tycoons turned their sights onto a new target: the middle market. And the biggest, wealthiest, most fluid middle market in the world was the United States. The question was: Where to start? Luxury had to find a place that had an abundant number of customers, didn't diminish the perceived status of the brand, and wouldn't cost a fortune if the store flopped. Las Vegas was the logical choice. It had buffed itself up, was growing exponentially, and, most important, was perhaps the lone place in America—and maybe the world—where the have-nots lived, if only for a few days, like the haves.

Las Vegas was in a sense the metropolitan equivalent of corporate luxury. Since nearly its inception, Las Vegas has hawked the dream of wealth, with Lady Luck as its conduit. But it's all a mirage. The sole objective for both Las Vegas and today's luxury brands is to take your money. It was only a matter of time until the two converged.

"As funky and tawdry as Las Vegas has been in the past, people come here and feel they can indulge themselves in personal pursuits of pleasure," Elaine Wynn explained. "Maybe they aren't the greatest gamblers, and maybe they can only play slots, but, boy, do they know how to shop. And it's a heightened experience here because it's judgment-free. No one is looking over their shoulder telling them they shouldn't be spending their money on this or that way. When they come here they are released from all those inhibitions, and it created a wonderful opportunity for retail."

IN THE UNITED STATES, President Ronald Reagan's tax breaks and the rising stock market kicked off the transformation of the middle class into the middle market. The Internet boom of the 1990s bolstered it that much more. America Online, in Dulles, Virginia, for example, had an estimated three thousand millionaires on staff in 1999. All this new money and spending power changed the American Dream: average Americans were no longer content being average. According to a University of Florida study in 1991, 85 percent of those surveyed aspired to be among the wealthiest 18 percent of American households, writes Juliet B. Schor, author of *The Overspent American: Why We Want What We Don't Need*. Only the remaining 15 percent said they would be content being "middle class." In a 1986 Roper Center poll, average Americans claimed to need $50,000 to fulfill their dreams. By 1994, it was $102,000.

Social priorities changed, too. According to a Roper Center study in 1975, a lot of Americans thought "the good life" meant a happy marriage, one or more children, an interesting job, and a home, reports Schor. By 1991, many of responses were more materialistic: "a lot of money," "a second car," "a second color TV," "a vacation home," "a swimming pool," and "really nice clothes."

Since 1970, real household income in America has risen by 30 percent; one-fourth of American households have an annual income of more than $75,000. By 2005, four million American households had a net worth of more than $1 million. What have Americans done with all that money? Gone shopping. Between 1979 and 1995, the average American's spending increased by at least 30 percent and up to 70 percent. And it was deeply satisfying: According to a 1997 study, 41 percent of Americans between the ages of twenty-two and sixty-one declared that shopping made them "feel good." To pay for it all, Americans went profoundly into debt. Between 1990 and 1996, credit card debt doubled; by 1997, American household debt was $5.5 trillion, Schor reports. Yet it wasn't enough: 27 percent of all American households with income over $100,000 claimed they couldn't afford to buy everything they needed.

Other industrialized nations have seen a similar trend, though not to the same extent. In the United Kingdom, disposable income has increased by 88 percent in real terms in the last twenty years. In Italy it increased fourfold from the 1970s to 2000, and in France nearly five times. Like Americans, Europeans went shopping, and they bought nice stuff. In 2004, nearly half the U.K. population claimed to have purchased as least one luxury product in the last twelve months.

THIS MADE THE luxury tycoons giddy with glee. Just as in Japan, they could roll out their stores across the United States and Europe, fill them with affordable, logo-covered products targeted to this new, shop-happy middle market, and watch their sales—and profits—mount. "[Expansion] was in the air and needed to be addressed," Tom Ford told me in 2006 about Gucci's expansion into the middle market in the 1990s. "Had we not done it, someone else would have."

Luxury brand executives applied their couture pyramid model to their retail expansion. First, they opened gleaming flagships in such cosmopolitan capitals as New York, Paris, Milan, London, and Beverly Hills to set the tone. They were big stores that contained the entire collection, from couture gowns to key rings, and were staffed with both the snooty salesclerks who knew the old-money regulars and friendlier sorts who could help the new middle-market customers. Like the couture shows in Paris and the made-to-order leather ateliers, the flagships—with their polished mahogany counters, plush carpeting, contemporary art, or antique decorated salons—reaffirmed the marketing departments' well-crafted image of luxury, reinforced the companies' brand power, and seduced legions of new followers from every economic level. Armani's flagship on Rodeo Drive, for example, draws hundreds of customers every day, from movie stars looking for something new to middle-market tourists who visit it like a museum.

The tourists may not fork out $3,000 for a suit then and there, but chances are when they get back to their hometown, they'll hit the lower-priced A/X or Armani jeans stores and buy into the dream.

Luxury brands clumped together on what were once streets filled with local merchants—Bond Street in London, Via Condotti in Rome, Rodeo Drive, and Madison Avenue—thereby changing the landscape and the local economics, in a sense creating luxury ghettos. In part the clumping was to draw the customers more easily: they came to see Dior and decided to check out Prada and Gucci, too. But there was also a financial consideration. Groups like LVMH, Gucci, and Prada negotiated blocks of real estate for their various brands. If you wanted Vuitton, you'd get Dior and Céline, Givenchy or Loewe, and offer a good price for the lot. "When we look to locate in a shopping mall . . . we define which mall is a luxury mall, because they need all of our brands," Arnault said.

In Beverly Hills the change was dramatic. Real estate value took off. Old local retailers and landowners sold or leased their space for a fortune to the only folks who could afford it: luxury brands. Even Fred Hayman, Mr. Rodeo Drive himself, cashed out. He leased the Giorgio building to Louis Vuitton. (No dummy, Hayman held on to the property.) "It's a very attractive company, an asset to Beverly Hills and certainly to Rodeo Drive," Hayman told me.

From there, the brands decided to roll out to the secondary cities such as Chicago, Miami, Hong Kong, Osaka—and Las Vegas. Vegas was a dream destination, and luxury brands were now in the business of selling dreams. It had the demand, and it didn't have much in the way of luxury retail—only Joseph Magnin, a small family-run boutique next to the Desert Inn, and Neiman Marcus, which had opened in 1981 as an anchor for Fashion Show, the Strip's first shopping mall. At first, Neiman Marcus catered to wealthy locals who had previously done their shopping on Rodeo Drive or during trips to New York. But soon tourists discovered it, in particular career women who were coming to Las Vegas for business and for pleasure and spending their hard-earned money as they pleased.

To tap into this new free-spending demographic, in May 1992 Caesars Palace and Simon Property Group, a major mall developer, opened the first retail mall at a casino. Reproducing ancient Rome, with colorful stucco houses and cobblestone streets, the Forum Shops offered a wide range of retailers from midlevel shops such as Ann Taylor and Caché to luxury brands Louis Vuitton, Gucci, and Bulgari. The target was tourists, plain and simple, and they bit big: the revenue from May to December 1992 was $500 to $700 per square foot—triple the national shopping mall average. By May 1993, it was approaching $1,000 per square foot. Five years later, Caesars inaugurated a thirty-five-shop extension that included the Atlantis show—an hourly Animatronics retelling of the legend of the mythic city, a five-hundred-thousand-gallon saltwater aquarium—and a range of retailers including Niketown, the Cheesecake Factory, and Dolce & Gabbana. They, too, did a bang-up business. Sales were $1,000 to $1,200 per square foot.

Steve Wynn took notice, and when he and his wife Elaine designed Bellagio, their $1.6 billion, 3,025-room luxury resort on the Strip, they decided to include a one-hundred-thousand-square-foot corridor called Via Bellagio, dedicated exclusively to luxury retailing. "We wanted brands that were at Neiman Marcus but didn't have a presence in Las Vegas like they did in Paris or Hong Kong," Elaine Wynn told me. "We started with the big triumvirate—Chanel, Armani, and Gucci—then filled in the blanks, adding Prada, Yves Saint Laurent. Chanel resisted coming. We had to give them a very big pitch. I remember my husband told Arie Kopelman [then president of Chanel Inc.], 'Arie, you think you are doing me a favor but, believe me, we are doing you a favor.' Arie wasn't familiar with the new Las Vegas. But he came to visit and he got it immediately. Armani was ready to go, but everybody was saying, 'Who else is coming? If you get a commitment we'll go.' They didn't want to be in a spotty neighborhood. Though they are competitive, they wanted to be together because that would assure a look. We didn't believe that this was an experiment. Neiman Marcus was already doing a terrific business and we were sure that there was a market to explore. When the audience changes every two and a half days, [business] grows. It was sure bet."

It sure was. For New York jeweler Fred Leighton, the Via Bellagio shop had its highest sales per square foot. "Bellagio kicked up the caliber of shopping in Las Vegas," remembers veteran Las Vegas retailer Terri Monsour. And it proved that luxury retail was a bona fide flourishing business in Las Vegas. In 1999 came the $1.5 billion Venetian hotel-casino with the five-hundred-thousand-square-foot Shoppes, where families glide down an indoor Grand Canal in genuine gondolas past palazzi that house not Casanova or Lord Byron but Burberry and Jimmy Choo. In 2003, Fashion Show completed a $1 billion renovation and expansion, and in 2004, the Forum Shops opened a third, sleek, modern section for sixty luxury retailers, including Harry Winston, Baccarat, Pucci, Kate Spade, and a second Coach store.

In a matter of a few seasons, Las Vegas became the second city in which a brand opened a store, after New York. For some brands, it was first. Christian Lacroix opened its first American store in the Forum Shops in August 2006. Juicy Couture, the California clothing brand that made its reputation by selling luxury velour sweat suits to Madonna and Gwyneth Paltrow, put its first freestanding boutique there, and Versace opened its only Home Collection store there. It was a wise move. With sales of $1,500 per square foot, the Forum Shops did nearly four times more business than the average regional shopping center in 2005, according to the International Council of Shopping Centers, making it one of the most successful in the country.

Since then construction of luxury shopping centers has not abated. The Wynns opened Esplanade with great fanfare on Elaine's sixty-third birthday in April 2005. Next door, Wynn is building Encore, a $1.4 billion hotel-casino, with a ninety-thousand-square-foot shopping mall for luxury brands, including Hermès. Across the street, the Sands Corporation, owner of the Venetian, is constructing a $1.8 billion, three-thousand-room resort called Palazzo, with three hundred thousand square feet of retail space that will include Christian Louboutin, Chloé, and Barneys New York, due to open in 2007. And MGM Mirage is building the $7 billion, sixty-six-acre Project City-Center to open in 2009, with eighty-plus stores that will have "all the major luxury suspects," said William Taubman, chief operating officer of Taubman Centers Inc. "We've come up with a plan that allows us to give the major international brands street frontage and brand identity similar to what they get on the Ginza in Tokyo and New York's Fifth Avenue." Though brands are sure to have several outlets along the Strip when the projects are completed, neither they nor the mall owners are worried about the idea of overexpansion. "People do not go up and down the Strip and comparatively shop," Terri Monsour told me. "They tend to stay close to their hotel."

Shopping in Las Vegas is, like gambling, a two-tiered world. There are hoi polloi, like Kris Stewart and Kathy Sorenson, the tourist sisters I met at the Esplanade, who play small stakes in the casino and cruise the luxury brand mall. For them, shopping in Las Vegas is a treat. The items for sale are far flashier than what they see back home, with lots of glitter and sparkle and not much hemline—all of which reinforce the idea of Las Vegas as a city of luxurious dreams. The stores themselves are much more inviting, with wide mall entrances and not a single menacing doorman to be seen. And the salesclerks are like the dealers in the casinos—they're friendly, and they take the time to educate you about the products; they don't assume that you know. "In New York I feel so uncomfortable walking in a store, like I don't belong there," Stewart explained. "Las Vegas is much more relaxed, casual." In part, that's because the staff can't always size up who's who. "You cannot be judgmental in Las Vegas," says Monsour. "The person in cutoffs and a holey T-shirt can open up a money belt and pull out $100,000 in cash. I've seen it many times." But also there is the great chance that if you don't buy this time, you might the next time you're in town. In its first year, half the customers at Wynn's Esplanade were repeat.

For Big Shoppers—the sorts, says Elaine Wynn, who fly in from far corners of the world and "buy thirteen pairs of Manolo Blahniks at a time"—it's a different experience altogether. Like the high-rolling gamblers—the ones casinos fly in on private jets, house in villas, and cater to attentively—Las Vegas's Big Shoppers get the royal treatment. Usually they call Justine Bach, head of Wynn's Personal Shopping Service, to announce that they are on their way. Bach clears her schedule, then goes to the stores in the Esplanade to pull clothes, shoes, handbags, jewelry, watches—anything and everything the customer might like—that she will either set up in a plush private salon just off the mall or send up to the shopper's room to try on. Sometimes the shopper visits the stores, too, with Bach in tow. There are two seamstresses and a tailor on staff to make immediate alterations because generally the customer wants to wear it *now*. Sometimes Big Shoppers ring down to Vuitton to order a new suitcase (or two or three) for their purchases. Monsour also ships worldwide. The hotel offers other perks to Big Shoppers, such as limousine service to and from the airport. "They are like the people who play baccarat," says Elaine Wynn. "They don't come often, but when they do it's a strong, strong business. So you have to have something available to satisfy their needs." In its first year of business, Esplanade did an astounding $1,800 worth of sales per square foot.

THE EXPANSION was racking up millions in sales and profits and making owners and shareholders extremely happy. But all these new stores created a new problem: unsold merchandise. When luxury brands sold their wares in their one flagship store and a handful of department stores, their inventory was limited. The little bit of ready-to-wear that went unsold was sent to discount chains like Loehmann's, or was burned. Leather goods changed so little that they remained on the shelves season after season.

However, to sell more merchandise and meet the quarterly turnover projections, designers churned out increasingly trendy collections of clothes, handbags, and shoes each season to draw customers more often to the stores. The downside was that the products had a much shorter fashion life span—six months max—before they were displaced by the new collection. And with hundreds of new stores around the world, the volume of leftovers was immense. Executives knew it was bad business to sell the leftovers for a pittance to the discount chains, and watch the Loehmann's and Syms of the world rake in the profits. Burning them and writing off the loss was out of the question; shareholders weren't about to watch their profits go up in smoke.

The answer lay somewhere between Rodeo Drive and the Las Vegas Strip—literally as well as figuratively. Two hours due east of Los Angeles, in the heart of the California desert on the way to Palm Springs, is a shopping center called Desert Hills Premium Outlets, which houses many of the same names you'll find in Beverly Hills—Dior, Prada, Ferragamo, Gucci, and Armani—but sell items at up to 75 percent less. It is part of Chelsea Property Group, a leading developer of more than forty upscale, fashion-oriented outlet centers around the world. When I visited Desert Hills in July 2005, there was a decent-size crowd, considering the sweltering desert temperatures. During the high seasons—October to March—you can wait in a long backup on Interstate 10 just to get into the parking lot. Approximately seven million people shop at Desert Hills each year, a great many who have bought into luxury's marketing of the dream but can't afford luxury goods at full or sale price, as well as those who can but want to get more for their money. "People are so into bargain hunting, and everyone loves luxury brands," Desert Hills general manager Kathy Frederiksen told me. "Customers sit down and look at the map and say, 'Wow! You have that and that!' They get so excited. 'We can buy so much more here with our money.' People leave with trunkfuls of merchandise. They make several trips to the car to load up the trunk."

Outlet shopping is perhaps luxury's greatest ploy to get its goods into the hands of anyone and everyone. "We have shoppers ranging from celebrities who can have it all but love the thrill of the hunt to value-conscious shoppers who aspire to wear these top brands," Chelsea Premium Outlets spokeswoman Michele Horner explained.

But outlet shopping is the antithesis of the flagship, the antithesis, in fact, of luxury itself. "It was jolting to view pieces from Prada's brilliant fall 2004 'extreme romanticism' collection withering on the vine," wrote columnist Karen Heller in the *Philadelphia Inquirer* in 2006 after visiting Woodbury Common Premium Outlets in New York. "The clothes were marked down, picked over and repeatedly pawed, the opposite of how they were originally displayed. Their power to enchant seemed minimized, even at a third the price, smashed together like produce in a storage hold."

Yet in today's luxury industry, outlets make good business sense: they sell goods that the movie stars, the flagships, the ads, and the billboards flack to the masses, but at a price that the masses can actually afford, sometimes in bulk. "The 1980s were all about status and how much you paid for something, but now it's prestigious to say how much you've saved," said Randy Marks, publisher for OutletBound.com, an online guide to outlet shopping. "Outlets are accessible. If you were to go to Rodeo Drive or Madison Avenue, you might be intimidated to walk into Michael Kors stores. But outlets are not as uppity. And retailers like that because they are opening their brands to people who might not get a chance or be willing to walk into a flagship store."

Outlet shopping began in the late nineteenth century as small company stores in factories where employees could buy items—often rejects—at a discount. It remained that way until 1970, when Vanity Fair clothing company opened the first factory outlet center in the United States in the old Berkshire Knitting Mill in Reading, Pennsylvania. It was a clever way to use the space that sat empty after manufacturing moved elsewhere. I remember my mother taking me there from our home outside of Philadelphia when I was a kid. We'd drive up early on Saturday morning, twice a year—spring and fall—to stock up on Vanity Fair brands such as Fruit of the Loom underwear and Lee jeans at a deep discount. The outlet was actually in the factory: mammoth hangar-like workrooms filled with busloads of frantic shoppers rummaging through giant bins of jeans, bras, T-shirts, tube socks, panty hose—the basics—all with defects, large and small. The labels were cut off roughly, leaving the seamed edges, inside and out. We always left with Hefty bags full of new clothes.

By the late 1970s, the entire town had become a giant outlet center. Developers, like Chelsea, saw what happened in Reading, realized that outlet shopping was a burgeoning business and by the mid-1980s, were constructing outlet shopping centers outside of towns across America. Desert Hills Premium Outlets began humbly in 1990 as a strip mall where midrange brands could unload overruns and leftovers. "Though we are in the middle of nowhere," says Kathy Frederiksen, "it was an instant success. It's a day trip from L.A. and Orange County, and we capture residents and tourists from Palm Springs."

As outlet shopping became a legitimate segment of the retail industry, American luxury brands such as Ralph Lauren, Donna Karan, and Oscar de la Renta, and department stores such as Saks—companies that knew the American bargain-hunting mentality well—opened stores at these malls and started sending their leftovers from each season there instead of to discount chains. Several of the brands sold so well that they began to produce less expensive lines to be sold solely in their outlet stores. Their success gave luxury brands from Europe—where outlets were still a foreign concept—the courage to give it a try.

In 1995, Desert Hills built a more highly designed addition. Gucci opened there in 1998, Tod's and Prada in 1999, and Tag Heuer in 2001. In 2002, Desert Hills opened a twenty-five-thousand-square-foot addition with a fancy brick outdoor esplanade lined with handsome storefronts dedicated to what Frederiksen calls "high-end tenants," bringing the total to 130 stores. Ferragamo, Bottega Veneta, Hugo Boss, and Sergio Rossi arrived in November 2002. Yves Saint Laurent came in March 2003, and Dolce & Gabbana in July. Dior opened in late 2004. "We promote the outlets as 25 to 65 percent off full retail price," says Frederiksen, "but a lot of these stores want to move the merchandise, and you can get it for a fraction of what it will cost in the store." Indeed, when I went into the Dior store, I was surprised to see that everything was 25 to 50 percent off full retail price, some items with an additional 75 percent off the reduced price. That meant that sexy lace bustiers cost a mere $25 instead of several hundred dollars. Desert Hills makes the shopping that much more interesting by selling coupon books for $5 that offer further discounts in particular stores.

The luxury brand outlet stores are often done up to look like their regular full-price boutiques, with blond wood floors, chrome-trimmed sales counters, and glass display cases. The salesclerks wear the same uniforms, and hip music is piped in. The stock usually comes from flagship stores around the region—Beverly Hills, Las Vegas, South Coast Plaza in Orange County, California—but it can come from as far away as Hawaii, Hong Kong, or Japan. It can be one month, one season, or a year or two behind. Sometimes the items have a slight flaw or a hem is ripped out or buttons are missing; shoppers must be diligent. "I once got home from the Ferragamo outlet only to find two mismatched silk evening pumps among my purchases," wrote reporter Laura Landrop in the *Wall Street Journal*. But, says Linda Humphers, editor in chief of *Value Retail News,* a monthly trade publication that covers the outlet business, "you will not see any fuchsia sweaters with three arms . . . because today outlet chains understand that is not good business. It's not the quality customers expect. And image is one of the reasons for opening an outlet, so excess goods don't end up [at a discounter] where goods are jammed together."

As a result, the array of goods at luxury brand outlets is choice. When I went into the Yves Saint Laurent shop in July 2005, it was as if I had stepped into a Best of Tom Ford store. Suits, shirts, dresses, gowns, and shoes from all four of his Rive Gauche collections from 2002 to 2004 were on the racks, and Ford's fashion shows played on a video screen, though he hadn't been with the company for more than a year. "They do a lot of sales by phone," Frederiksen tells me. "People call and then Saint Laurent ships it." At the Versace boutique a woman picked up a black leather gown that an A-list actress had worn to the Oscars and returned to the company. Some brands use outlets as their primary sales venue for more middle-market areas. Burberry, for example, had a dozen outlets in the United States in 2005, including a new one about forty miles outside Seattle. At the time, it was the only freestanding Burberry store in the entire state of Washington.

Desert Hills gets about 100 to 150 bus tours a month—80 percent are Japanese, and 10 percent come from other Asian countries. Bus tours originate out of Los Angeles, arrive at 10:00 a.m. and depart at 3:00 p.m., giving the customers five hours of concentrated shopping. Desert Hills has a Japanese-speaking customer relations representative, and several of the stores have Japanese-speaking sales associates. There are Japanese restaurants at the mall, too. But the average outlet center customer in the United States, according to OutletBound.com, is a forty-three-year-old white female with an annual income of

$50,000 or more. The reason for this, Humphers told me, is a mix of culture and marketing. "Men in the U.S. don't shop—90 percent of men's clothing is bought by women," she said. Furthermore, "outlet prices, while bargains, are still higher than those found in discount and off-price stores," she said, and that demographic is "the most targeted in marketing programs."

Desert Hills visits increased with the opening of the Morongo Casino Resort and Spa down the road in late 2004. Desert Hills does what it can to buff up the shopping experience: it has a VIP Shopper Club that allows shoppers to download exclusive savings offers from merchants, and in 2005 introduced Chop n' Shop, a helicopter service from Los Angeles to Desert Hills, for $770 per person. Each store has its perks too: good customers get e-mails and phone calls when new merchandise arrives, and customers can request to be notified when specific items come in. "The winning formula is to build a center big enough to keep out the competition, that's close to a major metropolitan area so it attracts local shoppers ten times a year instead of the four or five times a year they used to," said Humphers.

In the United States, luxury outlet malls are expanding. Las Vegas Premium Outlets is adding some 30 new stores to its 120-tenant list. In the rest of the world, outlet shopping is just taking off. Former Washington, D.C., real estate developer J. W. Kaempfer brought the notion of outlet malls to Europe in the early 1990s. Today his firm, McArthur-Glen, is the largest outlet mall developer there: its sixteen Designer Outlet malls, located in such former industrial towns as Troyes and Roubaix in France; Ashford, England; and just outside Florence, Italy, draw fifty million shoppers each year to such luxury brand outlets as Armani, Bulgari, Dolce & Gabbana, Hugo Boss, Prada, Roberto Cavalli, and Salvatore Ferragamo. Chelsea Premium Outlets has opened one mall in Mexico City and four in Japan. David Simon, CEO of Simon Property Group, the owners of Chelsea Premium Outlets, said in 2006 that it was building a premium outlets mall in Korea. And he added, "We believe in China."

WHILE MUCH of luxury's expansion to the middle market was created by the machinations of executives in corporate offices, the idea for luxury's newest and most promising retail avenue was, like so many great inventions, discovered by accident by an outsider. In 1998, freelance fashion editor Natalie Massenet told then–*Sunday Times Magazine* fashion director Isabella Blow that she wanted to produce an Edwardian-themed fashion shoot. The ever-creative Blow had one suggestion: "Think porcelain." Massenet went home that evening, sat down at her husband's computer, and for the first time surfed the Web, in search of Edwardian porcelain that might inspire her. Instead, she found something else: the endless possibilities of the Internet. "It was a mind explosion for me," Massenet told me over breakfast at the Westin in Paris in 2006.

How, she wondered, could she apply this to the world of luxury brands? Suddenly, the answer was obvious: online shopping, she said, was the "next logical step in the evolution" of luxury retailing. Before luxury e-tailing, she told me, "you had the whole media machine telling you what you needed to have, and then you had to travel to a city center to buy it. You had women in the Middle East who took shopping trips to London and Paris twice a year, women in the country going to the city." Wouldn't it be fantastic, Massenet thought, if they could order the luxury brand items they wanted from the comfort of their home and have them delivered in a matter of days? Wouldn't that be a true luxury?

Massenet, a pretty brunette who could pass for Sandra Bullock, immediately got to work on a business plan. Her idea: to do an online fashion magazine where you could buy the items you read about with a click of the mouse. She called it Net-a-Porter.com and describes it as "merchantainment—the convergence of impulse and media." Her plan was to hire buyers who would go to showrooms and order clothes at wholesale that she would sell for full-retail price online, just like a department store. To give the site more depth and hook interest, it would be set up like a Web magazine, with articles that "tell readers what makes the items for sale so special," she said. "You have to keep the magic. If you reduce it to a garment, you are missing the point of what that garment is about. It becomes a generic item."

Though new to the Internet, Massenet knew all about fashion and marketing. Born Natalie Rooney in L.A., the only child of a foreign correspondent-turned-film-flack and a Chanel showroom model, she was raised in Paris, studied English at UCLA, and worked as a film production assistant. In 1990, at twenty-five, she landed her first fashion job, as a stylist for a friend's fashion production company in Los Angeles. In 1993, she joined *Women's Wear Daily* as West Coast fashion editor, where she did styling and reporting, and covered events including the Academy Awards. In 1995, she met Arnaud Massenet, an investment banker based in London. She left *Women's Wear,* moved to London and married him, and became senior fashion editor for *Tatler,* a glossy women's fashion magazine, where she says she "learned about the high-fashion consumer." She went freelance in 1998, and began to work with Isabella Blow at the *Times.*

To get her Net-a-Porter idea going, Massenet called on designers she had worked with while at *Tatler* and the *Times* to ask if they'd participate. Among the first to sign on were London-based companies Jimmy Choo, Burberry, Matthew Williamson, and Anya Hindmarch. Once Massenet compiled a list of about thirty-five, she started looking for investors. It wasn't easy. "We didn't have a broad appeal to the investment community because we had a business plan that showed realistic sales projections and didn't show a public listing in six months," she told me.

Instead, she pulled together just over $1 million in start-up capital from friends and family in three months and sublet a quaint artist's studio in Chelsea, where the Chelsea Art School had been founded. "It had a beautiful studio room with a mezzanine where we kept the Jimmy Choo shoes and packaging, and one of the bedrooms was our stock room and the other the packing room," she remembered. There were five on staff. "We were a lean machine," she says.

Yet the luxury industry was averse to online retailing. Despite their rabid expansion in such middle-market retail spots as Las Vegas and far-flung outlet malls, luxury executives deemed Internet retail tacky. "The luxury industry couldn't get their heads around the idea that a three-dimensional retail experience they had spent years perfecting could be reproduced in two dimensions, so instead they stuck their heads in the sand," said Marc Cohen, director of Ledbury Research, a consulting firm that focuses on wealthy consumers.

And then there was the Boo.com fiasco. In the late 1990s, a trio of Swedish entrepreneurs jumped into the Internet start-up frenzy with a trendy sportswear e-tailer they called Boo.com. Boo got loads of press in such influential business titles as *Forbes* and the *Financial Times* and had impressive backers, including Bernard Arnault. Surprisingly, Arnault is a bit of a computer nerd who reportedly spends much of his free time surfing the Web. In the late 1990s, he put €500 million of his own money in an investment fund called Europ@web that backed various start-ups, including the online auction house QXL, the French search engine Nomade, and the music e-tailer Peoplesound.com.

But Boo was a badly managed company. It ran a huge overhead—its plush offices in London, New York, and Paris held 420 employees, an enormous number for a start-up. The founders lived large, flying on private jets or on the Concorde, traveling by limo, staying at hip four-star hotels. They had a $42 million marketing budget that they used on such follies as announcing their May 1999, launch on billboards across Europe and Scandinavia and hiring award-winning video director

Roman Coppola to make their television commercials. When they finally launched Boo.com, six months late and seven weeks before Christmas, it was a technical failure: fewer than 25 percent of attempts to access the site were successful. And it was a financial disaster: the company burned through an impressive $7 million a month. At its best, Boo made $1.1 million a month. Backers withdrew their support. There were layoffs, including the chief financial officer. Finally, in May 2000—just six months after it launched—Boo.com shut down and was liquidated. The founders had gone through $135 million in two years.

The Boo implosion didn't drive Arnault away from Internet retailing or teach him what mistakes to avoid when launching a site. *Au contraire*. He poured more than $100 million—from his personal Europ@web fund and LVMH—into eLuxury.com, a San Francisco–based Web site dedicated to showcasing and selling LVMH fashion brands. Arnault's idea was to produce an online version of a luxury department store, with each floor devoted to a different brand. It would sell everything from $20 Dior lipsticks to $20,000 Vuitton trunks, all wrapped beautifully in hard boxes with tissue paper and shipped from a warehouse in Memphis, Tennessee, where FedEx's worldwide distribution hub is located.

To get customers to return to the site regularly, Arnault and his team came up with the same idea as Massenet: an Internet fashion and lifestyle magazine that would be informative as well as highlight the brands available. Like the retail side, the webzine would be high-gloss—the online equivalent to *Vogue*. The eLuxury site hired top editors and journalists away from such prestigious titles as *Conde Nast Traveler, In Style,* and *Food & Wine* to create and write the content. No expense was spared. "We'd write articles like 'Celebrity Beauty Secrets' or 'Hot Spas' and to do it they'd send you some place for ten days, put you up at the best hotel, and pay for you to take in all the best restaurants, spas—everything," remembers one of eLuxury's original writers. "The amount of money they spent was dizzying."

ELuxury launched in June 2000—a month after the Boo.com flame-out and about the same time as a handful of other sites, including LuxLook.com, LuxuryFinder.com, and Net-a-Porter. Compared to the others, eLuxury was a monolith. "ELuxury launched a week after we did and I thought at the time, 'I have one week to make it, then this hugely funded machine will take over,'" Massenet remembers with a laugh.

Actually, it didn't work out that way. Though luxury online shopping made perfect sense—it appealed to wealthy customers who knew the products and wanted the ease of ordering from home, and it attracted a new middle-market clientele that had coveted the items but either didn't have access to or felt intimidated in the stores—it took a while to get going. "The market was nonexistent," says Massenet. "We had to create it." Not all the sites survived. Both LuxLook.com and LuxuryFinder.com went under in 2001; eLuxury acquired their URLs and customer databases. And eLuxury had its problems, too. Like Boo before it, the company ran far too high an overhead and was hemorrhaging money. Soon it began to make substantial cuts in the luxury side of its offerings: the fancy packaging disappeared, customers had to pay for return shipping, the editorial content started to shrink. "I remember in 2001 every time I attended an editorial meeting, there'd be one less person," one writer told me. In 2002, the magazine was completely phased out and only the e-tailing remained.

Only Net-a-Porter flourished. "Since we were small, we grew with the market," Massenet explained. Her overhead was tight, her staff top-notch: her main buyer, Sojin Lee, had worked for Bottega Veneta and Chanel before joining Net-a-Porter. The articles on the Web site were informative, the delivery time was fast—same day in London and within seventy-two hours around the world—and service was impeccable. "We don't just stuff the items in a Jiffy bag and send them out," Massenet explained. "The girls iron the white cloth bags, and stuff the sleeves with tissue paper. We use handmade, noncollapsible boxes. We knew that we could devalue brands by offering online without all the perks you get when you go shopping. We had to make Net-a-Porter more compelling than what you get in a store."

The company's advertising consisted chiefly of word of mouth and editorial mentions. "*Vogue* called us the chicest new boutique in the world," Massenet says proudly. With the rise of Google and other search engines, and affiliate Web sites like Vogue.co.uk and Vogue.de, Net-a-Porter's exposure grew. Business nearly doubled every year, and the number of new clients increased exponentially each month. To keep up, Massenet had to do "emergency fund-raising" six or seven times. "If we'd only had a few of Boo.com's millions," she says with a laugh.

In 2002, Net-a-Porter landed its retail angel. Chloé CEO Ralph Toledano agreed to let Net-a-Porter sell Chloé accessories. It was a real coup: Chloé's parent, Richemont, generally shied away from on-line retailing. Massenet bought fifty Bracelet handbags, which retailed at $1,000 a pop. Within three weeks, Net-a-Porter had a waiting list of two thousand for the bags. Toledano was so pleased with Net-a-Porter's results that he made the site Chloé's official online store. In 2004, Net-a-Porter did about $22 million in sales and posted its first profit. It's been earning a profit ever since, and sales are still doubling each year. By 2006, it did was doing about $70 million in sales.

In 2006, Net-a-Porter featured about 150 brands, including LVMH's Fendi, Céline, and Pucci. Massenet has carried Givenchy in the past and was currently looking at Dior. When I asked how she managed to have LVMH brands that are also available on eLuxury, she said, "We have a retail relationship with the individual brands and the individual management teams at those brands. Although we have positive relationships with each of the groups—Richemont, LVMH, Gucci Group—the decisions to go online with us are made at the brand level."

In August 2006, Net-a-Porter opened a fifty-thousand-sqare-foot warehouse U.S. distribution center in Long Island City, New York, eliminating the duty and taxes U.S. customers paid when orders were shipped from London, and speeding up delivery. Central Manhattan residents get same-day service; the rest of the United States receives orders within two days. By 2006, the company was attracting a hundred new customers a day from 110 countries and the average order totaled $850. Today Massenet's customers range from jet-set socialites to average middle-market consumers. The largest number—43 percent—are in the United Kingdom. North America accounts for 27 percent, continental Europe 15 percent, the Far East 8 percent, and the Middle East 7 percent. Surprisingly, ready-to-wear is the best-selling category. "Everyone thought it would be bags and shoes," Massenet explains. Clients regularly scan designer collections on Style.com and zap e-mails to Net-a-Porter requesting that the buyers select specific items. Net-a-Porter also alerts clients via e-mail about hot new arrivals. For many brands, Net-a-Porter sells more at full price than most department stores, which means more profit for the brands. Massenet's operations are still lean: she only has 250 employees, and does little advertising—primarily online banner ads. Massenet herself is perhaps the company's best publicity. A woman with great style and radiant beauty, she regularly poses for magazine fashion spreads, with Net-a-Porter plugged in the captions. When I met her, she was dressed in a white Chloé pencil skirt and black tee, a thin chocolate brown Céline cardigan, and Marni heels—"all from Net-a-Porter," she said proudly.

Net-a-Porter's success has finally removed the stigma of the e-tailing business for luxury executives. Since 2005, Louis Vuitton and Christian Dior have opened online boutiques in France, Germany, and the United Kingdom. (In the United States, the sites link to eLuxury.com.) Hermès launched its online retailing in 2002 in the United States and in 2005 in France to hawk its basics such as scarves, pocket squares, bracelets, and perfumes. Gucci Group began selling Gucci accessories online in 2003 and Bottega Veneta in 2005. And just in time. Forrester Research, an Internet research company based in Cambridge, Massachusetts, stated in a November 2005 study that thirty-nine million Europeans were buying clothing online and predicted that figure would double to seventy-three million by 2009, bringing the online share of total apparel sales to 18 percent. Analysts believe that online apparel sales in the United States will reach about $14 billion by 2009, making it more than computers and electronics. In 2005, online sales of jewelry and luxury goods in the United States rose by 31 percent. Furthermore, Forrester reported that in Europe, "for each euro of clothing sold online, an additional three euros of offline sales will be net-influenced," and concluded that luxury brands now "have no choice but to provide an online sales channel."

For Massenet, the future of online luxury retailing is what she calls "mass personalization"—essentially online couture. "Say you like that gray dress but you want it in red," she says. "We'll have it manufactured in red and deliver it to you. When you have a thousand women who want it in red, it becomes a viable business." The idea, she says, is "to offer customers exactly what they want. I think we will achieve that in the next five years."

While her method is new, Massenet's idea is quite old-fashioned: Net-a-Porter is a modern version of the classic department store. She has also proved a basic principle in luxury merchandising: a third-party retailer can reach out to the middle market and make a killing without hurting its reputation because it is simply a conduit and it sells a limited amount of items, giving both the store and the luxury brand the appearance of exclusivity. When luxury brands themselves go mass-market, however—selling a full range of goods in ubiquitous boutiques, outlets and duty-free stores and on their own Web sites—they undermine their well-crafted message. They become an everyday occurrence, a common presence. They aren't a luxury anymore.

OF COURSE, reaching out to the average consumer, hawking the dream, creating "democratic luxury" as Burberry's now-retired CEO

Rose Marie Bravo trumpeted in the late 1990s, was great for business. But going mass-market has had its drawbacks, too.

The most obvious is theft, known euphemistically in the business as shrinkage, and by carrying more stock in more places, luxury brands have made themselves increasingly vulnerable to it. The primary culprits are company employees, according to the National Retail Security Survey, conducted annually by the University of Florida. Garden-variety shoplifters who stash items in their coats or purses and slip out the door are still a problem, too. Luxury's most famous amateur shoplifting bust was in 2001, when twenty-nine-year-old movie star Winona Ryder was caught trying to steal $5,500 worth of merchandise at Saks Fifth Avenue in Beverly Hills, including a Gucci dress, a Dolce & Gabbana bag, and a Marc Jacobs top. She received three years of probation, a $10,000 fine, and 480 hours of community service.

That sort of theft is manageable: brands can simply add more security cameras and guards. What's become difficult is the dramatic rise in theft-to-order of luxury brand goods. "It's not normal shoplifting anymore, where they're stealing one or two items," said Joe Morrash, a detective with the stolen-property task force of the Alexandria, Virginia, police department. "They're stealing in volume and selling to fences and underground boutiques." Some capers are for-hire by private clients. In Minnesota, a dentist paid a professional thief to shoplift $250,000 worth of Baccarat, Chanel, and other luxury brand items. He was caught when, upon discovering that the loot included the wrong brand men's suits, he sent the thief back to steal Armani.

But a lot are staged by organized rings, many from Latin America. They move from New York to Washington to Chicago and steal in volume to supply boutiques elsewhere. They make off with a lot quickly. Andrew McColl, a Washington-based agent for the Federal Bureau of Investigation, arrested a thief taking $100,000 worth of items from the Tysons Corner mall in northern Virginia. At times, robberies can get dangerous: the Versace boutique in Boston was held up by two armed bandits, who attempted to make off with $750,000 worth of watches and jewelry before being caught. One of the gunmen struck an employee in the face with a .38 handgun, causing a gash that required seventeen stitches.

The pros have their tricks, like lining shopping bags with aluminum foil or duct tape to confound alarms or fleeing via little-watched side entrances. There are "girdle bandits" who slip most anything under their clothing. "One thief I know put a whole mink in a girdle," Gerald Dupree, a retired shoplifter, told the *Times*. Another, he said, "would go into a jewelry counter and, you know they have chains hanging on display racks? She could just lift the chains up all at once and drop them down her sleeves."

They also increasingly steal from the source. Cargo theft—when delivery trucks are jacked—is on the rise. And thieves routinely break into luxury brand showrooms and fashion magazine storage closets to steal samples. "They obviously had good taste," *Nylon* magazine's fashion director Michael Carl said after thieves swiped fifteen pieces of Prada and Chanel from the magazine's offices in 2004. "They systematically went through and picked out the nicest clothes."

Another problem luxury has faced from going mass-market has been attracting less-than-desirable customers and fans. Not all brands are thrilled with the sort of fervor their advertising, celebrity dressing, and retail expansion has created. Like Burberry—despite Rose Marie Bravo's "luxury for everyone" rhetoric. In Britain a few years ago, a working-class subculture emerged called Chavs, a term derived from the Romany travelers' word *chavi*, meaning "child." Young and usually with only a high school education, Chavs hang out at small-town shopping centers, smoke cigarettes, and intimidate passersby. Their uniform is a baggy tracksuit, clunky gold jewelry, and anything and everything with the Burberry check, much to the chagrin of Burberry executives. Chavs are "the same kind of slightly disenfranchised suburban kids" as punks were a generation ago, Lucian James, a brand consultant in San Francisco, told the *New York Times Magazine.* "In the same way in the 70s [punks] would sort of [snort] glue, now [Chavs] are all just sitting at McDonald's wearing Burberry hats." They are proud of their Chavness and have their own set of celebrity idols, the tops being Victoria Beckham, former Spice Girl and wife of soccer star David Beckham, and Daniella Westbrook, a working-class British TV actress who starred in the popular soap *EastEnders.* Westbrook was named the Queen of Chavs when she was snapped shopping in London dressed head-to-toe in Burberry check and pushing her Burberry check–clad baby in a Burberry check stroller. The Chavs became most obsessed with the Burberry check baseball cap. When Burberry stopped producing the caps, Chavs started buying counterfeit versions.

In the United States, the rap subculture, with its obsession for bling, embraced luxury's logo-ridden products, promoting brands in songs, onstage, or in music videos. They also began splurging on the clothes, jewelry, and handbags in very public shopping sprees. As Kanye West rapped, "I'm Kon, the Louis Vuitton Don. Bought my mom a purse, now she Louis Vuitton Mom." It shouldn't have been a surprise to luxury brands, since they created the obsession through design as well as marketing. Back in the early 1980s, at the nascence of the hip-hop movement, street kids in Harlem and the Bronx took the logos of Gucci, Dior, Louis Vuitton, and Chanel—back then very conservative brands for bourgeois white ladies—printed them on T-shirts, sweatpants, and baseball caps, oversized and in loud colors, and showed up at hip-hop clubs or on street corners garbed up in these spoofs. "Everything was very cartoon," says Kim Hastreiter, co-editor of *Paper,* the New York–based avant-garde pop culture magazine. "What a great way to devalue status. It wasn't bling. It was taking white status and taking the air out of it."

In the end, luxury picked up on the trend. In the early 1990s, Chanel designer Karl Lagerfeld used the house's double-C logo in the same way the ghetto kids did—dangling it from necklaces, hanging it from chain belts, stamping it on everything. Designers Marc Jacobs at Louis Vuitton, Tom Ford at Gucci, and John Galliano at Christian Dior incorporated this street take on old luxury into their work. As Kim Hastreiter and David Hershkovits recall in their book 20 *Years of Style: The World According to* Paper, "Ford immediately produced superfly coats, suits, hats, shirts and bags, all covered in the traditional Gucci-logo fabric."

And who became their best customers? The new superrich hip-hop stars such as Sean "P. Diddy" Combs, Jennifer Lopez, and Beyoncé Knowles, decking themselves out in Fendi furs, Fred Leighton diamonds, and anything with a Dior, Chanel, Gucci, or Vuitton logo on it. Logos—particularly luxury brand logos—represent "all the shit we don't have," said Def Jam Records founder Russell Simmons. "We're not ripped-dungarees-rock-n-roll-alternative-culture people. We want to buy into the shit we see on television but we want to put our own twist on it. Part of the fantasy of fashion is about being successful. It's aspirational. I put this on, I'm getting laid. Not because I'm cool and raggedy but because I'm cool and clean. Because I want to buy into this culture."

Some brands embrace the bling obsession. Gianni Versace once boasted that rapper Tupac Shakur "wore Versace on the day he walked into prison *and* on the day he walked out of prison." Dolce & Gabbana dressed Mary J. Blige for a concert tour, and, in 2005, Louis Vuitton hired hip-hop star Pharrell Williams to design its new sunglasses line. Some cringe silently and ring up the sales. And some speak out. "What can we do?" asked Frédéric Rouzaud, head of Louis Roederer, the last major family-owned champagne house and the makers of the top-of-the-line Cristal, which rappers swig, as well as sing about, often. "We can't forbid people from buying it. I'm sure Dom Pérignon or Krug"—both owned by LVMH—"would be delighted to have their business." In response to this apparent diss, rapper Jay-Z, CEO of Def Jam, took

Cristal off the wine list at his clubs in New York and Atlantic City and vowed to change the lyrics in the half-dozen songs in which he references the bubbly. "I view his comments as racist and will no longer support any of his products through any of my various brands," the rap star declared.

Perhaps the greatest problem luxury brands have created for their companies by going mass, banking analysts say, is financial instability. Before its global expansion to the middle market, luxury was immune to economic cycles. The companies were small and catered to a limited old-money clientele who were rich enough not to be affected by short-term drops in the stock market or economic downturns, and who shopped consistently and bought well. Luxury was a successful niche business. But when luxury changed its target audience to the cost-conscious middle market that shops when flush but stops cold when times get tough, it made itself dangerously vulnerable to recessions—as the industry would soon find out.

In the mid-1990s, luxury brand executives saw the Asian economic tiger as a hungry, deep-pocketed new customer base. "Anybody who had a name or wanted to make a name moved into Asia," Giancarlo Giammetti, then managing director of Valentino, told me. "If you opened one store, the next thing you knew, you opened five." Gucci had seven outlets in Hong Kong in 1998, three within a six-block radius. Prada had nine. New York City, in contrast, had just one Gucci and two Prada shops. It was inevitable that "these companies were going to get killed because of their overcapacity" in Asia, said Joanne Ooi, president of East from Seventh Ltd., a wholesale showroom in Hong Kong for Western designers trying to break into the Asian market. "Without tourism, Hong Kong is only a city of six million inhabitants. How is it going to support nine Prada stores?"

But in July 1997, Thailand's currency collapsed, triggering a two-year-long economic crisis across Eastern Asian, and luxury took a beating. Valentino's Giammetti immediately halted the construction of two Valentino stores in Singapore. Zegna closed three of its four shops in South Korea. Yves Saint Laurent pulled out of Seoul's Galleria department store, and Louis Vuitton shortened store hours in Hong Kong. Gucci's stock plunged a staggering 50 percent in a month. LVMH lost 45 percent of its stock value from July to October. At Hermès, sales in Southeast Asia dropped by 11 percent and its stock fell by 14 percent. "In South Korea," British designer Paul Smith told me, "our business [was] gone, completely. Overnight."

Four years later, the terrorist attacks of September 11, 2001, stopped leisure and business travel cold for weeks and diminished it greatly for two years, causing substantial losses for the luxury industry, which relies greatly on travel shopping. LVMH's net income plunged from €722 million in 2000 to a mere €10 million in 2001. As soon as the industry recuperated from those losses, SARS hit, in effect shutting down Hong Kong, one of its biggest markets in the world, for six weeks. Two years later, the threat of avian flu made luxury executives extremely nervous.

Since luxury has broadened its audience, middle-market brands such as Zara, Gap, H&M, and Banana Republic have taken advantage and moved in next door. "I wonder if Abercrombie being next to Prada on Fifth and Fifty-sixth Street will benefit Prada," mused Joel Isaacs, president of Isaacs & Company, a real estate firm in Manhattan that specializes in luxury retail placement. "From the view of foot traffic, it might. What I do suspect is that Abercrombie will benefit from Prada." This retail integration has turned once-chic shopping streets into tourist attractions and driven luxury brands to look for new, more "insider" addresses, such as the meatpacking and financial districts in New York and Melrose Place in Los Angeles, for big-spending luxury customers. Today there is not one bank, gas station, or drugstore on Rodeo Drive. Instead, there are more than thirty-five luxury brand fashion stores, twenty major jewelers, and a half-dozen high-end art galleries along the fifteen-hundred-foot, three-block retail stretch of

Rodeo Drive. In 2001, fourteen million people visited Rodeo Drive and it was averaging $1 million a day in retail sales. "We don't want to be on Rodeo Drive anymore," says Mario Grauso, president of the Puig Fashion Group, which includes Nina Ricci, Carolina Herrera, and Paco Rabanne. "That's not the shopping experience anymore. You don't want a busload of tourists out front taking pictures."

CHAPTER NINE

FAUX AMIS

"Being copied is the ransom of success."

—COCO CHANEL

$\mathcal{CK}$RIS BUCKNER pulled his gold Toyota Camry into the parking lot of a strip mall in the Little Tokyo section of eastern Los Angeles and walked up to the Starbucks for our appointed noontime rendezvous. We were going to tour Santee Alley, the street market in downtown L.A. where fakes are sold at wholesale and retail. Buckner is the founder, owner, and head of Investigative Consultants (IC), a private investigation firm that chases down manufacturers and distributors of counterfeit luxury goods. Medium height, the thirty-seven-year-old native Southern Californian was fit and tan like a surfer, his copper blond hair slicked straight back. He was dressed neatly and discreetly in a plain white polo shirt, newish jeans, and a pair of well-worn sneakers—nothing to draw attention. He's wise and quick, a real gumshoe, with a taut confidence that tells you he's seen it all.

Buckner grew up in Torrance, California, a charmless American urban sprawl just south of Los Angeles, and spent his teen years surfing the Pacific coastline and working part-time at Becker Surfboards in Hermosa Beach. At twenty-one, he entered the police academy and went on to become a deputy sheriff who walked the beat in Lennox and worked in L.A. County jails, keeping inmates in line. While he was a deputy Buckner qualified for his private investigator's license, so in 1994, at the age of twenty-six, he decided to go into business on his own. He set up his office in his home basement, and with his wife and mother helping out—answering phones, handling the books, even doing some undercover work—he took on basic assignments: witness interviews, litigation investigations, husband-and-wife matters. By the time we met in November 2004, he had ten PIs on staff and four administrative assistants who occasionally do investigative work, too.

The Los Angeles–based designer jeans company Guess was the first client to ask Buckner to go after counterfeiters. Today Buckner represents more than eighty clients, from toner products manufacturers to the Motion Picture Association of America. But his specialty is luxury goods: he handles more than thirty-five brands. Buckner's method is straightforward: he gets leads from the brands themselves, from informants, and from law enforcement officers who have seen something suspect. He also hears a lot from angry women who take a Gucci purse or a Rolex watch they received as a gift into the boutique for repairs or an exchange and are told it's fake. Buckner and his team gather the evidence through surveillance, serve "cease and desist" letters, and, if that fails, turn over the case to the LAPD or another law enforcement agency to execute search warrants and make arrests. "It's like the drug business—dirty like that," he told me in his raspy tenor. "A lot of people will drop dimes on the counterfeiters."

We met a few miles away because, as Buckner told me in his car on the drive over to Santee Alley, everyone knows him and if we wanted to see anything, we'd have to arrive quickly and discreetly.

With us was Buckner's associate, Hector Moya, a burlier and quieter sort, also in a casual shirt, jeans, and sneaks. We parked in a lot just off Los Angeles Street and hit the sidewalk at a good clip, heading toward Santee Alley, one and a half blocks up. The ambiance was like an outdoor bazaar in a developing nation: stalls selling everything from T-shirts to confirmation dresses, with designer handbags, jackets, and jeans hanging from the sun-bleached awnings. The banter and the bargaining were in Spanish and Korean. The heavy, pungent aroma of spicy sausages and onions grilling on beat-up carts filled the air; mango skins and watermelon rinds littered the gutter.

I sensed a bit of scurrying. "See that guy running ahead of us?" Buckner asked. A scrawny Hispanic in a white guayabera darted through the crowd a few steps in front, constantly looking over his shoulder. "He's going to warn them," Buckner said knowingly. Sure enough, when the kid got to the corner of Santee Alley, he let out a birdlike whistle. "They have spotters on rooftops, two-way radios," Buckner explained, "to keep a lookout for us."

When we turned the corner into the alley, the kid had disappeared into the crowd and the first stall we visited was empty. Minutes before, Buckner said, the place had been open for business. Though the front gate was still up, there was no shopkeeper and most of the merchandise had been stashed in duffel bags or big black plastic trash bags. As we walked down the concrete alley, Buckner pointed out a vendor named Ruben. "He was arrested two weeks ago for sales of counterfeit merchandise," Buckner said. "He was doing a deal in a parking lot nearby."

We headed toward another stall. A fellow in the street gave the shopkeeper a sign—whistled, then waved his hand. "She'll throw everything in bags and run it out of here," Buckner said. Sure enough, when we got to the stall, there were only a few Vuitton watches and handbags still on display. On the floor sat a couple of overstuffed trash bags and big cardboard cartons, sealed. The vendor, a small Asian woman well past fifty, stood at the counter, her hands resting nervously on a scrunched black plastic bag. Buckner's alert turquoise eyes zeroed in on it. "What's that?" he asked, and gently slid the sack from under her arm. Inside he found a well-worn Louis Vuitton catalog in Japanese. "They get this from Japanese tourism agencies," Buckner explained. "Chances are they have the merchandise hidden in the back."

IN THE TIMES of ancient Rome, Greece, and Egypt; the Mayans and the Incas; the American Indians and imperialist China, hallmarks and seals served as marks of origin: you knew who made your goods. In the Middle Ages, craftsmen joined professional guilds that provided marked goods with a seal of quality approval in addition to the craftsmen's personal stamps or signatures. When the Industrial Revolution arrived in the mid-nineteenth century, goods could no longer be traced back to a single craftsman—they were mass-produced in assembly lines. To distinguish as well as protect their products from the competition, companies trademarked their work and their logos, and trademarks became a guarantee of consistent quality. Since the 1950s, trademarks and logos have been increasingly used as marketing and advertising tools and have evolved into brand symbols.

Today logos brand people: by wearing or carrying an item emblazoned with a logo, you declare that you are a member of a tribe that subscribes to that particular brand's message and its ethics—essentially the dreams conjured up for you by the marketing department. Luxury-brand logos convey wealth, status, and chic, even if the bearer of the logo-ed product is a middle-market suburban housewife who bought it on credit. "I think it's completely impossible [to eliminate the logo] today," Miuccia Prada told me. "The recognition of the brand is too important. The more you want to enlarge your business, the more you have to use your logo."

By putting an emphasis on the logo and spending more than $100 million a year to advertise it, luxury companies made their brands, rather than the actual products, the objects of public desire. Unfortunately, they also created a demand they couldn't meet, and a product that average consumers craved but couldn't always afford. How many secretaries, teachers, or sales executives could really buy a new $500 Prada or $700 Louis Vuitton handbag *every season*? Counterfeiters stepped in, providing an endless supply of copies at 5 to 10 percent of the genuine product's retail price. And luxury's new hungry target audience started buying and buying and buying.

Counterfeiting is about as old as civilization itself. During the last century of the Roman Republic (100 BC), Romans grew rich and socially mobile, and one of the ways the upwardly mobile could gain acceptance by the patrician upper classes was to possess what old-moneyed Romans possessed. "Wealth itself didn't confer status," explains Jonathan Stamp, a classical historian and documentary film-maker. "You needed wealth plus something else, like objects." The politician and philosopher Cicero, for example, was an outsider who wanted desperately to be accepted by the establishment, so he spent a staggering one million sestertii on a citron wood table at a time when the average annual salary was a thousand sestertii. Suddenly Rome's nouveaux riches had to have tables just like it, and since they couldn't afford the real thing, they had carpenters copy it in lower-quality wood. Sculptors reproduced the great statues of the period in cheaper materials for the new moderately rich masses to use in decorating their homes and gardens. "People were spending money like never before and cared about superficial things," Stamp said. "All the old social structures had dissolved, and it was bemoaned by the patrician rich: 'People used to know their place.'"

Counterfeiting has long been a problem for modern luxury, too. Cheap knockoffs of checked and striped canvas Louis Vuitton trunks prompted Vuitton's son Georges in 1896 to design with the company's signature logo print of interlocking LVs and Japanese floral symbols. In 1948, a woman who had paid a small fortune to exclusively own one of

Christian Dior's designs arrived at a nightclub only to find another woman wearing an exact copy. "This is no joke," the woman wept, "but a tragedy." The French gendarmes launched an investigation that led six years later to the arrest of a counterfeiting gang. The thieves bribed seamstresses for patterns and models to borrow outfits that they would then copy.

Through much of the 1970s and 80s, counterfeiting was a small-time business. The luxury brand watches, sunglasses, and T-shirts sold by merchants on the street were obviously fake; the quality was lousy, the prices cheap. Luxury brands generally didn't get too worked up over it.

Two things changed the game: the democratization of luxury and the rise of China. When luxury brands went democratic, they thought they could satisfy the middle market with lower-priced handbags and perfume. What executives didn't count on was middle-market consumers satisfying their craving for higher-end items by buying fake versions that they could pass off as real. At the same time China evolved into a capitalist market economy and the world's manufacturing center, with a new class of entrepreneurs who saw counterfeiting as a viable business. The convergence of the two—big demand and big supply—was cataclysmic. And it took luxury executives—and executives in most other industries—by surprise.

Since 1993, the counterfeiting of all goods—from DVDs to pharmaceuticals—has increased by 1,700 percent, reports Indicam, an anticounterfeiting coalition based in Italy. The International Anti-Counterfeiting Coalition (IACC) in Washington estimates that up to 7 percent of today's global trade—$600 billion worth—is counterfeit. In 1982, the International Trade Commission estimated global losses from counterfeiting and piracy to be $5.5 billion; in 1988, it was $60 billion; and in 1996, it was $200 billion. In 2004, the U.S. Department of Commerce estimated that American companies alone lost between $20 billion and $24 billion annually. The loss of tax revenue due to counterfeiting is substantial, too: New York City police commissioner Raymond Kelly estimates that the city loses up to $1 billion in taxes annually.

While everything from Ferraris to mineral water is counterfeited today, fashion is one of the most popular sectors, because it is easy and cheap to copy and even easier to sell. In 2000, the Global Anti-Counterfeiting Group reported that 11 percent of the world's clothing and footwear was fake, and the World Customs Organization believes the fashion industry loses up to $9.2 billion (€7.5 billion) per year to counterfeiting. In 2002, the European Commission reported that trade in counterfeit clothing, footwear, perfume and toiletries reduces the European Union's gross domestic product by more than $6 billion (€5 billion) each year and costs 10,800 jobs.

The most popular and lucrative fashion knockoffs are those bearing luxury brand logos. You can buy fake Louis Vuitton handbags, Gucci sunglasses, and Burberry knapsacks in shops on Canal Street in New York and Santee Alley in L.A., in the souks of Marrakech and Istanbul, on the beaches of the Côte d'Azur, in flea markets, on the Internet, even in the living rooms of suburban America, where housewives host "purse parties" to make some extra cash. And people do buy. As a result, counterfeiting has ballooned from the small-potatoes local business of twenty years ago to a global racket today, one that is run by violent crime syndicates that also deal in narcotics, weapons, child prostitution, human trafficking, and terrorism. The FBI believes that terrorists financed the World Trade Center bombing in 1993 with sales of counterfeit T-shirts in a store on Broadway in New York City, according to the IACC. Interpol secretary general Ronald K. Noble told the U.S. House Committee on International Relations in 2003 that profits from counterfeit goods sales have gone to groups associated with the anti-Israel Shi'ite terrorist group Hezbollah, paramilitary groups in Northern Ireland, and Colombia's main rebel army, FARC. One of the suspects in the March 2004 Madrid train bombings is a known counterfeiter, according the United Kingdom–based Anti-Counterfeiting Group.

Investigators even believe that there may be a link between counterfeiting and the September 11, 2001, attacks on New York and Washington. The week after the attacks, fifteen hundred counterfeit vendor stalls—some purportedly owned and operated by al-Qaeda—at the Tri-Border Market in South America, where $70 million of business is done in cash every day, closed shop. And during a raid in early 2002 on a midtown Manhattan luggage store that was run by a man of Middle Eastern descent and sold fake luxury handbags and watches, New York security expert Andrew Oberfeldt and intellectual property rights lawyer Heather McDonald found a flight manual and simulator program and copies of technical schematics of a bridge. They immediately called the Joint Terrorist Task Force, which took over the case. "Profits from counterfeiting are one of the three main sources of income supporting international terrorism," says Magnus Ranstorp, former director for the Centre for the Study of Terrorism and Political Violence at the University of St. Andrews in Scotland.

Surprisingly, most companies didn't see this coming and didn't do much about it until the late 1990s. Some players still shrug. Louis Vuitton designer Marc Jacobs told me that he thinks counterfeiting is "fantastic," adding, "as long as I've been here, everything that we have done has been copied . . . We hope to create a product that is desirable." Prada CEO Patrizio Bertelli calls it part of "the game of fashion," and said, "I would be more worried if my product *wasn't* copied." They're not the ones who need to worry: today, most luxury companies have extensive legal departments that focus only on intellectual property theft, as it is called. They also have investigators on the ground, working the markets, chasing down leads on illegal factories, in China as well as in London, New York, Los Angeles, and other distribution centers. Louis Vuitton, one of the world's most copied brands, has forty lawyers in-house and 250 outside private investigators like Kris Buckner, and spends approximately €15 million ($18.1 million) each year fighting counterfeiting, despite Marc Jacobs's view. In 2004, Vuitton conducted twenty raids a day worldwide and put about thousand counterfeiters in jail. Companies that are active in raids, that seize merchandise and sue, definitely see a drop in their brand's fakes on the market. But the minute they ease up, the fake products, like a red tide, come right back. "This is a cost of business," McDonald told me. "Advertising is working. You'll never see something counterfeited of a brand you've never heard of."

BACK IN THE 1970S, before the advent of outlet malls, clothing wholesalers on Santee Street, a main thoroughfare in the garment district of downtown Los Angeles, began to sell leftovers out of the back-alley entrances to their stores. It was such a success that the owners redesigned their showrooms, creating a discount boutique in the back that opened onto the alley, and Santee Alley, as it was dubbed, became a bona fide retail street, several blocks long, open seven days a week.

In the 1980s, a surge of Korean immigrants arrived in Los Angeles and found the bazaar-like atmosphere of Santee Alley similar to the markets in Seoul. They began to take over leases and expand the businesses. Their business approach was the polar opposite of the cost-conscious American model: the Koreans manufactured clothes such as T-shirts and jeans fast, sold them cheap, and didn't worry about profit-and-loss figures. Profit came in volume. Today many leaseholders on Santee Alley are Korean, and they never quibble about rent, which is now approaching the levels of Rodeo Drive.

Slowly, counterfeit luxury brand items such as watches and handbags began to appear on the store shelves. At first, the fakes were easy to spot: they were cheaply made and lacked finesse. But as time went on, the quality got better and the demand increased. Soon Santee Alley was not only a cheap bazaar; it was L.A.'s premier counterfeit market. Today, twenty to thirty thousand people descend on Santee Alley daily to buy everything from inexpensive children's clothes to fake Chanel sunglasses, making it the third most visited destination in Los Angeles after Universal Studios and Venice Beach.

Counterfeit designer T-shirts and simple dresses are usually manufactured by Vietnamese or Latin American immigrants in nearby Riverside and Orange counties because turnaround is a mere matter of days. Some knockoff handbags are locally made, too: Santee Alley vendors go to neighboring Main Street, buy generic bags for a couple of dollars, stamp on a logo or sew in a label, and sell them for $20. But the good bags with the logo integrated into the design—as well as sunglasses, watches, and high-design garments like Burberry raincoats— are imported, primarily from China. Often you find a mix of both locally made cheapos and imported top-quality items within one shop, like the one run by a mild-mannered fifty-ish Indian vendor who, when we visited in 2004, was on probation. "I kept telling him to stop selling but he didn't," said Buckner as we walked into the shop.

By the looks of things, he still hadn't. On the shelves sat faux Vuitton-style bags stamped with colorful hearts rather than LVs and Chanel Cambon-style purses with a bold "OC" instead of the house's signature interlocking "CC," making them technically not fake. Next to them, however, were a couple of black leather handbags with regular Gucci labels on the front. Realizing he'd been caught, the shopkeeper quickly reached over and peeled off the Gucci labels; they were stuck on like Post-its. Buckner gave him a firm warning. "I treat all these guys with respect because it's nothing personal," Buckner told me. "These vendors shouldn't be selling counterfeits—what's wrong is wrong, what's right is right—but it doesn't make them bad people. The networks behind them are the slimiest."

When we walked out, Buckner spied one of his informants, who beckoned us into a discreet entry around the corner. He had just witnessed our visit and told Buckner that the "OC" is really a "CC"—that half the O peels off, leaving a Chanel-like double-C logo. "They do it like that to get it through U.S. Customs," he explained.

Then he showed Buckner a piece of fake Louis Vuitton hardware.

"You know where it's coming from?" Buckner asked.

"Yeah."

"I'll call you later."

The informant slid the gold fixture back into his shirt pocket.

Santee Alley attracts everyone. "Judges, prosecutors, defense attorneys shop here," Buckner said. "Affluent people from Newport Beach." A vendor named Peter concurs. "The whole world passes by here," he told me. "I sold some shirts to Chaka Khan three days ago. The police chief convention is in town and all the wives are down here buying Louis Vuitton."

Peter is a tall, handsome African-American in his early thirties. His shop is actually a one-by-three-foot sidewalk space in front of a store. He sells T-shirts with prized logos—when we visited, it was Abercrombie & Fitch. Most vendors in Santee Alley pay about $12,000 a month for their shops, then sublet the sidewalk to folks like Peter for about $1,000 a square foot, in cash. It's often on the sidewalk that you'll find the most blatant counterfeit goods, like Louis Vuitton and Chanel handbags and Gucci and Armani sunglasses.

Buckner told me that Peter was "the smartest man in Santee Alley." Peter just laughed. "I just know how to stay out of trouble," he said. A native of Rancho Cucamonga, a sprawling suburb on the road to Las Vegas, Peter started selling in Santee Alley in the early 1990s when he was a student at UCLA and needed some quick cash. He first sold fake handbags, but after three years switched to T-shirts. "When you are selling handbags, you are selling somebody else's designs," he reasoned. "I like designing things myself." He studied street fashion and would pick up on a new trend even before the main brands did. He printed "Tommy Sport" T-shirts and other products before Tommy Hilfiger trademarked it and made a killing.

In his fourteen years in Santee Alley, Peter has seen the market evolve. "What they used to sell here was garbage," he said. "Now you can get the same quality as in Nordstrom, because the consumer is smarter." I asked how much he earns. "I'm doing all right," he answered. When I asked him if he had any qualms about what he does, he shrugged. "Wherever there's a demand, you'll always have someone taking the chance."

What I realized from my tour is that people don't believe there is a difference between real and fake anymore. Bernard Arnault's marketing plan had worked: consumers don't buy luxury branded items for what they *are*, but for what they *represent*. And good fakes—the kind that can pass for real—now represent socially the same thing as real. I remember an American woman I saw one morning in the Peninsula Hotel in Hong Kong. She was a chic New Yorker in her fifties, well dressed in a designer pantsuit, good jewelry, and Chanel sunglasses, and obviously wealthy enough to pay $500 a night at one of the world's top hotels. She walked up to the concierge desk and asked its chief, "Where can I buy a good fake Rolex? You know, a really good fake." The concierge looked at her incredulously and said he didn't know. I looked at her and wondered, "Are the sunglasses fake, too?"

ONE WEEK AFTER my tour in Santee Alley, I boarded a train in the Hung Hom station in Hong Kong for a two-hour ride north to Guangzhou—which was known in the West as Canton—a city of eight million and the capital city of Guangdong Province. I was escorted by a luxury brand intellectual property expert and a local counterfeit private investigator. Once past the seemingly endless forest of high-rise towers of Hong Kong, we crossed the lush plains of the Pearl River delta into Guangdong Province, where fourteen million Chinese live on four thousand square miles, making it one of the most densely populated areas in the world. There remain some collective rice and duck farms, and we spied a few farmers out in the fields, working the fertile land with their oxen. But as we approached the city of Guangzhou, the farms gave way to enormous blocklike factories, hundreds of them, where workers make leather shoes, toys, clothing—everything. "This is why this region is called 'the Factory of the World,' " the expert told me.

Guangzhou has served an important international port for centuries. Arab merchants who traveled to China on the Silk Road in the seventh century settled in Guangzhou and turned the city into a trade center. In the sixteenth century, the Portuguese colonized nearby Macau and made it a base for foreigners who wanted to do business in China. The Portuguese, Dutch, French, British, and American traders would sail up the Pearl River from Macau to sell opium and buy Chinese porcelain, silk, and tea. In 1839, the First Opium War broke out when Qing Emperor Dao Guang shut down the opium trade. In the early twentieth century, it was the center for much of the republican movement that brought down the Qing Dynasty. The republic's first president, Sun Yat-sen, was from the region, and he was the head of Guangzhou's Kuomintang, the nationalist party.

During the first thirty years of communism, Mao Tse-tung neglected Guangdong, and the once prosperous and flourishing province became one of the poorest in the country. As Jasper Becker noted in his book, *The Chinese*, the state's investment per capita in Guangdong was the lowest in all of China. When Deng Xiaoping came to power in 1978, all that changed. Deng wanted to use Guangdong as a laboratory for his economic reforms. The following year, he changed the national one-child-per-family rule to two children in Guangdong and told the provincial government that it could keep its tax revenue rather than contribute to the central government. Factories sprouted across the delta like rice plants. As the demand for counterfeit versions of luxury goods in the West increased, legitimate manufacturers in the region began to produce fakes at night and on holidays. Eventually, workshops opened in Guangzhou solely to produce fakes. Today, Guangzhou is the capital of China's counterfeiting business.

Fighting counterfeiting in Guangzhou is not easy for several reasons. First, China does not have a history of intellectual property ownership. Confucius was the first to democratize education, and he encouraged the works of great scholars to be copied in order to spread knowledge to all classes. To further complicate the issue, China's communist leaders declared that the state—not individuals, not companies or corporations—owned all property. Since the economic reforms in 1978, the government has slowly embraced the notion of intellectual property ownership. The first patent and trademark laws were enacted in the early 1980s. "You have this strong heritage for many centuries [of copying], and then suddenly everyone tells you to stop," says Frederick Mostert, past president of the International Trademark Association. "It's a real cultural dilemma."

Anticounterfeiting was one of the subjects discussed during the U.S.-China Joint Commission on Commerce and Trade in Washington in April 2004. In response, the Chinese government announced the formation of a task force to tackle the problem, which implemented two new initiatives: it lengthened the prison terms of convicted counterfeit vendors to three years in order to deter counterfeiting, and it shut down the famed Silk Alley counterfeit market in Beijing to make way for a new five-story shopping mall that would ban counterfeit sellers. Both initiatives failed. When the new mall opened three months later, the international counterfeit syndicates moved in and took over the shops formerly occupied by small-time dealers. One vendor who squawked to the police was shot dead gangland-style. A month later, the U.S. trade representative declared that despite the Chinese government's efforts, intellectual property "infringements remain at epidemic levels," and that China's overall piracy rates have not dropped since the country's 2001 entry into the World Trade Organization.

In an effort to raise awareness in China, martial-arts movie star Jackie Chan starred in an international public awareness campaign called "Fakes Cost More." During the June 2005 press conference that kicked off the campaign, Chan fought off a group of faux assailants wearing Jackie Chan masks, attacked a staged counterfeiting stall with a chain saw, and ripped the fake Gucci, Armani, and Versace clothes off an actor dressed up as a tourist. "The ease with which authentic works can be copied in the digital world and the instant wealth it brings has given new rise to the second oldest profession in the world: piracy," Chan said. "It is easy to copy but difficult to create."

That was evident the moment we walked into Xinxing, the central wholesale market for counterfeit leather goods, just down the road from the domestic train station in Guangzhou. The market is a series of big warehouses with air-conditioned stalls filled with fake Louis Vuitton, Gucci, Chanel, Fendi, and Burberry products. One warehouse is for the Grade AA product—fakes that look so good it's hard for a non-expert to tell they aren't real. "Counterfeiters take the original item and do a three-D scan of it," the expert explained to me. "The process produces perfect copies of patterns."

The market stalls were clean and well appointed with glass display cases; vendors had catalogs, business cards, and a genial, courtly manner. It was hard to imagine that it was all completely illicit. The only differences between Xinxing and a legitimate wholesale market were the prices and the customers. I watched as a rotund middle-aged British man with a sweaty red face and balding pate negotiated with a Chinese vendor for an order of bogus Louis Vuitton bags. Going rate: 18 yuan ($2) for a monogram wallet, 150 yuan ($19) for the classic monogram purse. The price dropped by 30 percent for orders of more than one hundred. A pair of veiled Muslim women who were on our train from Hong Kong that morning were there, too, placing orders. "Gucci definitely has a problem," the expert said as he clocked the glut of double-G logo bags on display—almost as many as the ubiquitous LV fakes.

Across the street in another warehouse are the lower-quality goods: the stuff that looks fake and is often a bastardization or mélange of brand names—like Bossco or Emilio Valentino—and costs next to nothing. Small wholesale orders are taken along in a suitcase by the customer or a courier. Big orders are far more complicated. An order of ten thousand handbags would be divided into ten groups of a thousand to be made by workshops around Guangzhou. Counterfeit workshops are light and mobile; after two weeks, they pack up and move to escape detection. Once the order is completed, it is wrapped up and deposited in a neutral place, like the courtyard of a local school, where it will be picked up by a local transporter, often simply a guy on a bike with a cart. The local transporter will deliver it to the wholesaler in Xinxing, who will have it taken to another neutral place to be picked up by the international shipping agent and put in a shipping container. The goods are often packed in shipments of foodstuffs or legitimately manufactured clothing to escape detection by receiving customs officials. Sometimes the goods (particularly watches) are shipped in pieces or without labels or monograms, and are finished, assembled, or stamped by illegal immigrants in clandestine workshops at the destination. Each time the goods change hands, the prices double. All transactions are done in cash.

Hong Kong used to be the primary port, but its container fees have become prohibitive for counterfeiters, so more and more shipments leave directly from the ports of China: Shanghai, Dalian, and Guangzhou. From there, the ship goes to a "cleansing port" such as South Korea to change its point of departure and then onward to Japan, the United States, Italy, or Belgium. Shipments directly from China are more carefully checked; by passing through a cleansing port they become less suspicious.

On occasion, the shipment gets discovered during inspection by receiving customs officials. In June 2004, the U.S. Bureau of Immigration and Customs Enforcement (ICE) arrested a dozen people and seized six shipping containers—five with bogus handbags, luggage, and wallets, and the sixth with counterfeit cigarettes—coming into the United States from China, valued at $24 million. ICE agents also seized $174,000 in cash and eleven bank accounts. Officials said the suspects probably imported about two containers per week, each container earning $2 to $4 million in profit. That same month, seventeen Chinese men were arrested in a government sting operation for paying $1 million in bribes to undercover ICE agents at Port Elizabeth, New Jersey, to guarantee entry of thirty shipping containers of fake Louis Vuitton, Cartier, Gucci, and other luxury brand handbags, luggage, wallets, and sunglasses. The goods were to be sold by New York City retailers and street vendors. The smugglers, members of the Li Organization, one of the most powerful gangs on Canal Street, wired thousands of dollars in proceeds back to China.

The street value of Chinese goods carrying counterfeit trademarks seized by the United States doubled between 2005 and 2006 to $125 million, and counterfeit goods from China and Hong Kong made up 90 percent of all U.S. Customs and Border Protection's intellectual property seizures. The same is true in Europe: Nearly three-fourths of all counterfeit luxury goods seized at ports originated in China or Hong Kong.

While customs seizures of counterfeit goods continue to rise, a vast amount makes it through. The shipping containers are put directly onto trucks and hauled either to warehouses to be stored or to workshops to be assembled or stamped by clandestine workers. This is where human trafficking fits into the puzzle: the workers, sometimes children, have been sold into labor. They, too, have been shipped over and smuggled in. They are taken to tenement factories and often locked in. There they live, work, sleep. "I went on a raid in a sweatshop in Brooklyn, and illegal workers were hiding in a rat hole," Barbara Kolsun, senior vice president and general counsel for Kate Spade, told me. "It was filthy, and it was impossible to know how old the workers were."

The gangs then have the counterfeit goods transported to stores in wholesale markets like Canal Street and Santee Alley, where they are purchased by tourists, flea market merchants, purse-party ladies, and suburbanites who believe that buying, selling, or owning fakes is, as McDonald put it, "a victimless crime."

SHORTLY AFTER LUNCH in Guangzhou, we drove over to a Chinese law enforcement agency, a typical linoleum-floored, fluorescent-lit office that could be found anywhere in the world. The officers, most in their thirties or forties, were friendly and polite—offering us green tea as they spoke proudly of the success they had recently in fighting counterfeiting. After a few minutes the chief came in and announced that they'd gotten a tip about a counterfeit workshop across town. The informant was the landlord: he rents to the counterfeiter with full payment up front in cash, calls the cops and gets a reward for the tip, then rents the space again. "There are no ethics in this business," the expert tells me. "None." The cops strapped on their holsters, and a few put on bulletproof vests. Raids can be dangerous: sometimes workshop owners will pull a knife or have thugs there to beat up the cops. During one raid in Xinxing market, someone shot a gun in the air; when everyone hit the ground, the counterfeiters fled.

We all went downstairs, hopped into a pair of official vans and sped across town. Guangzhou is an industrial city with impenetrable smog, dingy high-rises, elevated highways slicing this way and that, and traffic congestion that would make Los Angeles look fluid. We pulled into the courtyard of a white stucco tenement. The cops jumped out, guns drawn, ran up seven flights of an open-air stairwell to the top floor, scurried across the balcony, looked through the window of one of the flats to confirm it was the right place, saw the door open, and went in. If it had been closed, the cops would have needed a warrant. Once they checked out the place to make sure it was safe, they waved us up.

We hoofed it up the steps, over empty Coke cans and other trash, and as we approached the top, the acute toxic smell of glue burned in our noses. We walked into the workshop—a long, wide room with barred windows—and before us stood two dozen Chinese boys and girls, roughly eight to fourteen, sitting at old sewing machines and standing behind plywood worktables littered with scraps of black leather, gooey pots of glue, and a cookie tin filled with stamps reading Versace, Boss, Dunhill. The children stopped midwork. One bag was stuck in a machine, half sewn. In the corner were big cardboard cartons filled with counterfeit luxury brand handbags in black leather. I picked one up and checked it out: the materials were cheesy, the sacks lined with plastic, the seams uneven. "Cheap fakes," the expert declared.

The cops told the children to line up single file. They looked at us with their sweet faces filled with confusion, their eyes tired and sad: they didn't know why they were told to stop working. As they walked out, some stopped to punch their time cards in hope of getting paid. Some glared at the owner, an overweight middle-aged Chinese man, and his factory manager, a Chinese woman in her thirties who sat in the small office next to the door, glum over a cold pot of tea. The investigators said it was rare to find the owner onsite. Both were arrested. The cops started to box up the handbags, the machines, the materials, everything. It would take two hours. A truck pulled up in the courtyard to haul it all off to a scrap yard, where it would be immediately destroyed. "They are out of business now," the expert said. The squad does at least two of these raids each day.

When it was time to leave, we had to run across the courtyard to the vans to shield ourselves from debris that the kids threw from the balconies. To the children, the cops are the bad guys. Many of the children in counterfeit workshops have been sold into labor by their families in the countryside. The children used to be picked up at the train station and taken to the factories, but the police started to stake out the stations and make arrests. Now factories hire agents, usually a man and woman who will pose as a married couple and go to the country in a truck to get one or two children. If the agents are stopped by police, the agents say that the children are theirs. Some families in the country sell their children because they believe that the children will have a better life in the city. But selling children has become a big business in China. The children work in factories or turn to prostitution and send their money home or bring it to their parents when they return home for the Chinese New Year. Most earn between $50 to $100 a month in factories.

The children who work in counterfeit factories are usually housed by the owners; the kids in the raid I witnessed lived across the courtyard in slum dorms. When a counterfeit factory is raided and the owner arrested, the children are left not only out of work but also homeless. One investigator who often assists on raids in China was so moved by the plight of the child workers that he and a handful of colleagues founded a charity, which helps place the children from shut-down factories in schools and underwrites their education and living costs.

Sometimes the cases are truly horrific. "I remember walking into an assembly plant in Thailand a couple years ago and seeing six or seven little children, all under ten years old, sitting on the floor assembling counterfeit leather handbags," the investigator told me as we drove away from the raid. "The owner had broken the children's legs and tied the lower leg to the thigh so the bones wouldn't mend. He did it because the children said they wanted to go outside and play."

ONE DAY IN 2004, New York security expert Andrew Oberfeldt and lawyer Heather McDonald were participating in a raid in a counterfeit mall on Canal Street in downtown Manhattan, when they saw a petite blond woman sobbing hysterically. In a thick Texas drawl, she pleaded with McDonald: "This is my first time to New York and this is awful! I just want to take my things and go home."

McDonald asked the police what the Texan's "things" were: "She had fifty-eight of the same bag," McDonald says incredulously.

McDonald said no, and the Texan left in a huff.

Five minutes later she returned, tears gone.

"I'm on the cell phone with my lawyer, and he says you can't do this without my day in court, so I'll take my bags and go," she declared.

"No," McDonald responded. "I'll take your bags and see you in court."

"Two weeks later we're doing a raid at a nearby location," McDonald recalled when we met in June 2005. "And who do we see? The same Texan. I told her, 'I thought you said you were never coming back here.' And you know what she said?"

"What?" I asked.

"'Bite me!' "

I laughed out loud.

"I'm sure," McDonald said, "that she was a purse-party lady."

Purse-party ladies are the drug dealers of the counterfeit trade: they buy from the wholesalers and sell to suburban users, folks with a craving for the goods but not enough dough for the genuine thing. Like teenagers gathering at a friend's upper-middle-class home to buy a couple of joints with their allowance or babysitting money, suburban women converge in well-appointed living rooms for wine, hors d'oeuvres, gossip, and fake Vuitton or Gucci handbags. The women hosting these fetes will make a killing—they double their investment—and never declare it to the IRS. Take Virginia Topper, the wife of a lawyer in Long Island, New York. When she was busted in 2003, she had $60,000 in cash stashed in her underwear drawer and a Jaguar in the driveway. She was found guilty and sentenced to community service. "She was the ultimate Amway lady," Oberfeldt laughed.

Most purse-party ladies don't see buying or selling fake handbags as a real crime. It seems so innocuous that churches, synagogues, and schools host purse parties to raise money for charities or in-house events. In a survey by the Anti-Counterfeiting Group, one-third of those questioned said they would knowingly buy counterfeit goods if the price and quality were right, and 29 percent said they saw no harm in the selling of fake goods unless the purchaser was at risk. "We'll go on raids in Chinatown wholesalers and we'll find five or six suburban women standing there—customers," Oberfeldt tells me. "We'll say to these women, 'The dealers take you down dark corridors, through locked doors. The police say, "Open up!" The lights are turned out, and everyone is told to be quiet. At what point did you realize that something was amiss here?'"

Some take it one step further, passing off fakes in stores as the real thing. Buckner had gotten a tip from an informant that the wife of a professional athlete sold fake luxury brand handbags in her northern California boutique for $1,800 a pop. Buckner had his operatives purchase a couple of bags, which he sent to the brands' headquarters to be verified. Turned out the bags were, as Buckner put it, "grade AA counterfeit. It's all counterfeit."

Back in 2003, Gucci discovered that Wal-Mart was selling counterfeit Gucci handbags and wallets as authentic in several of its stores around the United States. Gucci hired New York lawyer Steven Gursky, of the Gursky Group at Dreier LLP, to pursue Wal-Mart for "willful blindness," a practice in which the store buyer does not ask the wholesaler or middleman the origin of fake goods and then sells them as the real thing. It happens all the time: Gursky has handled willful blindness cases against Wal-Mart, Costco, and others on behalf of Tommy Hilfiger, Calvin Klein, Diesel, and Nike, to name a few. Generally, middlemen sell anything and everything they can get their hands on. "We've had cases where the vendor last sold the retailer toasters and now it's designer clothing," says Gursky, "and the buyers don't find this odd."

In the Gucci case, the middleman—actually a middlewoman— had attended the Las Vegas Off-Price Specialist Show, the largest American trade show devoted to selling odd lots of apparel and accessories at reduced prices, and picked up an order of Gucci handbags and wallets for a song. She testified later in the case that she believed the goods were authentic because she heard the people in the booth speaking Italian and assumed they were employees of Gucci. In fact, they were Israelis speaking Hebrew and had bought the wallets and purses at a factory in Romania. They were later arrested in Miami for selling other counterfeit goods. As they were already facing criminal and civil charges in Florida, Gucci decided to go after the middlewoman and Wal-Mart. Both settled on the eve of the trial in June 2005. "The sale of counterfeit merchandise by a reputable retailer is much more insidious than on Canal Street because often on Canal Street people assume what they are buying is fake," said Gursky. "But when you walk through doors of a $200 billion retailer, you believe that what they are selling is real. And sometimes it's not. The truth is, Wal-Mart is much more concerned about the buck than reputation—theirs as well as the trademark holder's."

Most luxury companies now have lawyers on retainer who spend each day surfing the Web, looking for fakes for sale. Companies such as AAA Replicas (www.aaareplicas.com) make Vuitton and Hermès knockoffs to order for $200 to $400 apiece. Amazon.com and eBay are two favorite places for counterfeit wholesalers to dump their stock. Amazon and eBay themselves cannot be held liable because they simply host a transaction between buyer and seller. But luxury brands are hoping to change that by making the Web sites liable for enabling the business. In 2004, Tiffany sued eBay in New York's federal court based on that principle, claiming that 80 percent of Tiffany products offered on the site were fakes. In 2006, LVMH filed a similar suit in Paris, stating that up to 90 percent of Vuitton and Dior items on eBay were counterfeit. By early 2007, both suits were still pending.

Many of the street-level hawkers in Europe and the United States—the guys you see with watches and bags spread out on blankets on street corners, or in trash bags slung on their backs on Riviera beaches—are Senegalese belonging to a two-million-strong Islamic sect called the Mouride brotherhood. They are illegal immigrants who sell Gucci watches and Vuitton baseball caps at a 400 percent markup, then send the cash—millions of dollars—back to Toube, their home base in Senegal and one of the fastest-growing cities in Africa. There, the money has contributed to constructing television and radio stations, a university, and one of the world's largest mosques, with an eighty-seven-meter tower covered in $10 million worth of imported marble. Rarely are Mourides prosecuted for peddling counterfeit goods. Like purse-party ladies, Mourides are, in the minds of cops, small-time dealers.

Counterfeiting flourishes because it is a high-return, low-risk business: Counterfeiters can earn millions and are rarely caught. "The markup is like heroin," says Oberfeldt. "Say I buy one ounce of heroin for $18,000. Diluted one to ten, I now have $180,000 worth. However, conspiracy to commit a crime and criminal possession of narcotics is an A–1 felony in New York. If I'm caught with any part of that ounce of heroin, I'm looking at eight to twenty-five years, and life if it's a multiple offense. It's mandatory sentencing. It's almost like murder.

"If I brought in $18,000 worth of handbags in from China"—which would retail for at least 10 times more—"you'd put me in jail overnight, maybe. And I'd call my lawyer and be out in the morning. Ninety-nine percent of the people caught in New York state selling counterfeit goods do not go to jail. The judges do not have the laws to sentence. The highest-level crime to be charged with in New York State is trademark counterfeiting, which is a C felony, like stealing a nice car. They never rat out their bosses. They just laugh at the cops.

"If you sell that heroin," he continues, "you'll have the DEA, the FBI, New York State and city police, Customs, and the IRS all looking for you—and you'll go to jail forever. If I sell counterfeit goods, all those people except the DEA *could* chase after me, but can't do anything once they get me. So most don't get involved."

Like the drug business, counterfeiting has become a professional racket run by organized crime. In New York in the 1980s until the mid-1990s, gangs—like a group of Asian American kids called the Born to Kill Gang—were in charge. "If we showed up to do a raid, women would take counterfeit watches, shove them up their shirts, and say, 'I'm pregnant, don't touch me!'" remembers Oberfeldt. "Once I saw a three-month-old baby in a milk crate that sat on top of a case of M-80 explosives. The gangs came after us with bats, they'd slash our tires, throw knives and significant explosives. It was terrorism. They tried to intimidate us. We videotaped them and locked them up and we got a lot of street cred when we manned up from ten to forty men and kept going."

Today Canal Street is run by grown-up gangs from China, like the Fukienese gang, as they are known in New York, whose members come from Fujian, a province along China's southeastern coast just across the straits from Taiwan. They speak a Fujian dialect among themselves and run the north side of Canal Street, west of Broadway. And they freely let the police seize goods rather than get arrested for fighting back. The network is tight. Like in Santee Alley, they all have direct-connect Nextel radio: if a police car turns a corner, the message is relayed down six blocks instantly and everything is shut down. They use homeless people as lookouts, giving them walkie-talkies. Random killings don't happen. "It's bad for business," notes Oberfeldt.

But things can get dangerous. During a two-day sweep in November 2004, New York police arrested fifty-one members of two violent gangs and charged them with a host of crimes ranging from racketeering to trafficking in counterfeit goods. Police seized $150,000 in cash and $4 million in counterfeit merchandise carrying the names of Chanel, Gucci, and Coach. U.S. Attorney David N. Kelley said the gangs "achieved their dominance through unflinching use of violence and fear." During their reign, a man who was suspected of cooperating with police received "a beating with pipes until his bones snapped," Kelley said. A rival gang member was shot in the head and survived only because the bullet miraculously shattered against his skull.

Buckner tells me that Los Angeles is less violent than New York, but dangerous nevertheless. When I visited his office in southern L.A., he showed me surveillance photos of a Hispanic vendor selling counterfeit merchandise in Santee Alley. The guy—a real muscled-up thug—had the number 18 tattooed on his fingers and his cheeks, signs that he is a member of the Eighteenth Street Gang, an L.A. gang that pays tribute to the Mexican mafia. Buckner has also seen guys with Hezbollah tattoos and pictures of Sheikh Nasrallah, the organization's political leader. Are they actually members of Hezbollah? No one knows for sure. What Buckner does know is that he has to watch his back. "We've had our tires slashed, our car windows broken. We've had surveillance on our office and on us to find out what we are up to," he said. "One of our men was driving a van in Santee Alley when gang members smashed the window and cut up his face."

To help crack down on the sale of counterfeit DVDs in Santee Alley, the Motion Picture Association of America donated ten cameras that were installed in and around the market in 2004, and the luxury companies profited from the initiative. That year alone, the Los Angeles Police Department seized $32 million worth of fake DVDs, watches, handbags, T-shirts, and more. "As we are a relatively new retail area, it's been the lawless frontier out there," admits the L.A. Fashion District's Kent Smith.

Some luxury corporations have decided to go after the counterfeiters more fiercely by pursuing big judgments; in January 2004, a New

York judge ordered the thirteen Chinese and Vietnamese defendants to each pay a record-breaking $18 million—totaling more than $500 million—to Cartier. The gang had a virtual monopoly on the counterfeit watch market in the United States and had been sending up to $100,000 a day back to their headquarters in Asia since 1988. Following the judgment, Cartier filed seizure orders on their houses, cars, and bank accounts. "We want to really hit them where it hurts: in the wallet," a Richemont executive told me.

Other countries are fighting the counterfeiting trade by targeting individual customers and retailers. In France, for example, tourists caught bringing counterfeit goods into France can receive a €300,000 fine (approximately $390,000) and up to three years in prison. And in Hong Kong, customs officials formed a task force of two hundred officers to stamp out counterfeiting and piracy on the retail level. In two years, the number of stores selling fake DVDs, software, and electronics in Hong Kong dropped from one thousand to one hundred. By 2004, there were only sixty. Counterfeit vendors in the Temple Street market in Hong Kong have been forced to move their bogus Vuittons and Guccis from the storefront tables to back rooms. Fake watch vendors closed up on Hong Kong's busy Nathan Road. Today, a hustler may hit you up on the sidewalk, but he has to take you down back alleys and up dark stairwells into rooms with steel doors to sell you a very good fake Rolex for a mere $45.

That's all well and good, says Oberfeldt, but in his view the wrong tack. "The only way to stop counterfeiting," he says, "is to get people to stop buying all this crap just to have these logos. We have to take it into our own hands."

CHAPTER TEN

WHAT NOW?

*"Luxury is the ease of a T-shirt in a very expensive dress. If
you don't have it, you are not a person used to luxury. You are
just a rich person who can buy stuff."*

— KARL LAGERFELD

ANDEL LEE is the modern American dream. His grandfather, for whom he's named, was a Chinese diplomat
who worked as an adviser for the American ambassador
in Beijing. Anticipating Mao's communist revolution, Lee's grandparents and his newlywed parents fled China in 1949. They lived in Japan
for several years and eventually settled in Washington, D.C., where
Lee's father served as the deputy assistant secretary for science and
technology for the Commerce Department and his mother worked as
an artist. Lee was raised in the comfortable Washington suburb of
Bethesda, Maryland, attended the University of Virginia, and earned
his law degree at Georgetown. He joined the prestigious law firm
Skadden, Arps in New York, and in 1991 was sent to Beijing to open its

office there—"not long after June 4," he points out, referring to the 1989 Tiananmen Square student protests two years earlier. "It was an interesting time, very quiet." He soon became the go-to man for Americans who wanted to do business in China. When I went to Shanghai for the first time in April 2004, he was my go-to man, too.

Lee invited me to lunch on the sunny rooftop terrace of M on the Bund, the trendy Western restaurant and preferred hangout for jet-set expats. When I arrived at one o'clock sharp, Lee stood to greet me, his manners as impeccable as his dark Armani suit. Lee is soft-spoken, straight-shooting, and seemingly honest: all things you do not associate with either lawyers or powerful businessmen. His strengths are knowledge—of the situations, the players, the hiccups—and patience. Both are as essential to doing business in China as air and water are to life.

"When I first came here, I planned to stay two to three years," he told me as we tucked into mesclun salads with smoked duck breast. "But every day you see something new and you hear something new— a new thought." In 1995, Lee had a new thought of his own: to open a gallery dedicated to contemporary art. "There was fresh new artistic expression that no one had seen in China, and the only places you could catch it was at art happenings, in underground art villages or in artists' studios," he said. "China has been an amazing civilization for five thousand years but that's because of its culture, not its military power. During the last sixty years, the most dynamic artists left or weren't allowed to show their work, and that was a tragedy."

In 1996, Lee opened the Courtyard, one of China's first privately owned contemporary art galleries, across from the east gate of the Forbidden City. The inaugural fete was a blowout, "with nine ambassadors and long-haired artists," Lee remembered with a laugh. "The police came, and they were shocked and surprised by the scene." Government officials, he said, "were afraid it could have been unhealthy art." And with just cause. "There was a lot of political content in the work," he admitted. Though Lee had all the permits required, the government shut down the gallery the next day. It took eight months to get permission to reopen.

In 1999, Lee decided to take the concept to Shanghai, but on a bigger, grander scale—"a place with a gallery and a restaurant," he said. During a Christmas call to a family friend, he mentioned his idea.

"You should look at our building," she offered.

Three years earlier, her family had purchased from the government a 1916 granite neoclassical building on the Bund that had served as the Union Insurance Company and later the Mercantile Bank of India. But the family had never figured out what to do with it.

A few days later, Lee checked out the place.

"I can do a whole building dedicated to setting the standards for contemporary art, luxury, and society in Shanghai," he thought to himself.

He wrote up a proposal that included restaurants, luxury retail, and an art gallery and presented it to the owner.

"This is fantastic," she told him, and gave him carte blanche.

He dubbed it Three on the Bund, after its address, and hired renowned architect Michael Graves to turn the proposal into reality.

Then he called Giorgio Armani.

IT TOOK THREE THOUSAND YEARS, but luxury has finally circumnavigated the world: it began in China and has now returned there, for consumption as well as production. And it is marching onward to India and Russia. The potential customer base is phenomenal. In 2006, China officially had three hundred thousand millionaires, Russia eighty-eight thousand, India seventy thousand. In 2004, Moscow had thirty-three billionaires, more than any other city in the world. "This is the century of emerging markets," Tom Ford told me. "We are finished here in the West—our moment has come and gone. This is all about China and India and Russia. It is the beginning of the reawakening of cultures that have historically worshipped luxury and haven't had it for so long."

When luxury business arrived in China in the early 1990s, the market was nearly non-existent. Forty years of communism and the Cultural Revolution had wiped out what was known as Chinese luxury, including the traditions of fine silk, delicate porcelain, and handcrafted wood furnishings. The Chinese didn't even have a word for luxury. They used the phrase *ming pai,* which means "famous brands." "When we opened here on Nanjing Road in 1995, people were pushing bicycles," Louis Vuitton president and CEO Yves Carcelle told me at the inauguration of the Louis Vuitton Global Store in Plaza 66 in Shanghai in September 2004.

At first, luxury brands opened stores in safe places like the lobby of the Palace Hotel in Beijing and the Plaza 66 luxury shopping mall in Shanghai to show off their wares. "It's cheaper than a billboard," said Paul French, a director of business consultancy Access Asia. "Just stick in some purses and some girls." In contrast to the rest of the world, the Chinese luxury market for much of the 1990s was male-driven: 90 percent of sales were to men, and male-oriented brands such as Boss, Dunhill, and Zegna thrived. Government officials and civil servants in Beijing, bankers and real estate barons in Shanghai, and manufacturing entrepreneurs in the northern provinces wanted all the trappings of Western businessmen. They bought Givenchy suits, Vuitton and Dunhill briefcases and money satchels, Rolex watches for themselves, and Cartier baubles for their wives and mistresses.

But in the early 2000s, Lee saw the luxury customer base broadening and believed that the market was mature enough to support a luxury retail-and-restaurant development. "Imagine that the luxury consumer is the top 5 percent of the population," he said. "In Shanghai, that's 900,000 people, in Beijing, it's 750,000—and that's not counting expats who are white-collar executives with nice packages. There are a half-million expats from Taiwan and Hong Kong alone." But rich locals weren't the only potential customers for Three on the Bund. "In Shanghai, you see secretaries dressed, out at night," Lee told me. "They save up and buy their Louis Vuitton bag. My secretary has a Prada bag. She displays it prominently on her desk and she's saving up for another one. And Beijing and especially Shanghai are the shopping Meccas for the wealthy from the north—Shenyang, Qingdao, and Harbin," he continued. "Most are private businessmen, in manufacturing and real estate—they buy an entire building at a clip. There are 250,000 millionaires in Wenzhou alone. They buy in cash. They have crew cuts and Dunhill bags stuffed with cash. They bring in their wife or girlfriend, say, 'What's the best?' and throw down the money."

Armani's presence in China in 2004 was minuscule compared to that of his competitors: a Giorgio Armani boutique in the Peninsula Palace Hotel in Beijing, Emporio Armani stores in Dalian and Wenzhou, and an Armani Collezioni in Shenzhen. For Lee, Armani was a natural choice for Three on the Bund. "He changed our aesthetic of contemporary fashion, and I thought it was important to bring him into China in a big way," Lee said. "He's vigorous and bigger than life, and that's important for China, the cult of the person. At the opening of Chanel, someone asked where Coco Chanel was. Armani would make a big impression on the Chinese."

When completed, Three on the Bund included a Giorgio Armani boutique; Emporio Armani; Armani Fiori (which sold orchids and calla lilies shipped from Holland); Armani Dolci (with Italian-made chocolates); two multibrand high-fashion boutiques; an Evian Spa; four restaurants, including Jean Georges Shanghai; and the Shanghai Gallery of Art. It would be the launchpad not only for Armani in China but also for the sort of Western-style retailing that luxury brands had cultivated and mastered in the rest of the world. "It's the moment to open here," Armani told me the day of the inauguration. "You can see things are happening. Last night when we went to dinner here in Shanghai, I was surprised by the way the people were so well turned out. Even Paris doesn't have this atmosphere, this spirit."

Armani made the most of his maiden voyage to the Middle Kingdom. He visited the Forbidden City, where Chinese tourists swirled around him, snapping photos. He was the guest of honor at a cocktail reception at the Italian ambassador's residence, with hundreds of impossibly hip Chinese twentysomethings dressed in Dior corset dresses and Armani suits, chattering endlessly, champagne in hand. In Shanghai, he staged a fashion show for a thousand people in a tent on the Pudong side of the Huangpu River, followed by a party in the Shanghai Gallery of Art at Three on the Bund with an abundant supply of good Chianti and heaping platters of carpaccio and prosciutto. Hundreds of young, beautiful Chinese danced to techno as American actress Mira Sorvino, British socialite Lady Helen Taylor, and Taiwanese movie idol Chen Chang—"the Johnny Depp of China," one girl swooned—held court in the VIP section. "Everything is alive here," Bao-Wen Chen, a forty-one-year-old Shanghainese investment banker, shouted to me over the booming music well after midnight. "There's a culture of young people who want to learn about luxury and fine dining. Shanghai is not New York or Hong Kong, but it's not far behind."

Three on the Bund kicked off the renovation of the elegant former banking district along the river, turning it into a luxury brand alley like the avenue Montaigne and Rodeo Drive in a matter of two years. In the first six months, sales of Armani at Three on the Bund were 50 percent more than Lee's initial predictions. Three-quarters of the clientele at Three on the Bund were local Chinese, and they dropped an average of $400 to $500 per visit. Chinese women began to take an interest in luxury goods: sales went up, and luxury brands began to putting more women's clothing and accessories in their stores. By 2004, women accounted for 40 percent of luxury goods sales in China, up from 10 percent in the 1990s. "In other provinces, they say people will buy food with their last penny, but in Shanghai, we'd buy clothes," local shoe designer Denise Huang told *Vogue* shortly after the Armani opening in 2004. Hong Huang, publisher of the luxury goods magazine *I-Look,* concurred: "A girl will spend a month's pay on a handbag. No one would do that in New York or London, but these girls have confidence. They know more money, more opportunity is coming for them."

Fashion magazines became the country's most important source of information on luxury goods. There are Chinese versions of *Elle, Cosmopolitan,* and *Vogue,* each which sell about half a million copies every month, primarily on newsstands. When *Vogue China* debuted in September 2005, it sold out its initial run in five days. The second printing sold out in three days. "The best-selling brands here are Chanel, Dior, and Louis Vuitton," *Vogue China* editor Angelica Cheung told me. "Most Chinese buy luxury as a status symbol rather than taste. They like logos. They want people to know they are carrying something expensive. You see people walk into stores and say, 'Where is this brand from? Italy? Must be good!' They can't pronounce the names and they don't know where it comes from. They just want it because it's expensive."

Brands began to expand into secondary and tertiary cities of six to eight million, such as Hangzhou, Guangzhou, Chengdu, and Xi'an. By the end of 2006, Louis Vuitton had fourteen flagships on Mainland China, including one in Xi'an, and had plans to open two to three new stores each year for several years to come. "We are still underrepresented in China," Vuitton managing director Serge Brunschwig said in 2005. "China's an underdeveloped market with good potential." Giorgio Armani grew from five stores in April 2005 to fifty-three in

2006, and planned to open another twenty-three in 2007. By the end of 2006, Greater China was Armani's second largest wholesale market in Asia, after Japan. Salvatore Ferragamo had thirty stores in China by early 2006 and scheduled another ten to fifteen in two to three years. Calvin Klein had twenty-four freestanding stores for its various lines in early 2006 with plans to open another eighty to ninety stores by 2008. Valentino opened its first mainland China store in 2006 in the secondary city of Hangzhou, along the famous West Lake near Dolce & Gabbana and Giorgio Armani. Most are doing very well. Since its arrival in Beijing in 1992, Louis Vuitton has "never lost any money in any store in China," boasted Vuitton's China CEO, Christopher Zanardi-Landi.

Today, luxury—like everything else in China—is booming. The Chinese economy has grown like no other in history. By 2006, China had become the world's fourth largest economy, after the United States, Japan, and Germany, and economists predict that it will be number one within a matter of a few decades. By 2005, the luxury market in China was worth about $1.3 billion, according to Bain & Company, an American consulting company.

The luxury customer in China has evolved into what Wilfred Koo, Givenchy's president for China–Asia Pacific, calls nouveau chic: young Chinese who "were born post–Nixon opening China, use the Internet, and have so much information." They spend money on themselves and buy top-of-the-line. The nouveau chic bought so much of Armani's more expensive Black Label at Three on the Bund that Lee decided in 2006 to transform the Emporio Armani store upstairs into Black Label space as well. Givenchy introduced a slimmer, more fashionably cut suit, and Zegna manufactures a men's wear line in China solely for the Chinese market. "And the women's business in China is going to boom-boom-boom!" Koo said with a smile.

When I met Koo, a third-generation retail merchant, in Hong Kong in November 2005, he was busy searching for new boutique locations in China. At that time, Givenchy had forty-eight men's wear stores, plus accessories boutiques in Beijing and Shanghai. All the stores there were franchises. "Three hundred shopping malls will open in the next three years in China," he said, incredulously. There were six big malls planned in Beijing alone, making up six million square feet of shopping, most to be open in time for the Summer Olympics in 2008. Givenchy was planning to open two LVMH-owned flagships, in Beijing and in Shanghai, in 2006. "You will see Beijing and Shanghai transformed," Koo assured me.

Handel Lee is a major force in the transformation of both. In the fall of 2007, he plans to open Legation Quarter in Beijing, the city's first luxury complex outside a hotel, at a four-acre compound on the southeast corner of Tiananmen Square that served as the American Embassy from 1903 to 1949 and where Lee's grandfather worked for several years. Legation Quarter, as it is called, will include a 180-seat repertory theater; a twenty-five-thousand-square-foot art gallery; seven restaurants, including one by star New York chef Daniel Boulud; and a handful of "superluxury" brand boutiques, as Lee calls them. "Destination luxury like Brioni and Patek Philippe," he said, "brands that don't want to congregate with their competitors."

In Shanghai, Lee is constructing another luxury destination on the six-acre site of the former British consulate just north of the Peace Hotel on the Bund, a neighborhood that is currently undergoing a major facelift. Among the upscale projects under way are the Peninsula Hotel, Saks Fifth Avenue, and a retail-residential-office complex developed by the Rockefellers. When Lee's complex opens in late 2009, it will have a small concert hall, art museum, luxury retailers and a boutique hotel. Like Three on the Bund, both Legation Quarter and the new Shanghai project should do a bang-up business. Analysts at Ernst & Young predict that in 2010 there will be 250 million Chinese who will be able to afford luxury goods, and by 2014 the Chinese will displace the Japanese as the world's premier luxury brand consumer.

"We started early because we were really convinced that modernization was going on in China," Bernard Arnault said at the opening of the Louis Vuitton Mansion at the China World Trade Centre in Beijing in November 2005. "We knew [China] would someday be the biggest market in the world. Whether it would be in twenty, thirty, forty years, it was irreversible."

The Chinese domestic retail market is only part of the story. Like the Japanese, the Chinese like to travel and shop. Mainland China represented only 2 percent of the luxury market in 2006, but the Chinese accounted for 11 percent of world sales. That figure will likely double within a decade, according to Merrill Lynch. "There are 25 million Chinese traveling [now] and there will be 100 million in 2020," Antoine Colonna, luxury analyst for Merrill Lynch in Paris, said in 2004. "They spend an average of $1,000 on luxury goods [per person per trip]. They might save on dinner or lodging, but not on luxury goods." Vuitton chairman and CEO Yves Carcelle told me at the Vuitton store inauguration in Shanghai in 2004, "Mainland Chinese are one of the most eager to buy when they travel. Each time we sell 100 in China, we sell 150 to Chinese abroad."

The Chinese travel boom began in July 2003, when the Chinese government eased travel restrictions to Hong Kong. By 2005, 76 percent of all mainlanders traveling abroad headed to Hong Kong, and their preferred activity was and is shopping: there's more choice in Hong Kong, and prices are 10 percent lower than back home, where they pay luxury taxes. "Three years ago, Hong Kong accounted for 2 percent of our sales," Bulgari CEO Francesco Trapani told a luxury-brand roundtable in 2004. "Now it accounts for between 15 and 20 percent."

Luxury brands have expanded in Hong Kong to meet the demand. In a matter of weeks in late 2005, both Louis Vuitton and Chanel opened Peter Marino–designed megastores. Louis Vuitton now has six stores in Hong Kong and one in nearby Macau. In comparison, it has three in Paris. DFS is opening a Galleria in Macau in 2008, primarily to target the Chinese. Dior has nine boutiques in Hong Kong, including a flagship on Peking Road in Kowloon that is a massive eleven thousand square feet. "Mainlanders go to Hong Kong with one goal— to buy," said Tom Doctoroff, director for JWT advertising in Shanghai. "Chinese people will gladly spend a price premium for goods that are publicly consumed. But it's like buying a big glob of shiny glitter. They know which brands are famous, but they can't tell you the difference between them in terms of quality or design. [They buy] to burnish their credentials as someone of the modern world by stocking up on a year's supply of prestige."

That doesn't perturb Bernard Arnault. "I think, ultimately, the customers of luxury in China will be sophisticated customers," he said at the Vuitton opening in Beijing in 2005. They are certainly trying. Mainlanders are enrolling their five- and six-year-olds in private lessons (golf, music, ballet, horseback riding, ice skating, polo), etiquette schools, and fast-track courses that bill themselves as junior MBA programs. "These people are rich economically but lacking in basic manners, and they are not very fond of their own reputation," Wang Lianyi, an expert in comparative cultural studies at the Chinese Academy of Social Sciences in Beijing, told the *New York Times*. "These new rich not only want money, they want people to respect them in the future."

A RUSSIAN MAN buys a big new Mercedes. Two weeks later he brings it back to the dealer and says, "I want a new one."

"But sir, you just bought that car," the dealer sputters. "What's wrong with it?"

"The ashtrays are full."

That joke epitomizes Russia's new wealth today: young billionaire oligarchs with a taste for *richesse* to rival the Romanovs'. "I have customers coming in to the store and buying seven hundred socks because they wear them once and then throw them away," said David Gisi, managing director for men's wear at Mercury, one of Russia's largest retail groups. "They consider Rolex to be almost like Swatch."

At first, wealthy Russians spent their wealth overseas. They bought the Côte d'Azur's grandest villas, Ferraris by the dozen, French couture by the collection. So many wealthy Russians have settled in London, Europe's primary financial center, that it is sometimes referred to in the British press as Londongrad or Moscow-on-Thames. The chic neighborhood of Chelsea has been dubbed "Chelsky" and the luxury department store Harvey Nichols is now known as "Harvey Nicholsky." When I asked a Dior employee at the avenue Montaigne store in Paris who were the best customers, she told me without hesitation, "Russians." They came in regularly and dropped $10,000 to $20,000 in an hour. The salesgirls who speak Russian were among the store's busiest. At many of Armani's ready-to-wear stores, Russians bought more than Americans and Japanese.

Now luxury brands are bringing their wares to Moscow, taking advantage of the extraordinary baroque architecture erected when luxury last flourished in the Russian Empire, during the Romanov period. Outside of Moscow and Saint Petersburg, there is no wealth— Russia's minimum wage was about $27 a month in 2005, and wage arrears in 2004 were $820 million—and therefore no luxury market. But there is enough money in Moscow to make luxury tycoons rich and happy. After the 1998 financial crisis that led to the collapse and disappearance of most banks, Russians hoarded an estimated $50 billion in cash, much of which they now spend in luxury brand stores in force. Merrill Lynch analysts have called Russia "a young consumption economy unwilling to save." Pambiamco Consultants, a top fashion marketing and strategy firm in Milan, stated in 2004 that the luxury market in Russia was about $600 million, with an annual increase of 6 to 8 percent. According to AT Kearney, a Chicago-based consulting firm,

Moscow was the most attractive emerging market for retailers in 2003 and 2004, and second, after India, in 2005. By 2009, analysts believe Russians will account for 7 percent of all luxury brand sales.

Across Red Square from the Kremlin and Lenin's Tomb is GUM, the historic nineteenth-century galleria that, during the Communist era, was the State Universal Store. It sold government-issued clothes and food to locals and *matryoshka* nesting dolls to tourists, and was known for its empty shelves and grumpy personnel. Today it is a luxury mall. Among the tenants along the marble walkway are Louis Vuitton, Dior, and Moschino. For the Dior opening in October 2006, actress Sharon Stone cut the ribbon with Christian Dior's own scissors. Then the company hosted a lavish cocktail party for 600 and, later, an intimate dinner of Beluga caviar, roasted lamb, Belvedere vodka, and vintage Dom Perignon for 250 at Turandot, Moscow's new gold-encrusted imperial Asian restaurant.

Nearby, Mercury Group built a one-hundred-thousand-square-foot arcade-like mall in an old cobblestone street called Tretyakovsky Proyezd (Tretyakov Drive). There you'll find wildly rich Russians cleaning out dozens of luxury brand boutiques, including Gucci, Prada, Dolce & Gabanna, and a three-floor Armani spread, replete with a VIP salon. In the evening, they return to Tretyakovsky Proyezd in their darkened-windowed Mercedes SUVs, dressed in their luxury brand purchases, to dine at Mercury's haute-priced haute cuisine restaurant, Tretyakov. "We are building Via Montenapoleone," Mercury's vice president and retail director, Alla Verber, said, referring to the luxury shopping street in Milan. "We deal only in luxury, luxury, luxury. That means luxury cars, luxury fashion, luxury jewelry, luxury food and luxury home products. We are a luxury empire."

A thirty-minute drive from downtown Moscow is Crocus City, a gigantic 690,000-square-foot luxury mall that opened in 2002 and has 180 boutiques, including Armani, Pucci, Céline, Chloé, Versace, and Gianfranco Ferré. "Before we designed Crocus City, we went to Bal

Harbour [in Miami] and Short Hills [New Jersey], and we visited luxury malls across Europe. Then we combined everything we liked together in one vision," Crocus International co-owner and commercial director Emin Agalarov said. "Crocus City is a place where you can walk in on a cold day and find yourself in a tropical paradise where you can shop, relax and be entertained. There's a huge swimming pool with professional synchronized swimmers who do shows every three hours. There's a river that streams down the limestone hallways." It is in the midst of expanding, adding another 120 boutiques, a thousand-room hotel that Agalarov said will be like "the Venetian or the Bellagio, with Russia's biggest casino, and . . . Russia's biggest movie theater with 20 to 25 screens." When finished in 2010, Crocus City will encompass 10.8 million square feet.

The Russian expansion is working. Christian Dior reported sales growth there of more than 50 percent in 2004, and said that its Moscow flagship was the fifth most profitable of its 170 stores. Louis Vuitton CEO Yves Carcelle said that the company sells more ready-to-wear in Moscow than anywhere else in the world. No wonder Christian Lacroix took his haute couture collection to Saint Petersburg in 2005. "And it sold very well," a Lacroix spokeswoman told me cheerfully.

"IF YOU THINK CHINA is something," Yves Carcelle told me, "wait until you see India."

Unlike Russia or China, which both underwent communist periods that all but erased the social and economic class system and cultural heritage, India has always had a wealthy elite that lived well. The maharajas often shopped in Europe and patronized luxury companies, including Louis Vuitton, Chanel, and Cartier, which established the names back home.

What has changed in India in the last few years is the economic rise of the Middle Class. Companies around the world have out-sourced to India, creating jobs and an economic boom. In 2005, ana-lysts estimated that twenty-two million Indians join the middle class each year. For them, just as for middle-market Americans, Japanese, Chinese, and others, logo-covered luxury brands are symbols of their new prosperity. "People have the money and they want to spend it, not save it," said Rachna Mehra, account executive for business develop-ment for Nicole Miller in India.

And luxury brands have flocked to India to meet the new de-mand. By 2006, Louis Vuitton had two stores there, one in the Oberoi Hotel in Delhi and another in the swank Taj Mahal Hotel in Mumbai. Chanel inaugurated its first boutique there, designed by Peter Marino, in April 2005 at New Delhi's Imperial Hotel. The French press reported that its supply of No. 5 sold out before the store even opened for business. Fendi opened a store in the Taj Mahal Hotel in November 2006 with accessories designer Silvia Venturini Fendi—mother of the Baguette bag—cutting the ribbon, followed by a gala dinner at the Taj Mahal Palace. Versace arrived in June 2006; Armani, Valentino, Ferragamo, and Hermès all have plans to expand there.

According to banking analysts at Merrill Lynch, India has about five million luxury customers and is about ten years behind China in market development. As in China, the potential growth for the luxury sector in India is boundless. Both countries have more than one billion people and, combined, account for nearly 40 percent of the world's population. Both have explosive economies and a new class of wealthy entrepreneurs who want to embody Western ideals and an emerging middle market with—as luxury executives like to say—aspiration. There are more than four hundred million with the means to spend on luxury and high-end goods, and says Mehra, "this 400 mil-lion is ripe to shop."

A study by Bain & Company consultants reported that luxury business in India increased by 25 percent in 2005, second in growth only to China. "The growth of luxury in India should be four times higher than the world average in the next five years," Bain & Company reported in 2006. "The number of households with revenues higher than $230,000 a year should nearly triple between 2005 and 2010." In 2006, India's shoppers bought $434 million worth of luxury clothing and accessories, and that figure was expected to double to $800 million by 2010. Goldman Sachs reported that over the next fifty years, India will be the fastest-growing major economy in the world.

What makes India easier for luxury brands to crack than China is its culture and its knowledge of Western luxury: it never closed its doors to the world. The most coveted luxury brand in India in 2006 was Gucci, followed in descending order by Armani, Dior, Versace, Vuitton, Ralph Lauren, Yves Saint Laurent, Chanel, and Prada, according to an ACNielsen study. "In just the last year, our client profile has definitely been expanding," said Karen Wilson Kumar, of Louis Vuitton in India. "We still have a customer that travels widely and shops abroad. But we're now seeing a new wave of clients that are young, upwardly mobile, double-income couples with expendable money. We're also seeing a young generation that looks for the fashion side of Louis Vuitton—the new looks, brighter colors and latest bags. There are a lot of youngsters buying the *pochette* as their segue into Vuitton." There is also a love and tradition of jewelry in India, particularly gold. Analysts at McKinsey & Company believe that sales of branded jewelry such as Cartier and Boucheron will increase by 40 percent annually, to more than $2 billion by 2010.

The only hitch seems to be infrastructure. "The chance of an avenue Montaigne developing in India is very low," said Prasanna Bhaskar, India retail manager for Louis Vuitton. "We do not have the kind of roads and promenades here that customers could easily walk down." India does not have shiny, newly renovated cities like Shanghai or Moscow either. As Valentino Fashion Group CEO Michele Norsa noted, "When you come out of [Mumbai's Taj Mahal Palace & Tower] or a store in New Delhi, the streets are congested and filthy."

Local developers are hoping to change that, or at least offer luxury brands an alternative. State governments are offering tax breaks and discounted loans to help developers fund the construction of malls across the country: more than 375 malls are slated to be completed by 2008. The finance ministry reported in 2006 that the country would receive $150 billion over the next five years for infrastructure improvements, and private construction companies have been busy building a $38 billion network of new roads. That said, analysts and luxury brands see India as a long-term market. "If you ask the firms that are already there, business isn't that great," Hermès International CEO Patrick Thomas said in 2006. "But the potential is there, and it will become an important market."

DOWN A SHORT, nondescript street just behind La Scala opera house in Milan is the epicenter of what's next in luxury branding: the Bulgari Hotel. Housed in a former convent that had been bombed to bits during World War II and rebuilt in the charmless postwar style of public housing, the Bulgari has become, since its opening in May 2004, the preferred gathering place for the city's chic and fashionable. There are only fifty-eight rooms, done up by renowned interior designer Antonio Citterio, with perks that were once de rigueur in luxury hotels: superthick doors that make the room truly soundproof, four-poster oak beds with feather bedding, oak-paneled walls, big bathrooms, and walk-in closets with beechwood hangers. There are modern touches, too, like a motion sensor in each room that lets housekeeping know when someone is there and a spa with a lap pool with gold-leaf tile steps. The Bulgari brand has a discreet presence: a catalog on the coffee table, Bulgari toiletries in the bath, Bulgari green tea candles on the bedside tables, which housekeeping lights for turn-down service. "It's a PR machine for the brand," Bulgari CEO Francesco Trapani said in 2005. "We do not expect that this will be a huge moneymaking venture. It's more of an image thing."

Trapani is one of luxury's most savvy executives. When he was hired by his uncles, Bulgari president Paolo Bulgari and vice president Nicola Bulgari, to become CEO in 1984, Trapani decided, like his fellow luxury tycoons, to take the one-hundred-year-old jewelry company that his great-grandfather Sotirio Bulgari founded to a broader market. He introduced lower-priced jewelry, watches, and perfume; made ad campaigns more accessible; revamped the vaultlike shops into airy, less intimidating spaces; expanded into new markets; and stuck prices next to items in window displays to show middle-market passersby that they, too, could afford Bulgari. In 1995, he listed 32 percent of the company on the Milan stock exchange. Two years later, he launched Bulgari leather goods, followed by boutiques dedicated solely to the new line. By 2005, accessories made up 8.4 percent of all Bulgari sales. In the ten years since Bulgari went public, turnover has increased four times, to more than $1 billion a year, (€919 million in 2005), and profit has risen five times, to $154 million (€116.4 million). "When I took over, we were not part of the big game," Trapani says quite frankly. "Today we are."

Hotels were the next logical step. After all, tycoons like to boast that their companies aren't brands, they are lifestyles, and their creative directors/designers are today's ultimate arbiters of taste. If they can dress you and your home, why shouldn't they envelop you on vacation, too? In 2000, Versace and the Australian property developer Sunland opened Palazzo Versace, a 205-room, 72-condo resort on the Gold Coast of Australia, with three restaurants and a private marina. The place is a temple to the Versace aesthetic, with neoclassical furnishings, parquet floors, and vibrant rococo-print drapes, bedcovers, sheets, and throw pillows. In late 2006, Versace and Sunland signed a deal to roll out another fourteen Palazzo Versaces in the next fifteen to thirty years, starting with Dubai in 2009. "Our hotels aren't for business," Versace CEO Giancarlo Di Risio said. "They're luxury."

Giorgio Armani announced a licensing agreement with Dubai-based Emaar Properties in 2005 to develop a dozen Armani hotels and resorts. Armani himself will handle the design and decor; Emaar, which is investing $1 billion in the project, will manage. The first will open in Burj Dubai, the world's tallest building, and the second in the Emporio Armani complex in Milan, both in 2008. Ferragamo has a handful of boutique hotels in Florence under the Lungarno brand, and Italian brands Missoni and Byblos are reportedly working on hotel projects. Miuccia Prada told me that she had been approached to do a Prada hotel but declined. "For me, doing decoration of a chain is not enough," she told me. "We have to have something to say."

In 2001, Trapani signed a deal with Marriott: Bulgari would do the decor and Marriott's Ritz-Carlton group would handle management. They opened the Milan hotel three years later, followed in 2006 by a plush resort in Bali. "We believed it was an innovative yet legitimate way of leveraging our brand and enhancing its awareness in the luxury market," Trapani told me. "A hotel gives us the opportunity to serve our clientele better with a complete lifestyle experience." In 2005, the Bulgari in Milan generated about $17.5 million (€15 million) in revenues. Bulgari's 65 percent share—€9.6 million—was consolidated into its financial statements. Other projects include boutique hotels in London, Paris, New York, and Tokyo, and by the end of 2005, Trapani was in talks with Handel Lee to open a Bulgari hotel in Lee's British consulate project in Shanghai.

ON A FRISKY FRIDAY night in September 2004, Paris's hip set flocked to the rooftop restaurant of the Centre Pompidou to celebrate fashion's coolest new collaboration: Chanel designer Karl Lagerfeld and H&M, the Swedish low-priced retail chain. Like his work for Chanel, Lagerfeld's H&M clothes were slick and savvy: skinny black pantsuits, crisp white shirts, mod shifts, and chiffonlike cocktail dresses. Unlike his Chanel pieces, however, they were all priced under $150—and most under $100. Lagerfeld wanted to prove that cheap can be fabulous, too. In the end, good fashion isn't about price, he said, "It's all about taste."

Since luxury broadened its reach to the middle market, it has encountered something it had not counted on: serious competition from "fast fashion" companies, such as H&M, Zara, Target, Mango, and Topshop, which produce trendy new clothes and accessories year round and ship to their stores weekly. Their secret weapon is computer technology. Zara uses data from its 426 stores to spot new trends and offers ten thousand new products a year. Topshop generates up to three hundred new designs a week. The shelf life of a garment has fallen from six months to a couple of weeks, creating what *Vogue* editor Anna Wintour calls "a seasonless cycle" for fashion.

To compete with luxury fashion, fast fashion has enlisted the help of top designers. Target hired Issac Mizrahi; Topshop has had Hussein Chalayan and Sophia Kokosalaki; H&M brought in Lagerfeld, Stella McCartney, and Viktor & Rolf. Fashion darling Roland Mouret, who quit his eponymous London-based firm in 2005 after a dispute with its owners, designed a capsule collection for Gap, and in 2006, former Chloé designer Phoebe Philo was reported to be quietly consulting for the company, too.

One snowy winter morning in 2006, I visited H&M's marketing director, Jörgen Andersson, at the company's modern Stockholm headquarters, to find out how luxury fast fashion works. Hennes & Mauritz—or H&M as it is known now—is a Swedish phenomenon. It started out in 1947 as a single store owned and run by an entrepreneur named Erling Persson in Västerås, a town about an hour's drive from Stockholm. In the 1970s, Persson's son Stefan joined the business and expanded it; in 1982, he became CEO, in 1998 executive chairman. The company was listed on the Stockholm stock exchange in 1974, and is one of the country's top-performing companies, along with Ericsson. In early 2006, there were 1,193 stores in twenty-two markets with plans to expand to Dubai and Kuwait. H&M's business is based on high turnover. New garments are delivered to stores every day, which draws customers back regularly. More than 750 people work at the Stockholm headquarters, including a hundred designers who churn out collections nonstop, fifty-five patternmakers, and a hundred buyers for the company's stores. "We usually work on designs a year ahead but we can turn something out in two to three weeks if something hits fast," Andersson explained.

Everyone I met there was young, beautiful, and fashionably dressed in groovy clothes from the new H&M collection by Stella McCartney. Andersson—a tall, handsome Swede, just like you'd imagine—told me that he and the company's creative director, Jan Noord, came up with the idea of inviting luxury designers to do capsule collections for the brand. "We wanted to do a big campaign for Christmas, something different, and we asked ourselves, 'What would be the ultimate gift to women that would exemplify our motto of fashion quality at the best price?'" he explained. "And we started to talk about Karl. Women admire him, and he has constantly proven to be innovative. We called Karl and he loved the idea. He said, from his point of view, H&M is deciding what's in fashion as much as Chanel does, that fashion is created by big fashion houses, but trends are set in the street by how people wear clothes. We came up with the idea of a limited edition, a tight collection, to combine mass distribution with exclusivity: 'massclusivity.' We want to be democratic, but you have to be there on a special day. You could never find Karl on sale."

Lagerfeld did the designs and worked with H&M to choose the fabric, which came from Italy, and the clothes were manufactured in Turkey, Romania, and the Baltic states. Prices were 20 to 30 percent higher than regular H&M prices because, Andersson explained, "we wanted to do the best quality possible." When the collection went on sale, the public reaction was explosive. "We created a fashion event," Andersson remembered. "People would have breakfast and then queue up at H&M. Some items sold out in two hours, like the sequin evening jacket for women. It was all sold out by Christmas, which is what we had hoped for. As Karl says in a video we did, 'Taste has nothing to do with money.' "

The success of fast-fashion luxury designer collections like Lagerfeld's H&M line has rattled the luxury industry, and several companies have changed the way they do business to keep up. Ferragamo centralized inventory and established computer links to suppliers, cutting the design-to-delivery cycle by 20 percent, to ten weeks. Burberry began to offer four to five capsule collections each season. Other fashion houses, including Escada, have come up with midseason collections they call "hot fill-ins," and are delivering clothes to retailers even before the seasonal fashion shows in Paris, New York, and Milan. To keep fashion shows relevant, French fashion association head Didier Grumbach has proposed holding them much earlier in the seasonal cycle.

More important, the emergence of luxury designer fast fashion has finished off whatever division was left between high-end and low-end fashion. These days, the rich buy Isaac Mizrahi designs at Target while the middle market shops at Gucci. Mizrahi calls the phenomenon "bipolar shopping disorder." Lagerfeld thinks it's just terrific. "We live in a time when expensive and inexpensive—not cheap, I hate that word—can live very well together," he told me. "It's the first time in fashion this has happened."

"Before, cheap clothes looked cheap," Andersson told me. "Today, it's nearly impossible to see the difference, and that's what we are trying to prove. We can never be as luxurious as Chanel, but luxury is more in your perception than what it says on the label. We see ourselves as competitors with everyone—Gap, Zara, but also Chanel. Why shop at Chanel if you can shop at H&M?"

CHAPTER ELEVEN

NEW LUXURY

The saddest thing I can imagine is to get used to luxury.

— CHARLIE CHAPLIN

ODAY, THE LUXURY INDUSTRY is like Monopoly. The focus is no longer on the art of luxury; it's on the bottom line. In early 2006, Prada sold the money-losing Jil Sander to a London-based private equity fund called Change Capital Partners for a reported $119.1 million. The Hamburg-based line is now designed by a young, well-regarded Belgian named Raf Simons, while Jil Sander herself, who lives next door to the headquarters, plots her return to fashion. Since 2000, Arnault has unloaded several of his brands. He sold LVMH's stake in Michael Kors fashion to Sportswear Holdings, Ltd., the group that owns Tommy Hilfiger and jewelers Asprey and Garrard; Ebel watches to the Movado Group; Pommery champagne to the Vranken Monopole champagne group; and Christian Lacroix to the Falic Group, the Florida-based duty-free retailers. Most are thriving. At the time I was completing this book, it was rumored that

LVMH's weakest fashion brands—Givenchy, Céline, and Kenzo—may have been on the block. Procter & Gamble shut down the Rochas atelier in 2006 but held on to the perfume license. Designers—once the founders and owners of luxury companies—are now hired hands that are as disposable as the clothes and handbags they create. "All these big companies don't care about you as a person," former Givenchy designer Alexander McQueen said. "You're only a commodity and a product to them and only as good as your last collection."

Presidents and CEOs primarily come from the global corporate world, and the revolving door spins so fast that there are now a handful of headhunter agencies that specialize in placing executives at luxury companies. Business schools now offer degrees in luxury business management. The job of luxury CEO is extremely well paid: Burberry CEO Rose Marie Bravo earned $9.2 million in 2002, and, according to *Forbes,* Coach's CEO Lew Frankfort raked in $55.99 million in fiscal year 2005, making him the thirteenth highest paid chief executive in the world.

Brands are expanding their reach by licensing their names on anything and everything once again. Versace designed a limited edition Nokia telephone (covered in one of its rococo prints) and a Lamborghini. In early 2007, Prada introduced a signature mobile phone with the South Korean electronics firm LG. "A mobile phone is more and more an accessory . . . an object of design and style, a status symbol which almost defines a person—definitely one of the most important objects in a woman's handbag," a Prada spokesman said.

Some applaud the democratization of luxury. "It means more people are going to get better fashion," Anna Wintour, editor of *Vogue,* told me. "And the more people who can have fashion, the better."

But not everyone in the business agrees. "What was once exclusive in Beverly Hills is now everywhere," Fred Hayman told me. "It's lost its cachet. The Gucci store in Beverly Hills was one of the most extraordinary experiences in retailing. Now it is just another Gucci store. When you get greedy, that's what happens."

"To me, luxury is something you want to reach for, that is unattainable," said Ilse Metchek, executive director of the California Fashion Association. "Way back when, luxury was something you really wanted. You looked at society's ladies and you wanted to live like them, and it was unattainable. Now we have Ikea and Desert Hills mall. Where is the difference between Jimmy Choo and the C. H. Baker? Three straps and a high heel at $700 and it'll still be out of fashion at the end of the season. There's always a new heel and a new color. Luxury used to have a shelf life."

Miuccia Prada's mother concurs. "She says that the things [at Prada today] are not well made, that the fabrics are not as good, that everything was much better in her time," Miuccia once said.

A handful of major brands—Hermès and Chanel in particular—strive to maintain and seem to achieve true luxury. The quality comes through in their products—the handmade Kelly and Birkin bags, Joseph Mul's roses in No. 5—and in their philosophies. Both firms over the years have bought or invested in old, traditional luxury brands that produced "exceptional products," as Jean-Louis Dumas calls them, not for simply profit but because the executives wanted them to continue to exist. At Hermès, the brands included John Lobb shoes, Saint-Louis crystal, Puiforcat silversmiths, and Leica cameras. Chanel has a subsidiary that acquires esteemed French specialty companies that have provided fine handcrafted details and accessories for couture for decades and keeps them in business. Known as Paraffection, or 'By Affection', it includes the embroidery house Lesage, shoemaker Massaro, milliner A. Michel, feather and art-flower house Lemarié, costume jeweler Desrues, fabric-flower maker Guillet, and gold- and silversmith Robert Goossens, who collaborated with Coco Chanel to create jewelry for the house from 1955 until her death in 1971. "You cannot advertise a couture dress then put garbage on it," Karl Lagerfeld explained. "Indian embroidery is not bad. But French embroidery from Lesage is another story. As long as we are doing couture, we needed those craftsmen."

The philosophy behind the move is the same as that which sets these two companies apart from their competitors. "Luxury is exclusivity—it is made for you and no one else has it," Françoise Montenay, Chanel's former president for Europe, explained to me. "At a minimum, it must be impeccable. Maximum, unique. It's the way you are spoken to, the way the product is presented, the way you are treated. Like the tea ceremony in Japan: the ritual, the respect, the transmission from generation to generation. At Chanel, luxury is in our chromosomes. It's our credo, something we try to achieve all the time."

The desire by customers to find that impeccable uniqueness for less than the price of a car or a house has created a new subsection in fashion: vintage. When I was a college student, "vintage" was a fifteen-year-old skirt that you bought from the Salvation Army for a buck. Today, "vintage" is a twenty-year-old Yves Saint Laurent haute couture velvet coat with a mink collar for $3,000. Collecting and selling vintage couture has become a good, bona fide business. Shop owners attend auctions and paw through closets of old-time couture clients to find gems for young Hollywood actresses, New York socialites—in fact, anyone who wants something beautifully made and most likely one-of-a-kind. "Buying modern luxury has become an investment," says Cameron Silver, owner of Decades, one of Hollywood's top vintage shops. "Vintage allows women to wear unique, high-quality clothes for a fraction of the price."

Silver, a tall, dark and stylish thirty-six-year-old from Beverly Hills, got into the vintage business by chance. Back in the early 1990s, he was a singer who specialized in German cabaret, and while touring the United States, he spent his free time in thrift stores and charity shops in cities such as Minneapolis, Seattle, and Miami, looking for hip designer men's fashion. "On the racks I'd see all this great women's wear and a lightbulb went off," he told me. "I was looking at vintage not as vintage but as modern clothing that happened to be thirty or forty years old." He returned to L.A. and saw a 1926 Deco building on Melrose a block east of the fashion mecca Fred Segal with a For Rent sign in the window. Silver signed the lease and opened Decades in 1997.

At first, Silver specialized in 1960s and 70s fashion, because, he says, "that's the birth of modern fashion: Courrèges, Cardin, Rudi Gernreich, Yves Saint Laurent, Studio 54." But as he learned more about the history of fashion, he said, "I could see the sexiness of a twenties beaded flapper dress or the glamour of a 1930s bias-cut gown." He started carrying a bit of pre–World War II Chanel, Lanvin, and Schiaparelli as well as anonymous pieces that were of extremely high quality. "When I buy something, I ask, 'Does it look modern and does it look sexy?'" he says. "Every woman at every age wants to look sexy."

In addition to the Melrose boutique, Silver now has a corner in the Dover Street Market in London and does trunk shows in department stores around the world. Prices run from about $200 to $4,000, but can go as high as $35,000 for an early Dior couture evening gown. He has about two thousand regular customers, including celebrities, their stylists, writers, producer's wives, businesswomen. "Basically, anyone with great fashion sense," Silver says. His biggest sellers are original Yves Saint Laurent, Pucci, Halston, and James Galanos. "Glamorous fashion," as he calls it. "There's not much glamour left in contemporary luxury fashion, and if there is glamour, it's mass glamour."

IN THE LAST FEW YEARS, there has been the emergence of a new tribe in the luxury business, what I call luxury refugees: designers, perfumers and executives who grew so disillusioned with the compromises and greed of the luxury corporate world that they fled and started something small and independent that would allow them to do what drew them to the business in the first place: create the best that money could buy. "Luxury fashion brands today are too available, everything is too uniform, and customer business is too pedestrian," Tom Ford, luxury's most recent high-profile refugee, told me recently. "It's like Mc-Donald's: the merchandise and philosophy behind it is very similar. You get the same hamburger and the same experience in every McDonald's. Same with Vuitton. We helped create that at Gucci. It was the right thing at that time. Had we not done it, someone else would have it. The world was becoming a global culture. It was in the air and needed to be addressed, and I'm proud of what we accomplished. But it's not what I'm interested in now. I'm in a backlash. All these handbag ads make me sick. It's so formula. And it's foolish to think that customers are not going to tune out, that they aren't as bored with it as we are. I believe that the little companies are the big ones. There are lessons we can learn from small, old-fashioned luxury."

When Ford left Gucci in April 2004, he took a year off to figure out what he was going to do next. He started a movie production company called Fade to Black with the goal of producing and directing films. He published a coffee-table book of his work. He designed sunglasses and created Tom Ford Beauty, a cosmetics and perfume line with Estée Lauder. And he wrote a business plan for a men's luxury fashion brand known simply as Tom Ford that will include made-to-measure, high-end ready-to-wear, accessories, and leather goods. "We'll have $25,000 watches, custom-made jewelry, and hand-made suits," he told me in May 2006, a year before he opened his first store, in New York. "We'll be closed to the public part of the day, and you have an appointment and meet with your fitter. It's a way to do a new big luxury. I'm not try-ing to create something for everyone. I am creating something for the highly visual, highly urbane customer, and I believe there are enough of these customers out there that business will be just as great as when you go mass."

Perhaps my favorite luxury refugee is French shoe designer Chris-tian Louboutin. He may be the most defiant voice in luxury fashion today. "I'm just back from a meeting with someone who wanted to buy my company again," he told me when we met at his headquarters office one freezing April evening in 2006. "I said no, again."

Louboutin is a rare bird in today's luxury goods industry: a highly successful, purposefully small, designer-owned-and-run company that produces impeccably made items. Louboutin's silk satin stilettos and crocodile pumps can be found on the feet of the beautiful, the famous, and the fashionably in-the-know. Among his regular high-profile clients are Jennifer Lopez, Queen Rania of Jordan, Madonna, Elizabeth Taylor, and *Today* show news anchor Ann Curry, who occasionally flashes Louboutin's signature scarlet soles on camera. Louboutin's company is tiny by luxury standards. After fifteen years in business, he only has seven stores and thirty-five people on staff, including his salespeople. He sells in several upscale department stores, including Barneys New York, Bergdorf Goodman, Neiman Marcus, and Saks Fifth Avenue in the United States and Harvey Nichols, Selfridges and Harrods in the United Kingdom. He does no advertising. He has no marketing department. He does not actively pursue dressing stars for the red carpet. He sells about 100,000 pairs of shoes a year. When I ask him what he does in sales annually, he looked at me blankly. "I have no idea."

What sets Louboutin apart from his confreres is his business philosophy. "I see these men who build luxury brands to make money, and I am working in the same industry but I feel I have nothing in common with that," he explained. "Luxury is the possibility to stay close to your customers, and do things that you know they will love. It's about subtlety and details. It's about service. I cannot accept a place where people are badly received. I can't imagine spending several thousand dollars on something and the salesclerk gets annoyed because you take fifteen minutes to look. Luxury is not consumerism. It is educating the eyes to see that special quality."

This philosophy has been instilled in Louboutin since childhood. He was born and raised in a working-class neighborhood in east Paris.

His mother looked after him and his four sisters. His father was a wood craftsman who made fine furniture and prototypes of French train car interiors. "There were models of interiors of trains all over the house," Louboutin remembered. Louboutin spent afternoons hanging out at the nearby Musée national des Arts d'Afrique et d'Océanie. On the door was a sign with the image of a stiletto shoe crossed with a big red X; spike heels wrecked the parquet. At the time, platforms were all the rage. What on earth, Louboutin wondered, was this steep, slim shoe? He began to sketch it on schoolbooks and scraps of paper.

One day a friend gave him a book about Roger Vivier, the shoe designer for Christian Dior in the 1950s, who is credited with inventing the stiletto. Paging through the book, Louboutin realized he'd found his calling. At sixteen, he was hired to design shoes for the famed Folies Bergères cabaret, and learned how to make them solid enough to withstand professional dancing and high kicks. In his twenties, he worked as a shoe designer at Chanel, Yves Saint Laurent, and Charles Jourdan, which at the time produced Dior's shoes, and helped curate a museum retrospective for Vivier, who was by then in his seventies. "Vivier taught me that the most important part of the shoe is the body and the heel," says Louboutin. "Like good bone structure, if you get that right, the rest is makeup."

When the exhibit concluded, Louboutin needed a job. He knew he didn't want to return to working for the big brands. "It was no longer my dream," he told me. "I asked myself, 'Do you want to work for others for the rest of your life?'" He thought about founding his own shoe company, but he says, "I didn't want to show my shoes to retailers in an old leather suitcase in an office in a bad building in New York." While he was shopping in the passage Véro-Dodat in Paris's Second Arrondissement, he ran into antique gallery owner Eric Philippe, who mentioned that a retail space was available down the way. Louboutin raised approximately $200,000 from his savings and the investments of two friends, signed the lease and in November 1991 opened his shop.

It was a jewel box of a design, with cubbyholes in the walls, each containing one shoe or two shoes. "If you make a precious environment, then what's inside is precious, too," he told me.

He produced his first shoes in a little factory called Evelyne Shoes in Nice. "They were nice, but they were not taking me seriously and they were really too slow," Louboutin remembers. They were also quite expensive: a single pair of shoes cost about $110 if Louboutin supplied the skin and $125 if the factory supplied the skin. "First cost!" Louboutin recalled, rolling his eyes. "Can you imagine?" His retail price was double, plus 20 percent VAT, making his shoes a pricey $270 to $300 a pair.

One of his first customers was Princess Caroline, who, while trying on Louboutin's pumps, declared to her friend that they were "so Anouk Aimée," referring to the chic French movie star. As it happened, the other person in the boutique was a reporter from *W* magazine. When the article was published with Princess Caroline's public anointment, Louboutin became an instant luxury star. The American retailers came that March to buy for the winter 1992–1993 season, and, as Louboutin remembers, "I had no shoes. I had never considered retailers wanting to buy my shoes. There are no luxury department stores in France. The French do not go to a department store for luxury goods. I was like Guerlain, who had his boutique and no distribution." The buyers found Louboutin's shoes to be quite expensive. When he explained that his source was costly, they said, "Why don't you go to Italy?"

He took their advice and found a factory in Lombardy that was more efficient and half the price. He liked the place because it was spotless and they made gorgeous shoes. "If you do luxury," Louboutin explained, "you have to treat people in a human way and you have to be elegant. You can't ask poor people in bad conditions to make beautiful things." Though his reputation and production were rising, his company was still minuscule: himself, an administration person, and a part-time salesgirl in the shop. "When I wasn't in Italy," he remembered, "I was in the store, selling."

His third season, he added his signature scarlet sole. Within three years, he broke even and paid off his debts. In 1997, he opened a store on the Left Bank in Paris. Then came stores in London, New York, and Beverly Hills. In 2003, he opened a franchise in Moscow. "I wasn't excited about doing a franchise," he said, but "franchises are good for places you don't visit, or are foreign to you. A franchise is like a translator in a country you do not understand." In 2007, he is opening in Las Vegas.

The secret to Louboutin's success is his ability to balance the industrial and the exclusive. He will turn out twenty thousand pairs of an elegant, classic pump, but he also designs what he calls Cinderella shoes, delicate treasures that he produces in an extremely limited run. "I have a small piece of batik from Mali that I want to use," he told me. "I think I can do twenty pairs of shoes with it: ten for two different stores. This way, a woman can have the pleasure of having a shoe she'll never see anywhere else and another shoe that is a great shoe." In addition to the Cinderella shoes, Louboutin offers a made-to-measure service where, like couture, you can change the height or the color of a design or come up with something brand new and have it fitted to your foot. "That's why I keep the company on a human scale," he says. "If I lost the laboratory, I'd lose the pleasure of design."

The other reason his company flourishes is simple: integrity. "I remember my father cutting wood," he told me. "If you sculpt in the vein, it's beautiful. If you go against the grain, it breaks. Same goes with business. If you go with the flow, it grows naturally. But if you try to grow your company in an unnatural way, it breaks . . . I did not do a company to make money. I made shoes and it became a company."

Naturally, the luxury tycoons have been circling for a few years now. The first bite came at a dinner party for eight at a private home in Paris in 2000. Louboutin found himself sitting on the sofa surrounded by four top businessmen.

"When can we buy a bit of your company?" one asked eagerly.

"I felt like a girl being invited to dance," Louboutin recalled. "I blushed and said, 'No thank you.'"

"My company grew little by little, and one of the reasons is because I handle everything," Louboutin told me. "I don't have any desire to rush, to concentrate on too many markets. If I did, I would lose the core of my work, which is designing shoes."

Yet Louboutin doesn't completely dismiss the idea of selling. "If there is a moment I no longer want to play this game and I could cash out and do something with that money to help the poor and the sick," he said, "then I'd sell."

ON A COOL SPRING morning in Paris, I was chatting with a Hollywood producer friend who was in town and told him about this book.

"Fine," he said, sizing up the story like a movie pitch. "I see where you're going with this: luxury companies have gone mass and along the way forgotten their original mission, which was to provide the rich with truly exceptional products. So here's what I want to know: What do the rich do now?"

"That's a good question," I answered. "I'll find out."

I thought back to my visit to the Vuitton factory in Asnières. Along with watching the seamstresses and technicians churn out hundreds of logo bags, I saw the craftsmen making a large square wooden jewelry case covered in python. Nothing on the box identified it as Louis Vuitton—no monogram, no label—and though I am not particularly keen on reptiles, I found it to be exceptionally beautiful. It was a one-of-a-kind special order, I was told, for a "good client." Anyone with enough jewelry to fill it, I said to myself, must be a very good client indeed.

For the ultimate in lingerie, the rich go to Alice Cadolle in Paris, a couture house specializing in undergarments run by Poupie Cadolle, the great-great-granddaughter of founder Herminie Cadolle, who invented the bra back in 1889. The experience of having a custom-made bra at Cadolle is luxury in the old-fashioned sense of the term: genuine personal attention, exquisite materials, beautiful handcraftsmanship, all to create something just for you. Poupie, a genial blonde with a knowing smile, receives you in her salmon-colored salon with plum velvet drapes and Herminie's Napoleon III sofas, asks you what you're looking for, and takes your measurements. She has four hundred basic designs to choose from and then alters the pattern to fit your body. You select the fabric—although she prefers to work with lace and tulle—and you choose the color, although Poupie pushes black. "I find that 95 percent of the women look beautiful in black," she told me. "It looks good against their skin."

Poupie makes about 550 made-to-measure bras a year, 100 strapless bras, 50 girdle-like foundations ("for ample women to wear under couture gowns," she said), and 30 traditional lace-up corsets for clients who include several movie stars, one queen, and a few of the showgirls from the Crazy Horse Saloon in Paris. She makes corsets for films as well, including for Juliette Binoche in *Chocolat,* Monica Bellucci in *How Much Do You Love Me?*, and the cast of the French retro whodunit *8 Women.* Four times a year, Poupie travels to New York to see her regular American clients. The basic bra requires three fittings and costs about $800. Matching underwear is $160 to $400, depending on the fabric.

A few years ago, a corporation offered to buy Cadolle. "I said no," Poupie told me. "We have been independent for 120 years, we can be for another 50." She's grooming her pretty twenty-eight-year-old daughter Patricia to take over when she retires. In 2005, Poupie had to move out of the building where her great-grandmother Alice set up shop in 1911. It was a charming old place with a clackety gated elevator and a plush salon with red-velvet drapes. Today, it is part of a half-block-long Roberto Cavalli store.

The really rich still buy and wear couture, which runs from $20,000 for a basic suit to $100,000 for an evening gown. But the regulars generally do not pay full price. "We're dickering, we're in the Armenian rug dealer stage," life-long couture client Nan Kempner told me a few years ago regarding a Dior couture jacket she loved but found to be overpriced. "One has one's priorities," she said.

She got the jacket.

I remember attending a fitting for one of Dior's best clients one afternoon in the avenue Montaigne couture salons. She ordered eight or ten gowns with matching made-to-measure shoes. When she was presented the bill, the vendeuse made sure to point out that these were special prices. The message was clear: if you buy couture in bulk, you get a discount.

The really rich do not attend the couture shows either. "Most of the Chanel clients are not here," Karl Lagerfeld told me after the Chanel couture show in July 2006. "They have other things to do, you know? But the oceans are crossed by private jets for fittings."

"Who are they?" I asked.

"New fortunes. Huge fortunes. People who are richer than air. People we don't really know—we know if the money is clean—but people who don't want to be identified. It's not the red carpet. Whenever you have the dress on the red carpet, those women, they cancel their order immediately. The women who buy couture don't want to be identified with actresses."

"Where do they live?"

"China, there are more than a couple."

A few days later, Chanel's head seamstress and one of its vendeuses were flown with the collection to China for the weekend on a private jet. "There will always be a need for haute couture," socialite São Schlumberger told me, "because there will be people who, if it exists in red, will want it in white, who want quality, something special for themselves, something where there aren't dozens of the same."

In the United States, the rich shop at Giorgio Armani. The wealthiest 5 percent of Americans account for 47 percent of all sales in Armani-owned stores, Victoria Cantrell, senior vice president and chief information officer for Giorgio Armani Corporation, said in 2006.

For jewelry, the rich prefer custom-made. The French fine jeweler Boucheron, owned by Gucci Group, reported in 2005 that special orders were up 15 percent a year.

For handbags, they order Hermès.

Yet they also shop at outlets. When I was at the Desert Hills Premium Outlets in August 2006, I spotted a shiny young couple loading shopping bags into the trunk of their ivory Maybach 62 sedan—which at the time sold for more than $380,000 new. When I tried on a pair of black leather mules at the Sergio Rossi outlet later that afternoon—which, at half price, still ran $200—the saleswoman told me, "We had a princess in here the other day who so loved those shoes she bought them in every color. She comes here every season."

They demand and take advantage of perks, such as personal shoppers who not only pull clothes for private viewings and fittings in plush salons but also cater to a customer's every whim. Danielle Morolo, a personal shopper at the Americana Manhasset luxury shopping center in Manhasset, New York, packs customers' suitcases. She runs errands—once it was all the way Palm Springs—and she spent part of her vacation in Florence to hunt down lace for a customer. "I've had people call me from the office and ask me to go to their homes and pick something out of the closet because they didn't like what they were wearing," she said. "I have the security codes to clients' homes."

They don't even have to show up to shop. "My best customer lives in Atlanta, but hasn't been in the store since the Super Bowl 2000," said Jeffrey Kalinsky, owner of the trendy fashion boutique Jeffrey in Atlanta and in downtown New York. "We mail her a package every week, she picks out what she wants, and sends the rest back. These days, we go to them." Los Angeles retailer Tracey Ross regularly secures tickets to *American Idol* or movie premieres for customers, and sends customized gift baskets to their homes or hotel rooms.

Hong Kong luxury retailer Lane Crawford opened a VIP suite that connects to its neighboring Four Seasons hotel in 2005 for its best clients. The three-thousand-square-foot Platinum Suite, as it is called, is spacious and modern, with commanding views of Hong Kong harbor. Among its perks are the hotel's concierge and restaurant services as well as stylists and makeup artists to help you choose just the right outfit from Lane Crawford and get dressed for an event. The suite is often booked for private meetings and dinner parties, but Bonnie Brooks, president of the Lane Crawford Joyce Group, told me during visit, "If you are in Hong Kong for the day, and want a place to park, you can come here. And you don't have to spend."

Saks Fifth Avenue invites its top-spending clients to an annual dinner at a top New York restaurant—in 2006, it was at Le Cirque—and sends them home with goodie bags stuffed with cashmere blankets, Baccarat crystal vases, or Fabergé eggs. Neiman Marcus's customers who spend $5 million a year on their Neiman Marcus credit card receive complimentary memberships to Exclusive Resorts, a luxury residence club, and three weeks at one of the properties. "[Big-spending customers] like to be coddled," a Saks spokeswoman said. "Getting VIP treatment makes you feel special. It's human nature. You love to get the prize."

In Las Vegas, the really rich stay in hidden villas that are furnished with European antiques and include twenty-four-hour butler service, private pools, private gyms, saunas and steam rooms, and entourage rooms for their nannies, pilots, chefs, and whoever else is in tow.

They have perfume made just for them, like Louis XIV did three centuries ago. Each year, Patou receives a handful of orders for in-house nose Jean-Michel Duriez to create a made-to-measure perfume bottled in a Baccarat crystal flacon. The service costs approximately $70,000.

And if they live in or visit South America, they shop at Daslu, the world's most luxurious store.

OVER THE LAST FEW YEARS, I had heard about Daslu, the luxury fashion emporium in São Paolo, Brazil, owned and run by a savvy, ambitious woman named Eliana Tranchesi, and, to me, it sounded like everything that luxury brands professed to be.

Daslu started, like most other successful luxury ventures, quite humbly. Back in 1958, Tranchesi's mother, a high-society lawyer's wife named Lucia Piva de Albuquerque, would fly from São Paolo to Rio de Janeiro to buy Brazilian high fashion. Then she'd invite her lady friends to her modest 1940s home in the posh Vila Nova Conceição neighborhood to sell them the clothes, donating a portion of her profits to charity. At the time, Brazil was closed to imports. If South Americans wanted European luxury, they would travel to Europe or the United States to buy it. Over the years, Lucia's living room business grew. Official store hours were 1:00 to 5:00 p.m. She hired her friends' daughters to help with sales. Her uniformed maids scurried about, serving tea and coffee and fetching clothes from various rooms. It became known as Daslu, which translates to "In Lu's House."

In 1977, Eliana, then twenty-one, began to get involved. She worked as a salesgirl and launched an in-house label, which she designed and had produced in Brazil. Lucia bought the house next door to expand the retail space. As the business grew, Lucia added another, and another, and another, and connected them, creating a warren of salons filled with shoes, clothes, handbags, and jewelry. Eventually Daslu took up the better part of a tree-lined block. "It didn't have any windows, and there were no signs outside," Tranchesi told me over tea at the Plaza Athenée one October afternoon in Paris in 2005. "There was an awning with a big D on it, and that's it." When Lucia died in 1983, Eliana took over.

In 1989, Brazil's new president, Fernando Affonso Collor de Mello—the first democratically elected leader in twenty-six years—implemented an economic plan to battle the country's rampant inflation that included freezing assets and bank accounts, and easing restrictions on imports. For Tranchesi, it was an answer to her prayers. "I said, 'We are going to have Chanel, Gucci!'" she remembered. "And my friends said, 'Are you crazy? No one has any money.'" Tranchesi didn't care. "I knew we had clients with taste," she told me, "that there would be a market." She jumped on a plane and flew to Europe to meet with fashion houses. "The first collection we bought was Claude Montana," she remembered. It was followed by Valentino and Moschino. In the mid–1990s, a Chanel bigwig traveled to São Paolo and stopped by Daslu to see what the all the hubbub was about. He was bowled over.

"We have to have a Chanel store in here," he told Tranchesi when they met in her little office upstairs. "But where?"

Tranchesi looked around.

"Here," she said.

"There were thirteen other important retailers in São Paolo at the time with big display windows on the street," Tranchesi told me, "and he chose Daslu, inside, on the third floor, in the middle of the men's department! He came to the opening and at the end of the day he was on his knees putting shoes on clients' feet. We sold 70 percent of the collection in the first day. I asked friends to leave behind some of what they had purchased so I could show it the second day."

Though Chanel was a roaring success, Tranchesi still had trouble getting brands to sell to her. "They didn't see Brazil as a good market," she said. "But then they'd come here and were overwhelmed." Eventually, she snagged Gucci, Prada, Zegna, and Dolce & Gabbana, which all set up in-store boutiques. To make room for them, Tranchesi had to keep buying and renting neighboring houses. By 2002, she had twenty-three houses, for a total of 135,000 square feet, and seventy thousand clients. Their armored limos with bulletproof glass clogged the street. Neighbors started to complain. When Tranchesi needed to expand even more, the zoning commission said no, so she decided it was time to move. In June 2005, she closed the old, rambling Daslu and inaugurated the new Daslu, a 180,000-square-foot Florentine-villa-like fashion emporium in Vila Olímpia, a bustling business district about a mile from the original location. In the first four months, she added fifteen thousand new clients.

In April 2006, I traveled to São Paolo, the world's fifth largest city, with eighteen million people, specifically to visit the new Daslu. Even with all I knew about the store, I was still knocked out.

You enter by a long private driveway and pass through two security gates. The economic disparity in Brazil is radical and divisive: the poorest 40 percent of the country's 188 million possess only 8 percent of its wealth, many living in sprawling urban shantytowns known as *favelas*. The richest—the country's ruling class—live like pre-revolution aristocrats with fortified homes where they entertain lavishly, with armored limos and bodyguards. "We have a lot of problems with security here," Mônica Mendes, Daslu's international director of marketing, explained to me. "The really rich don't go out and walk in the streets." Most cars have darkened windows not to block sunlight but for security, and you never, ever roll your window down. Locals will drive through red lights rather than stop and take the risk of being carjacked. Mendes was so nervous sitting at one red light where there were a few squeegee guys that when it turned green and we drove on unharmed, she crossed herself and said a prayer of thanks. "São Paolo is one of the most important markets for bulletproofing," she said. "Everybody has it."

Once you arrive at the store's entrance, a valet takes your car and you are whisked inside the vanilla marble hall to the concierge desk, where a hostess will sign you in. If you are a regular, you have probably already alerted your regular salesgirl that you are coming, and the hostess will ring to tell her you've arrived. If not, you will be assigned a salesgirl for your visit. The salesgirls are known as Dasluzettes and are the daughters of São Paolo's best families. They are *très soigné*—tall and thin, with smooth butternut skin and long glistening hair—and they move in the city's rarefied social circles, attending smart dinner parties and extravagant galas nightly. "The salesgirls live the life that the customers live," Tranchesi explained. "So they understand."

If you're a regular customer, chances are your Dasluzette has already pulled several pieces that you will probably love and put them aside in a private salon for you to try on. New clothes arrive often, which is why Daslu's best customers tend to come to the store four times a week. "Women in Brazil are completely crazy about fashion," Mendes told me during my visit. "Clients buy American *Vogue,* tear out the pages, give them to the salesgirl and say, 'When that arrives, I want it.' When the Fendi Baguette first came out, we sold them all in presale before we received them."

If you are a new customer, like I was, your Dasluzette will give you a tour, collecting items that interest you as you move from room to room. Like the old Daslu, the store layout is like a house with interconnecting salons. The decor is in soft off-white tones with thick champagne-hued carpeting—it's as if you've plunged into a vat of *crème anglaise*—and white orchids everywhere. On the ground floor are the designer boutiques, including all the regular suspects: Vuitton, Dior, Gucci, Valentino, Jimmy Choo, Sergio Rossi, Chloé, Pucci, Valentino, Manolo Blahnik. "Every young Brazilian woman knows Manolo Blahnik," Tranchesi said with a laugh. "And Valentino sells well because the husbands love their wives in Valentino dresses." For most of the brands, Daslu owns the franchise and chooses the clothes. But the brands usually handle the decor themselves, to maintain continuity; Peter Marino designed the Chanel and Dolce & Gabbana boutiques. Vuitton, Burberry, Armani, and Ferragamo lease their space from Daslu. The Vuitton store, at four thousand square feet, is the largest in Latin America.

On the second floor you'll find fine jewelry, perfume, lingerie, swimwear, vintage wear, a few more luxury brands, a champagne bar, the Leopolldina restaurant, and Daslu private label for women, known as Daslu Collection. No men are allowed in the Daslu women's department, and there are security guards posted at the entrances to make sure. There are no dressing rooms on the women's floor. Instead, customers strip down to their lacy underwear and try on the clothes right there on the sales floor. "My mother only received friends, so there was no problem changing in front of one another," Tranchesi explained. "I did the same: friends receiving friends, so no need for changing rooms. It's natural for Brazilians. You aren't ashamed if men aren't around."

The Daslu collection has become a pillar of the store. It accounts for 60 percent of sales there and is now carried by several international retailers including Bergdorf Goodman, Saks-Jandel in Washington, Tracey Ross in L.A., and Harrods and Browns in London. Tranchesi still designs the collection and has it made in Brazil, mostly in locally produced materials. The clothes are casual chic: swishy jersey dresses, sexy stretch jeans, towering strappy sandals decorated with big faux jewels, filmy gowns flecked with crystals. As you settle into one of the cozy corners with comfy sofas to try them on, the maids, known as the "uniform girls" because of their black dresses with white aprons and stockings, will serve you refreshments. "When Daslu was in my mother's house, the maids, who wore the same uniform, helped and served," Tranchesi explained. "They started by giving coffee or water. Then they started to put the clothes back." Now there is an army of three hundred.

The ambiance at Daslu is clubby and delightfully upbeat. Customers come from Rio and Salvador, Argentina and Peru. Everyone knows everyone—there are plenty of air kisses. They shop for a few hours, meet up for high tea in the Leopolldina restaurant or for a drink in the champagne bar, catch up on gossip, then shop some more. Six times a year, Daslu hosts a festive fashion show/party for ten thousand of its best customers. "The women dance, shop, and have a great time," Mendes says. On Tuesday evening, Daslu stays open until ten, and chic Paulistas meet there for dinner and shopping. The wealthy and famous like Daslu, she explained, "because you have a lot of privacy, you have everything you need, and everyone is treated like a VIP." Celebrities particularly like the safety of the Daslu compound. "Nothing happens to them here," Mendes said. "No one notices or bothers them. [Formula One champion] Michael Schumacher came here last year and nobody said anything. [Brazilian soccer star] Ronaldo is one of the most important clients we have at Daslu and nothing happens. No autographs. No photos. Nothing." A few years ago, Tranchesi had a study done of shopping habits at Daslu. "Normally, in a Brazilian shopping mall, 20 percent buy," she told me. "At Daslu, 75 percent of people who walk inside buy something."

On the third floor is the men's department. There's a Johnnie Walker whiskey bar, a bookstore with a fireplace and sofas, and even a La Perla lingerie boutique, "so they can buy for their wives and girl-friends," Mendes says. There's a men's Daslu ready-to-wear line; departments dedicated to electronics, athletic wear, and gym equipment; a travel agency; a luxury real estate agency; Mitsubishi, Volvo, and Maserati dealerships; a Ferretti yacht broker; a Daslu helicopter dealer (one hangs on display in the atrium); a tobacconist; a music department; a Japanese restaurant called Kosushi that is considered the best in São Paolo; and a wine department with a selection of vintages to rival the best caves in Paris.

On the fourth floor, you find the children's clothing and toy department, with a playroom and a kid's-height bar with bowls of gumdrops and plates of chocolate chip cookies, a bank, a pharmacy where you can fill your prescriptions, a hairdresser where each client has a private room, and a spa: "Brazilian women are crazy about the body and skin care—it's unbelievable," Mendes said. "They have facial massages regularly." Daslu of course has the best facialist in town. "It takes four or five months to get an appointment." She adds. In addition, there is Casa Daslu, with table-, glass-, and silverware as well as refrigerators, barbecues, and a Viking showroom; a stationer to do your engraved notepaper and invitations; a chocolate shop run by Tranchesi's sister, where all the chocolates are made by hand; and a bakery called Pati Piva that does extravagant tiered wedding cakes. On the ground level, there is a consecrated wedding chapel, and on the fifth floor is a series of immense terrace-like reception rooms and a ballroom that can seat thirteen hundred, all with a view of the city. "I think Daslu is the only place in Brazil where you can do everything for your wedding, including holding the ceremony and the reception, booking the honeymoon, and buying the house," Mendes said.

When it is time to pay, you are ushered into a lounge-like room where you sit on one of the comfortable Louis XVI chairs, have a coffee brought to you by a uniform girl, and chat with your salesgirl while everything is run up. On the counter sits a pile of the latest Daslu CDs, a compilation by the Daslu deejay of hip Brazilian and Latin music, which you can buy for a few reales. On the wall is a flat-screen TV broadcasting Daslu TV. Throughout the store, Daslu radio is playing. You pay the bill and are escorted out by your Dasluzette, empty-handed. Everything has been sent down to your car, or up to the helipad.

There are seven hundred Daslu employees, including the uniform girls; a thousand others employed by brand shop-in-shops, travel agencies, restaurants, and so on; and nine hundred third-party service providers such as valets, janitors, and security guards. Next door, Daslu has an employee day care center called the Villa Daslu Educational Center with a nursery where female staff can come and nurse

their babies three times a day, and a school for children up to age fourteen. Some two hundred attend. The children receive instruction in
English, art, sewing, piano, guitar, and ballet—often by clients. When
I visited the school, I met two tall, elegant clients who had just finished teaching a group of eight-year-old girls in the ballet studio.
There is also a pediatrician, a dentist, and a psychologist. After a hot
lunch in the school cafeteria, children seven and older go to the local
public school. Younger children stay and play. They have snack time
on picnic benches in the garden. "The uniform girls were unhappy
with the schools and the quality of life for their children, so we opened
the school," explained Mendes as we walked down the hallway and
visited classes. "This is even better than my children's school."

But what really sets Daslu apart from other luxury retailer's is
Tranchesi's personal involvement with the business. Chances are,
you'll run into her while you are shopping, and she'll ask how the kids
are, help you pick out a few things, or assist in fittings. "In America, in
Europe, retailers know what they've sold by looking at the numbers in
the computer," she told me. "I know what we sell here because I'm on
the shop floor. I don't sit in an office. I run the business from here"—
and she tapped her belly. "In luxury brand stores, when you pay, they
forget about you. They completely forget about you," Mendes told me.
"Eliana doesn't just know the name of the client, she *knows* the client.
Daslu is her house, and the customers are her guests."

Shortly after the opening at the new location in July 2005, Daslu
was raided by federal police agents and Tranchesi was arrested for alleged tax evasion. The government alleged that import-export firms
falsified invoices listing prices of imported goods far below market
value to allow Daslu to pay less in duty. "It was crazy—280 police came
to the office," said Mendes. "You never see that in a *favela*, even when
there is a big drug trafficking bust. But Daslu, yes. It was to show off
in the press, to draw attention from Lula and his problems," she said,
referring to President Luis Inacio Lula da Silva, the country's socialist

president, who has been embroiled in a series of corruption scandals. Tranchesi was released shortly after. In December 2006, Daslu was ordered to pay $110 million in back taxes. The store planned to appeal.

On the second day I went to Daslu—it took three entire days to see the place—I had lunch with one of its good customers, a chic woman named Cristiane Saddi, the marketing director for the local Mercedes dealership that her husband owns. She also volunteers at a local Syrian-Lebanese hospital that her grandmother and her great-aunt founded. Saddi is one of those remarkable women who give Brazil its reputation as the land of stunningly sensual women: thin, tan, and taut, with long black hair as slick as oil and eyes to match, she was dressed in a tight white Dolce & Gabbana blazer over a lacy white camisole, skinny white Diesel jeans, big diamond stud earrings, and towering heels. We met in Leopolldina, Daslu's elegant restaurant and one of São Paolo's top power spots, packed daily with celebrities, businessmen, and socialites. The chef is Italian, and the cuisine is a Best of Europe tour: filet mignon with red wine sauce, wild mushroom risotto, lobster-stuffed ravioli, prosciutto and melon, and seviche.

We talked of her Daslu experience. "My mother used to go to the original one and would take me," Saddi said as she tucked into an ample lunch of beef filet and pasta. "I started shopping there myself when I was fifteen. Now I'm forty-three. It grows and grows and never loses that family feel. You're not received as a client but as a family friend. When I got married, we lived just down the street. I would call and say, 'I need a gift for this or that,' and they would pull something. Salesgirls are your friends. They are in the same social swirls. When you go to Daslu, it's not to buy a new pair of shoes. It's to see your friends. You can't find this service anywhere else in the world."

And we talked about life as a São Paolo socialite: "You can be everything all together—work, mother, hostess—because you have staff," she said. "In return, you help with the schools, houses, everything. My driver has been with me twenty-one years, since I married, and I have watched his children grow up. When he was sick I put in him in the hospital and got him the best doctors, the best treatments. You help them, because they help you. All the families here do that. It's an exchange."

What I really wanted to know, though, was this: what, for Cristiane Saddi, is luxury today?

"Daslu is a luxury because you can do what you want," she explained, pouring dark chocolate sauce over two slices of cake. "They have the best brands and the best choice in the world, from bras to evening gowns to housewares. Everything you need for everything. How many fashion stores also sell cars? You just think about a product—you can buy it at Daslu."

After two days at Daslu, I understood what she meant. Daslu may have been dreamy, but it wasn't a dream.

As she dug into her cake, I began to think about the state of the luxury business, how it seemed over the last two decades to have lost its soul. I wondered where it would go: what would it do once the Japanese and Americans had grown weary of luxury brands and emerging markets were saturated? When gimmicks like art galleries and gala concerts would no longer draw crowds in the stores? When there were no more corners to cut and there was no more growth to be had? Was there enough integrity or value left in these brands to allow them to continue to call themselves "luxury"? Or, more important, to maintain their legitimacy, I asked Saddi, would they be able to keep the wealthy like her and her peers as customers?

"Yes," she said. "The Louis Vuitton here carries only its most expensive items," she said. "Daslu clients don't need the logo entry-level handbag or to wear labels or logos. We buy from luxury brands, but not ordinary products. Special items. There's always something special. You can see what is mass and what is special. Luxury is not how much you can buy. Luxury is the knowledge of how to do it right, how to take the time to understand and choose well. Luxury is buying the *right thing*."

And with that, Saddi wiped the chocolate off her lips, reapplied her lipstick, got up, and kissed me good-bye.

"Must get back to work," she said, and she clicked off in her stilettos.

ACKNOWLEDGMENTS

Deluxe exists thanks in large part to two extraordinary women: Nina Hyde, the legendary fashion editor of the *Washington Post,* who gave me my first job as a fashion reporter in the late 1980s, and taught me that fashion was as serious and respectable a beat as covering the White House; and Amy Spindler, style editor of the *New York Times Magazine,* who assigned me a series of major investigative pieces about the fashion industry in the late 1990s, and said to me, "You should turn this into a book." She was right. Sadly, like Nina Hyde a decade earlier, Amy Spindler succumbed to cancer far too young and before she could see it happen.

Peter Riva helped shape the idea for *Deluxe* and gave me the kick I needed to sit down and write the proposal. My agent, Tina Bennett at Janklow & Nesbit, had the patience to keep rereading it for what seemed like forever until it sparkled, then sent it to Ann Godoff and Emily Loose at Penguin Press in New York and Stefan McGrath at Penguin Press in London, who—on my fortieth birthday, no less—courageously took me on and guided me into authorship. Penguin Press editors Jane Fleming and Helen Conford tag-teamed me, asking all the right questions and adding needed structure, both to me and the manuscript. Happily, their interpretation of "a couple of more months" was as elastic as mine.

Deluxe would not contain half the information it has without *Newsweek.* My editors Fareed Zakaria, Nisid Hajari, and Susan Greenberg and my Paris bureau chief Christopher Dickey allowed me to wander the planet on behalf of the magazine in search of the real story behind the luxury industry, and published early versions of these reportages in *Newsweek's* international edition. Sue Greenberg further gave up weekends and part of her New Year's vacation to gently shape the manuscript into a seamless read, as she has done with my *Newsweek* copy for more than a decade. Longtime *Newsweek* Paris bureau photo editors Ginny Power and Jacqueline Duhau helped to choose and find just the right pictures to accompany my words and popped up my spirits when they started to wane.

A slew of young, hungry reporters helped me with research, including Marie Valla, Jenny Barchfield, Remi Hoki, J. J. Martin, Erin Zaleski, Florence Villeminot, Nicole Martinelli, Laura Czigler, and Lauren Greenwald. These dynamic young women spent hours chasing down obscure numbers, setting up interviews in far-flung places, and, when needed, translating foreign languages. Fact-checker supreme Austin Kelley pored through mountains of documents, deciphered my scribble, and followed up with sources to make sure I got it right. And several luxury brand PR folks—including Amee Boyle at Giorgio Armani, Olivier Labesse at DGM Conseil, Marie-Louise de Clermont-Tonnere and Claire Chassard at Chanel, Annelise Catineau and Olivier Monteil at Hermès and the unflappable Nathalie Tollu at Louis Vuitton—answered my seemingly endless barrage of follow-up questions with speed and aplomb. I could have never pulled this book together without them.

I am deeply grateful to the hundreds of people I interviewed for *Deluxe* on the record, including Wanda McDaniel, Kenneth Fang,

Tom Ford, Laudomia Pucci, Kris Buckner, Handel Lee, Menehould de Bazelaire, Leslie Caron, and Olivia de Havilland, and those who spoke to me off the record and told me the secrets of the luxury industry. Mônica Mendes was right to insist that I travel to São Paolo to see Daslu firsthand, and was extraordinarily welcoming when I did, and Jennifer Woo and Bonnie Brooks of Lane Crawford, Wilfred Koo of Givenchy, and David Tang helped me negotiate Hong Kong and Guangzhou, making what seemed impossible achievable. Several friends, including Laurie Sprague, Cathy Nolan, Kevin Mulvey, and Mike Medavoy, read *Deluxe* in rough form or debated its premise with me, and their input shaped its outcome. I must also thank photographers Don Ashby, Marcio Madeira, and Patrick Demarchelier and artist Tom Sachs for generously providing beautiful images for *Deluxe*, Andre Balazs, Philip Pavel and everyone at the Chateau Marmont for putting up with me as I tried to channel the hotel's writing ghosts, and the indefatigable June Newton, who kindly invited me into her home and took the most honest portrait of me ever.

More than once while reporting and writing *Deluxe* I thanked the heavens above for allowing me to start my journalism career in the Style section of the *Washington Post*—the writer's section of the writer's newspaper—during the reign of the *formidable* Ben Bradlee. Editors Mary Hadar, Deborah Heard, Rose Jacobius, and Gene Weingarten and music critic Joseph McLellan took me as a green and eager college student, gave me terrific assignments, and pushed me to dig deeper and write better. It was journalism boot camp and finishing school all in one, and I use all that they taught me every day of my career.

Most important, I could have never written *Deluxe* without the encouragement of my family and the profound support and love of my husband, Hervé, and our incredibly patient daughter, Lucie—my light—who gamely accompanied me on many of my reporting adventures and spent half of her six-year life waiting for me to finish this project.

Now, honey, now we can go play in the park.

NOTES

INTRODUCTION
Page

3　**The luxury goods industry:** Claire Kent, luxury goods analyst, Morgan Stanley London, e-mail, April 18, 2005.

3　**Thirty-five major brands:** Claire A. Kent et al., "Making the Sale," Morgan Stanley Dean Witter, March 11, 1999, p. 10.

4　**In Asia:** David B. Yoffie and Mary Kwak, "Gucci Group N.V., (A)" Harvard Business School, case 9–701–037, September 19, 2000; revised May 10, 2001, p. 4.

6　**The Chinese enriched:** Palmer White, *The Master Touch of Lesage: Embroidery for French Fashions* (Paris: Editions du Chêne, 1987), p. 16.

7　**As Diana Vreeland:** Diana Vreeland, *D.V.* (New York: Da Capo Press, 1997), p. 47.

7　**"I'm no philosopher":** Stanley Karnow, *Paris in the Fifties* (New York: Random House, 1997), p. 263.

10　**In 2005:** "Best & Most 2005," Generation DataBank, www.generation.se.

11　**In their best year:** Rana Foroohar, with Mac Margolis in Rio de Janeiro, "Maximum Luxury," *Newsweek Atlantic Edition*, July 25, 2005, p. 44.

11　**The Swiss bank:** Rana Foroohar, "Going Places," *Newsweek International*, May 15–May 22, 2006, p. 54.

11　**The private security:** Ibid., p. 58.

12　**By 2011:** Foroohar, "Maximum Luxury," p. 44.

12　**When Arnault:** Deborah Ball, "Decisiveness and Charisma Put Yves Carcelle in the Hot Seat at LVMH's Principal Division," *Wall Street Journal Europe*, October 1, 2001, p. 31.

13　**"What I like":** "Arnault, in His Own Words," *Women's Wear Daily*, December 6, 1999, p. 11.

CHAPTER ONE: AN INDUSTRY IS BORN

17　**"Luxury is a necessity":** Anna Johnson, *Handbags: The Power of the Purse* (New York: Workman, 2002), p. 21.

18　**Its flagship:** Eric Wilson, "Optimism's the Point, Not Excess Baggage," *New York Times*, October 13, 2005, p. G1.

18　**"Luxury is crossing":** Joshua Levine, "Liberté, Fraternité—but to Hell with Egalité!" *Forbes*, June 2, 1997, p. 80.

20　**"High profitability":** Suzy Wetlaufer, "The Perfect Paradox of Star Brands," *Harvard Business Review*, October 2001, p. 123.

22　**Louis XIV dressed:** Stanley Karnow, *Paris in the Fifties* (New York: Random House, 1997), p. 268.

22　**Louis XVI's wife:** Judith Thurman, "Dressed for Excess: Marie-Antoinette, Out of the Closet," *New Yorker*, September 25, 2006, p. 138.

22　**She was "an object":** Palmer White, *The Master Touch of Lesage: Embroidery for French Fashion* (Paris: Editions du Chêne, 1987), pp. 20–21.

22　**"French fashions":** Karnow, *Paris in the Fifties*, pp. 268–69.

23　**At the age of thirteen:** Paul-Gérard Pasols *Louis Vuitton: The Birth of Modern Luxury*, (New York: Abrams, 2005), p. 13.

23   **The 292-mile trek:** Ibid., p. 21.

23   **"Here you find":** Ibid., p. 24.

23   **Vuitton became:** Ibid., p. 30.

23   **In 1854:** Ibid., p. 354.

23   **Throughout the mid-1800s:** White, *Master Touch of Lesage*, p. 24.

24   **"Women will stoop":** Karnow, *Paris in the Fifties*, p. 270.

24   **Worth's dresses:** White, *Master Touch of Lesage*, pp. 24–25.

24   **His prices:** Karnow, *Paris in the Fifties*, p. 271.

24   **Louis Vuitton's business:** Pasols, *Louis Vuitton*, p. 88.

26   **To keep up with:** Ibid., p. 76.

26   **"In those days":** Maria Riva, *Marlene Dietrich: By Her Daughter* (New York: Knopf, 1993), p. 111.

26   **In the 1920s, France:** White, *Master Touch of Lesage*, p. 56.

27   **In five years:** Ibid., p. 51.

27   **In the 1930s:** Ibid., p. 62.

27   **"The huge skirt":** Diana Vreeland, *D.V.* (New York: Knopf, 1984), p. 98.

27   **But couturier Lucien:** Marie-France Pochna, *Christian Dior: The Man Who Made the World Look New* (New York: Arcade, 1996), p. 78.

27   **"You can force us":** Ibid., p. 77.

28   **The Vuittons were:** Kim Willsher, "Louis Vuitton's Links with Vichy Regime Exposed," *Guardian*, June 3, 2004, p.15.

28   **"The styles [during]":** Karnow, *Paris in the Fifties*, pp. 266–67.

29   **I remember Ivana:** Nina Hyde, "Lacroix's Curtain-Raising Couture; Kicking Off the Fall Shows with Soft Chiffon & Crepe," *Washington Post*, July 24, 1988, p. G1.

30   **The swanlike models:** Karnow, *Paris in the Fifties*, pp. 258–59.

30   **"After all the horrors":** Ibid., p. 264.

30   **The Parisian clients:** Ibid., p. 263.

32   **Couture houses:** Ibid., p. 260.

33   **By 1951:** White, *Master Touch of Lesage*, p. 80.

33   **Soon licensing:** Richard Morais, *Pierre Cardin: The Man Who Became a Label* (London: Bantam, 1991), p. 91.

33   **"I was staying":** Vreeland, *D.V.*, pp. 106–7.

34   **"Bloomingdale's":** Ibid., p. 134.

34   **By 1977:** Nadège Forestier and Nazanine Ravaï, *The Taste of Luxury: Bernard Arnault and the Moët-Hennessy Louis Vuitton Story* (London: Bloomsbury, 1992), p. 54.

35   **Finally, in 1977:** Hugh Sebag-Montefiore, *Kings on the Catwalk: The Louis Vuitton and Moët-Hennessy Affair* (London: Chapmans, 1992), p. 82.

35   **He decided:** Ibid., p. 16.

36   **Recamier expanded:** Pasols, *Louis Vuitton*, p. 280.

36   **In 1984:** In 1984, Vuitton sales were 1.25 billion French francs and profits were 197 million French francs. Chris Hollis (Investor Relations, LVMH), e-mail with the author, February 5, 2007.

36   **In 1986:** Sebag-Montifiore, *Kings on the Catwalk*, p. 115.

CHAPTER TWO: GROUP MENTALITY

41   **The result:** Suzy Wetlaufer, "The Perfect Paradox of Star Brands," *Harvard Business Review*, October 2001, p. 122.

42   **The France:** Jennifer Steinhauer, "The King of Posh," *New York Times*, August 17, 1997, Sec. 3, p. 1.

42   **"You have to":** Joshua Levine, "Liberté, Fraternité—but to Hell with Egalité!" *Forbes*, June 2, 1997, p. 80.

42   **Upon graduating:** Nadège Forestier and Nazanine Ravaï, *The Taste of Luxury: Bernard Arnault and the Moët-Hennessy Louis Vuitton Story* (London: Bloomsbury, 1992), p. 10.

43   **Arnault fled:** Ibid., pp. 13–14.

44   **"I can be":** Ibid., p. 11.

44   **Its only hope:** Hugh Sebag-Montefiore, *Kings on the Catwalk: The Louis Vuitton and Moët-Hennessy Affair* (London: Chapmans, 1992), pp. 23–24.

44   **He convinced Lazard:** Levine, "Liberté, Fraternité," p. 80.

45   **It was perhaps:** Sebag-Montefiore, *Kings on the Catwalk*, p. 41.

45   **He shocked:** David D. Kirkpatrick, "The Luxury Wars," *New York Megazine*, April 26, 1999, p. 24.

45   **Unlike Dior's:** Sebag-Montefiore, *Kings on the Catwalk*, pp. 30–31.

45   **When he took:** Forestier and Ravaï, *Taste of Luxury*, p. 17.

46   **"I don't want":** Sebag-Montefiore, *Kings on the Catwalk*, p. 37.

47   **In 1988:** Nina Hyde, "The Battle of Lacroix," *Washington Post*, April 7, 1988, p. C1.

47   **Feeling beaten:** Sebag-Montefiore, *Kings of the Catwalk*, pp. 50–58.

48   **In the spring:** Ibid., p. 137.

48   **At one point:** Ibid., p. 220.

48   **The French daily:** Forestier and Ravaï, *Taste of Luxury*, p. 93.

48   **Finally, in April:** Sebag-Montefiore, *Kings on the Catwalk*, p. 232.

49   **His motivation:** Forestier and Ravaï, *Taste of Luxury*, p. 106.

49   **He expanded:** Wetlaufer, "The Perfect Paradox," p. 121.

49   **Carcelle was:** Deborah Ball, "Decisiveness and Charisma Put Yves Carcelle in the Hot Seat at LVMH's Principle Division," *Wall Street Journal Europe*, October 1, 2001, p. 31.

50   **"You think of Vuitton":** Zoe Heller, "Jacob's Ladder," *New Yorker*, September 22, 1997, p. 109.

52   **"If you control":** Levine, "Liberté, Fraternité," p. 80.

52   **By 2004:** "LVMH: Full of Potential, Will It Be Realized?" Merrill Lynch, November 2002.

52   **Dior's sixty-three-year-old:** Sebag-Montefiore, *Kings on the Catwalk*, p. 192.

53   **"[Audrey] Hepburn":** Kirkpatrick, "The Luxury Wars," p. 24.

53   **In 1996:** Levine, "Liberté, Fraternité," p. 80.

54   **"For a European":** Steinhauer, "King of Posh," p. 1.

54   **"[Arnault] is":** Ibid., p. 1.

56   **He travels:** John Marcom Jr., "The Quiet Afrikaner behind Cartier," *Forbes*, April 2, 1990, p. 114.

56   **"We concentrate":** William Hall, "Companies & Finance: When Time Is a Business's Ultimate Luxury," *Financial Times*, June 9, 2000, p. 34.

56   **"It's not just about":** James Fallon, "Rupert's Way: While Competitors Spend for Acquisitions Like There's No Tomorrow, Richemont CEO Johann Rupert Plans for a Rainy Day," *Women's Wear Daily*, May 30, 2000, p. 8S.

57   **"Product integrity":** Ibid.

57   **"We are not":** Hall, "Companies & Finance," p. 34.

57   **"In five to ten":** Fallon, "Rupert's Way," p. 8S.

57   **Cartier accounts for:** Miles Socha, "Milking Fashion's Cash Cows," *WWD The Magazine*, November 3, 2003, p. 88.

58   **By the late 1980s:** Kirkpatrick, "Luxury Wars," p. 24.

58   **"It was pretty much":** David Yoffie and Mary Kwak, "Gucci Group N.V. (A)," Harvard Business School case (9–701–037), May 10, 2001, p. 2.

59   **Gucci sales:** Ibid., p. 9.

60   **De Sole declared:** Kirkpatrick, "Luxury Wars," p. 24.

60   **Arnault said:** Ibid.

60   **Pinault laughed:** Sarah Raper, "LVMH's Arnault: The Tower and the Glory," *Women's Wear Daily*, December 6, 1999, p. 8.

61   **When PPR took:** Yoffie and Kwak, "Gucci Group N.V. (A)," p. 14.

65   **Her father, Gino:** Myriam de Cesco, "Galeotta fu una borsa," *Lo Specchio*, January 8, 2000, pp. 76–80.

65   **"We passed":** Ibid.

68   **"It can be":** Michael Specter, "The Designer," *New Yorker,* March 15, 2004, p. 112.

68   **Once Bertelli:** Cathy Horyn, "Prada Central," *Vanity Fair,* August 1997, p. 96.

69   **By the end of 2001:** Specter, "The Designer," p. 114.

CHAPTER THREE: GOING GLOBAL

76   **In February 1976:** Kyojiro Hata, *Louis Vuitton Japan: The Building of Luxury* (New York: Assouline, 2004), p. 7.

76   **"The serenity":** Ibid., p. 11.

77   **Hata came:** Ibid., p. 23.

78   **"During the first ten years":** Ibid., p. 75.

79   **But the economic boom:** Claire Kent, Sarah Macdonald, Mandy Deex, and Michinori Shimizu, "Back from Japan," Morgan Stanley Equity Research, Europe, November 14, 2001, pp. 3, 7.

80   **They were the only:** Ilene R. Prusher, "Japanese Retailers Turn to 'Shetailers,'" *Christian Science Monitor,* August 29, 2001, p. 1.

80   **It was a wise:** Deborah Ball, "Decisiveness and Charisma Put Yves Carcelle in the Hot Seat at LVMH's Principal Division," *Wall Street Journal Europe,* October 1, 2001, p. 31.

82   **In 2006:** www.moodiereport.com/pdf/tmr_may_06_6.pdf.

82   **In 1960:** Stephanie Strom, "LVMH to Buy Duty-Free Empire for $2.47 Billion," *New York Times,* October 30, 1996, p. D1.

82   **Between 1977 and 1995:** Judith Miller, "He Gave Away $600 Million, and No One Knew," *New York Times,* January 23, 1997, p. A1.

83   **"This was not":** Jon Nordheimer, "Slaughtering the Cash Cow: Millions of Dollars Couldn't Keep DFS Group Together," *New York Times,* March 12, 1997, p. D1.

83   **Feeney, the more:** Miller, "He Gave Away $600 Million," p. A1.

83   **Miller, by contrast:** Jerry Adler, "He Gave at the Office," *Newsweek,* February 3, 1997, p. 34.

83   **In 1994:** David D. Kirkpatrick, "The Luxury Wars," *New York Magazine,* April 26, 1999, p. 24.

83   **Feeney and Parker:** Vicki M. Young, "Miller Threatens Suit after LVMH Pulls Out of Talks for DFS Stake," *Women's Wear Daily,* March 20, 1997, p. 1.

85   **In 2003:** "Japanese International Travelers: Trends and Shopping Behavior," 2003 JTM/TFWA Japanese Traveler Study, Executive Summary, p. 1.

88   **"Andy was":** Joshua Levine, *The Rise and Fall of the House of Barneys* (New York: Morrow, 1999), p. 118.

88   **For those who:** Ibid., p. 199.

91   **"Rule No. 1":** Kate Betts, "The Retail Therapist," *Time,* May 30, 2005, p. 53.

91   **Sales at the Osaka:** Ibid.

91   **After Marino renovated:** Miles Socha, "King Louis: Louis Vuitton's New Clothing Store," *Women's Wear Daily,* October 10, 2005, p. 1.

92   **Hata has long:** Hata, *Louis Vuitton Japan,* pp. 40–43.

93   **"It's luxury":** Elizabeth Heilman Brooke, "Tokyo Club: A New Way to Shop," *International Herald Tribune,* February 27, 2004, p. 14.

95   **The total cost:** "Chanel Opens Flagship Shop in Tokyo's Ritzy Ginza," Agence France Presse, December 4, 2004.

CHAPTER FOUR: STARS GET IN YOUR EYES

101   **Gucci nearly:** David B. Yoffie and Mary Kwak, "Gucci Group N.V. (A)," Harvard Business School, case 9-701-037, September 19, 2000; revised May 10, 2001, p. 10.

101   **LVMH spent:** Federico Antoni, "LVMH in 2004: The Challenges of Strategic Integration," Stanford Graduate School of Business, case SM– 123, March, 17, 2004, p. 12.

102 **"We are the largest":** David D. Kirkpatrick, "The Luxury Wars," *New York Magazine*, April 26, 1999, p. 24.

102 **At Gucci:** Yoffie and Kwak, "Gucci Group N.V. (A)," p. 10.

103 **Silent-screen siren:** Patty Fox, *Star Style: Hollywood Legends as Fashion Icons* (Santa Monica, Calif.: Angel City Press, 1995), pp. 76–77 and pp. 83–90.

104 **When Crawford:** Ibid., p. 24.

104 **Grace Kelly's:** Ibid., p. 96.

104 **Hollywood stars:** Ibid., p. 92.

104 **sold their signatures:** Marian Hall, with Marjorie Carne and Sylvia Sheppard, *California Fashion: From the Old West to New Hollywood* (New York: Abrams, 2002), p. 92.

104 **He originally settled:** Salvatore Ferragamo, *Shoemaker of Dreams: The Autobiography of Salvatore Ferragamo* (Florence: Giunti Gruppo Editoriale, 1985), pp. 37–48.

105 **In the early 1920s:** Ibid., pp. 51–54.

105 **"Valentino would drop":** Ibid., pp. 89–92.

106 **But in 1955:** Marie-France Pochna, *Christian Dior: The Man Who Made the World Look New* (New York: Arcade, 1996), pp. 161–162.

107 **For most of the twentieth century:** Scott Huver and Mia Kaczinski Dunn, *Inside Rodeo Drive: The Store, the Stars, the Story* (Santa Monica, Calif.: Angel City Press, 2001), p. 12–18.

109 **The Gucci store:** Sara Gay Forden, *The House of Gucci; A Sensational Story of Murder, Madness, Glamour, and Greed* (New York: HarperCollins, 2001), p. 39.

110 **By the late 1970s:** Anthony Cook, "Wheeling and Dealing on Status Street," *New West*, February 27, 1978, p. 20.

110 **Beverly Hills:** Ibid., p. 19.

110 **Hayman was once:** Karen Stabiner, "Spring Fashion: King of the Hills," *Los Angeles Times Magazine*, February 15, 1998, p. 18.

112 **The neighborhood boys:** Judy Bachrach, "Armani in Full", *Vanity Fair*, October 2000, p. 193.

114 **Fred Pressman:** Joshua Levine, *The Rise and Fall of the House of Barneys* (New York: Morrow, 1999), p. 90.

114 **In 1979:** Michael Kaplan, "Blame It on Armani," *Movieline*, September 19, 1999, p. 74.

115 **When *Time*:** Levine, *House of Barneys*, p. 92.

118 ***Vogue's* Anna Wintour:** Author interview, Paris, July, 2001.

118 **Jennifer Meyer:** Jareen Stabiner, "Dressing Well Is the Best Revenge," *Los Angeles Times Magazine*, December 11, 1988, p. 42.

122 **"Those girls":** Gaby Wood, "She's Got the Look," *Observer*, July 16, 2006, p. 12.

124 **Zoe has even:** Booth Moore, "In Her Image: Rachel Zoe's Clients (Lindsay, Nicole, Jessica) Often Look Like . . . Her," *Los Angeles Times*, July 16, 2005, p. E1.

126 **According to a study:** *Lifestyle Monitor*, January, 2005.

127 **Sir Elton:** Shawn Hubler and Gina Piccalo, "The Heirarchy," *Los Angeles Times*, March 1, 2005, p. E5.

129 **One prominent stylist:** Libby Callaway, "Red Carpet Catfighting: The Seamy Side of the Stars' Style Wars," *New York Post*, February 29, 2004, p. 48.

129 **One stylist reportedly:** "Fat Chance," *People Hollywood Daily*, February 26, 2005, p. 14.

132 **Chopard's:** Booth Moore, "Red Carpet Revenue," *Los Angeles Times*, February 22, 2005, p. E12.

CHAPTER FIVE: THE SWEET SMELL OF SUCCESS

135 **"A woman enveloped":** Janet Wallach, *Chanel: Her Style and Her Life* London: Mitchell Beazley, 1999), p. 162.

139 **"[Dior's perfume]":** Federico Antoni, "LVMH in 2004: The Challenges of Strategic Integration," Stanford Graduate School of Business, case SM–123, March, 17, 2004, p. 6.

140 **Prehistoric man:** Diane Ackerman, *A Natural History of the Senses* (New York: Random House, 1990), pp. 56–59.

140 **In Crete:** Ibid., pp. 60–61.

141   **French king Louis XIV:** Ibid., p. 62.

144   **"The industry has":** Caroline Brothers, "The Precise Smell of Success," *International Herald Tribune*, October 21–22, 2006, p. 12.

144   **In 2003:** Miles Socha, "Milking Fashion's Cash Cows," *WWD the Magazine,* November 3, 2003, p. 88.

145   **She was born in:** Wallach, *Chanel*, pp. 5–18.

145   **She made her way:** Ibid., pp. 19–31.

146   **First she did a test:** Alex Madsen, *Chanel: A Woman of Her Own* (New York: Henry Holt, 1990), p. 135.

147   **Théophile Bader:** Ibid., p. 136.

147   **Throughout the 1920s:** Stanley Karnow, *Paris in the Fifties* (New York: Random House, 1997), p. 273.

149   **Her first collection:** Wallach, *Chanel*, p. 150.

149   **Even Christian Dior:** Ibid., p. 154.

153   **Together, they do:** Chandler Burr, "The Scent of the Nile," *New Yorker*, March 14, 2005, p. 78.

153   **In late 2006:** Brid Costello and Matthew W. Evans, "Givaudan-Quest: Creating a New Number One," *Women's Wear Daily*, November 27, 2006, p. 3.

154   **Take Dior's brief:** Burr, "Scent of the Nile," p. 78.

162   **"All I see":** "Fashion Scoops: In the Flesh," *Women's Wear Daily*, July 11, 2001, p. 5.

164   **They can be:** Burr, "Scent of the Nile," p. 87.

164   **When Alain Lorenzo:** Joshua Levine, "Liberté, Fraternité—but to Hell with Egalité!" *Forbes*, June 2, 1997, p. 80.

CHAPTER SIX: IT'S IN THE BAG

169   **Handbags have:** Andrea Lee, "Bag Lady," *New Yorker*, September 25, 2006, p. 80.

169   **"It's like you've":** Anna Johnson, *Handbags: The Power of the Purse* (New York: Workman, 2002), p. 54.

169   **I read about:** Reggie Nadelson, "Out of the Box," *Departures*, May–June, 2002, p. 146.

169   **In September 2005:** Ben Widdicombe, "Gatecrasher," *New York Daily News*, September 10, 2005, p. 20.

170   **At the Venice Biennale:** Farid Chenoune, *Carried Away: All About Bags* (Paris: Le Passage Paris—New York Editions, 2004), p. 72.

171   **Jackie Onassis:** Nadelson, "Out of the Box," p. 143.

171   **Maryvonne Pinault:** Ibid., p.176.

171   **Carrying into a jury:** Robin Givhan, "Martha's Moneyed Bag Carries Too Much Baggage," *Washington Post*, January 22, 2004, p. C1.

173   **Among the more:** Nadelson, "Out of the Box," p. 146.

173   **In 2003:** Pascale Renaux, "L'Ange Guardian," *Numéro*, October 2003, p. 302.

174   **"We are frightened":** Nadelson, "Out of the Box," p. 150.

174   **Whereas Gucci Group's:** Lisa Lockwood, "Polet's Prescription for Changing Gucci," *Women's Wear Daily*, November 16, 2005, p. 45.

174   **In 1995:** Christopher Dickey, "C'est Chic, C'est French," *Newsweek International*, March 17, 1997, p. 38.

181   **This persecution:** Nadelson, "Out of the Box," p. 177.

184   **As he likes:** Dickey, "C'est Chic, C'est French," p. 38.

184   **Sales were so slow:** Bridget Foley, "Full Galop," *W*, March 1998, p. 230.

184   **He found the rue:** Helmut Newton, *Autobiography* (New York: Doubleday, 2003), pp. 241–42.

186   **The modern handbag:** Chenoune, *Carried Away*, passim.

187   **"Listen, Diana":** Diana Vreeland, *D.V.* (New York: Knopf, 1984), p. 89.

187   **It had no monogram:** Johnson, *Handbags*, p. 7.

188   **"We've got into the":** Chenoune, *Carried Away*, p. 32.

189 **In 1986:** Palmer White, *The Master Touch of Lesage: Embroidery for French Fashion* (Paris: Editions du Chêne, 1987), p. 134.

191 **As Holly Brubach:** Holly Brubach, "In Fashion: Forward Motion," *New Yorker,* June 25, 1990, p. 77.

193 **It became:** Andrea Lee, "Bag Lady," *New Yorker,* September 25, 2006, p. 80.

194 **Market sources:** Miles Socha, with contributions by Jennifer Weil, "LVMH Profits Pass $1 Billion," *Women's Wear Daily,* March 10, 2005, p. 9.

196 **Between 1994 and 1998:** David B. Yoffie and Mary Kwak, "Gucci Group N.V. (A)," Harvard Business School, case 9–701–037, September 19, 2000; revised May 10, 2001, p. 11.

199 **That year, Frankfort:** Barbara Woller, "First-Class Coach," *Journal News,* May 23, 2005, p. 1D.

199 **From 2001 to 2006:** Claire A. Kent, Mandy Deex, Rachel Whittaker, Angela Moh, and Andy Xie, "Luxury Goods in China: A Long-Term Investment," Morgan Stanley, February 27, 2004, p. 13.

202 **A brown leather tag:** Alessandra Galloni, Cecilie Rohwedder, and Teri Agins, "Foreign Luxuries: Breaking a Taboo, High Fashion Starts Making Goods Overseas," *Wall Street Journal,* September 27, 2005, p. A1.

202 **In May 2005:** Adam Jones,"Prada Ponders Outsourcing to China," *Financial Times,* May 20, 2005, p. 10.

CHAPTER SEVEN: THE NEEDLE AND THE DAMAGE DONE

209 **It has been used:** Nina Hyde, "Silk, the Queen of Textiles," *National Geographic,* January 1984, p. 48.

213 **Back in the 1920s:** Pietra Pietrogrande, *Antico Setificio Fiorentino* (Florence, Italy: Le Lettere, 1999), p. 71.

213 **Back in the factory's:** Ibid., p. 95.

214 **On some farms:** Hyde, "Silk, the Queen of Textiles," pp. 14–19.

214 **The Chinese began:** Ibid., pp. 27–30.

215 **One recounts:** Ibid., p. 36.

215 **Another tells:** Pietrogrande, *Antico Setifico Fiorentino,* p. 21.

215 **One of the early centers:** Ibid., pp. 33–43.

221 **In 2004:** Alessandra Galloni, Cecilie Rohwedder, and Teri Agins, "Foreign Luxuries: Breaking a Taboo, High Fashion Starts Making Goods Overseas," *Wall Street Journal,* September 27, 2005, p. A1.

227 **One-fourth of Hong Kong's:** Ted C. Fishman, *China Inc.* (New York: Scribner, 2005), p. 88.

227 **By the mid-1990s:** Ibid., p. 89.

228 **In September 2006:** "In Brief: Actor Appeals to Burberry," *Women's Wear Daily,* November 27, 2006, p. 2.

228 **In November:** David Cracknell and Jonathan Leake, "Charles Joins the Burberry Revolt," *Times* (London), November 26, 2006, p. 4.

229 **Peter Hain:** Samantha Conti, "Burberry to Close Factory," *Women's Wear Daily,* January 11, 2007, p. 15.

229 **Today, there are:** "Swatches: Canton Connection," *Women's Wear Daily,* January 3, 2006, p. 8.

229 **China's textiles:** John Zarcostas, "China's Textile Exports Soar 23.8 Percent," *Women's Wear Daily,* January 10, 2006, p. 8.

230 **In late 2005:** George Wehrfritz, "A River in Reverse," *Newsweek International,* January 30, 2006, p. 53.

231 **The constant pressure:** John Zarocostas, "Global Labor Study Cites Human Rights Violations," *Women's Wear Daily,* October 19, 2005, p. 19.

232 **"Chinese factories":** Jane Perlez, "Vietnam Arrives as an Economic Player in Asia," *International Herald Tribune,* June 20, 2006, p. 2.

232   **"China is no longer":** Luisa Zargani, "China Trains Eye on Italian Firms," *Women's Wear Daily*, February 22, 2006, p. 13.

CHAPTER EIGHT: GOING MASS

239   **America Online:** Annie Groer, "The New Gilded Age," *Washington Post*, August 1, 1999, p. F1.

239   **According to a University:** Juliet B. Schor, *The Overspent American: Why We Want What We Don't Need* (New York: HarperPerennial, 1999), p. 14.

239   **According to a Roper:** Ibid., p. 16.

239   **Since 1970:** Michael J. Silverstein and Neil Fiske, with John Butman, *Trading Up: The New American Luxury* (New York: Portfolio, 2003), pp. 25–26.

239   **By 2005:** Sharon Edelson, "Chasing Big Spenders: Stores Step Up Services for Key Luxe Customers," *Women's Wear Daily*, August 1, 2006, p. 1.

239   **Between 1979 and 1995:** Schor, *Overspent American*, p. 12.

239   **According to a 1997 study:** Ibid., 159.

239   **Between 1990 and 1996:** Ibid., p. 72.

239   **Yet it wasn't enough:** Ibid., p. 6.

240   **In 2004:** "Accessible Luxury—What It Is and Why It's Working," Ledbury Research, November 8, 2004.

241   **"When we look":** David D. Kirkpatrick, "The Luxury Wars," *New York Magazine*, April 26, 1999, p. 24.

244   **And MGM Mirage:** Sharon Edelson, "Taubman Plans for Big Names at Vegas Center," *Women's Wear Daily*, September 21, 2005, p. 5.

247   **"It was jolting":** Karen Heller, "On Deep Discount, Prada Has Never Looked Worse," *Philadelphia Inquirer*, January 6, 2006, p. M3.

247   **"The 1980s":** Booth Moore, "Outlet for That Energy," *Los Angeles Times*, September 1, 2005, p. 28.

249   **"I once got home":** Laura Landro, "Style—Hunting & Gathering: Catwalk Chic on the Cheap," *Wall Street Journal*, September 17, 2005, p. 11.

250   **But, says Linda Humphers:** Moore, "On Deep Discount," p. 28.

250   **But the average:** Ibid.

251   **"The winning formula":** Ibid.

254   **"The luxury industry":** Vanessa Friedman, "An Online Business Model Dressed to Kill," *Financial Times*, May 30, 2006, p. 10.

254   **It ran a huge overhead:** Karen Lowry Miller, "Hitting the Wall at Boo," *Newsweek Atlantic Edition*, July 17, 2000, p. 42.

259   **Analysts believe:** Cathy Horyn, "Point, Click and Strut," *New York Times*, December 15, 2005, p. 1.

259   **Furthermore, Forrester:** Luca S. Paderni, with Jaap Favier and Manuela Neurauter, "Louis Vuitton Takes Online Luxury Shopping Mainstream," Forrester Research, November 8, 2005.

260   **The primary culprits:** Lisa Bertagnoli, "To Catch a Thief: Independent Retailers Forgo High Tech Gizmos and Gadgets in Favor of Old-Fashioned Security Measures," *Women's Wear Daily*, October 13, 2004, p. 58S.

260   **Luxury's most famous:** Adam Tschorn, "Hollywood's Walk of Shame," *Women's Wear Daily*, February 24, 2004, p. 34S.

260   **"It's not normal":** Guy Trebay, "Shoplifting on a Grand Scale: Luxury Wear Stolen to Order," *New York Times*, August 8, 2000, p. B1.

260   **In Minnesota:** Schor, *Overspent American*, p. 40.

260   **Andrew McColl:** Trebay, "Shoplifting," p. B1.

260   **At times, robberies:** Rosemary Feitelberg, "Two Nabbed in Versace Hold-Up; Boston Boutique Site of Armed Robbery," *Women's Wear Daily*, May 12, 1997, p. 23.

261   **The pros:** Trebay, "Shoplifting," p. B1.

261 **"They obviously":** Greg Lindsay, "Sticky Fingers," *Women's Wear Daily,* January 27, 2004, p. 23.

261 **Chavs are:** Rob Walker, "The Good, the Plaid and the Ugly," *New York Times Magazine,* January 2, 2005, p. 20.

263 **As Kim Hastreiter:** Kim Hastreiter and David Hershkovits, *Twenty Years of Style: The World According to Paper* (New York: Harper Design International, 2004), p. 34.

263 **Logos—particularly:** Teri Agins, *The End of Fashion: How Marketing Changed the Clothing Business Forever* (New York: Quill, 2000), p. 111.

263 **Gianni Versace:** Ibid., p. 139.

263 **"What can we do?":** Gideon Rachman, "Bubbles and Bling," *Economist,* Summer 2006, p. 20.

264 **"I view":** George Rush and Joanna Molloy, "Daily Dish," *New York Daily News,* June 15, 2006, p. 26.

266 **In 2001:** Scott, Huver and Mia Kuczinski Dunn, *Inside Rodeo Drive: The Store, the Stars, the Story* (Santa Monica, Calif.: Angel City Press, 2001), p. 34.

CHAPTER NINE: FAUX AMIS

273 **In 1948:** Stanley Karnow, *Paris in the Fifties* (New York: Random House, 1997), pp. 260–61.

274 **In 1982:** International Anti-Counterfeiting Coalition, white paper, January 2005, p. 3.

274 **In 2004:** Ted C. Fishman, "Manufaketure," *New York Times Magazine,* January 9, 2005, p. 40.

275 **In 2002:** IACC white paper, p. 20.

276 **Prada CEO:** Robin Progrebin, "Reality Check," *Connoisseur,* n.d., p. 140.

281 **As Jasper Becker:** Jasper Becker, *The Chinese* (New York: Free Press, 2000), pp. 74–75.

282 **A month later:** Evan Clark, "U.S. Report Calls for Action on Intellectual Property Laws," *Women's Wear Daily,* May 2, 2005, p. 16.

285 **That same month:** "U.S. Charges 17 with Trafficking in Counterfeit Goods, Money Laundering, Attempted Bribery of a Public Official," United States Attorney Southern District of New York, press release, June 4, 2004.

285 **The street value:** Progrebin, "Reality Check," p. 140.

285 **The same is true:** Peter S. Goodman, "In China, a Growing Taste for Chic; But Fakes Also Vex Developing Market," *Washington Post,* July 12, 2004, p. A1.

292 **Many of the street-level:** Marcus Mabry and Alan Zarembo, "Africa's Capitalist Jihad," *Newsweek Atlantic Edition,* July 7, 1997, p. 42.

293 **During a two-day:** Julia Preston, "U.S. Charges 51 with Chinatown Smuggling," *New York Times,* November 13, 2004, p. B2.

CHAPTER TEN: WHAT NOW?

299 **In 2006:** Emily Flynn Vencat, "Shaping the New Looks," *Newsweek International,* May 15–22, 2006, p. 82.

299 **In 2004:** Paul Klebnikov, "Russia's Richest People: The Golden Hundred," Forbes.com, July 22, 2004.

300 **The Chinese didn't:** Claire A. Kent, Mandy Deex, Rachel Whittaker, Angela Moh, and Andy Xie, "Luxury Goods in China: A Long-Term Investment," Morgan Stanley, February 27, 2004, p. 4.

300 **"It's cheaper":** Lisa Movius, "Shanghai's Bund 18 Luring Luxury Brands," *Women's Wear Daily,* January 11, 2005, p. 18.

303 **By 2004:** Kent, Deex, Whittaker, Moh, and Xie, "Luxury Goods in China," p. 6.

303 **"In other provinces":** Sarah Mowar, "Dressed to Shanghai," *Vogue,* October 2004, p. 336.

303 **"We are still":** Lisa Movius, "China's Luxury Rush: Expanding Vuitton Shows Market's Growth," *Women's Wear Daily,* December 29, 2005, p. 12.

304 **By the end of 2006:** Amanda Kaiser, "Tilling the Luxury Landscape," *Women's Wear Daily,* March 21, 2006, p. 2B.

304 **Calvin Klein:** Lisa Movius, "Valentino Unveils Women's for Mainland China," *Women's Wear Daily,* September 26, 2006, p. 17.

304 **Since its arrival:** Zhu Ling, "Louis Vuitton to Open Three New Stores in China," www.chinadaily.com.cn/bizchina/2006–05/15/content_589908.htm, May 15, 2006.

306 **Mainland China:** Luisa Zargani, "Luxury and the Lands of Opportunity," *Women's Wear Daily,* November 29, 2004, p. 4.

306 **"Three years ago":** Lisa Movius, "Bulgari Continues Expanding in China," *Women's Wear Daily,* September 29, 2006, p. 22.

307 **"Mainlanders go":** Tom Miller, "Shopping Is the Lure for Mainlanders," *South China Morning Post,* November 7, 2005, p. 16.

307 **Mainlanders are enrolling:** Howard W. French, "In China, the Upper-Class Quest Starts Low—at Age 5," *International Herald Tribune,* September 22, 2006, p. 1.

307 **"I have customers":** "Seeking Russian Gold: Despite Turmoil, Brands Rush to Booming Market," *Women's Wear Daily,* September 30, 2004, p. 1.

308 **At many of Armani's:** Miles Socha, "Couture's New Hope: Russia, Asia and the Mideast," *Women's Wear Daily,* January 23, 2006, p. 5.

308 **Outside of Moscow:** Natasha Singer, "Russia's Luxury Mania: Stores Grab Real Estate to Build New Empires," *Women's Wear Daily,* October 4, 2004, p. 1.

308 **After the 1998:** Robert Galbraith, "Courting the New Russian and Indian Luxury Consumers," *International Herald Tribune,* September 30, 2005, p. 14.

309 **For the Dior opening:** Miles Socha and Brid Costella, "Christian Dior's New Flagship on Red Square," *Women's Wear Daily,* October 24, 2006, p. 3.

309 **Nearby, Mercury Group:** Singer, "Russia's Luxury Mania," p. 1.

309 **"Before we designed":** Ibid.

310 **Christian Dior reported:** "Seeking Russian Gold," p. 1.

311 **In 2005:** Galbraith, "Courting the New Russian and Indian Luxury Consumers," p. 14.

311 **"People have the money":** Rosemary Feitelberg, "On to India, China," *Women's Wear Daily,* December 5, 2006, p. 17.

311 **There are more:** Ibid.

312 **A study by Bain:** Ibid.

312 **The most coveted:** Cecily Hall, "Far East Fashion-Forward," *Women's Wear Daily,* June 1, 2006, p. 12.

312 **"In just the last year":** Betsy Lowther, "The Treasures of India: As Luxe Brands Rush In, Prime Space Runs Out," *Women's Wear Daily,* November 7, 2006, p. 1.

312 **Analysts at McKinsey:** Vencat, "Shaping the New Looks," p. 82.

312 **"The chance of":** Amy S. Choi, "Eyeing India's Riches: As Barriers Come Down, Luxury Brands Go Slow," *Women's Wear Daily,* March 13, 2006, p. 1.

313 **State governments:** Ritu Upadhyay, "Bombay Dispatch: Expanding Malls," *Women's Wear Daily,* March 13, 2006, p. 11.

313 **The finance ministry:** Choi, "Eyeing India's Riches," p. 1.

314 **"It's a PR machine":** "Talk about Branding," *Time,* June 2005, Bonus Section, p. A4.

315 **"Our hotels":** J. J. Martin, "Travel with Style," *Harper's Bazaar,* Fall 2006, p. 89.

316 **Fashion darling:** Miles Socha, "Philo Said Working with Gap," *Women's Wear Daily,* November 27, 2006, p. 2.

318 **Burberry began:** Claire Kent, Mandy Deex, Elke Finkenauer, Rachel Whittaker, "Luxury & Apparel Retail," Morgan Stanley Equity Research Europe, March 7, 2005, p. 17.

318 **Mizrahi calls:** Ibid., p. 10.

CHAPTER ELEVEN: NEW LUXURY

321 **In early 2006:** Amanda Kaiser, "Jil Sander Loss Hits $46.3 Million in 2005," *Women's Wear Daily,* May 30, 2006, p. 3.

322 **"All these big":** Sarah Raper, "LVMH's Arnault: The Tower and the Glory," *Women's Wear Daily,* December 6, 1999, p. 8.

322 **Burberry CEO:** "Continental Compensation," *Women's Wear Daily,* July 17, 2003, p. 14.

322 **according to *Forbes*:** www.forbes.com/lists/2006/12/Rank_1.html.

322   **"A mobile phone":** Luisa Zargani, with contributions by Alessandra Ilari, "Prada Calling Via Venture with LG," *Women's Wear Daily*, December 13, 2006, p. 11.

323   **"She says":** Holly Brubach, "In Fashion: Forward Motion," *New Yorker*, June 25, 1990, p. 79.

334   **The wealthiest:** Sharon Edelson, "Chasing Big Spenders: Stores Step Up Services for Key Luxe Customers," *Women's Wear Daily*, August 1, 2006, p. 1.

334   **Danielle Morolo:** Ibid.

334   **"My best customer":** Ibid.

335   **Saks Fifth Avenue:** Ibid.

BIBLIOGRAPHY

Ackerman, Diane. *A Natural History of the Senses*. New York: Random House, 1990.

Agins, Teri. *The End of Fashion: How Marketing Changed the Clothing Business Forever*. New York: Quill, 2000.

Arnault, Bernard. *La Passion Créative: Entretiens avec Yves Messarovitch*. Paris: Plon, 2000.

Becker, Jasper. *The Chinese*. New York: Free Press, 2000.

Bindloss, Joseph; Sarina Singh; Deanna Swaney; and Robert Strauss. *Mauritius, Réunion & Seychelles*. Victoria, Australia: Lonely Planet, 2001.

Bloch, Phillip. *Elements of Style: From the Portfolio of Hollywood's Premier Stylist*. New York: Warner, 1998.

Bonvicini, Stéphanie. *Louis Vuitton: une saga française*. Paris: Fayard, 2004.

Brubach, Holly. *A Dedicated Follower of Fashion*. London: Phaidon Press, 1999.

Burr, Chandler. *The Emperor of Scent: A Story of Perfume, Obsession and the Last Mystery of the Senses*. New York: Random House, 2002.

Celant, Germano, and Harold Koda. *Giorgio Armani*. New York: Solomon R. Guggenheim Foundation, 2000.

Chenoune, Farid. *Carried Away: All About Bags*. Paris: Le Passage Paris—New York Editions, 2004.

Ferragamo, Salvatore. *Shoemaker of Dreams: the Autobiography of Salvatore Ferragamo*. Florence, Italy: Giunti Gruppo Editoriale, 1985.

Fishman, Ted C. *China, Inc*. New York: Scribner, 2005.

Forden, Sara Gay. *The House of Gucci: A Sensational Story of Murder, Madness, Glamour, and Greed*. New York: HarperCollins, 2001.

Forestier, Nadège, and Nazanine Ravaï. *The Taste of Luxury: Bernard Arnault and the Moët-Hennessy Louis Vuitton Story*. London: Bloomsbury, 1992.

Fox, Patty. *Star Style: Hollywood Legends as Fashion Icons*. Santa Monica, Calif.: Angel City Press, 1995.

Galbraith, John Kenneth. *The Affluent Society*. New York: Houghton Mifflin, 1998.

Hall, Marian, with Marjorie Carne and Sylvia Sheppard. *California Fashion: From the Old West to New Hollywood*. New York: Abrams, 2002.

Hastreiter, Kim, and David Hershkovits. *20 Years of Style: The World According to Paper*. New York: Harper Design International, 2004.

Hata, Kyojiro. *Louis Vuitton Japan: The Building of Luxury*. New York: Assouline, 2004.

Huver, Scott, and Mia Kuczinski Dunn. *Inside Rodeo Drive: The Store, the Stars, the Story*. Santa Monica, Calif.: Angel City Press, 2001.

Johnson, Anna. *Handbags: The Power of the Purse*. New York: Workman, 2002.

Karnow, Stanley. *Paris in the Fifties*. New York: Random House, 1997.

Kennedy, Shirley. *Pucci: A Renaissance in Fashion*. New York: Abbeville Press, 1991.

Krannich, Ronald L. *The Treasures and Pleasures of China: Best of the Best*. Manassas Park, Va.: Impact Publications, 1999.

Levine, Joshua. *The Rise and Fall of the House of Barneys*. New York: Morrow, 1999.

Madsen, Alex. *Chanel: A Woman of Her Own*. New York: Henry Holt, 1990.

Mally, Ruth Lor. *China Guide*, Cold Spring Harbor, N.Y.: Open Road Publishing, 2002.

Morais, Richard. *Pierre Cardin: The Man Who Became a Label*. London: Bantam, 1991.

Newton, Helmut. *Helmut Newton, Autobiography*. New York: Doubleday, 2003.

Pasols, Paul-Gérard. *Louis Vuitton: The Birth of Modern Luxury*. New York: Abrams, 2005

Pietrogrande, Pietra. *Antico Setificio Fiorentino*. Florence, Italy: Le Lettere, 1999.

Pochna, Marie-France. *Christian Dior: The Man Who Made the World Look New*. New York: Arcade, 1996.

Rawsthorn, Alice. *Yves Saint Laurent*. London: HarperCollins, 1996.

Riva, Maria. *Marlene Dietrich: By Her Daughter*. New York: Knopf, 1993.

Schor, Juliet B. *The Overspent American: Why We Want What We Don't Need*. New York: HarperPerennial, 1999.

Sebag-Montefiore, Hugh. *Kings on the Catwalk: The Louis Vuitton and Moët-Hennessy Affair*. London: Chapmans, 1992.

Silverstein, Michael J., and Neil Fiske, with John Butman. *Trading Up: The New American Luxury*. New York: Portfolio, 2003.

Smith, Sally Bedell. *Reflected Glory: The Life of Pamela Churchill Harriman*. New York: Simon & Schuster, 1996.

Twitchell, James B. *Living It Up: Our Love Affair with Luxury*. New York: Columbia University Press, 2002.

Veblen, Thorstein. *The Theory of the Leisure Class*. New York: Penguin, 1994.

Vreeland, Diana. *D.V.* New York: Da Capo Press, 1997.

Wallach, Janet. *Chanel: Her Style and Her Life*. London: Mitchell Beazley, 1999.

Watson, Albert. *Prada a Milano*, Milan: Grafica di Italia Lupo.

White, Palmer. *The Master Touch of Lesage: Embroidery for French Fashion*. Paris: Editions du Chêne, 1987.

INDEX

PHOTO CREDITS